Colm Peter McGrath

The Development of Medical Liability in Germany, 1800–1945

Studien zur
europäischen Rechtsgeschichte

Veröffentlichungen des
Max-Planck-Instituts
für europäische Rechtsgeschichte
Frankfurt am Main

Band 314

Vittorio Klostermann
Frankfurt am Main
2019

Colm Peter McGrath

# The Development of Medical Liability in Germany, 1800–1945

Vittorio Klostermann
Frankfurt am Main
2019

Umschlagbild / Cover Art:
Bench dispensing scales, 19th century
S. Maw, Son and Thompson (1870–1901)
Type commonly used through the 19th century
Credit: Wellcome Collection. CC BY

Bibliographische Information der Deutschen Nationalbibliothek
Die Deutsche Nationalbibliothek verzeichnet diese Publikation in der Deutschen Nationalbibliographie; detaillierte bibliographische Daten sind im Internet über *http://dnb.dnb.de* abrufbar.



Druck und Bindung: docupoint GmbH, Barleben
Typographie: Elmar Lixenfeld, Frankfurt am Main

Gedruckt auf Eos Werkdruck.
Alterungsbeständig ISO 9706 und PEFC-zertifiziert

Printed in Germany
ISSN 1610-6040
ISBN 978-3-465-04367-6

# Contents

# Preface

A number of debts have been incurred during the process of writing this book and the doctoral thesis on which it was based, and substantial thanks, both professional and personal, is owed to numerous people.

Turning to the professional: First, to the Arts and Humanities Research Council who funded my research as part of the European Legal Development project. Being involved with this project provided a vital springboard for my academic interests and gave me an unparalleled opportunity to engage with other systems beyond the English common law. Secondly, to Professor Dr Dr (hc mult) Reinhard Zimmermann, whose early direction and ongoing willingness to discuss parts of this work were invaluable in its completion, and the tremendous staff of the Max Planck Institute for Comparative and International Private Law in Hamburg, Mrs Halsen-Raffel in particular. It was there that, over the course of 13 months, the research that underpins this book was undertaken. Their collective warmth towards a young, bumbling common lawyer was, and remains, deeply appreciated. Thirdly, to Professor Ken Oliphant, Professor Dr Dr hc Helmut Koziol and all my friends and colleagues during the five years that I worked at ETL/ECTIL in Vienna, I owe a debt for their tireless patience in helping me find my feet in a foreign land (and legal system), and their support through some very difficult times. To Dr Barbara Steininger, who was kind enough to read and comment on an early draft of this volume, and Sonja Akbal, who makes all things possible, particular thanks is owed. Only so much knowledge of a foreign legal system may be gained from books in one's home jurisdiction and the chance to work at one of the nerve centres for comparative tort law in Europe helped me flesh out what I had so gleaned as an undergraduate, and delve deeper into the '*mentalité*' of the civil law. Fourthly, to Professors Paula Giliker and Stefan Vogenauer who acted as the examiners for the doctoral thesis on which this volume is based. Their collective insight and commentary proved inestimable in refining and illuminating the way forward for this project. Finally, I wish to thank the Master and Fellows of Trinity Hall, Cambridge, where, between 2015 and 2017, and due to the very generous support of the WYNG Foundation, I was the WYNG Research Fellow in Medical Law and Ethics. This post, and the freedom that came with it, allowed me to undertake the work necessary to complete this volume in the peace and beauty of that place; a rare privilege indeed.

Turning to the personal: thanks are due to Dr Christopher Brookes, the Tutor for Advanced Students at Corpus Christi College, Cambridge, where I studied as both an undergraduate and postgraduate. Corpus has indelibly affected my life and I am grateful to have been able to spend so many happy times there. Beyond the college, there is, of course, the Faculty of Law where all the staff of the Squire Law Library provided a constant welcoming and supportive home for my studies and, later, my research. Further, I am grateful to Alison Hirst who, throughout my postgraduate studies, was a source of constant good grace and assistance. I am blessed to be part of an academic circle that has always been comforting and challenging in equal measure. To Stelios Tofaris, Jonathan Morgan, Daniel Carr, Sandy Steel and Matthew Dyson – with whom I hope to share many more trials! – thank you all. To Professors David Ibbetson and John Bell, who have given me more than I can ever repay, I am forever in your debt. A further teacher, Tony Carlin, who taught German at St Malachy's College, Belfast, is owed a special thanks for giving a recalcitrant student the gift of language so as, in time, to be able to engage with another legal system and put to work the skills that David and John would later help me develop. Beyond academia, John, Imelda, Patrick and my wider family have been an inspiration, I love you all with all my heart. To the staff of the Bridgewater Suite in Belfast City Hospital, whilst I wish we did not know you at all, I am forever grateful that we do.

Finally, thanks are due to my wife Helen, without whose constant love, support, good humour and encouragement this book – and much else besides – would have been, simply, impossible. You are my North Star, my fixed point and the reason that anything I do is worth doing.

Somerset House, November 2018
C. P. McGrath

# Introduction

'Every method has its adherents and detractors'[1]

## 1. The subject at hand

Liability for negligent harm caused by medical treatment is a subject familiar to all legal systems, although not all systems treat it alike. It seems customary when discussing the subject at any length to note that such liability is an ancient feature of legal systems given the Code of Hammurabi contained both harsh sanctions for such liability alongside provisions fixing the cost of treatment;[2] even in ancient Mesopotamia, it seems, the legal regulation of medical practice and the consequences of injurious practice went hand in hand. Evaluating the strength of that connection during a different period of legal history lies at the heart of what follows.

This work is a legal history of the development of civil liability for medical error in Germany between 1800 and 1945. Within that, it focuses on one central aspect of that subject: the definition and interpretation of the requirement that the defendant medical practitioner was at fault. The aim of this inquiry is to examine the development of the law in relation to changes within the legal system and the broader context of medical practice and regulation, identifying, where possible, the drivers behind legal change. Thus, it investigates the relationship between the legal and medical discourses concerning what may be termed medical error and, in doing so, reveals a rich interaction between the two out of which the law-in-practice emerged. It aims to provide not simply an understanding of what the law was and how it changed, but rather what drove its development; why and how did it come to be?[3]

Having set out, briefly, what this book does, it is important to be clear as to what it does not do. Medical liability is here circumscribed to errors in diagnosis and treatment, its classical core. We do not consider the closely-related topic of liability based on failure to obtain the patient's consent. Furthermore, we are concerned only with the substantive doctrinal understanding of fault; we do not consider the various tools developed to provide the plaintiff (as they will be referred to) with a procedural indulgence. These are valuable in their own right, but must await further study. It is hoped that unpacking how liability for errors

1 *RG 09.10.1936*, Hübner/Warneyer (1939) 113.

2 §§ 215–225; H-D Viel (2002) 647.

3 On development and legal change, see Bell/Ibbetson (2012) 1–10.

in diagnosis and treatment was understood provides much groundwork towards such efforts.

From this, three choices must immediately be defended: Why focus on medical liability? Why in Germany? Why during the period 1800–1945?

As to the first, the genesis of this study was as a contribution to an emerging literature within European private law, which seeks to better understand the developmental patterns within different doctrinal areas, often by adopting a historical analysis, as the basis for better understanding the modern law.[4] The fact that medical liability is a common and, inevitably, long-standing problem with which legal systems have had to wrestle suggests a natural testing ground for those interested in how private law has developed over time; in a mature legal system it is a subject that is likely to present a rich amount of data over a long enough period. Furthermore, if one wishes to test the relationship between legal change and extra-legal changes, then medical liability, again, naturally suggests itself given the ever-present but ever-changing nature of medicine and medical practice across different systems; just as there are clearly different approaches to law across the legal systems of the world, there are different national approaches to medicine, medical practitioners and medical provision. This last point may not be immediately obvious to some, certainly in the developed world. Nevertheless, even within Europe, the process of medicine's development has varied in line with various cultural and historical contingencies, no less so in the case of Germany.[5] Finally, these matters are often intimately related to choices (or, at least, inertia) within the legal system: Who can practice medicine? What it is they are offering? How do patients access healthcare? These are all susceptible to the unintended interference of, or regulation by, the legal system, and offer an excellent chance to study the relationship between legal and extra-legal change.

But why turn to Germany as the focus of this study? The answer to this is that there are several features of Germany's respective medical and legal histories that suggested a study of the relationship between them here would yield a suitably rich result. First, the modern German law on medical liability is a voluminous and, increasingly, systematised body of specific rules within broader private law. Whilst the *Patientenrechtegesetz* 2013 – long in coming[6] – has now codified much

4 Hondius (2010).

5 In Germany's case this revolves centrally around the considerable degree of state control over medical practice maintained well into the nineteenth century, the role of the university and, associated with it, the laboratory in medical education, and the persistence of unorthodox medical practice, see Kater (1985); Huerkamp (1990); Bonner (1995) 232, 281; Weisz (2006) 60–63, 243. In the absence of further detailed comparative work it is important not to overstate the case for a German *Sonderweg* in all medical matters, see Maehle (2009) 129–130.

6 Kubella (2011) 15–25; Katzenmeier (2001) 85 f.

of the law within the *Bürgerliches Gesetzbuch* (*BGB*),[7] this was possible only because of considerable work by the German courts in shaping the contours of liability before that point.[8] Thus, there is sufficient legal material to provide a thicker account than would be possible in other legal systems.[9] Secondly, substantive German doctrine has proven itself willing to strongly challenge the claim that the defendant medical practitioner was not at fault because they did what other practitioners would have done in the same circumstance;[10] their analysis of fault has now restricted this essentially sociological approach, replacing it, at least in part, with what may be termed an ethical appproach;[11] it is now based on a court-driven ethic that stands analytically separate from internalised, medical views of appropriate behaviour. This represents a key doctrinal shift, yet how and why this process occurred is poorly understood. When one examines the standard German texts, explanations of this process, brief as they are, often focus on a change in terminology in the latter half of the twentieth century, from '*Kunstfehler*' to '*Behandlungsfehler*', which reflected the shift away from an older interpretative model that indulged ideas of *medically* accepted practice, to the current interpretative model.[12] Given there is no specific historical treatment of the relevant German law here, indeed there has been surprisingly scant scholarship on this topic generally,[13] there is a gap in the literature that invites further detailed study of how and why the German law reached this position, which is what this book seeks to provide. Indeed, as will be shown below, the explanation for this takes the legal historian to a much earlier period than has, up to now, been thought worth studying, a rebuke to the idea

7 *Gesetz zur Verbesserung der Rechte von Patientinnen und Patienten,* BGBl I (2013) 277.

8 Stauch (2015). Not that some had gone unnoticed beforehand, see Shaw (1968); Stauch (2008).

9 Hondius (2010) 13.

10 Stauch (2008) 43–45.

11 Montrose (1958).

12 'The "*Kunstfehler*" was, for a long time, the foundation of medical liability', Katzenmeier/Laufs/Lipp 335; Katzenmeier (2002) 273 f; Giesen (1983) 11 f; Riegger (2007) 15–17.

13 An unpublished German doctoral thesis amounts to the closest available literature, which covers some of the same ground. In contrast to the present study, that thesis offers an essentially descriptive, historical account of the whole scope of medical liability in Germany to 2000, Riegger (2007). Other works offer brief commentaries on individual parts of the history here, but none in a comprehensive fashion and none offer more than a cursory recounting of the terminological shift identified above. An indicative example is Katzenmeier (2002) 273–274. A broader account of the surrounding legal, intellectual development in liability law as a whole is available in Jansen (2003). By contrast this study offers only a specific, contextualised analysis of medical error.

that medical liability, '…is a rather new phenomenon'.[14] Thirdly, turning to the relevant features of Germany's medical history, Germany's position (commonly alongside the United Kingdom, the United States and France)[15] as one of the powerhouses behind modern, scientific,[16] hospital-based medicine suggests that the legal system would be presented with sufficiently numerous challenges throughout that process, as the nature and delivery of medicine changed, to justify a developmental study. It allows the study of a key player within the western medical tradition.[17] Fourthly, the occupational development of what we refer to in this study as orthodox medical practitioners – those who sought to establish themselves as the intellectual and occupational guardians of medical services – has long been thought to differ in Germany in key ways from that of their counterparts in similar systems.[18] The extended, delayed path of orthodox practitioners away from considerable control by the state towards the freedom of occupational hegemony is a unique feature of German medical history,[19] and, as such, it is important to understand the degree, if any, to which it influenced legal change here. Fifthly, that this came at the cost of decades of medical practice being defined in law as a 'trade' open to anyone meant the medical marketplace in Germany remained populated by a bewildering range of unorthodox practitioners, from the homeopathist to the empiricist to the outright charlatan, well into the twentieth century. A measure of the extremity of this situation was that there was no necessary bar on allowing such practitioners to play a role in the emerging, modern public health structures. Given access to orthodox, scientific medicine was also largely dependent on whether one lived in a city or the countryside throughout the early twentieth century, the lived experience of German medical practice demands a better understanding of whether and how, in assessing the question of fault, German courts accounted for the vastly differing occupational and intellectual models of medicine on offer.

Finally, why only study the German law between 1800 and 1945? The answer here is that to understand the relationship between legal and medical change over time, a sufficiently broad period is required to account for a suitable degree of dynamism in both spheres. The period covered here allows us to study their relationship to one another at a time when both were in flux and going through the final iterations before settling in their broadly current forms, and easily satisfies this. Even so, four immediate further questions arise: First, why study

14 Hondius (2013) 8.
15 Bonner (1995).
16 Broman (1997); Cunningham / Williams (2002).
17 On the idea of a discrete *western* medical tradition see, Jacyna (2006) 28 ff.
18 Kater (1985); Huerkamp (1990); Neal / Morgan (2000).
19 Huerkamp (1990) 66-67; Weindling (1986) 290.

the law before 1945? In answer to this, it is immediately clear that many of the key changes in this subject had taken place by the early 1950s. As the *Bundesgerichtshof* (*BGH*) put it succinctly in *BGH 27.11.1952* when discussing how to assess whether the defendant practitioner was at fault:[20]

> 'From the fact that expert practitioners of dentistry ordinarily work with unsecured needles, the conclusion may be drawn that the defendant demonstrated the degree of care *customary* within his occupation. Yet, as noted, this is not determinative. Rather, more decisive is whether the objective required care has been observed. Presently, the protection of patients from incidents during treatment, which threaten avoidable injury, is the highest imperative.'

That they cited a range of earlier decisions from the era of the *Reichsgericht* in justifying this makes clear that any account of our chosen topic must seek its answers in that era. Secondly, why then study the law before the enactment of the *BGB*? It, after all, is the touchstone of modern German civil law. To this we can say that in focusing on the development of the law here – the why, not simply the what – it is necessary to pre-empt the code to understand the extent to which codification, one of the key moments of formal change in the basis of the law here, made any difference at all.[21] Thus, some coverage of the nineteenth century is necessary at least. Thirdly, then, why stray into the murky, fractured world of the law before unification in 1871? Or, if one is interested in the impact of the *Reichsgericht*, why not begin in 1879? The answer here is that both the medical discourse surrounding error and the beginning of efforts to standardise medical education and regulation emerged at the start of the nineteenth century and continued throughout it. There is considerable discussion of the appropriate definition given to medical error in both the relevant legal and medical sources in the early part of the century, and in the latter half, the vast Pandectist literature provides a window into the emerging civil rather than criminal treatment of medical error. Thus, 1800 presents itself as a natural starting point to ensure these matters are given proper attention. Finally, and returning to the twentieth century, why include the post-1933 law as it developed under the Nazi regime? More detailed justification may be found in chapter five, but a brief explanation is required here: In short, the increasing use of technology and reach of medicine into the human body repeatedly came before the courts throughout the 1930s. Including this period allows us to present the two case studies on these questions that conclude this volume and demonstrate the role of technology as a driver of change here. Furthermore, both the early case law of the *BGH* and the literature of that post-war era as it relates to the subject matter at hand draw on cases from

20 BGHZ 8, 138, 141, emphasis added.

21 Zimmermann (2001) 98, sagely noting the possibility that in some areas the *BGB* brought no change at all.

that period without prejudice or comment; they played a key contemporary role in understanding the development of the law here. As to why we end at 1945, there is no point at which the narrative presented in this study can be easily broken, any such point is artificial at best and, at worst, blinds us to a possible explanation for the shape of the law. Once it is recognised that the post-1933 law is a necessary part of understanding the development of the law here, 1945 suggests itself as a suitable terminus given both the abolition of the *Reichsgericht* and the natural break in Germany's constitutional history that it heralds. Whilst further study of the post 1945-era, particularly given the establishment of the 1949 Basic Law, would greatly enrich the findings presented here, we offer only a brief comment on this era in the conclusion and leave that work for later scholars. As we will demonstrate, the issue of medical error was very much alive in the pre-1945 German law, itself dominated by the arrival of the *BGB*, and, earlier, throughout the jurisprudence of the *Reichsgericht*. As will be shown, it is in this earlier period that a clear break with a sociological approach to fault was made, even if sustaining it required the later courage of others.

## 2. Why study this at all?

This study provides an account of why and how German law concerning medical error developed as it did, uncovering the intimate link between the legal development and parallel changes in the medical arena. By doing so, it rehabilitates this earlier period as deserving as much attention for this aspect of the development of medical liability as it commonly receives when one considers other aspects of German medical liability.[22] It achieves this by demonstrating that the medical and legal discourses surrounding medical error were, for a considerable period, entwined across contract law, criminal law, the law of delict, and the medical regulatory sphere. The *Reichsgericht* came to exploit the tension within that medical discourse, and, in doing so, provided analytical space for courts to challenge accepted medical behaviour. Whilst the law was, for a long period, passively receptive, it was the existence of that medical discourse and its interrelation with the legal discourse that played a key role as a driver of legal development, albeit to the eventual chagrin of its originators.

The last century has witnessed three fundamental changes in healthcare. It has become institutionalised, its reach has intensified,[23] and a highly self-organised and regulated class of practitioner bound to a collective ethic of practice has emerged. No less than in other western countries, the contemporary German

22 See, for example, *RG 31.05.1894* RGSt 25, 375; Franzki (1982) 57–61; Helbron (2001) 23–23, 80–82.

23 Katzenmeier (2002) 11–17.

law is commonly accompanied by a rhetoric of crisis;[24] litigation rates have jumped in recent decades and there is a pressing need to focus on the present, not explain its genesis.[25] The knowledge offered in this book will not provide better rules; it does not offer any normative solution to this 'crisis' and may be thought useless as a result; such is the risk of any academic endeavour, particularly – if unfairly – legal history. In asking whether the law's development here is the product of legal or extra-legal factors, a German with an interest in the positive law may respond that understanding *how* and *why* the law developed is superfluous. Indeed, there may be few insights to be gained from this endeavour for those from other systems with a different iteration of medical or legal history; inevitably, further study will be required before more detailed comparative insights can be made. But to the extent that what follows offers a commentary on contemporary law, it is as a reminder that formal legal rules can be easily changed, but if the formal rules are not themselves drivers of the law, they are susceptible to be undermined by those drivers, unnoticed, which are.

## 3. A brief map of what follows

The course of argument may be stated briefly: The German civil law in the nineteenth century was heavily imprinted with long-irrelevant Romanist ideas about medical practice and the value of labour, with medical error largely sidelined. The criminal law, however, had historically maintained a considerably more specific treatment of medical liability and, in that context, an ongoing debate over conceptually defining error amongst the rapidly self-organising orthodox medical practitioners resulted in the *Kunstfehler*, a view of error rooted in the medical discourse. This internal medical discourse was readily co-opted by the nineteenth-century law as the formal fault standard shifted from gross to simple fault. The result was, thus, an informally indulgent stance towards orthodox medical practitioners. As the twentieth century progressed, an increase in the frequency of civil law actions placed that understanding of a *Kunstfehler* under pressure. But the concept provided the courts with a standard to push back against and, in the context of institutionalised and advancing medical practice, they did just that, adopting their own variation to help patients receive appropriate treatment. The book progresses as follows:

Chapter one traces the organisation of healthcare throughout this period, as well as the changing nature of medical practice, practitioners and regulation. It does this by mapping the emergence of modern orthodox medical practice

24 Giesen (1983) 7; Katzenmeier (2001) 40; Stauch (2008) 2; Oliphant (2013) 551.

25 Katzenmeier (2001) 40–41, noting the jump from 6,000 claims per annum in the 1960s to 20,000 by late 1990s. The trend continues, see Stauch (2013) 204.

alongside their less orthodox brethren, marked by the *Gewerbeordnung* 1869. It will be shown that, even in its modern institutional form, German medicine and medical practice was intensely pluralist in terms of the actors who provided medical services. The chapter then examines the emerging internal disciplinary and regulatory apparatus of the Honour Courts (*Ehrengerichte*), established as part of the paraphenalia of occupational development surrounding the orthodox practitioners. We identify the emergence of a lively internal medical discourse surrounding the definition of error, in the medical parlance a *Kunstfehler*, spurred by a single prosecution in 1811, the so-called *Fall Horn*. Internal medical discussion of what constituted an error worthy of legal reproach continued throughout the nineteenth century before settling on a broad acceptance of the idea of a failure to comply with generally accepted rules of medical science. Finally, the chapter traces the development of the procedural rules that governed how this medical discourse entered courts, drawing on published medical opinions presented in evidence. It becomes clear that as the modern procedural rules emerged, this internal medical discourse on error played a central role in the liability process.

Chapters two, three and four examine the analysis of medical error during the nineteenth century within criminal law, contract law and the law of delict respectively.

Whilst the focus of this study is upon German civil law and its approach to fault, chapter two provides important context in that it examines the history of the *Carolina*, from which the root of the *Kunstfehler* may be traced, the treatment of liability for medical error within the various criminal codifications of the era and the availability of the criminal law as a route for compensation in the form of a fine (*Buße*) in opposition to the civil law. It then considers the *Fall Horn* in greater detail. It demonstrates that, in parallel with some civil law scholars, an often-indulgent standard of fault appeared to apply before the *Reichsstrafgesetzbuch* 1871. Post-1871, however, the *Reichsgericht* adopted the language and logic of the *Kunstfehler* as it had been defined by the medical discourse, most visibly in a series of decisions in the 1880s, concerning antiseptics.

Turning to the civil law, chapter three begins by considering Roman medical practice and law before addressing the categorisation of the practitioner-patient relationship and, finally, the attendant fault standard that would result. Beginning in *Rome* is necessary to fully understand the nature of the debate surrounding medical error in nineteenth-century contract law and scholarship, which was frequently driven by discussion concerning different forms of labour, medicine's place within them, their respective categorisation within Roman law and the appropriateness (or not) of the author's chosen modern analogy. The contemporary debate is captured in one part, which examines the two leading scholarly contributions beyond mainstream Pandectists. Amongst Germanist scholarship there was considerably greater clarity, albeit variously expressed, and realism about how the relationship should be categorised. This modernist approach was also visible in the contemporary codifications. As to fault, the approach differed depending on the nature of the contractual solution being advocated, and in some cases a prejudicial choice about the fault standard led an author analytically back to the category rather the other way around. The idea of compliance with the standards of one's occupation, judged against expert evidence, was often relied on to fill out how various contractual standards would be applied in practice, whether codified or not, and, although the language of the *Kunstfehler* was largely absent, the underlying logic was often present. The result was that continued conceptual confusion about the nature of the contractual relationship left this part of the civil law slow to develop any specific approach to the practitioner-patient relationship and, ultimately, weak against the encroachment of the extra-legal influences on the subject.

In chapter four, again working from the Roman inheritance, we find that in delict there was markedly less confusion as to whether and how a claim against a medical practitioner might sound, but whether it offered recovery beyond what might be claimed under a contract, specifically damages for immaterial harm, was, beyond the various codified pockets of law in the era, contested. As such there was less discussion of delictual liability, but the fault standard, as in contract, settled on simple fault assessed against expert evidence drawn from orthodox medical practice. The chapter then turns to a discussion of the *sui generis* solution proposed by *Zimmermann* in 1873, which posited medical liability as being based on the old Roman *actio in factum contra mensorem qui falsum modum dixerit*. The supposed advantage of this was the higher degree of fault required to sustain a claim against a medical practitioner. Whilst there is some evidence that this quasi-delictual solution was adopted elsewhere in Germany, there are cases which suggest that it was, at best, exceptional. The chapter then considers the liability of unorthodox practitioners and notes an emerging tendency to hold such practitioners to the standards of their orthodox brethren, thus demonstrating a quasi-regulatory use of the private law to deal with pluralism in the medical marketplace. As with chapter three, the long reach of the Roman law appears to have stunted discussion of medical error as a specific legal problem, again opening the civil law to outside influence from the medical discourse.

Chapter five then examines the categorisation of medical liability in the *BGB* and the resulting standard of fault. As to the former, the *BGB* settled the default contractual position for the bulk of medical practice and, with some minor contortions, provided a flexible solution for the modern model of insurance-based practice, which had come to dominate healthcare. Equally, the unrelated decision to restrict damages for immaterial harm to claims in delict, and the fact that a contractual relationship was impossible in some prevalent forms of public healthcare provision, preserved the relevance of delict here. As such, courts were required to rationalise their analysis of why negligently performed treatment satisfied the wrongfulness requirement in § 823 (1) *BGB*, a process that drew on the discussions surrounding the '*Körperverletzungsdoktrin*' developed within the criminal law. As to the standard of fault, we find that whilst the *BGB* provided, in § 276, a relatively clear definition of negligence, the approach inherited from the nineteenth century of relying, in practice, on the contours of the *Kunstfehler* to define the boundaries of medical liability, blossomed in the twentieth, undermining the text of § 276 in practice. Nevertheless, the courts began to shift from that position over subsequent decades as open debate emerged over how the *Kunstfehler* related to the concept of fault (*Verschulden*). This resulted in clear analytical ground being put between the two concepts such that, whilst generally overlapping, a practitioner could be condemned to liability without, according to accepted medical practice, having committed a *Kunstfehler.* In a key shift, the courts came to exploit rather than indulge uncertainty as to what constituted accepted practice. Furthermore, as the previous definition faltered, academic commentary began to question the correct scope of what ought to be considered a question of *medical* behaviour in the first place. The chapter provides two case studies drawn from common fact patterns from this period. In each, the courts demonstrated their willingness to disregard evidence of accepted medical practice and instead craft their own standards. That each case study involved treatments that were characteristic of the advances in medical science and technology, and saw the courts articulate a standard based on patients' expectations of safe and modern treatment, supports the argument that these developments were key normative justifications for the courts' behaviour here. The chapter closes with a detailed consideration of the possible impact of the Nazi regime on the developments in the latter part of this period.

Chapter 1

# Medical Organisation, Regulation and Discipline in Germany: 1800–1945

'His art is conjectural, his path untrodden.'[1]

## 1. Introduction

We begin by examining medical practice, its regulation, its internal disciplinary mechanisms and how German law accessed medical expertise. Establishing how these features developed contextualises the legal discourse on fault and error and, ultimately, allows us to assess whether the legal system was influenced by that medical discourse. The following topics are here addressed: First, organisation of care and the division of medical practice between a range of orthodox and unorthodox practitioners; secondly, the process of professionalising medical practice, the development of the medical Honour Courts (*Ehrengerichte*) and the internal, medical debate over defining consequential medical error, the so-called *Kunstfehler*; thirdly, the role of expert evidence and the way it reflected that internal medical discourse in court. It will be shown that the occupational goals of the orthodox medical practitioner in the nineteenth century came to fundamentally affect the regulation of medical error.

## 2. The organisation of care

The following two sections examine the nature of medical organisation in the nineteenth and early twentieth centuries. The first looks at access to medical services. The second examines practitioners themselves, whether orthodox or otherwise, alongside changes in education and training and, finally, the changes wrought by Nazi health policy under the *Reichsärzteordnung* 1935. The evolving relationship between the state and medical practitioners emerges as a key feature of this period, given it allowed other forms of medical practice to compete alongside the scientific, university-based '*Schulmedizin*' of what we will refer to as orthodox practice.

1 Kalisch (1860) 27, quoting renowned psychiatrist JC Reil's characterisation of medical practice in the Fall Horn, discussed below.

## (A) Accessing healthcare

The nineteenth century saw the widespread medicalisation of the general populace;[2] but focusing on *Bismarck's* 1883 social insurance reforms, which formally opened up access to healthcare to a greater proportion of the population, can distract from the daily reality of accessing care earlier in the century.[3] Private practice, often in the form of taking on a position as a *Hausarzt* or *Leibarzt* for a family or individual, remained the default in the early nineteenth century; indeed, most healthcare interactions took place, even where the patient relied on public care,[4] at home, by the bedside. Provincial ordinances regulated costs, with access to orthodox medicine skewed towards the upper classes.[5] *Huerkamp* characterises the patient–practitioner relationship here as doubly asymmetric to the patient's advantage. First, patronage by the benefactor patient was emphasised over reliance on the practitioner's claimed expertise.[6] Secondly, orthodox practitioners were forced to compete alongside family members and unorthodox practitioners; each offering supposedly equal hope at the bedside.[7] Status and success often had more to do with social mores than learning;[8] a '*Hausarzt*' was advisor rather than simply a healer.[9] Providing free practice to the poor could be made a prerequisite for private practice,[10] but at the lower end of the market, competition with unorthodox practice was rife.[11]

Key to the process of medicalisation was the hospital. Particularly in the second half of the nineteenth century it provided the necessary observation and technology to implement medical advances, and enable orthodox practitioners to assert control over the patient.[12] In *Prussia* there had been a marked increase in the use of hospitals in the first half of the nineteenth century despite the fact that hospital-based advances, such as antiseptic and anaesthesia were products of the late 1800s; 155 hospitals in 1822 became 1,122 in 1876 and by 1855 the number of patients treated in hospital once a year had risen to 1:86 from 1:1841

2 Foucault (1979); Spree (1988) 182–183.

3 Dross (2002) 69; Weindling (1997) 119–121.

4 Dross (2002) 76, discussing the *Krankenbesuchanstalten* as a measure for poor relief, noting its adoption in Hamburg and the support the idea enjoyed in Berlin around 1900.

5 Huerkamp (1985) 27.

6 Huerkamp (1985) 24–26.

7 Ibid. 74.

8 Kater (1985), noting the relevance of duelling corps to progression for a young practitioner.

9 Huerkamp (1990) 70–71.

10 Stolberg (2002) 122.

11 Weindling (1997) 123.

12 Bleker (1997) 18.

in 1843.[13] Nevertheless, there was little standardisation across hospitals, particularly earlier in the century.[14]

Alongside the poor, working migrants were central to evolving healthcare mechanisms.[15] They motivated, in part, *Bismarck's* 1883 legislation on health insurance.[16] Existing private insurance funds, based on guild membership,[17] did not always provide medical treatment.[18] That 1883 legislation doubled the number of workers who had been covered by insurance to around 10% of the population, connecting them with hospital-based orthodox practitioners.[19] Over subsequent expansions, the percentage of the population covered by these schemes would rise to 23% in 1914 including family members following the *Reichsversicherungsordnung* 1911.[20] By the start of the 1930s, this had jumped to 20 million insured and, including their family members,[21] covered two thirds of the population. *Bismarck's* reforms coincided with the shift to the hospital as the dominant forum for practice as the growth of scientific medicine from the 1870s provided a justifiable, objective basis to undermine previously individualistic approaches to diagnosis and treatment.[22] Rural areas, however, often remained a 'medical desert',[23] populated by unorthodox or itinerant practitioners.[24] Neither were unorthodox practitioners necessarily excluded from insurance practice.[25] Vague drafting in the social insurance legislation meant there was no requirement that the medical treatment that was guaranteed was given by orthodox practitioners.[26] Nevertheless, insurance practice reduced orthodox practitioners' dependence on individual patronage,[27] and the resulting shift away from treatment in the patient's home reinforced medical control the patient's choices.[28]

13 Bleker (1997) 19.
14 Dross (2002) 82; Spree (1996) 59.
15 Dross (2002) 73.
16 Labisch (1997) 40, stressing that the legislation concerned labour and poverty rather than health and medical aid; Dross, (2002) 90.
17 Frevert (1985) 646, noting the existence in *Prussia* by 1874 of 4,641 local authority sick funds in addition to the private trade union funds.
18 Dross (2002) 79. See also the *Geselleninstitut* model in Bavaria, Stolberg (2002) 125.
19 Huerkamp (1985) 178; Huerkamp (1990) 75; Labisch (1997) 39–40, noting earlier, limited models.
20 Maehle (2009) 8; Huerkamp (1985) 2–3.
21 By 1925 over 85% of funds offered it as an optional benefit, Leichter (1979) 125.
22 Bleker (1997) 32.
23 Frevert (1985) 649.
24 Spree (1998) 178.
25 McClelland (2002) 80.
26 Spree (1998) 171.
27 Huerkamp (1985) 178; Huerkamp (1990) 70–71.
28 Huerkamp (1985) 131, 137, 163–164.

## (B) German medicine and medical practitioners

In this section, we look at changes in the educational requirements of orthodox medical practice. The importance of universities becomes clear as the genesis of the scientific medicine that characterised the largely homogenised orthodox practitioners that resulted. This contrasts with the continued presence of a broad range of unorthodox practitioners, who played a key role in healthcare provision.

### *(i) Medical training in the German-speaking world*

The German-speaking world had, since the seventeenth century been characterised by a complex, multi-tier system for training and regulating orthodox medical practitioners. This continued into the nineteenth century.[29] Alongside the university-educated '*Arzt*', the '*Wundarzt*', a practical surgeon, would have attended one of the many remaining practical schools rather than university.[30] There, lower class students received training to return to work in poorer areas.[31] This host of medical and para-medical practitioners was a legacy of the eighteenth century and, as a measure of their importance, one estimate calculated 12 '*Wundärzte*' for every university-trained practitioner, without counting less skilled (or unskilled) practitioners.[32] In part, this created the defining feature of German medical training: control by the state over the right to practice.[33] In Prussia, a 1725 statute removed universities' right to issue medical licences and required a fixed set of university courses, whilst, in Bavaria, state schools were established.[34] The Prussian model of statism proved particularly influential.[35] But it was not without its drawbacks: the state licence for one state (the *Approbation*) was not necessarily recognised by others until 1869.[36] Reform of the Prussian examination curricula in the *Medizinalordnung* 1825 completed the process removing the distinction between medicine and surgery.[37] Indeed, it was not until 1798 that a practical requirement was introduced at the *Charité*; again making universities suddenly all the more relevant.[38] The 1825 reforms had

29 Weindling (1997) 121–122.

30 17 remained by 1786, Bonner (1995) 21.

31 Bynum (2006) 138.

32 Bonner (1995) 21–22. One survey counted over 200 practical schools.

33 McClelland (2002) 35.

34 Bonner (1995) 27–29; Labisch (1997) 35.

35 Bonner (1995) 160.

36 McClelland (2002) 38.

37 Weisz (2006) 45–46; Huerkamp (1985) 45–46.

38 Huerkamp (1990) 67–68 candidates were required to treat two patients for one month.

maintained the division of medical practice between various classes of trained practitioner but signalled their decline by creating a university-trained competitor with broader competence.[39] By 1852 the leading practical schools had closed and a single standard was legislatively fixed with licensed practitioners taking one of three titles: *Praktischer Arzt*, *Wundarzt* or *Geburtshelfer*.[40]

University had, thus, become the single route into orthodox practice. As *Bonner* observes: 'Nowhere at mid-century was the new faith in science as the basis for medical education, mastered through experiment and the use of the laboratory, more advanced than in Germany'.[41] This linked orthodox practice with scientific research and development, inclining it towards the abstracted, laboratory science that symbolised German medicine and a progressive *mentalité*.[42] This also had drawbacks. The prevailing approach to academic training, that both teachers and pupils ought to be allowed total freedom to decide the form and content of their course ('*Lehrfreiheit*' and '*Lernfreiheit*'),[43] made it difficult to establish any sort of uniformity between curricula until at least mid-century.[44] Even *Virchow*, the great practitioner and Prussian politician, was scathing of this emphasis on freedom given that it seemed to create a poor-quality majority with a superlative minority at the top.[45]

The influence of the university saw the agglomeration of scientific subjects such as chemistry onto many curricula in 1861.[46] Following Prussia, an 1869 regulation for the North German Confederation refreshed the state examination and created the first uniform, nation-wide standard for certification.[47] This supplied the new, single, standard for the Empire post-unification.[48] The explosion in research and teaching matched an explosion in the number of university-trained practitioners, with states experiencing a huge increase between 1887 and 1939,[49] as the growth of the medical profession 'vastly outstripped' that of the population as a whole.[50] But, in these formative years

39 Kater (1985) 678; Huerkamp (1985) 42.

40 Huerkamp (1985) 57–58; Bonner (1995) 188; Bynum (2006) 138.

41 Bonner (1995) 187–188; Bynum (2006) 140.

42 Lenoir (2002) 14.

43 Bynum (2006) 140.

44 Simmer (1970) 44.

45 Ibid. 45

46 Huerkamp (1985) 102.

47 McClelland (2002) 118. It was at this point that the academic degree was separated from the ability to pass the *Staatsexamen*.

48 Bonner (1995) 254.

49 Breuer (1963) 12–13. *Breuer* demonstrates that Prussia, for instance, went from 9,310 practitioners servicing 28,375 residents in 1887 to 28,232 servicing 45,328 in 1939.

50 McClelland (2002) 80; Breuer (1963) 7; Bonner (1995) 270, 335–336.

of scientific medicine, orthodox practice did not necessarily come with a guarantee of safe practice; horizons were being expanded and with that came risks. *Krähe* reported a prosecution from 1852 whereby a surgeon shot his patient in the knee to stimulate bone growth. The act had the desired effect and the patient later pronounced themselves cured, the surgeon escaping, somewhat amazingly, with only disciplinary sanction.[51]

From the 1840s, state control, the grant and withdrawal, of the licence, was increasingly unwelcome; all licensed practitioners were, additionally, regarded as civil servants.[52] Tariffs issued by local authorities set fees,[53] and § 200 of the *Preußisches Strafgesetzbuch* 1851 (*PStGB*) imposed a fine for failure to offer medical assistance to those in 'urgent danger'; the so-called *Kurierzwang.* Although lacking a centralised representative body,[54] extensive lobbying resulted in the *Gewerbeordnung* 1869 passed for the North German Confederation and, in 1871, extended to the Empire.[55] This measure had profound implications for the practice of medicine, the sociological conception of orthodox practice and the nature of argument by legal scholars over categorising medical liability.[56] The *Gewerbeordnung* 1869 abrogated the *Kurierzwang*, but designated medicine a free trade, protecting only the use of titles such as '*Arzt*', '*Wundarzt*', or equivalent, without a licence; creating the so-called *Kurierfreiheit*,[57] and setting the scene for the early twentieth century.

### *(ii) The persistence of unorthodox practice*

Despite the criminal ban on quackery in § 199 *PStGB*, the nineteenth century remained a highpoint for such practice. Understanding this clarifies that the legal regulation of medical error concerned a world in which a vast range of practitioners populated the medical marketplace well into the twentieth century.[58] Several factors explain this persistense:

51 Krähe (1984) 85–87.
52 Huerkamp (1985) 242. It was noted that whilst they suffered the burdens they did not enjoy the benefits such as pensions.
53 Huerkamp (1985) 242–243. *Prussia* had first issued such a table in 1693 and had reissued it in 1815 setting both a floor and a ceiling for all medical practice.
54 Maehle (2009) 8; Huerkamp (1985) 255; Huerkamp (1985) 256–257. McClelland (2002) 78.
55 McClelland (2002) 78.
56 Maehle (1999) 313.
57 *Gewerbeordnung* 1869 § 29.
58 Frevert (1985) 638. *Huerkamp* describes a 'network of non-qualified healers', Huerkamp (1985) 36.

First, university-educated practitioners persisted with urban practice, leaving empirical and quack practitioners to fill the rural gaps.[59] For many, unorthodox practice was often the only available, and trusted, option.[60] Whilst in 1899 *Berlin* boasted 12.7 orthodox practitioners per 10,000 inhabitants, *West Prussia* had merely 3.1; for unorthodox practitioner, business was clearly there if one was willing to risk prosecution.[61] Secondly, the home-based nature of much practice would have served to validate unorthodox practice alongside orthodox practitioners.[62] Thirdly, it was, arguably, not until the second half of the century that university-based medicine's advantages became clear.[63] Fourthly, following the *Gewerbeordnung* 1869 many took advantage of the legal freedom granted to them, with numbers peaking in the decade following 1869.[64]

Unorthodox practices were manifold. Alongside exorcists, charmers, lay brothers, birth helpers, wise men, wise women, mesmerists and 'piss prophets', there were hydro-therapists, herbalists, homeopaths and lay midwives.[65] Many of these tapped into support for a humoral, vitalist '*Volksmedizin*', which for many patients entailed 'medicine'.[66] Practices such as homeopathy – the most powerful challenge to orthodox medical authority in the nineteenth century[67] – electro-homeopathy and hydropathy proved particularly popular in second half of the century.[68] Key to their success was casting these practices as similar to orthodox practice, with the administration of medicines and application of devices to the body;[69] homeopathy, just like university medicine aspired to present itself as a system, with a code of conduct and organisation locally and nationally.[70] Indeed, often advocates of some unorthodox practices such as homeopathy were, in fact orthodox, university-educated practitioners themselves.[71]

Unorthodox practice bloomed into the twentieth century.[72] Prussia, having begun registration in 1902, registered 4,104 such practitioners that year; 7,549 in

59 McClelland (2002) 39; Stolberg (2002) 123.

60 Spree (1998) 178.

61 Frevert (1985) 638. *Frevert* suggests that the migrant rural population carried with them their preference for unorthodox practice into the cities during the mid-century, at 648–649.

62 *Aerztliche Sachverständigen-Zeitung* (1896) 232.

63 Huerkamp (1990) 68; Frevert (1985) 640.

64 Stolberg (2001) 146.

65 Spree (1998) 161; Huerkamp (1985) 36.

66 Huerkamp (1985) 36–37; Spree (1998) 173.

67 Jütte (2001) 142.

68 Stolberg (2001) 153.

69 Ibid. 153.

70 Jütte (1995) 46 ff.

71 Jütte (1995) 45; Stolberg (2001) 143.

72 Kater (1985) 678.

1908.[73] The Minister of State ruled out formally barring unorthodox practitioners from insurance practice in 1887,[74] (on the basis that the many members of the public still preferred the latter),[75] a position which continued into the twentieth century.[76] It was not until 1939 that a regulation banned the remunerated, unlicensed practice of medicine and, even then, the corollary was, in effect, permanently legitimised unorthodox practice.[77]

### *(iii) Nazi medicine and medical practice*

The Nazi programme saw a vital role for medicine and medical practice.[78] Regarding the former, they emphasised a naturalism in contrast to, but confusingly, alongside scientific, orthodox practice.[79] This included an emphasis on de-specialising (and often de-urbanising) orthodox practitioners in favour of generalist, less technical medicine, enforced through compulsory continuing education.[80] As to practice, one of the defining features of the Nazi era medical hierarchy was a new grade of practitioner: the lay healer (*Heilpraktiker*); in essence formalised unorthodox practice. By 1935, when legislation asserted full Nazi control over the medical profession, there were at least 14,000 lay healers, three for every ten orthodox practitioners.[81] To curry favour, the German Natural Healer's Union reduced its membership by one third, expelling more quackish elements.[82] Following the *Heilpraktikergesetz* 1939, states' health officials could designate otherwise unorthodox practitioners as lay healers, who could take payment and provide healthcare within the local area. Particularly skilled, (an administrative rather than expert medical assessment), lay healers could entitle themselves, 'physicians of natural healing'; train at a university faculty without having a basic school diploma; and request aid from orthodox practitioners.[83]

This period shows that the era of the modern law's emergence was one in which treating patients in an institutionalised and scientific fashion arrived relatively late. Escaping the state's yoke had necessitated permitting unorthodox

73 Huerkamp (1985) 277.
74 Ibid. 274. The situation was fiercely criticised by the 15th *Ärztetag* in 1887, *Aerztliches Vereinsblatt* (1887) 199.
75 Spree (1998) 167.
76 McClelland (2002) 181.
77 Huerkamp (1985) 277.
78 Leichter (1979) 133; McClelland (2002) 223.
79 Haug (1989) 123.
80 Weisz (2006) 124–125.
81 Kater (1989) 37.
82 Ibid. 37.
83 § 2 (2) *Heilpraktikergesetz* 1939; Kater (1989) 38.

practice to continue. Finally, as the shift to hospital-based care continued into the twentieth century, the Nazi emphasis on alternative forms of medicine alternate to the university-based '*Schulmedizin*' saw some unorthodox practitioners formalised within the medical hierarchy.

## 3. Internal regulation and conceptions of error

Having established the nature of the medical marketplace, in this part we examine the disciplinary mechanisms overseeing orthodox practice and the internal, medical discussions, throughout the nineteenth century, concerning the definition of medical error. It will be established that, during the nineteenth century, both a standardised approach to medical regulation, and agreement of a standard hinging on the infringement of a generally recognised rule of medical practice emerged. Although formally unrelated, these developments characterise orthodox practice as primarily focused on intra-professional matters rather than the practitioner-patient relationship and keen to stress the need for grossly negligent behaviour as a requisite for imposing liability.

### (A) Regulation and the Honour Courts

As is clear from the preceding part, orthodox practitioners were increasingly subject to regulation concerning qualification; this was no less the case when it came to disciplinary regulation. In this section, we examine that regulation. Understanding how it operated reveals a tension between the ethics of orthodox practice and marketplace reality.[84] Establishing how poor practice was defined internally, and whether those regulatory structures targeted actionable error within the patient–practitioner relationship, allows us, in due course, to contrast the scope of protection offered by these internal mechanisms with that of the external regime imposed by the criminal and civil laws.

#### *(i) The regulatory background of the nineteenth century*

The fragmented nature of medical practice makes a detailed picture of nineteenth-century regulation difficult, but the broad shape is clear. Since the fourteenth century, medical practice had often been regulated through local ordinances and the establishment of local Medical Colleges (*Medizinalkollegia*).[85] These institu-

84 Maehle (1999) 309.

85 Dross (2002) 71, noting the establishment in *Prussia* of the central *Ober-Collegium Medici* in 1725 to take over from its provincial forerunners.

tions focused primarily on healthcare provision and policing quackery and, although they could regulate simply poor practice, sanctions were rare.[86]

The nineteenth century saw these ordinances refreshed or renewed, with over thirty states and provinces passing a new one. The underlying reason in many cases, such as the 1825 Prussian *Medizinalordnung*, was to ensure practitioners were better qualified,[87] and these ordinances often focused on improving intra-professional etiquette as a means to raise the occupation's standing.[88] Many did not contain any regulation of injurious practice, but some, like the Hamburg *Medizinalordnung* 1818, allowed withdrawal of permission to practice for repeated sloppy practice, meaning evidencing gross negligence or questionable morals.[89] *Rodegra* notes that whilst precise numbers of prosecutions under the *Medicinalordnung* 1818 are unavailable, there were a wide range of claims against local general practitioners.[90] In Prussia, which had been a latecomer in that it had not adopted a *Medizinaledikt* until 1685 followed by a further *Medizinalordnung* in 1725,[91] the *Gewerbe-Ordnung* 1845 made provision for revocation of a practitioner's licence if they clearly lacked the qualities licensure presumed.[92] In due course the *Gewerbeordnung* 1869, originally applicable within the North German Federation, was extended to cover the entire Empire from April 1871.[93] As noted above, this classified medical practice as a free trade, regulating only the titles associated with orthodox practice. Abandoning the approach of the *Gewerbe-Ordnung* 1845 towards medical practitioners, § 53 of the 1869 ordinance clarified that a medical license could only be revoked where it had been granted on false evidence. § 147 provided for a fine of up to 100 thalers or, in default, imprisonment for up to 6 weeks. Central regulation was, thus, limited.

Beginning with *Lübeck* in 1809, the nineteenth century saw also the growth of local medical societies, strengthening the collective cohesion of orthodox medical practitioners, leading to the creation, in 1873, of the *Deutsche Ärztevereinsbund*, the first centralised body to represent medical interests at the national level.[94] These societies clearly played a role in regulating medical practice given many possessed an Honour Council, (*Ehrenrat*) and, additionally, had adopted an enforceable code of conduct (*Standesordnung*). *Huerkamp* notes that whilst in 1877 only 24 of the 156 affiliated societies had such a code, by 1890 the number

86 Weindling (1997) 121–122; Riegger (2007) 58.
87 Riegger (2007) 72.
88 Huerkamp (1985) 129.
89 Riegger (2007) 72.
90 Rodegra (1986) 74.
91 Arztbach (1960) 3–4; Broman (1997) 53–55.
92 § 71 *Gewerbe-Ordnung* 1845.
93 Maehle (2009) 7.
94 Arztbach (1960) 4,6; Maehle (2009) 7.

stood at 105 and, of those which lacked a code, 61 still possessed an Honour Council, leaving only 53 without either.[95] In unaffiliated societies, the majority lacked either a council or a code, but a sizeable minority possessed both.[96] The emphasis on adopting this voluntary apparatus increased in the 1890s, as the chances of establishing a compulsory regime had diminished. To that end, in 1889, the *Ärztevereinsbund* adopted a standardised model code at its annual meeting in *Brunswick*.[97] There had already been a degree of overlap between some codes of conduct in that many had drawn from the codes in place in *Munich* (1875) and *Karlruhe* (1876), the former having been a translation of the American Medical Association's own 1847 'Code of Ethics'. These served, in part, as the basis for the *Brunswick* model.[98] By 1890, of the 352 societies in the Empire, 225 were part of the *Ärztevereinsbund*,[99] 135 had a code of some sort, and 194 an Honour Council.[100]

Despite these increasing efforts to put in place standardised disciplinary mechanisms, two criticisms can be made: First, the drawback of a voluntary system of regulation was that a practitioner could simply leave the relevant society to escape punishment.[101] Those who took the *Gewerbeordnung* 1869, and its promise of medicine as a free trade, at its word would be slow to consider their colleagues over their own economic wellbeing.[102] Secondly, it is important to understand that increased disciplinary mechanisms and use of codes of conduct did not bring with it an emphasis on patient safety. Rather, the opposite appears to be true, subordinated as patient safety often was to intra-occupational relations; many codes of conduct focused on occupational courtesy and etiquette.[103] Where they did touch on the practitioner-patient relationship it was often in very short, general provisions, in contrast to the detailed and elaborate provisions on how to treat one's colleagues.[104] Taking the *Karlsruhe* code as an example, the former required six to the latter's twenty-six paragraphs and, even then, patient-centred provisions dealt mainly with matters of etiquette towards a

95 Huerkamp (1985) 128.

96 Graf (1890) 54.

97 Maehle (2009) 15–16.

98 Ibid. 16. *Graf* listed the adoption of the *Karlsruhe* code as one of the topics surveyed in his 1890 census of the *Ärztevereine*, Graf (1890) 138.

99 Huerkamp (1985) 251.

100 Maehle (2009) 16–17, citing Graf (1890) 138–160.

101 Ibid. 13. *McClelland* makes this same criticism generally of the state's ability to control medical practice given, again, a practitioner could simply move, McClelland (2002) 36, 83.

102 Maehle (1999) 317.

103 Taupitz (1991) 278.

104 Huerkamp (1985) 128.

fellow practitioner in and around a patient.[105] Some other codes were incredibly concise, and focused merely on intra-professional conduct.[106] Indeed, the standardised model agreed in *Brunswick* was entirely focused on such matters alongside suppression of unorthodox practice.[107] This all might be explained on the basis that, fighting for control of the marketplace, the logic of orthodox practitioners was that, '... honourable = competent'.[108] But the result was that where a practitioner's view conflicted with that of their colleague, the thrust of their internal regulatory mechanics ranked silence and professional courtesy higher than the patient's health.[109]

For a variety of reasons then, these attempts at voluntary disciplinary regulation did not meet the hopes and expectations of practitioners, or offer much solace to the patient. Neither did the increased existence of disciplinary mechanisms mean greater use of them. An 1881 report to the *Ärztevereinsbund* noted that, of 92 medical societies surveyed, 52 had disciplinary panels of some sort but that only 32 cases had been reported between them.[110] This dissatisfaction on the part of orthodox practitioners would lead to attempts throughout the last three decades of the century to put in place a compulsory, and therefore necessarily state-backed, system for medical discipline.

### *(ii) Medical Chambers, Honour Courts and standardisation*

Compulsory, state-backed systems could be found throughout the late nineteenth century in some states such as *Baden* (1864), *Brunswick* (1865) *Saxony* (1865), *Bavaria* (1871) and *Hesse* (1876).[111] These bodies were recognised as occupational representatives by the government, responsible for providing advice on medical legislation, but were not always imbued with disciplinary powers.[112]

Alongside these local, state-backed models, the final two decades of the century saw concerted efforts by orthodox practitioners to establish more rigorous disciplinary structures along the lines of the Honour Courts, which were commonplace in the nineteenth century as disciplinary fora in the military, for civil servants, and lawyers.[113] For lawyers, the *Rechtsanwaltsordnung* 1878

105 Huerkamp (1985) 128.
106 Taupitz (1991) 278 discussing the four-paragraph code for Leipzig from 1888.
107 Maehle (2009) 16.
108 Taupitz (1991) 271.
109 Huerkamp (1985) 130.
110 Maehle (2009) 12–13.
111 Ibid. 10–11.
112 Huerkamp (1990) 78; Maehle (2009) 11.
113 Maehle (2009) 8.

established a series of state-authorised chambers, which resident practitioners were required to join. These chambers exercised a disciplinary jurisdiction over their members, overseen by an *Ehrengerichtshof* linked to the *Reichsgericht.*[114] It was the lawyers' model that formed the basis for the medical reform efforts.

The question of formal regulatory structures for orthodox medical practice was wrapped up in the standing of the occupation itself. Both the impact of lifting restrictions on medical practice through the *Gewerbeordnung* 1869, and an increased degree of intra-practitioner strife caused by greater density of practitioners, and competition under *Bismarck's* compulsory health insurance system post-1883 contributed to orthodox practitioners' desire to improve their image and standing within wider society.[115] The *Ärztevereinsbund* argued this could be achieved, in part, by ensuring practitioners were bound to a fixed set of norms through which 'proper' practice would be guaranteed and departures from it penalised. In 1880 they began to lobby for the creation of a model similar to that enjoyed by lawyers.[116] The *Ärztevereinsbund's* first draft of a *Reichsärzteordnung* had lifted directly from the *Rechtsanwaltsordnung* 1878, which presumed that a standardised, defined code of professional practice could be established, against which practitioners could be measured. These renewed attempts by orthodox practitioners to improve their social standing and distinguish themselves from their unlicensed competitors, in effect seeking to reverse, in part, the long-sought freedom that had been achieved with the *Gewerbeordnung* 1869, all contributed to the creation of new disciplinary structures and the standardisation of orthodox medical practice. However the 1880 draft was not unanimously supported upon its adoption. Some feared that as an Honour Court would require state involvement in the regulation of the profession, endangering hard-won freedoms; that these bodies would too quickly punish innovators or junior practitioners (unfamiliar with occupational mores) and too slowly punish the professors; or that greater use of Honour Councils was a less confrontational way of resolving intra-occupational disputes.[117] The attraction of voluntary mechanisms also remained strong with 1882 seeing a renewed draft adopted, which replaced state-authorised chambers with merely voluntary ones.[118]

Nevertheless, on the 25th of May 1887, after years of lobbying and increasing dissatisfaction with the voluntary regime, *Bismarck* issued a Royal Decree establishing 12 provincial Medical Chambers (*Ärztekammern*) for Prussia, each of which had jurisdiction over all of the orthodox practitioners resident in the

114 Maehle (2009) 8–9.
115 Huerkamp (1990) 78; Maehle (2009) 8.
116 Maehle (2009) 9–10.
117 Ibid. 12.
118 Ibid. 13.

province, who in turn were enfranchised for that Chamber.[119] The disciplinary mechanism for the Medical Chambers allowed for warnings, or, temporary or permanent withdrawal of voting rights where a practitioner, '…seriously or repeatedly violated the duties of their calling',[120] or was found to have, '…proven themselves unworthy of the respect their calling demanded'.[121] In the event these (inflexibly too harsh or too lenient) powers were rarely deployed.[122] Alongside procedural lethargy – in *Westfalia*, that sanction had been used twice in a decade, whilst in *Berlin / Brandenburg* it was only used seven times between 1898 and 1900 – by 1891 only 52 cases had been reported in *Prussia* as a whole with only ten resulting in sanction.[123] In any case, where a practitioner had burned their bridges or cared little for their voting rights, this state of affairs would likely have been quite ineffective and prompted continued efforts towards reform.[124]

In 1889, *Bismarck* rejected a request by the *Deutsche Ärztevereinsbund* for a national *Ärzteordnung*; the different approach of some states suggesting it was best left to individual states to decide.[125] The renewed emphasis this placed on standardising the voluntary structures of the medical societies has been explored above and, in 1890, the *Ärztevereinsbund* reinstated state-backed Honour Courts into its platform for reform. Opposition remained, with some pointing to fears the system, open as it would be to both practitioners *and* the public, might result in patients clogging the system with damaging, unsubstantiated claims.[126] The original 1880 draft had proposed action only where the state medical authorities, the public prosecutor or three practitioners had applied for prosecution.[127] Nevertheless, a draft Law on Honour Courts (*Ehrengerichtsgesetz*) emerged in 1896 and was passed into law in 1899, coming into force on the 1st April 1900.[128] The establishment of the Honour Courts helped orthodox practitioners regain a degree of status lost to the *Gewerbeordnung* 1869.[129] This final push was not limited to *Prussia*: both *Hamburg* (1894) and *Saxony* (1896) had had established state-backed Honour Courts (and in the case of the latter, followed up in 1904

119 Huerkamp (1985) 263.
120 Ibid. 264.
121 Maehle (2009) 14.
122 Maehle (1999) 317.
123 Maehle (2009) 16.
124 Huerkamp (1985) 264.
125 McClelland (2002) 83.
126 Maehle (2009) 17.
127 Ibid. 11.
128 Ibid. 18.
129 Huerkamp (1990) 78.

with a regional *Ärzteordnung*).[130] A raft of similar legislation followed in many states during the next decades.[131]

The Prussian *Ehrengerichtsgesetz* 1899 established an Honour Court for each of the 12 local chambers, membership of which was compulsory for practitioners within the region.[132] These were to be staffed by four practitioners drawn from the respective chamber and a professional judge, who took on the role of investigating the claim.[133] The *Ehrengerichtshof für Ärzte* (*EGHA*), some of whose decisions were published in both the relevant periodicals and as freestanding collections by the court itself,[134] was, in turn, staffed by the legally trained director of the ministry for Medical Affairs, four practitioners drawn from the chambers and two appointed by the King.[135] Echoing the phrasing of § 28 of the *Rechtsanwaltsordnung*, § 3 of the *Ehrengerichtsgesetz* required conscientious practice and that a practitioner, '…showed himself worthy of the respect that his calling demanded, in his conduct both during and outside medical practice',[136] although it did not define more precisely when these duties would be breached.[137] § 3 clarified that: '*Politische, wissenschaftliche und religiöse Ansichten oder Handlungen eines Arztes als solche können niemals den Gegenstand eines ehrengerichtlichen Verfahrens bilden*', so the intellectual, political and social views of a practitioner appeared, as such, beyond disciplinary procedures. Where these duties were breached, the court could levy fines up to 300 marks where the proceedings were informal along with warnings and reprimands, and up to 3,000 marks where they were formal (a potentially astronomical sum given only 40% of practitioners in *Berlin / Brandenburg* earned more than 5,000 marks per year in 1900, rising to 53% by 1906, and ten-fold greater than the criminal law could levy for a negligent injury),[138] alongside withdrawal of voting rights – either temporarily or permanently – from the guilty party.[139] The basic right to practice, however, the *Approbation*, could only be withdrawn by the state, normally on the basis of criminal conviction.[140] The Prussian scheme thus allowed for the largest fines and, along with Saxony, had the highest degree of

130 Huerkamp (1985) 265; Maehle (2009) 20.
131 Arztbach (1960) 6–7.
132 Maehle (1999) 309–338.
133 Maehle (2009) 19.
134 Ibid. 21.
135 Huerkamp (1985) 268–269.
136 *Aerztliches Vereinsblatt für Deutschland* (1897) 301–310; Maehle (1999) 320.
137 Arztbach (1960) 10.
138 Huerkamp (1985) 214.
139 Maehle (2009) 19.
140 Ibid. 19, 26.

formal organisation,[141] but had a broad flexibility in the sanctions it could deploy, as well as recognition that some cases could be dealt with summarily.[142] The fact that the *Ehrengerichtsgesetz* had not, as in Saxony, legislated for a binding code of conduct also provided broad scope for the Honour Courts to use § 3 to regulate Prussian medical officials.[143]

Turning to what can be gleaned from the practice of the Honour Courts, it is immediately clear that, unlike the preceding voluntary system, the courts were subject to much greater use, providing 'lively activity' in disciplining practitioners.[144] Before the First World War the courts received around 480 to 560 complaints per year rising to around 600 in 1920 and 1921. Taking into account the ever-rising number of practitioners this gives a fairly steady annual rate of around 3–3.5% of practitioners before and after the war being subjected to disciplinary proceedings.[145] A substantial number also involved the use of formal proceedings (1,357 between 1903 and 1913) and in total *Maehle* estimates that as many as one in ten practitioners were subject to proceedings during the years up to WWI.[146] Indeed *Huerkamp*, who gives slightly differing figures covering 1904–1909, suggests around 800 complaints were received per year, of which around 500 went to some sort of proceedings, and that between 1904 and 1909 around 20% of all Prussian practitioners would have been disciplined.[147] As to how the actions were initiated, between 1903 and 1921 around 20–30% came from private persons, and a similar number from the state authorities leaving a plurality of allegations stemming from other medical practitioners.[148] If the aim had been to improve collegial behaviour, practitioners themselves had, it seems, certainly taken the opportunity to report on their brethren.[149]

Looking at the types of cases that were reported gives us a final insight into the role of internal disciplinary measures. Here, we find two key features: First, a small handful of offences accounted for most proceedings before the Honour Courts, and these were predominantly focused on intra-professional problems. In *Berlin / Brandenburg*, between 1903 and 1920, advertising was the most frequently cited reason for punishment outstripping maltreatment by 18:1.[150] This was equally reflected in both the practice of the *Ehrengerichtshof*, the

141 Maehle (1999) 321.
142 Maehle (1999) 331.
143 Huerkamp (1985) 270.
144 Maehle (2009) 31; Huerkamp (1985) 271.
145 Ibid. 32–35.
146 Ibid. 33.
147 Huerkamp (1985) 272.
148 Maehle (2009) 34.
149 Huerkamp (1985) 272.
150 Maehle (2009) 37.

equivalent Saxon institutions and the later situation in the Weimar Republic.[151] Where a complaint concerned the practitioner-patient relationship, sexual misconduct, which could attract a stiff fine,[152] and negligent certification predominated,[153] and, where they conflicted, such concerns would often be subordinated to intra-professional mores. For instance, in a decision from the *Westfalia* Honour Court in 1905, a practitioner, who had provided a report on behalf of a patient regarding their allegation against the district physician, was sanctioned for having believed the word of the patient against a fellow practitioner; the charge against the physician having been dismissed.[154] Despite the *Gewerbeordnung* 1869 repealing the legal compulsion to aid passersby, the *Ehrengerichtshof* declared, in an early decision, that the failure to supply medical aid to a person in a life-threatening situation would bring disciplinary, if not legal, sanction.[155] There, the practitioner had turned down two requests for aid despite knowing that the patient, a three-and-a-half year old child was sick. His appeal, that a sudden worsening of the illness had instead caused the situation, was rejected. As to what might be regarded as failing to show the necessary conscientiousness in treatment, one case, in which a practitioner had treated their patient for gonorrhoea by mail, saw this condemned as a 'gross lack of scruples', although it is unclear whether the patient actually suffered any harm.[156] Certainly, the court seemed slow to punish a practitioner on the basis of long-held opinions, at least where considered appropriate: Where a practitioner had allegedly given insufficient advice to a patient about the contagiousness of scarlet fever, the *Ehrengerichtshof* accepted that, in the absence of official advice about using disinfectant, the advice to wash and air the infected child's clothes could not be considered a breach of the duty to provide conscientious practice.[157] In some cases the use of the conscientious practice test could be used to punish what was, in effect, negligent practice, such as where a practitioner had carelessly filled in a certificate by simply crediting the account of the patient in whose interest it was being made, rather than establishing the facts for themselves.[158] Indeed, in another certification case, the court made clear that in light of the duty of care imposed by §§ 222 and 230 of the *Reichsstrafgesetzbuch* by reason of a medical practitioner's calling, discussed at greater length in

151 Maehle (2009) 38–39 n 120.
152 *EGHA 15.05.1906* EPE (1908) 107; *EGHA 15.05.1906* EPE (1908) 108.
153 Maehle (2009) 38–39.
154 Maehle (1999) 330.
155 *EGHA 01.12.1902*, EPE (1908) 81.
156 *EGHA 07.01.1907*, EPE (1908) 85.
157 *EGHA 02.12.1905*, EPE (1908) 99.
158 *EGHA 11.01.1904*, EPE (1908) 89.

chapter two, there could be no excusable mistake where a practitioner negligently failed to meet the standard expected of them. There, the practitioner had negligently certified his patient, deaf-mute from childhood, as having functional sensory organs. He claimed that whilst he had made notes on which to base the certificate, he had failed to note the deaf-muteness. This negligence was sufficient to ground his punishment for failure to practice conscientiously.[159]

The second key feature is that the regime was rigorously applied to sharpen the blurred line between orthodox and unorthodox practice in favour of the former. Indeed, although jurisdiction over activities and beliefs outside of the simple practice of medicine had seemingly been denied, a decision of the *EGHA* in 1902 had stressed that the '*als solche*' in § 3 *Ehrengerichtsgesetz* permitted the *form* in which the views were expressed to fall under disciplinary jurisdiction.[160] Thus, whilst the holding of differing medical viewpoints was not, as such, punishable, practitioners still needed to be wary in their advocacy. In 1904, the *EGHA* disciplined a supporter of homeopathy on the basis of the offensive, spiteful and dishonourable way in which he had expressed his opposition to scientific – or in his description, allopathic – medicine.[161] It could also be said that the association of advertising with unorthodox practice lay behind the vehemence with which it was pursued by orthodox practitioners and punished by the Honour Court.[162] Any actual business association with a quack or naturopath who the orthodox practitioner knew, or ought to have known, was such was, without more, regarded as an infringement against professional honour (*Standesehre*).[163] A quack, for the purposes of the *Ehrensgerichtshof*, was anyone who had not received a formal medical education.[164] Practitioners were penalised for taking posts at institutions overseen by known quacks (there a mesmerist),[165] for giving speeches at associations known to be associated with quackery, and for working alongside a quack even where the local population had customarily gone first to see said bone-patcher (*Knochenflicker*).[166]

Such unorthodox practitioners were, by their nature, subject neither to regulation as a prior requirement for entering the medical marketplace nor for their continued place in it. Even those who tried to form themselves in the image of their orthodox colleagues could neither agree nor meaningfully

159 *EGHA 04.05.1903*, EPE (1908) 87.

160 *EGHA 30.05.1902*, EPE (1908) 165; Huerkamp (1985) 270. See also *EGHA 08.01.1907*, EPE (1908) 166–168.

161 *EGHA 08.11.1904*, EPE (1908) 166; Maehle (2009) 39.

162 Maehle (2009) 36.

163 *EGHA 14.05.1906*, EPE (1908) 140.

164 *EGHA 14.05.1906*, EPE (1908) 140.

165 *EGHA 30.05.1902*, EPE (1908) 138; *EGHA 05.05.1903*, EPE (1908) 139.

166 *EGHA 28.05.1907*, EPE (1908) 142.

enforce common standards. Rather it was left to the criminal or civil law to control dangerous practice and offer remedies for damage caused by it. Thus, the scope of liability for injurious practice becomes central in this early period as the only effective means of regulating the less high-minded practitioner. For orthodox practitioners, criminal liability was also important as, by the 1850s, it could, as noted above, lead to the withdrawal by the state of one's license entirely. The quasi-regulatory nature of the criminal law, which for a long time had provided for a ban from practice amongst the possible punishments, will be examined in chapter two.

Through their rigorous policing of these activities on the part of orthodox practitioners, the Honour Courts succeeded in creating an ersatz version of the legal distinction between orthodox and unorthodox practice that had been abandoned in the *Gewerbeordnung* 1869.[167] Equally, despite the fact that the *Ehrengerichtsgesetz* had not provided a standardised code of conduct, as *Maehle* notes, the fact that the decisions made under its aegis were published, allowed a binding code of medical ethics to accrete over time.[168] The decisions fed back into the development of the Prussian code of conduct of 1911, which later informed the national, model code of conduct adopted by the *Ärztevereinsbund* in 1926.[169] Amongst other things, this had, loftily, declared, in a common but trite medical trope, the irrelevance of monetary gain.[170] Unsurprisingly perhaps, the nature of the ethical and regulatory framework developed by the Honour Courts was one that focused on improving the lot of orthodox practitioners as a class by imposing a centralised, idealised form of practice centred on intra-occupational behaviour, and minimising competition for the benefit of practitioners rather than ensuring safe practice for the patient as an end in itself.[171] Conscientious practice meant careful practice but, more tellingly, required a practitioner to consult their own conscience as to what to do in a challenging situation, and so decide what was best for their patient, rather than treating the patient as being competent to decide for themselves.[172]

### *(iii) The Reichsärzteordnung 1935*

Some states, such as Saxony, had established an *Ärzteordnung* imposing a legally-binding professional code as early as 1904, but this model remained an outlier in

167 Huerkamp (1985) 273.
168 Maehle (2009) 39.
169 Maehle (1999) 337.
170 Taupitz (1991) 288.
171 Maehle (1999) 329.
172 Ibid. 334.

the era. It was not until December 1935, under the Nazi regime, that orthodox practitioners succeeded in their long-held goal of a single regulatory ordinance, the *Reichsärzteordnung* (*RÄO*).[173] This came not as the result of successful lobbying by practitioners but, rather, as part of the Nazi policy of coordination (*Gleichschaltung*), with the rhetoric of self-regulation used as a vehicle to realise the corrupting theories that underlay the regime. Indeed, any claim to self-regulation must be carefully viewed in light of the extensive control over professional occupations, medicine in particular, that resulted from this rhetoric in practice.[174] The *RÄO* brought with it the effective end of any independence that the medical profession had enjoyed up to this point: for instance, the *Ärztevereinsbund* was forced to disband in April 1936, replaced by the *Reichsärztekammer*, which fell under the direct ministerial control.[175] The era of medicine as a free trade, which had begun in 1869, ended as the *RÄO* set aside the relevant provisions of the *Gewerbeordnung* 1869 for medical practice,[176] and, to a much greater degree than with other occupations, brought it under the control of the state:[177] § 1 (2) *RÄO* pithily declared, '*Der ärztliche Beruf ist kein Gewerbe*'. This had, as will be shown in subsequent chapters, long been effectively overlooked in questions of liability, but had also been put under pressure by the courts, who had been increasingly unwilling to overlook the stated higher goals of serving a public purpose in favour of the muckier, more base focus on monies that designation as a *Gewerbe* brought with it.[178]

The work of the Honour Courts had continued undisturbed through to the withdrawal of their jurisdiction and abolition in 1936 under the *RÄO*.[179] That instrument established a uniform system of medical professional courts in every medical chamber throughout the country with a central appeal court in *Munich*, the *Ärztegerichtshof*.[180] In some of many changes under this new regime, proceedings could only be initiated by the local overseeing authorities, the *Reichsärztekammer*, or the practitioner themselves;[181] and the courts were overseen by a judge in the local district court.[182] The possible measures available were warnings, reprimands and fines up to 10,000 marks as well as excluding a practitioner from the public health sector and assessing their fitness to practice

173 RGBl I S 1433; Arztbach (1960) 13; Taupitz (1991) 288–289.
174 Taupitz (1991) 290.
175 § 80 *RÄO* 1935; McClelland (2002) 217.
176 Arztbach (1960) 5.
177 Ibid. 12–13.
178 Ibid. 14 discussing *RG 11.06.1907* RGZ 66, 143.
179 Taupitz (1991) 289.
180 Maehle (1999) 337.
181 § 57 *RÄO* 1935.
182 Arztbach (1960) 16.

medicine.[183] Whilst the *RÄO* made clear that practice was conditional on respecting civil regulations, and the disciplinary courts were broadly empowered to expel practitioners considered to be '*unwürdig*', the racist and anti-Semitic goals underlying these rules were clear in practice.[184]

In establishing a single national regime for medical regulation and discipline, the *RÄÖ* also abrogated the various state codes of conduct.[185] In its place, § 14 *RÄO* empowered the *Reichsärztekammer* to enact a professional ordinance for the entire *Reich*, which duly followed in November 1937, in the form of the *Berufsordnung für die Deutschen Ärzte.* Far from being a purely Nazi-driven document it leant closely on the document that had been promulgated, drawing on the developed practice of ethics, as a voluntary code by the now extinct *Ärztevereinsbund* in 1926. That code had in fact already been administratively adopted in 1935 by the organisation that oversaw insurance practice but was thus, in parts, broadened to all practitioners by the 1937 order.[186] This may be contrasted with the clearly Nazi preamble, which made explicit the envisaged role of medical practitioners as guardians of the ethnic and racial '*Volk*', subordinate to the regime's evil ideology, and a number of provisions, which, characteristically, emphasised the rights of the state over those of individual patients.[187] Yet, once shorn of these elements, the 1937 order formed a model for post-war disciplinary regulations enacted by various local chambers,[188] which filled the vacuum left by the suspension of the *Reichsärztekammer.*[189]

### *(iv) The Heilpraktikergesetz 1939*

The reinstatement of a formal legal connection between remunerated practice and orthodox practice proved problematic for Nazi ideology. The regime placed particular emphasis on an organic, natural, and holist medical ideology, and had attempted to turn away from the technological and scientific model that had so characterised orthodox German medicine up to that point.[190] As discussed above, this was, in part, drawing on a ready body of support for natural health movements and other forms of medicine that had continued to flourish

183 § 52 *RÄO* 1935; Maehle (1999) 337.
184 Arztbach (1960) 13. See Majer (2003) 310–312.
185 § 86 *RÄO* 1935; Taupitz (1991) 289.
186 Taupitz (1991) 289.
187 For instance, § 3 emphasised the duty to emphasise procreation for the greater good of the regime
188 Hübner/Drost (1955) 1–3, noting its use in 1950 by *Bayern*; Taupitz (1991) 291, who notes the 1956 adoption of a version by the *Hesse* medical chamber.
189 Hübner/Drost (1955) 1; Taupitz (1991) 294.
190 Lawrence (2006) 374.

throughout Weimar Germany.[191] But placing a renewed emphasis on homeopathy and folk medicine was at odds with the statutory declaration that, '*Der ärztliche Beruf ist kein Gewerbe.*'[192] An attempt at finding a middle ground was made with the *Heilpraktikergesetz* 1939 which, as discussed, created the new rank of lay healer (*Heilpraktiker*). These practitioners were granted a degree of ersatz professional clothing in the form of compulsory membership of the new German Natural Healer's Union, but no new recruitment was permitted.[193] Most worryingly from the orthodox perspective was that the new law blurred the clear distinction between licensed and unlicensed practice and indeed, echoing the old *Kurpfuschereiverbot* in § 199 *PStGB*, permitted the old ways to continue provided an unorthodox practitioner did not take payment. Those who fell afoul of the statute could be imprisoned for up to one year or fined.[194]

## (B) Medical conceptions of error: The *Kunstfehler*

The defining feature of the internal medical discourse on error in the nineteenth century was a fierce, on-going debate over its definition, or to use the word that was coined to describe it, the meaning of a *Kunstfehler*.[195] The term had its etymological roots in the language used by the first comprehensive criminal code for the Empire, the *Carolina* in 1532, discussed further in chapter two. There, in a statutory article dealing with negligent medical conduct, a punishment was levied against those whose caused death through practice that was '*unfleiß oder unkunst*'. Over time it was used to describe medical error generally, and by the nineteenth century, had come to be used as a synonym for it.[196] But it was the nineteenth century, which saw an extended engagement by the medical profession in trying to define what should be regarded as a *Kunstfehler*. In this section, we examine this debate and the definition upon which orthodox practice eventually settled.

### *(i) The Fall Horn*

Although the majority of medical texts discussing the subject appear in the latter half of the century,[197] the spur to these discussions was the criminal prosecution

191 Lawrence (2006) 375.
192 Kater (1989) 37.
193 Ibid. 38.
194 § 5 (1) *Heilpraktikergesetz* 1939.
195 Krähe (1984) 3, 54 noting its earliest use in a medico-legal text of 1797 but its emergence in the medical literature of this period and its absence up to that point from the lexicon.
196 Katzenmeier (2002) 273.
197 Riegger (2007) 80.

of one *Dr Ernst Horn*, the head of psychiatry at the *Charité* in 1811. The legal ramifications of the case will be examined in greater detail in chapter two but it suffices here to briefly explain the facts and the result. *Horn* was accused of criminal negligence following the death of one of his patients as a result, it was alleged, of the treatment he had prescribed. This had involved securing the patient, a mentally ill woman, in a restraint sack (*Zwangsack*), which was itself placed within another sack for a period of an hour. Shortly upon being removed from the sacks, the patient died. The possibility of an eminent medical practitioner, rather than a quack, being held criminally liable for a treatment he had often used in the past led to uproar in the medical world, and began a discussion that would span the rest of the century. Thanks to the presence of the earlier rule in the *Carolina*, it was hardly the first criminal prosecution of a medical practitioner, but, as it concerned the definition of a *Kunstfehler*, it was, '...the most spectacular case of its time, and was the origin of the scholarly argument concerning the issue'.[198] Key to the finding that he had not been criminally negligent had been a succession of expert opinions that regarded his treatment methods as relatively common and identified the cause of death as the result of an independent medical problem suffered by the victim. Adding to its notoriety was the fact that the prosecution had been motivated by a rival practitioner at the *Charité* sending a letter to the authorities accusing *Horn* of criminal negligence.[199] We will return to the opinions delivered in the *Fall Horn* in more detail below.

### *(ii) The struggle for clarity*

Despite discussion in the literature concerning the practitioner-patient relationship, from the seventeenth century onwards, there had been, at least by the early nineteenth century, little attempt to actually define what a *Kunstfehler* was, and even less agreement on a fixed definition. *Krähe* recounts *Henke's* 1830 list of eight texts back to 1601, which had addressed the issue of medical error but which lamented that this had failed to provide a satisfactory account.[200] Indeed, the term was not to be found in some contemporary regulatory documents, such as the 1818 Hamburg *Medizinal Ordnung*, at all.[201] The earliest definition by *Fahner*, in 1797, had defined it as '...behaviour that is contrary to the authoritative and general rules of medical practice accepted by teachers of the same',

198 Krähe (1984) 38.
199 Kalisch (1860).
200 See Henke (1830) 86–93.
201 Rodegra (1986) 72.

without discussion of how these generally accepted 'rules' were to be arrived at.[202]

The first half of the nineteenth century saw several definitions proffered, with discussion often centring around whether the state of medicine admitted such general rules as *Fahner*, and in 1814 *Gossler*,[203] had suggested as forming the boundaries of acceptable practice. In 1818 *Skalley*, who had been the investigating judge in the *Fall Horn*, rejected such an approach on the basis that such rules were not possible and, looking to the tripartite schema of fault that had been adopted in the Prussian *Allgemeines Landrecht* 1794, that, in any case, criminal liability should be restricted to *culpa lata*. He was less clear on the standard in civil cases but it was certainly not that a practitioner would be liable for 'minor fault'.[204] In 1830 *Henke*, the renowned medico-legal author, again raised concerns that fixed rules were both impractical given the current state of medicine, and that they would restrict the necessary freedom of medical practice required for progress. Furthermore, he supported a framework that punished unorthodox practitioners to a greater degree than orthodox practitioner who, it had to be presumed, were operating in the patient's interests.[205] Like *Skalley*, *Henke* restricted liability to gross negligence but eschewed offering a free-standing definition of a *Kunstfehler* beyond that. Nevertheless, he gave an example that such would be the case where a practitioner had killed or injured a patient through the, 'absence of, or, disregard for, the knowledge or skills appropriate to the respective science or art'.[206] Drawing on the old approach of the *Carolina*, evidence of such a failing on the part of an orthodox practitioner, could be proven only by an opinion from the 'higher medical authorities [...] or the medical faculties'. In particular they would be well placed to rule on whether a new method was appropriate or not.[207] The inability to define the extent of the ever-changing foundations of medical knowledge, or indeed guarantee that licensed practice ensured only safe practice was a theme, which appeared in the work of many other medico-legal authors in the era who struggled to define a *Kunstfehler*, leading some to even eschew liability for negligently inflicted harm altogether on the basis that it was simply the patient's bad luck.[208] As the literature continued to increase, the various different definitions abounding in this early period led the leading criminal lawyer of the age to label the concept of

202 Riegger (2007) 81.
203 Goßler (1814).
204 Krähe (1984) 43.
205 Ibid. 46.
206 Henke (1830) 142.
207 Ibid. 145–146.
208 Krähe (1984) 49–50.

little use for defining the boundaries of liability, particularly where it was focused on establishing fixed rules for medical practice.[209] Summing up the results up to mid-century, common practice was less to seek to define a *Kunstfehler* but rather use it as a catchall for punishable conduct in order to facilitate discussion of the extent to which terms of art rooted in the law should be applicable to medical practitioners.[210] Indeed the fact, overlooked by *Krähe*, that *Henke's* example given above is almost precisely the same language as that in article 67 of the *Bayerische Strafgesetzbuch* 1813, which defined the breach of a duty owed by reason of one's calling or trade as gross negligence, demonstrates the extent to which nascent legal, rather than medical definitions informed the discourse. *Krähe* noted, further, that, whilst the frequently given reason for failing to fix upon a definition was the difficulty in trying to reconcile the idea of a mistake (something defined by not doing that which ought to be done in the circumstances) with a setting in which fixed rules were thought a hindrance rather than a help, this was often phrased in terms of hindrance to the *general* progress of medicine, not the *particular* good of the patient. The latter was often relegated, rhetorically, behind the 'salvation of scholarship and humanity'.[211]

### *(iii) Virchow's resolution*

Such was the state of affairs to which the medical scholars of the second half of the nineteenth century bent their minds. In 1857 *Casper* sought to define medical error not in terms of a *Kunstfehler*, but rather in the legal terminology of the 1851 Prussian criminal code. As the general subject matter of a *Kunstfehler* was negligent practice, it was necessary to grapple with the law on its own terms but, unfortunately, a definition had been omitted by the legislator.[212] He rejected the idea that medicine had a fixed codex of norms, although he did note that that law had provided such a schema for builders,[213] but conceded that a medical license did not grant a practitioner a free pass and expected the law to respect a practitioner's school of thought, experience, talent and conscience.[214] He preferred to define negligent medical conduct as that which *totally* diverged from what the 'overwhelming majority' of practitioners would do in the same situation *and* what the 'overwhelming majority' of medical writers regarded as

209 Mittermaier (1853) 179.
210 Krähe (1984) 62.
211 Ibid. 63–63.
212 Ibid. 82.
213 Casper (1957) §70, 635–636.
214 Ibid. §72, 644.

the appropriate course of action.[215] Although, by shifting focus to the lived practice of medicine rather than pre-ordained rules, progress of a sort had been made, the obvious problem of how to reconcile this with developing new treatments proved a stumbling block.[216] As *Krähe* noted, in the example of the pistol-based treatment described earlier, *Casper's* test would surely have resulted in a guilty verdict rather than the more measured balancing of risks and benefit that saw that practitioner acquitted.[217] What it did provide, however, was grist for later medical scholars to mill.[218]

The most significant contribution to the debate was made in 1870 by leading medical practitioner and Prussian statesman *Rudolf Virchow*. The expert opinion (*Gutachten*) from which it had been taken had been written as a contribution to the drafting process for the criminal code of the North German Federation, and discussed the applicability of the corresponding paragraphs of the 1851 Prussian criminal code to medical practitioners, a prestigious task undertaken by a respected medical genius. Recognising that there could be no argument as to whether medical practitioners were caught by the provisions, examined in detail in the following chapter, *Virchow* instead proposed an additional sentence for the section dealing with negligent homicide, which would have enacted two bases for finding a culpable *Kunstfehler*: '1) Breach of the generally recognised rules of the medical arts, 2) The absence of required attention or care'.[219] As to the first, he conceded there was no fixed codex, but that was not equivalent to saying that there were not a number of generally accepted rules. He offered as examples: drugs having maximally allowed doses, or the un-tackled rupture of the stomach or bowels during surgery. He regarded the second criteria as necessary to ensure a practitioner was not criminalised for merely making a mistake or suffering a misfortune; the most careful practice could not account for the vagaries of the body's complexity.[220] Where a practitioner had not transgressed generally recognised rules, then *Virchow* was clear that liability ought only to arise in cases of gross negligence otherwise medical progress might be hindered.[221] As will be discussed at a later point, *Virchow's* actual suggestion did not have the desired impact on the statutory wording of the various criminal codes it could have influenced, nor did it, at a single stroke, stop later medical authors railing against the idea of fixing a definition or rejecting the idea of establishing a codex

215 Casper (1957) §73, 648–649.
216 Krähe (1984) 86–87.
217 Ibid. 87.
218 Kalisch (1860).
219 Virchow (1879) 519.
220 Ibid. 516, 520.
221 Ibid. 520.

of supposedly binding rules.[222] Yet this short, authoritative text made a lasting impression on the medical, and legal conceptions of a *Kunstfehler* in that it decisively secured the concept against an idea of the generally accepted rules of medical practice, a theme adopted by subsequent scholars[223] and, in due course, by the *Reichsgericht*.[224] The contemporary insistence that liability should ultimately be restricted to grossly negligent conduct was a continuing theme, albeit that some defined failure to show the degree of care that one could customarily expect from a medical practitioner as grossly negligent in and of itself.[225] Others, in an attempt to preserve a broad experimental discretion, insisted that neither the law, nor medical scholarship should place any formal limits on the scope of permissible medical conduct.[226] As to why *Virchow's* position enjoyed the success that it did, *Krähe* suggests the influence of the natural sciences and medical progress in this period. The discovery of cellular pathology by *Virchow* himself, and the advent of anaesthetics and asepsis in particular, contributed to a radically different degree of medical engagement in the body that differentiated the self-image of medical practitioners in the latter half of the century from that of their earlier brethren a few decades beforehand. The 1870s onwards marked the coming into full blossom of the scientific work of German universities who were churning out the practitioners to whom these concepts would apply.[227] This maturation, and the realisation that with complicated operations came the risk of hugely increased harm from medical error drove the efforts to establish praxis-rooted rules for medical practice.[228]

As a guide then, the *Kunstfehler* in the form proposed by *Virchow* thus provided a much more flexible tool, which had the capacity to move with accepted medical practice rather than ossify it and was met with a receptive audience more prepared to settle on the existence at any given moment of accepted norms of medical practice. Indeed, in practice, as we shall see below, it reflected some of the versions proposed subsequently, which often focused on medical experts examining in each case what accepted medical practice would

222 Deneke (1888) 253–254; Fuld (1898) 351.

223 Oesterlen (1882) 611; Emmert (1900) 530; The idea had been recently rehabilitated to a degree in some of the legal literature, see Berner (1867) 30; Krähe (1984) 95–97.

224 *RG 03.07.1884* RRGSt (1884, vol 6) 506.

225 Kühner (1886) 28; Ehrenzweig (1892) 42, citing three definitions from *Oesterlen*, *Casper* and *Schürmayer* respectively, the latter two of which stress the gross nature of any breach as a requirement from criminalisation.

226 Deneke (1888) 258–259

227 Bonner (1995) 253.

228 Krähe (1984) 80.

have been and judging the defendant against that.[229] As *Krähe* noted, cases reported by medical authors towards the end of the century saw practitioners imprisoned for the similarly aggressive treatment of a mentally ill woman as *Dr Horn* had used at the start of the century;[230] the accepted norms could, clearly, change. Like *Casper*, *Virchow* did not think that mere qualification to be a medical practitioner granted a right to unbounded practice, nor could one continue to do that which the great majority of your fellow practitioners took to be pointless or dangerous.[231] Nevertheless, as we will see in the rest of this work, legal scholars would, particularly in the mid-nineteenth century, stress the absence of any binding rules for medical practice. This was often said, as it had been by medical authors, to allow the necessary degree of experimentation and progress to take place and led in some cases to suggestions that mere licensing *was* indeed sufficient to justify a medical prerogative over the patient. These mid-nineteenth-century views, never wholly accepted even then, were clearly contradictory to the prevailing medical view of the concept and waned as the century ended.[232] But these discussions demonstrate the gap between legal and medical reasoning. As had been observed by *Casper*, the *Kunstfehler* was, in this period, primarily a concept rooted in medical rather than legal thought. One legal scholar, writing in 1867 listed 17 medical texts and only two legal texts discussing the standard of (criminal) fault expected from a medical practitioner. There were two ways that this line could be blurred. First, the extent to which the legal analysis of medical error chose to define itself as or as opposed to the *Kunstfehler*. This subject will be discussed at some length in subsequent chapters, but it is important to note here the apparent disinterest of the medical scholarship in civil liability; their focus was, overwhelmingly so, on criminal liability and criminal standards, but there is nothing to suggest that the discussions were intended to be limited to criminal prosecution or that the same logic would not apply in civil cases, as can be seen in practice.[233] Secondly, the degree to which this medical discourse, if not formally co-opted by the law, played an *evidential*, procedural role in the legal process. This will be considered in the following part of this chapter.

229 Deneke (1888) 255–256.

230 Krähe (1984) 39.

231 Ehrenzweig (1892) 36.

232 Ibid. 40.

233 *Aerztliche Sachverständigen-Zeitung* (1897) 171–172. There, an orthodox practitioner was civilly liable for blinding a new-born, infected with gonorrhoea, through the incorrect administration of chemical drops.

## 4. Medicine and the legal system

The use of expert evidence was a long-standing feature of actions for medical error, no less so in this period.[234] Article 134 of the *Carolina* had, in 1532, enshrined the role of medical practitioners as advisers to the court on matters of medical error.[235] Yet it was only in the late nineteenth century that this arrangement, a choice by the legal system, was complemented for the first time by sustained and increasingly coherent internal medical discussions about the assessment of error. The coincidence of these two features of nineteenth-century life, and the procedural and cultural mechanics which permitted their interaction to such a high degree, reflexively characterised both medical and legal discourses concerning medical error. The fact that the second half of the nineteenth century saw a marked rise in the number of actions for medical error provided plenty of scope, as the following chapters will demonstrate, for such interaction. The preceding parts of this chapter have helped build a picture of the sociological role and status of those orthodox medical practitioners who would be called on to provide expertise in this period; we now turn to examine the use of such experts in the legal system during this era by doing two things that will help lay the ground for the following chapters.[236] First, examining the way in which the medical discourse detailed above made its way into the court process. This will require analysis of both procedural and cultural features of Germanic legal systems, and the development of forensic medicine in the nineteenth century. Secondly, analysing the way in which questions of medical error were, at this point, framed by courts and answered by medical experts respectively.

### (A) The procedural and cultural-historical role of expert evidence

The nineteenth century saw a wide range of variations of the inherited, Romano-canonical nature of Germanic legal proceedings.[237] In some parts, legislative instruments governed procedural rules, whereas, in others, the organically-developed procedure of the *gemeines Recht* applied.[238] The latter was a continuation of the earlier practice of the *ius commune*. The hallmarks of this approach were a primarily written, documentary procedure with the conduct of the case, the determination of the issues and the presentation of evidence being primarily

234 Ehrenzweig (1892) 66.

235 Schumann (2009) 557, 564.

236 Dwyer (2008) 183, 197. These factors are key to understanding the role of the expert in court.

237 Wieacker (1995) 137 f; Oberhammer/Domej (2005) 103–104, 110.

238 Philips (1895) 271.

in the hands of the parties themselves.[239] Particularly important, with regard to the presentation of evidence, was the greatly restricted ability of the judge to direct questions to, or indeed call, witnesses;[240] the judge played a very passive role.[241] This relative powerlessness was rooted not only in the procedure for the laws that the judge administered but also in the fact that the Germanic judge was, for a considerable time, a layman. This had certainly incentivised a reliance on legal expertise, with the local law faculty often being asked to supply an opinion on the law in a given case. The practice of these *Aktenversendungen*, permitted by article 219 *Carolina* in 1532, had continued right up to the reorganisation of the Imperial court system in 1878,[242] inculcating a high degree of reliance on, '...higher authority in all doubtful matters'.[243] Such opinions, as they were described, were not formally binding, but, in reality, often tended to be treated as such by the courts and were even occasionally described as a 'judgment'.[244] When it came to the role of evidence in the procedure of the *gemeines Recht*, experts, medical or otherwise, wielded considerable power. Judges were restricted from coming to their own view of the evidence, a question that was often heavily regulated by abstract criteria, which ascribed a given weight to different forms of evidence,[245] and confined to deciding questions of law. Even then, as discussed, this was, in practice, often delegated.[246] Against the *ius commune / gemeines Recht* model stood the liberal French *Code de Procédure Civil* 1806 which had remained in force in the left bank of the Rhine until 1877.[247] It emphasised a public, oral hearing and whilst it shared the emphasis on party control over proceedings and the presentation of evidence,[248] provided the judge with greater powers to control and dictate not only the nature of the proceedings, but also to freely assess the evidence before them.[249]

The first German state to break with the foregoing *gemeines Recht* approach was *Prussia*. The *Allgemeine Gerichtsordnung für die Preußischen Staaten* 1793, (*AGO*), blended parts of the *gemeines Recht* and the French model with its own enlightened-absolutist ideology.[250] This could best be identified in providing the

239 Wieacker (1995) 140 n 9.
240 Oberhammer / Domej (2005) 296.
241 Ibid. 295.
242 Wieacker (1995) 137; Oberhammer / Domej (2005) 108.
243 Crawford (1994) 104.
244 Wieacker (1995) 137.
245 Kwaschik (2004) 73; Oberhammer / Domej (2005) 108; Stürner (2010) 815; Crawford (1994) 96.
246 Oberhammer / Domej (2005) 296.
247 Dwyer (2008) 199; Oberhammer / Domej (2005) 108.
248 Wieacker (1995) 368.
249 Prütting (2008) 251.
250 Ibid 251.

judge with considerably greater power to control proceedings.[251] Following the French code of 1806 many later German codifications were heavily influenced by it as in the case of the *Prozessordnung in bürgerlichen Rechtsstreitigkeiten für das Königreich Bayern* 1869 (*BPO*), which accordingly also adopted the free judicial assessment of evidence.[252]

As to the treatment of the relevant forms of evidence in these various regimes, again there was no single unitary picture. Two forms of evidence were most relevant to the subject at hand here, the evidence of the plaintiff themselves, and the role of expert evidence. As to the first, whilst the plaintiff would always have been able to answer questions in order to clarify the facts and allegations, (*Parteianhörung*), the ability of, say, an injured patient to give evidence as to the defendant's actions was hampered by the Roman rule from D.22.5.10: *nullus idoneus testis in re sua intelligitur*, which had been adopted by the *gemeines Recht*.[253] Even where such testimony was admitted it was given negligible formal evidentiary value, requiring the corroboration of two 'untainted' witnesses,[254] an impossible standard for many patients to meet. The only way around this was to swear an oath, regarded as dispositive of the claim entirely rather than related to the truth of the facts.[255] Oaths were distinguished from one another according to whether they were ordered by the judge, shifted from another party or undertaken by the party themselves, with each bearing different implications for the burden of proof.[256] The *BPO* 1869 had made the first significant exception to this rule in simply allowing a party to make, on oath, a full and exhaustive statement regarding their own behaviour or views,[257] but it was not until the late nineteenth century that pressure to abandon the Roman rule began to mount in earnest.[258]

As to the second form, expert evidence had played a more accepted and consistent part in many of the forerunning, smaller local or regional procedural

251 Oberhammer/Domej (2005) 107, 109 noting the so-called '*Untersuchungsmaxime*', in contrast to the '*Verhaltensmaxime*' of the *gemeines Recht*; Wieacker (1995) 140. Although superseded by further legislation in 1833 and 1846 this feature remained unchanged.

252 § 328 *BPO* 1869; Prütting (2008) 251; Wieacker (1995) 368. *Wieacker* lists the following regions as having been influenced: *Hanover* (1850), *Oldenburg* (1857), *Baden* (1862) *Württemberg* (1868) and notes it's stamp on the drafts codes for *Prussia* (1868) and the nascent Confederation (1870).

253 Kwaschik (2004) 73.

254 Kwaschik (2004) 73–74; Wetzell (1878) 218–219.

255 Oberhammer/Domej (2005) 255.

256 Ibid. 255.

257 § 454 *BPO* 1869; Kwaschik (2004) 75.

258 Oberhammer/Domej (2005) 256.

codifications as one form of evidence alongside others,[259] but, again, different approaches were taken. As to the various codifications, the Prussian *AGO* allowed for the court to call experts, if requested by the parties, where knowledge of a particular skill or science was required.[260] The parties could agree on an expert but, where they could not, the court would do so and, where the authorities had designated someone as an expert, they could not refuse to serve where approached.[261] Whilst this might be thought to amount to little difference in practice, one commentator suggested that there was a close connection between the higher ranks of medical practitioner and the court, noting that whilst the parties could, if they agreed, choose a second class veterinarian, if left to the court, the court was bound to choose a first class one.[262] An appellant was free to request a second opinion, but had to specify the grounds why it might support his claim, and where there was discord between the opinions delivered at first and second instance the judge could appoint a third expert whose view was decisive.[263] The *BPO* 1869, reflecting the French model, allowed parties to agree on the use, nature and number of experts, called and, where agreement could not be reached, the court could call three experts.[264]

The *gemeines Recht* understood and relied on experts (*Sachverständige*) in a considerably broader fashion than the Roman law, defining them as simply those who possessed a particular technical, scientific or trade-acquired knowledge.[265] Where such knowledge was required to answer a particular claim by one of the parties the judge would request an expert opinion (*Gutachten*) from a suitable qualified person or persons who then stood in the role of aid(s) to the judge;[266] there was little agreement on how many ought to be called in any given situation.[267] In questions of medical error the courts were heavily reliant on expert evidence to help ascertain what had happened. Here the opinion would have been provided by a single, nominated practitioner or, often, collegiately from the University medical faculty or from within the various organs of a state's medical-administrative apparatus.[268] Examples of the latter,

259 See the *Allgemeine Gerichtsordnung für die Preußischen Staaten* 1793 Title 9 § 38; §§ 433 ff *BPO* 1869.
260 IX § 38 *AGO* 1793.
261 Reimer (1822) 182.
262 Alker (1846) 168–169.
263 XIV § 60 *AGO* 1793.
264 §§ 433–434 *BPO* 1869.
265 Wetzell (1878) § 44, 528.
266 Mittermaier (1819a) 125.
267 Wetzell (1878) § 44, 530 n 21, although *Wetzell* does suggest that in trivial cases a single expert would suffice.
268 Wetzell (1878) § 44, 531; Krähe (1984) 66, noting the emphasis many medico-legal authors placed on the importance of expert evidence. Legal practitioners

often born from the earlier public health infrastructure, could be seen in the Prussian medical colleges of the eighteenth century and, later, the Scientific Deputation for Medical Matters, established in 1808 as a source for expert opinion on all manner of medical concern.[269] Indeed, contemporary medical authors had stressed, as we have seen, the need for an opinion from this latter, seemingly more authoritative source, rather than simply relying on a University opinion to damn a practitioner for medical error. Any opinion had to be motivated but, particularly where provided by an official body, it could be delivered in written, collegiate form;[270] thus channelling a single, accepted view of the matter under discussion.[271] As to the weight given to such evidence, the combination of the formal constraints on the judge and the concomitantly authoritative position of these state institutions in the nineteenth century rendered their opinion nigh-on determinative of the questions that were put to them, whether this was delivered as a single opinion, or, reflected the majority view where more than one opinion was sought. The renowned mid-century legal scholar *Mittermaier*, referring to a local medical authority, stressed the official nature of these institutions as justifying treating their opinion as an unquestionable finding.[272] There were limited grounds on which the judge could refuse an opinion such as where it suffered from significant, procedural or material flaws such as failing to give reasons or was ambiguous.[273] Indeed, in order to appeal against the findings in an opinion it had to be shown that there had been an error in the instructions and the premise on which it was given.[274] In such a situation a further opinion was to be secured.[275] But where it was correctly delivered and gave a clear answer it was the case, '...that an opinion duly arrived at in the ordinary course of matters permits no counter evidence'.[276] A medical

had, on occasion, stressed a preference for decisions from the collegiate bodies rather than individual practitioners, see *Aerztliches Vereinsblatt* (1894) 573.

269 Krähe (1984) 67–68; See XXXVIII § 6 *GPO* 1793 concerning declaring someone a lunatic or a wastrel. A *Kreisarzt* was not bound to appear as an expert if requested and, if no-one could be found, the court could require the local *Medicinalbehörde* to nominate someone, Reimer (1822) 804; Alker (1846) 169.

270 Wetzell (1878) § 44, 532.

271 The French code had, in article 318, explicitly adopted this requirement that, even where there were more than one experts, only one report was to be drawn up as a means of avoiding the uncertainty of conflicting opinions, see Hammelmann (1947) 37.

272 Mittermaier (1819a) 140.

273 *OAG Lübeck 20.07.1849* Seuffert's Archiv 3, 158.

274 *Cassationshofes zu Wolfenbüttel 01.05.1855* Seuffert's Archiv 9, 299.

275 See also § 448 *BPO* 1869 which allowed the nomination of a technical expert.

276 Wetzell (1878) § 44, 534.

expert was privileged as, in essence, the '*judex facti*'.[277] A less indulgent strand could be identified in the French-influenced codes, with the *BPO* providing that the court was not to simply accept the majority verdict nor indeed even a unanimous one, rather it was to assess the differing opinions and the underlying reasons behind them.[278]

The *Reichszivil-* and *Reichsstrafprozeßordnung* (*RZPO, RStPO*) enacted in 1877 and in force from 1st October 1879, brought the first settled unity to this area. For the criminal law an inquisitorial style of proceedings was retained.[279] For civil proceedings, on the other hand, the French approach to the parties' control over presentation of evidence, and basic control over proceedings was adopted,[280] but the role of the judge was also strengthened in two ways. First, they assumed greater control over the conduct of proceedings themselves, with powers to direct and lead the parties in various ways.[281] The powers of control enjoyed by the judge were further strengthened by legislation and reform in 1909, 1924 and 1933, undermining, somewhat, the more liberal nature of the 1877 statute.[282] Secondly, § 259 *RZPO* and § 260 *RStPO* enshrined the default position that the judge could freely assess the evidence presented according to their own discretion and conviction, gone were the formalistic restrictions on the weight the judge could give to various forms of evidence:[283]

> '*§ 259 ZPO 1877*
> *Das Gericht hat unter Berücksichtigung des gesamten Inhalts der Verhandlungen und des Ergebnisses einer etwaigen Beweisaufnahme nach freier Ueberzeugung zu entscheiden, ob eine thatsächliche Behauptung für wahr oder für nicht wahr zu erachten sei. In dem Urtheile sind die Gründe anzugeben, welche für die richterliche Ueberzeugung leitend gewesen sind. An gesetzliche Beweisregeln ist das Gericht nur in den durch dieses Gesetz bezeichneten Fällen gebunden.*'

> '*§ 260 RStPO 1877*
> *Über das Ergebniß der Beweisaufnahme entscheidet das Gericht nach seiner freien, aus dem Inbegriffe der Verhandlung geschöpften Ueberzeugung.*'

Despite the example of the *BPO*, and the successful use of party testimony as evidence in Austria, the German legislator had remained sceptical in 1877, regarding it as too inquisitorial for civil procedure. As such the basic structure of

277 Katzenmeier (2002) 397.
278 § 437 *BPO* 1869.
279 v Seuffert (1906) 170–171; v Liszt (1906) 223.
280 Dwyer (2008) 203–204; Oberhammer / Domej (2005) 297.
281 Oberhammer / Domej (2005) 297.
282 Oberhammer / Domej (2005) 299; Dwyer (2008) 204–205. The 1924 act, the so-called *Lex Emminger*, 'dramatically' expanded the role of single judge courts, see Dubber (1995) 236.
283 Stürner (2010) 809; Katzenmeier (2002) 397.

the oath system was enacted into the *RZPO*.[284] This was somewhat mollified by the fact that, with the adoption of free judicial assessment, the plaintiff's testimony took on greater importance if still not truly an evidential nature.[285] The weight that could be given to their account was strengthened in the 1924 reforms, in line with a general strengthening of the judge's position, but it was not until the comprehensive reform of the *Zivilprozessordnung* in 1933 that party testimony was accepted as true evidence.[286] Even then, however, it was simply substituted into the existing schema in place of oaths and categorised as a subsidiary form of evidence.[287] As such the German law distinguished awkwardly between party testimony at the behest of the judge, at the request of the opposing party and on behalf of the party bearing the burden of proof.[288]

Expert evidence on the other hand was given clear and comprehensive regulation in both the 1877 statutes. In each case, the general provisions on witnesses were applicable alongside more specific rules.[289] The choice, and number, of experts now lay, by default, firmly in the hands of the court, although in civil cases the parties could still agree on an expert, and where official experts were designated in particular fields, then special circumstances had to be shown to shift the presumption that they would be chosen.[290] The confirmation of expert evidence as addressed to the court, rather than on behalf of one of the parties would have been particularly helpful in situations where one practitioner had been called on to remedy the allegedly shoddy job of another, and so could be led as a witness.[291] In principle, the court could choose whether the opinion was to be given in written or oral form but, where the former, the expert could, in the case of the civil proceedings, be called to explain the opinion in court, albeit that did not entail the fierce cross-examination, which characterised the common law.[292] Where the requested opinion was unsatisfactory, the court could require a second be produced or a different expert be approached as, in line with the free assessment of evidence, it was no longer bound to follow the opinion, but had to explain its decision to reject one.[293] This fact in particular had, during the drafting process, met with resistance from orthodox practitioners who felt that a legislative guarantee was necessary to ensure that, if a

284 §§ 410 ff *RZPO* 1877 (§§ 445 ff after 1910) ; Oberhammer/Domej (2005) 256.
285 Oberhammer/Domej (2005) 257.
286 Ibid. 257.
287 Kwaschik (2004) 76.
288 Oberhammer/Domej (2005) 258; Kwaschik (2004) 83.
289 § 72 *RStPO*; § 367 *RZPO*.
290 § 73 *RStPO*; § 369 *RZPO*.
291 Hanauer (1897) 423–425.
292 § 82 *RStPO*; § 376 *RZPO*. Dwyer (2008) 195.
293 § 83 *RStPO*; § 377 *RZPO*; Auerbach (1899) 482.

judge wished to go against an opinion, the case be heard afresh with a new judge and opinion.[294] Some argued that despite the newly expanded analytical powers of the judge, a clearly worded, thorough opinion from a medical expert should, in effect, bind them nevertheless.[295]

Thus, whilst the importance of the patient's own evidence was undervalued in evidential terms, there was consistent reliance on, and weight given to, expert evidence. This would have been particularly authoritative before 1877, constrained as the judge then was, but was diminished in the regime established by the legislation of that year. As judges lost their previous lay characteristics over the late nineteenth century they were given greater powers to balance all the evidence before them in a case. Nevertheless, the social standing and connection between officially established bodies and the provision of evidence would have helped them to retain their respected, valued position.

### (B) Medicalising law: *Kunstfehlergutachten*

It was in this period that German medico-legal science had come to fruition.[296] One of the primary tasks of medico-legal work was to provide courts with expert evidence, giving medico-legal practice a key role in the escalating number of claims against medical practitioners for medical error over this period.[297] Some noted the irony that the diminishing mystery of the body opened practitioners to greater frequency of claims.[298]

As to why there was a rise in actions over this early period, much of the medico-legal literature of the nineteenth century suggested that actions against a medical practitioner were only seldom brought by the patient themselves and often had their roots, as in the *Fall Horn*, in disputes with fellow practitioners who would report their brethren's activities to the authorities,[299] or had, Iago-like, poured poison in the patient's ear against their practitioner.[300] Given the

294 'Der Entwurf einer Straf-Prozess-Ordnung für das Deutsche Reich', (1875) *Aerztliche Sachverständigen-Zeitung* 28.

295 Deneke (1888) 255–256.

296 Krähe (1984) 69. *Krähe* notes the foundation of the first university chair in medico-legal studies came in the late nineteenth century; Huerkamp (1985) 106; Wagner (2004) 89; Fischer-Homberger (1988) 83 ff.

297 Dettmeyer/Preuß/Madea (2004) 265, noting that this fact did not go overlooked by contemporary medico-legal scholars.

298 Ehrenzweig (1892) 35. But he later noted that, particularly with internal medicine and the administration of drugs, it remained very difficult to identify the causal mechanisms at play, 46–47.

299 Krähe (1984) 65.

300 Hanauer (1897) 425.

concurrent effort to improve their social standing, the use of actions for medical error in order to discipline aberrant behaviours in the name of collective 'collegiality' is highly plausible.[301] *Mittermaier* suggested that often in fraught situations the patient's family were more likely to advocate litigation, and, so, were not to be trusted when it came to evidence.[302] The increasing number of claims being brought can be seen partly through the number anecdotally reported in the medical and legal literature of the time. In 1853, *Mittermaier* had discussed eight Germanic cases in one article, whilst a medico-legal survey found 22 cases reported in the press between 1852 and 1856.[303] In 1882 *Oesterlen* had listed 82 cases mostly published after 1850 but of those only 37 resulted in a conviction and, in nine, there was, despite the finding of a *Kunstfehler*, an acquittal for lack of causation.[304] Certainly by mid-century, rhetorical reference to the increasing number of action could be found in medical and legal journals.[305]

The practice of German courts in referring appropriate questions to external medical institutions shared as august a heritage as the practice of consulting the local law faculty, having been common practice by 1600.[306] By the nineteenth century this close link between the courts and both medical educational and administrative structures ensured that the medical practice procedurally represented in court was the university-research-driven model outlined above. The documentary nature of proceedings and the long-standing interaction of criminal justice and medical practitioners had further enabled medical science to orient itself to the needs of the legal system, and allowed the legal system to fully incorporate, unadulterated, the technical evidence that medical experts could supply.[307] This crucial nexus of reliance, created by wholly coincidental choices in legal procedure, spurred the breakneck growth of medico-legal science and medico-legal literature in Germany throughout the eighteenth- and nineteenth-centuries.[308] More importantly, it provided German medical practitioners with extensive exposure to, and interaction with, legal thought processes. The styles of legal and medico-legal thought were highly similar; each system sought to provide authoritative guidance on legal matters and, by the

301 Rodegra (1986) 77.

302 Mittermaier (1853) 187.

303 Reported by *Virchow* in Virchow (1879) 515.

304 Krähe (1984) 40, 99–100.

305 Obergutachten des Königlichen Medicinalcollegii für Pommern (1858) 43; Hanauer (1897) 425; *Aerztliches Vereinsblatt* (1896) 444.

306 Crawford (1994) 104.

307 Ibid. 98, 104.

308 Ibid. 89, 105 noting that the, '...practice of *Aktenversendung* meant that German courts did not so much stimulate medico-legal studies as commission them'.

nineteenth century, medico-legal scholarship could be considered a subset of legal literature on proof and procedure.[309] It was in medico-legal literature of the age that many of the scholarly treatments of the *Kunstfehler* question explored above took place, and it was the consumers of this literature that provided the opinions on which courts based their judgments. The combined effect of the concretised definition given to a *Kunstfehler* by *Virchow* in the medical discourse and the innate connection between this scholarship and court process posits several consequences for liability. First, it was likely to be very difficult to demonstrate fault where a practitioner was behaving in a manner accepted by their medical peers. Indeed *Ehrenzweig*, in 1892, noted that medical practitioners accused of an offence ought not to worry as they would always be able to rely on an expert opinion from the medical college to identify whether they had infringed any generally accepted rules or not.[310] Equally, where, in an era of the rapid expansion of, and experimentation with, the reach of medical science, if no accepted practice could be identified, then a practitioner might be in a position whereby, '…the doctor who has once been permitted to practice, may be considered his own legislator'.[311] Secondly, the view of medical practice that was reflected in court was the orthodox one. Thirdly, this view could be monolithic in that, in the ordinary course of events, a single opinion, even where delivered in a collegiate form, would not be required to canvas the various possible approaches that the accused practitioner could have adopted and, where further opinions were sought by appeal courts the tendency to rely on opinions from officially sanctioned bodies would, in theory, provide an increasingly authoritative view. The written, collegiate form rendered the medical-cultural mores of orthodox practitioners reflective of a legal norm in that *their* answer to the question of whether there had been an error was determinative.

Given the extent to which the *Kunstfehler* was a prevalent part of medical literature, the degree to which the legal analysis of fault relied on this medical one becomes a key factor not only for the scope of liability but, also, in its ultimate control by medical practitioners.[312] More comprehensive analysis of this question from a legal perspective is the business of later chapters, but here we examine a number of opinions from throughout the nineteenth century as a

309 Crawford (1994) 99.

310 Ehrenzweig (1892) 43; *Aerztliches Vereinsblatt* (1888) 266, noting that if medical practitioners were often escaping liability the reason had less to do with the basis of the law and instead lay in how the law was being applied in practice, which is to say, relying on such an opinion.

311 Mittermaier (1858) 14. A similar point was also made by *Virchow* to the effect that the first person to undertake a procedure that caused injury would not be liable, but, after that, those who did the same would be, Virchow (1879) 519.

312 Ehrenzweig (1892) 35–36.

means of studying the way in which the court phrased the relevant questions when consulting outside medical expertise, and how these were answered. This will allow us to understand the degree to which the medical discussions outlined above really entered the decision-making process surrounding claims for medical error and whether one discourse dominated, or yielded to, the other. This is made possible as a number of these opinions were published in their entirety in the medical press, often in the official journal of the Prussian Deputation, the *Vierteljahrsschrift für gerichtliche und öffentliche Medicin.*

The first set of opinions, from 1853, was issued by the Prussian Deputation.[313] The case involved a claim for the negligent homicide of a 12-year-old child by a local orthodox practitioner, Dr *M*, in 1845. The child was injured in a cart accident, breaking his femur and tearing his knee ligaments. The practitioner opted to treat this with anti-inflammatories, leeches and compresses for 17 days before setting the bone, applying a bandage and placing him in a fracture apparatus. A few days after that, the wound began to suppurate. Here the defendant's evidence was confused. Called back to the patient again, he had either removed the apparatus and applied a compress or had torn the splints apart by force in an attempt to excite the leg. The wound worsened and the district surgeon was called. Upon examination, it was clear that the knee, the foot and much of that leg were gangrenous. The district physician was called a few days later and confirmed this finding. The foot having begun to fall off, a few weeks later the child died from infection, although no post-mortem was undertaken. The appeal court requested an opinion examining whether the defendant was guilty of, '...negligent and unskilled treatment' of the child.[314]

The local medical college had previously answered the question affirmatively, stressing that the negligence was to be found in only having visited three times in the first, crucial days. Delivering the opinion on appeal, the Deputation came to the same result, but rejected the idea that a fixed number of visits could be dictated. Were one to do so, it would be placing an unjust and often unachievable burden on the local *Wundarzt.* Rather it was best left to their judgment and skill to decide how often to attend.[315] Whether this case was one where more visits ought to have been made was impossible to answer from the files given that the lapse of time between the events and the father's interrogation, which rendered his evidence incomplete and partial. Considering an outbreak of scarlet fever in the district at the time of the treatment, it could not

313 Superarbitrum der Königlichen wissenschaftlichen Deputation für das Medicinalwesen (1854) 185.

314 Ibid. 190.

315 Ibid. 191.

be said that the treatment evidenced negligence.[316] Treating the question of whether practice was unskilled separately, however, they agreed with the medical college that there could be no such claim against his behaviour during the first 17 days. Nor was the choice of the particular apparatus itself questionable so long as it, or any other course of action, had been done with necessary care. However, his admitted manipulation of the apparatus was clearly unskilled in that, having done it with such little care, it must necessarily have caused injury and necrosis.[317] In this opinion we see the relevance of accepted practice, not as a set of prescriptive rules but as a retrospective peer review. That they treated the question of negligent and unskilled treatment as two separate points is interesting in that this appears to treat negligence as a measure of the attentiveness of the practice, rather than the skill involved, the latter being a question of compliance with the appropriate degree required. This approach mimics, as we shall see in chapter two, the approach of the *Carolina*, which sanctioned practice that was either '*unfleiß*' or '*unkunst*' roughly along similar lines.

The second opinion, again delivered by the same authoritative body, is from 1858 and concerned an obstetrician (*Geburtshelfer*), *Dr H*.[318] He attempted to deliver a child by forceps and then by hand for over ninety minutes with the patient bleeding. With the child still *in utero*, the patient lost consciousness. *Dr H* realised nothing could be done to deliver the child and, thinking the mother dead, removed himself. Both the woman, having in fact only fainted, and the child died that evening. The question from the court was simply, 'Whether and in what way *Dr H* could be charged with the death of *R*?' The college noted two potential criticisms. First, his use of the forceps and then his attempts by hand, despite the constriction of the mother's pelvis.[319] Neither could be regarded as any sort of fault on his part as this was to ascribe the obviousness of hindsight to the practitioner in the challenging circumstances in which he found himself.[320] Secondly, nor was there anything to criticise in his withdrawal. The key was that he believed nothing more could be done rather than having left without having tried to do anything he thought might save her.[321] In each case the Deputation described these actions as a mistake (*Irrtum*) or 'incorrect view', but did not regard such occurrences as blameworthy. Casting the situation from the start as a difficult one in which other practitioners could not have done better set the stage for the result.

316 Superarbitrum der Königlichen wissenschaftlichen Deputation für das Medicinalwesen (1854) 193.
317 Ibid. 194.
318 Ibid. 1.
319 Ibid. 25.
320 Ibid. 26.
321 Ibid. 27.

To the contrary, where, the situation was stable, despite the acknowledged difficulties that could arise during labour, a practitioner who was unsure of what to do should call for aid rather than pressing ahead. In such a case, where an obstetrician had, through delay, ended up killing his patient by causing sufficient injury trying to remove her placenta that she bled to death, the Deputation was clear that the accused had acted, '...with a gross, inexcusable degree of ignorance and lack of skill in the matter' and in doing so had failed to fulfil the duty owed by him by reason of his medical practice.[322] In a further case, the *Oberlandesgericht Frankfurt am Main*, in holding a practitioner liable to pay compensation to an injured child, was critical of a general practitioner who had failed to call a specialist despite the unhurried situation of the patient.[323]

One of the clearest advantages enjoyed by the orthodox medical practitioner was the fact that court procedures could set them in judgment over their less orthodox brethren, as two further opinions, reported in 1889, demonstrate.

In the first, an experienced quack midwife (*Winkelhebamme*), *L*, was prosecuted for the negligent homicide of a young crippled woman, *R*, who had experienced a difficult and prolonged labour.[324] Having, earlier during the fateful day, examined the patient and declared her confidence that a trained midwife was not necessary, after a few hours *L* changed her mind. The situation was so grim this second, trained midwife instantly called for a physician, but the patient died soon thereafter.[325] The first opinion had regarded *L*'s practice as negligent in that she was not in such a pressing position that calling further, orthodox, help had been impossible, and that her attempts to turn the child when she realised it was in breech had been both greatly mistaken and dangerous. An *Obergutachten* from the local medical college was requested to clarify the causal relationship but it concurred that L's actions were clearly negligent on two grounds: the failure to earlier call for aid and her injurious manipulation.[326]

In a second case, a wagoner, *S*, suffered a compound fracture to his leg.[327] He declined orthodox medical attention and called a local stationmaster, *H*, who was also an unorthodox practitioner (*Medicaster*). *H* recommended orthodox care as the fracture would be difficult and slow to heal but *S* refused and, so, *H*

322 *Aerztliche Sachverständigen-Zeitung* (1897) 183.

323 Ibid. 171–172.

324 Obergutachten des Königlichen Medicinalcollegii für Pommern (1858) 58.

325 Ibid. 61.

326 Ibid. 67–68. The question of causation was regularly referred to as one of the most challenging and important that a medico-legal practitioner could be called on to address, Deneke (1888) 257–258.

327 Ibid. 43.

undertook treatment.[328] This consisted of wrapping part of the leg in cardboard, and, having washed it with camomile tea, applying a wad of lint and unguents to the wound itself. This went on for six weeks, during which the patient seemed neither in significant pain, nor did the wound suppurate. Suddenly one day, *S* complained of heart pain, passed out and died.[329] *H* was prosecuted. The question put by the court was, 'Did the curative treatment given to *S* play a role in the tragic outcome of the broken leg and, if so, could that be tied to negligence on *H's* part?'. The opinion noted that, whilst the treatment was clearly inappropriate for such an injury (*'ganz fehlerhaft und falsch'*), and death would likely have been avoided with appropriate treatment, whether this amounted to negligence was a question for the judge.[330] Although the court exonerated *H* by reason of doubts over causation,[331] an *Obergutachten* from the *Superarbitrium des Medicinalcollegiums* felt less constrained and reported that the accused's treatment, which had in their view consisted of applying absolutely worthless measures – in effect an omission to treat – was clearly incorrect (*'fehlerhaft'*).[332]

It was clear that whatever the formal standard to be applied was, its answer was, at least evidentially, filtered through orthodox medical practitioners, regardless of the type of practice. As is clear from the opinions discussed above, it was not uncommon for the court to simply put the question of whether the defendant had been negligent in precisely those terms, leaving if for the medical experts to assess whether this was in fact the case against their own rubric. This use of legal terms was, on occasion, the subject of some grumbling on the basis that it might either make the author of an opinion appear to be a co-accuser (particularly sensitive where it concerned a claim based on a *Kunstfehler*),[333] or, because it risked the author's authority being undermined through accidental misuse of such a 'foreign', legal term.[334] The use of opinions from the medical-administrative bodies suggests they were often required to provide guidance.[335]

328 As noted above, the prevalence for trusting, or being economically limited to unorthodox practice continued throughout the century. See *Aerztliche Sachverständigen-Zeitung* (1896) 232. There, the patient had been so won over by her *Naturheilkunde* that she would only see orthodox practitioners the *Naturheilkunde* had approved.

329 Obergutachten des Königlichen Medicinalcollegii für Pommern (1858) 45.

330 Ibid. 51–52.

331 Ibid. 58.

332 Ibid. 55–56.

333 *Aerztliches Vereinsblatt* (1894) 573, reporting a speech by a lawyer who recommended that opinions ought only ever be sought from multiple leading practitioners or the collective organs of the state medical administration.

334 Merner (1888) 32.

335 Deneke (1888) 261, reporting to the third *Ärztetag*, and noting that an opinion from higher medical authorities was required in the overwhelming majority of cases.

In the final decades of the century, the language of *Virchow's* definition of a *Kunstfehler* began to appear as the crux of the question on which opinions were based, making even more clear the degree to which the legal analysis of medical error had been subsumed within the medical one.[336] The praxis of the *Kunstfehler*, and its potential importance to orthodox practitioners as a brake on liability, was clear. The patient's own evidence, often criticised as confused and untrustworthy by lawyer and medico-legal author alike where alive,[337] was, predictably, devalued where they had died, but this had the corollary effect that, as the patient's body itself became the evidence which was being interpreted, the definitional powers of orthodox expertise were further elevated.

## 5. Conclusions

It has been necessary to establish how standardised medical practice of the form recognisable in the present day emerged in Germany to better understand the extent to which the legal discourse on medical error reflected the state of actual medical practice or treated only with its own, internalised image of idealised practice. The emergent theme from this chapter is that the creation and development of both a standardised practitioner and form of practice in the model of hospital-based care was a complex and extended process, which occurred within a medical marketplace where the orthodox practitioners' social standing, power and claims to knowledge were constantly developing and being challenged. These challenges came from both the state, in the form of government control of the educational framework, and from a host of unorthodox practitioners. The reaction on the part of orthodox practitioners was the swiftly regretted legislative 'victory' of 1869, which allowed them to escape the former at the cost of lowering themselves to the level of the latter; as a result, the need to sociologically differentiate themselves became ever more pressing. This promoted renewed, and eventually successful, efforts to establish a binding form of disciplinary apparatus. That process marked the crystallisation of efforts to create an underpinning and increasingly standardised set of ethical and behavioural norms for orthodox practice. It has been established that the central concern of these norms was the maintenance of collective honour and the reputation of orthodox medical practice rather than the abstract quality of care the patient received.

Part of the surge in medico-legal scholarship was a concurrent discussion focused on defining an internalised, medical concept of injurious error. The *Kunstfehler*, as it came to be understood, settled on a model that privileged a

336 *Aerztliches Vereinsblatt* (1885) 39; *Aerztliche Sachverständigen-Zeitung* (1898) 356.
337 Mittermaier (1853) 186–187.

sociological rather than an ethical understanding of error; it looked to what practice was, not what it should be. A practitioner would fall foul where it could be shown that they had failed to abide by a practice that was generally accepted by fellow practitioners. Furthermore, the common medical view was that liability ought to only result where there had been grossly negligent conduct on the part of the practitioner. As is clear in this era, considerable weight was given to broader concerns about intra-practitioner relations rather than patient safety, and it is no surprise to see this reflected in both disciplinary proceedings and the discussion surrounding the *Kunstfehler*. The frequently voiced fears when discussing the latter, that 'fixed' rules would stymie medical progress, were slowly abandoned as the importance of identifying 'accepted' practice in both a professional and a practical sense came to be realised in the final decades of the century. A medical concept of error predicated on 'accepted' practice certainly permitted the law to be coterminous with the scope of the internal disciplinary apparatus.

The *Kunstfehler* as understood in this period was thus capable of supplying an operative, organising concept of error for the law to draw on, built around the rules and practices of orthodox practitioners and providing a readily available intellectual framework for the content of the legal duty owed by a practitioner, orthodox or otherwise. The position accorded to expert evidence invited this medical discourse into legal proceedings. The close link between the judicial process and medical expertise created a relationship between the structure of legal analysis that was at least symbiotic, if not one that actively engendered in medico-legal scholarship a tendency towards such conceptual exposition. An expert opinion had to be motivated, but the motivation then became an extended syllogism based on internally accepted notions of medical practice. For much of the nineteenth century, the judge had little ability to challenge these views of what constituted an actionable error but was empowered, to a degree, to do so after 1879. Nevertheless, a hierarchy of administrative medical bodies ensured that as a case progressed through the court system, an equally progressing and authoritative hierarchy of medical expertise could be engaged to reflect a monolithic view of what actually constituted accepted practice. The result of all this is to understand that the nature of medical practice, practitioners, regulation, and internal discipline were key features in shaping the medical discourse surrounding medical error. The relationship of this discourse to legal doctrine and practice is the subject of the rest of this book.

Chapter 2

# Medical Error and the Criminal Law

> '...currently the subject of great disagreement before the courts in all states'[1]

This book seeks to explain the development of the fault standard in civil law. But the criminal law played an important role in this era in helping to contextualise the civil law. Several features are notable: First, it was in the criminal law of the *Carolina* that the *Kunstfehler* had its linguistic and conceptual roots, and in a single criminal prosecution that its relevance was reignited. Secondly, unlike civil law, criminal law had specific legislative tools dealing with medical error. Thirdly, the criminal law remedy overlapped with civil law in the form of a fine (*Buße*). Finally, it was in the *Reichgericht's* criminal case law that the *Kunstfehler* came to judicial prominence. Each topic is examined in this chapter.

## 1. The *Carolina* 1532

### (A) Medical error in the *Carolina*

Criminalising medical error had long roots in the German legal memory, and beyond.[2] The genesis of this was the *Constitutio Criminalis Carolina* of 1532 (hereafter, *Carolina*). Little analysis of the relevant article, 134, is available.[3] It explicitly regulated medical conduct, which negligently, or intentionally, resulted in the death of the patient, but was understood by contemporary jurists as also having regulated simple injury so-caused:[4]

> *'Item so eyn artzt auß vnfleiß oder vnkunst / vnnd doch vnfürsetzlich jemandt mit seiner artzenei tödtet / erfündt sich dann durch die gelerten vnd verstendigen der artzenei / daß er die artzenei leichtfertiglich vnd verwegenlich mißbraucht / oder sich vngegründter vnzuolessiger artzenei / die jm nit gezimbt hat vnderstanden / vnd damit eynem zuom todt vrsach geben / der soll nach gestalt vnd gelegenheyt der sachen vnd nach radt der verstendigen / gestrafft werden / vnnd inn disem fall allermeyst achtung gehabt werden /*

1 Mittermaier (1853) 1, discussing the criminal liability of medical practitioners.
2 For a summary of the various ancient civilisations that adopted a criminal approach, see v Gerlach (2000) 389; Kehr (1972) 32–38; Riegger (2007) 33–37.
3 We rely heavily on *Kehr's* study, Kehr (1972).
4 Kehr (1972) 48, 53–54.

*auff leichtuertige leut / die sich ärtzenei vnderstehn / vnd der mit keynem grundt gelernet haben. Hett aber eyn artzt solch tödtung williglich gethan / so wer er als eyn fürsetzlicher mörder zuo straffen.'*

The key feature of article 134, as *Kehr* notes, was its quasi-regulatory use, deploying liability to control an otherwise unregulated marketplace.[5] The provision applied to orthodox practitioners, empiricists and charlatans.[6] Negligent practice, as well as practices that offended moral customs and good sense, or caused harm as a result of using prohibited or baseless medicines were caught by the first sentence.

Although the *Carolina* sought to regulate all medical practice, status made a key difference to the question of guilt, as the judge was required to seek expert medical advice ('*durch die gelerten vnd verstendigen*') on matters relating to the activities of learned practitioners. This was not obvious from the text, which appeared to separate the decision as to whether practice was '*unfleiss*' or '*unkunst*' from ('*dann durch…*') a decision by medical experts as to whether such practice offended moral customs and good sense.[7] In practice this was the basis on which all of these questions were assessed. *Kehr* stresses the explicit aim (in article 150) of ensuring that decisions were as similar as possible; individual judges could not be trusted to assess questions of medical skill and custom.[8] Where a case concerned a layperson or unorthodox practitioner who did not have the benefit of any formal learning their fault appears to have been presumed in taking on the treatment itself.[9] As such, the provision set the boundaries of orthodox medical knowledge as demarcating the bailiwick of non-criminal practice.[10] This is perhaps explicable on the basis that the *Schöffen* courts were manned by lay judges whose legal – let alone medical – knowledge was questionable,[11] and worked well alongside the establishment of medical colleges in many cities, which, as we have seen, provided a body of practitioners willing to supply answers.[12]

As punishment, the *Carolina* allowed both capital and severe physical, alongside civil, punishments, which included jail, expulsion, and forfeit.[13] The latter in particular, often taking the form of paying a fine to the injured

5 Ibid. 41–48; 92–93.
6 Ibid. 49, noting this reading by later jurists such as *Michaelis* in 1739.
7 Ibid. 63–65.
8 Ibid. 63, 65–66.
9 Ibid. 69.
10 Ibid. 63.
11 Wieacker (1995) 82–83.
12 Kehr (1972) 52–53.
13 Ibid. 97–100. Although as *Kehr* notes, prison terms played a smaller role in practice compared to the other options on offer.

party themselves, was the customary civil penalty.[14] Practice suggested that civil penalties were the norm for breaches of the first sentence and the lesser the degree of fault involved, the greater the chance that a financial penalty was appropriate.[15] Despite the specificity of article 134, *Kehr* notes that actual prosecutions were difficult to find but instances can be found described if one turns to the medico-legal literature.[16]

### (B) Fault in the *Carolina*

As to fault, article 134 required proof of practice that was *'unfleiss'* or *'unkunst'*, and use of medicines that was *'leichfertiglich'* and *'verwegentlich'*. *'Unfleiss'*, used in other parts of the code,[17] required a practitioner not to have exercised care and due diligence in the performance of their duties.[18] *'Unkunst'* spoke to the absence of the, 'knowledge skill and experience', that was expected of a practitioner.[19] It was from this that the common nineteenth-century language of the *'Kunstfehler'* ultimately flowed. As a juridical understanding of fault *Kehr* notes that *'unfleiss'* or *'unkunst'* equated to the modern understanding of negligence,[20] requiring only failure to meet the objective standard of current medical practice.[21] Such was the enthusiasm of the era for tackling the social evil of charlatanism, practice by an unorthodox practitioner was deemed inherently negligent,[22] with the Roman rule re-appearing in the later literature: *Culpa enim est, immiscere se rei ad se non pertinenti.*[23]

## 2. Medical error before 1871

### (A) Criminal codification before 1871

The subsequent history of the *Carolina* is largely untroubled by change. Until the Enlightenment, article 134 was either taken as a whole or in the form of its individual offences into regional legislative provisions.[24] Thus it remained, in

14 Ibid. 100.
15 Ibid. 105.
16 Ibid. 172.
17 Ibid. 54–55.
18 Ibid. 55. See also, Grimm/Grimm, 565–570.
19 Ibid. 56–57; Riegger (2007) 55.
20 Ibid. 89.
21 Ibid. 89.
22 Ibid. 69; 82.
23 Ibid. 69, citing D.50.17.36.
24 Ibid. 160–161.

some form, the basis for criminalising medical error into the nineteenth century,[25] and continued to be applied to a broad class of medical occupations.[26] We will examine the regional codifications, which were the first to break with this influence, as well as the *Reichsstrafgesetzbuch* (*RStGB*) 1871, the first of the sweeping *national* codifications that preceded the *BGB*. This reveals a movement away from the specific regime of the *Carolina*.

Late eighteenth- and nineteenth-century codes largely eschewed specificity regarding legislative punishment of medical error. Some thought this a pity: medico-legal scholar *Henke* groused that it contributed to uncertainty over when a patient might have an action.[27] *v Kreittmayr's Codex iuris Bavarici criminalis* 1751, and the Austrian *Constitutio criminalis Theresiana* 1769 both opted for a single provision applying to all persons generally.[28] This continued in the *Bayerisches Strafgesetzbuch* 1813 (*BayStGB*, often called *Feuerbach's Strafgesetzbuch*). The final, revised *Bayerisches Strafgesetzbuch* (*BStGB*) 1861 contained only a general provision for both negligent homicide (article 232) and negligent bodily injury (article 239).[29]

A modified Carolinian approach, *was* enacted in the *ALR* 1794.[30] Although there was no single clause covering medical error,[31] numerous specific provisions on the misuse of medicines and poor practice supplemented a general clause for bodily injuries.[32] Many were contained in Chapter 11 of Title 20 of the *ALR's* Second Part. § 795 of that Chapter supplied the necessary link to the civil provisions of the *ALR's* First Part (I VI § 98) and so allowed for compensation for the victim or their family in proportion to the degree of fault exhibited. Where prosecution stemmed from the breach of a official or occupational duty, § 799 provided for a ban from practice (*Berufsverbot*):[33]

25 For instance, it was still discussed as a basis for the law in Mittermaier (1819b) 355; Riegger (2007) 57, 69. *Riegger* lists seven regions where it applied in the absence of their enactment of a local, state regulation.

26 Kehr (1972) 152, 158.

27 Henke (1830) 107.

28 Kehr (1972) 171.

29 Laufs/Eichener (1991) 93.

30 Riegger (2007) 67.

31 Krähe (1984) 64.

32 II XX § 691, '*Ein jeder ist schuldig, sein Betragen so einzurichten, daß er weder durch Handlungen, noch Unterlassungen, Andrer Leben oder Gesundheit in Gefahr setze.*' Cited by *Henke*, Henke (1830) 81. Chapter 11 was titled '*Von körperlichen Verletzung*'. Indeed, whilst the '*Arzt*;' only appears once in the First Part of the *ALR* (and the *Apotheke* twice) the Second Part is riddled with references to medical practitioners of all persuasions, orthodox or otherwise.

33 Kehr (1972) 171. *Kehr* notes that a *Kunstfehler* would suffice.

*'II XX § 799:*
*Ist die schwere Beschädigung eines Menschen durch grobe Vernachläßigung gewisser besonderer Amts- oder Berufspflichten veranlaßt worden: so soll der Uebertreter, noch außer der nach vorstehender Verordnung ihn treffenden Strafe, zu einem solchen Amte oder Gewerbe auf immer für unfähig erklärt warden.'*

Chapter 20 was quasi-regulatory rather than purely punitive for, whilst it aimed at the regulation of medical practice, it supplied criminal sanctions. Equally, the need to subordinate unorthodox practice was visible in II XX § 706: less orthodox practitioners such as dentists and herbalists had to submit themselves to the supervision of orthodox practitioners:

*'II XX § 706:*
*Zahn- und Augenärzte, Bruch- und Steinschneider, Quacksalber, Wurzel- und Olitätenkrämer, Hebammen, Hirten, Schäfer, Scharfrichter, und alle andere, die aus innern oder äußern Curen, ohne Erlaubniß der Obrigkeit, oder ohne Zuziehung und Genehmigung eines approbirten Arztes, ein Gewerbe machen, sollen, nach Bewandniß der Umstände, und nach der mehrern oder mindern Gefährlichkeit der gebrauchten Mittel, mit Gefängniß auf vierzehn Tage bis sechs Wochen bestraft warden.'*

The influential *Preussisches Strafgesetzbuch* (*PStGB*) 1851 moved away from the *ALR's* detailed approach. Medical error would, as in the *BayStGB*, be regulated through the general provisions on negligent homicide and bodily injury (§ § 184, 198 *PStGB* respectively).[34] In the former, punishment took the shape of a prison sentence of between two months and two years; in the latter, a fine of between ten and one hundred *Thalers* or imprisonment for up to one year.[35] The offence set out in § 198 would only be pursued at the request of the injured party unless it involved a serious bodily injury,[36] or the breach of an occupational duty ('*Berufspflicht*'). Where, as it naturally would for an orthodox practitioner, intentional or negligent bodily injury resulted from the breach of such a duty a practitioner could, under § 203 *PStGB*, be barred from practice permanently, or for up to five years.[37]

That approach could be also found earlier in some of the smaller regional codifications.[38] The original *Württembergische Strafsgesetzbuch* of 1839 had used a similar model in articles 251 (negligent homicide) and 267 (negligent bodily

34 Berner (1867) 26.

35 § 193 *PStGB* provided a heavier sentence of up to 15 years of hard labour in cases of serious injuries.

36 Defined in § 193 *PStGB* as an injury causing a longer-than-twenty-day illness, or unfitness for work, or which caused either mental illness or robbed the victim of their sight, speech, or hearing.

37 § 203 *PStGB*. This provision was taken as applying generally to medical practitioners of various strands, see Riegger (2007) 68.

38 *Beseler* notes the indebtedness of the *PStGB* to the *ALR* for § § 199–203, Beseler (1851) 384.

injury). The former provided for a prison term of no less than six months in cases where there was a high degree of negligence but, in lesser cases, a fine of up to three hundred guilders. The latter provided a term of up to eight months or in the case of minimal infringements, a fine between five and twenty guilders. A ban from practice, either limited or permanent, was provided for under article 251, where it concerned those whose practice was officially controlled. Indeed, article 453 provided a general power to impose a limited or enduring ban from practice where a publically licensed person was convicted. Of the pre-1871 codifications it was only the *Strafgesetzbuch für das Grossherzogtum Baden* (*BadStGB*) 1845 that contained a specific provision concerning the liability of medical practitioners for negligently causing death or bodily injury. The purpose of that provision, § 543 *BadStGB*, was to supply, in addition to the usual penalties for those offences found in the generally applicable provisions of § § 211 and 237 respectively, a limited or perpetual ban from practice.[39]

The *PStGB* also retained some of the specific provisions from the *ALR*. In § 199 it preserved the weight of criminal sanction behind a bar on the unlicensed, remunerated practice of internal or external medicine, or midwifery.[40] This was explicitly intended, by the article's title, to deal with quackery (*Kurpfuscherei*).[41] It would also stretch to cover a qualified practitioner dabbling beyond their area of qualification.[42] The penalty was a fine of between five and fifty *Thalers*, or six month of imprisonment.

Taken together, there was a high degree of specific consideration of medical practitioners in the criminal codes of the era, albeit most of which was designed to single out forms of liability closely connected to medical practice or to ensure appropriate punishment. The continued presence of a ban from practice rooted in the criminal law gave these codes a quasi-regulatory character in an era where centralised regulation of orthodox practitioners was not yet the norm.

39 This was supplemented by § 542, which allowed a similar punishment for practitioners who had committed any other crime punishable with at least three months of imprisonment in the pursuance of their duties.

40 Although *Oppenhoff's* commentary suggests that the courts would be easily satisfied on this count noting that taking on treatment in the expectation of payment was enough, and payment could be found in the higher price charged for any medicaments. Oppenhoff (1867) 308, n 8. See also the discussion over the possible other approaches during the drafting process in Beseler (1851) 382; Mittermaier (1853) 5.

41 Before 1873, Bavaria, on the other hand, criminalised unorthodox practice even where it went unremunerated, see Stolberg (2001) 140.

42 Berner (1867) 16.

### (B) Criminal fault before 1871

This section contextualises the changes heralded by the *RStGB* 1871. First, we sketch the approach adopted in the earlier codifications. Secondly, we revisit the seminal *Fall Horn* from 1811, and examine it for what it revealed about the standard of care. Thirdly, we consider the scholarly literature on medical liability. Spurred by the *Fall Horn* this was a frequent theme to which several writers returned before 1871.

#### *(i) Early codifications and occupational duties*

Throughout the nineteenth century, many of the codifications set out above formally required gross negligence, *culpa lata*. However, this often simply meant a failure to comply with the behaviour expected of the defendant in the practice of their calling rather than a particularly egregious or flagrant breach of these standards.[43] Examples can found in article 67 *Feuerbach's StGB* and the attendant provisions of the Württemberg and Hanoverian codes.[44] These provisions laid down a presumption of gross negligence where the injury flowed from a failure to meet the attendant knowledge and skills pertaining to their science, art or occupation. The relevant standard was, thus, certainly, informally, indulgent, relying as it did on the assessment of the defendant's behaviour against the benchmark of orthodox medical standards, but the continued language of gross fault speaks to a quasi-formal indulgence in addition.

#### *(ii)* The *Fall Horn*

The scholarly discussion of criminal fault as it concerned medical error in this era took place in the shadow of the *Fall Horn.*[45] It provides an excellent insight into the mechanics of an action for medical error as many of the documents involved were later made available and widely circulated.[46]

The psychiatrist *Dr Ernst Horn* was, at the time of his prosecution in 1811, the director of the medical school at the *Charité. Luise Thiele*, 21, had been earlier admitted to the hospital suffering from an unspecified mental illness. To prevent her causing a disturbance through her screaming and frenzy, and in line with *Horn's* general practice, she was left on the floor inside two restraining sacks, as

43 Berner (1867) 22–23.

44 Ibid. 21–22.

45 Riegger (2007) 72.

46 Two examples may be found in: Henke (1830) and Kalisch (1860). Each extensively reproduced various documents associated with the case.

she had been, albeit inside one, on at least four earlier occasions for periods of up to three hours.[47] The second sack was removed after an hour and *Thiele*, reportedly flushed and unable to drink, convulsed and died. Scandal resulted, leading to an investigation by the police.[48] An initial report to the authorities by one of *Thiele's* relatives had been rejected as the case did not involve violence,[49] but following a letter from one *Dr Kolrath*, himself a surgeon and obstetrician at the *Charité* – and someone who had a history of disagreements with *Horn* – to a senior Prussian official accusing *Horn* of causing the patient's death, the *Kammergericht* opened an investigation. This investigation, relying on the expert opinion of one *Dr v Könen* exonerated *Horn* on the basis that death had been caused by a stroke following asphyxiation and this was a common cause of death for hysterical, raving patients.[50] The question had been put as: 'Furthermore, whether in the concrete case the use of a restraining jacket and sack was entirely improper, or in what circumstances (not reported here) would this be permitted?'[51] He noted that the precise form of treatment – the sack – was unknown to him and insufficiently little information could be deduced from the investigation files to answer whether it was a common treatment or not.[52] Yet is noteworthy that he felt in a position to state that, having been ordered by *Horn*, a practitioner as established an academic and author as *Horn* deserved the benefit of the doubt.[53] The minister of justice intervened and demanded the *Kammergericht* obtain two further expert opinions. The report of *Dr Reil*, wholly supported in the event by *Dr Merzdorf*,[54] confirmed that the use of the sack was a common treatment. Furthermore, having experimented on his own dog,[55] the sack was shown to be permeable and so the cause of death was not asphyxiation but rather a self-induced stroke that had stopped her breathing.[56] As *Reil* then put it: 'She died in a sack as others die in their shirts, but it does not follow that she died as a result of that.'[57] *Reil* characterised orthodox medical practice as inherently uncertain and noted that the, '…means by which he experiments are often more heroic than a mere sack'; indeed *Reil* lamented what

47 Mittermaier (1819b) 347.
48 Ibid. 346.
49 Riegger (2007) 77, citing Kalisch (1860) 11.
50 Mittermaier (1819b) 348.
51 Kalisch (1860) 7.
52 Henke (1830) 180.
53 Ibid. 180.
54 Kalisch (1860) 27.
55 Ibid. 12. The unfortunate hound was placed in such a sack for 12 hours and emerged fresh.
56 The court's failure to investigate the sack for themselves was one ground on which their conduct of the case was later criticised, Mittermaier (1819b) 353 f.
57 Kalisch (1860) 17.

might happen if every fatality resulted in a criminal investigation of the practitioner concerned.[58] In short, the practitioner ought to be able to experiment with the aim of furthering his noble aims without fear of criminal censure where, through mere accident, harm befell his patient. *Horn* was vindicated and the case dismissed.[59]

Whilst the case cast a long shadow throughout the century, the immediate feature of it for our purposes is not just the extent to which questions of medical fault in a criminal context depended upon expert evidence of the customary nature of any practice, but also what it reveals about the nature of the fault analysis itself. *Skalley*, the investigating judge, in his own later writings on the case had argued that it would have been impossible to establish liability unless it could be shown that the sack was an '...entirely impermissible and inherently dangerous tool',[60] a high standard indeed. Given this would have been judged against the opinion provided by the medical experts, the *Carolina's* approach clearly remained influential.[61]

### *(iii) Medical error and early criminal scholarship*

*Mittermaier* noted that, whilst criminal liability for negligent medical treatment had been the, '...subject of great disagreement before the courts', there was little by way of academic consideration of the topic.[62] The majority of such academic work was clustered at the end of the century and almost solely considered intentional bodily injury, which lies beyond the scope of the present inquiry.[63] But there is some earlier scholarship on which we may draw and that provides an insight into the developments up to 1871.

*Mittermaier* had been spurred to write by the *Fall Horn*.[64] As he saw it, the criminal law required gross negligence measured against the standard of the general prudence of a practitioner.[65] For him, the *gemeines Recht* applied no

58 Kalisch (1860) 27.

59 *Krähe* notes that the matter did not hinder *Horn's* career given he was appointed as a Professor at the University of Berlin in 1812 but that *Kolrausch* persisted with his accusations, failing twice to have the matter later reopened, Krähe (1984) 37.

60 Mittermaier (1819b) 352, reviewing *Skalley's* account of the case from 1818.

61 Schmidt (1900) 40–41.

62 Mittermaier (1853) 1; See similar sentiments by Geiß (1838) 584. Writing in 1867 *Berner* lists only *Geiß* and *Mittermaier* as having written on the subject and indeed, omits the latter's earlier 1818 piece considered here. This contrasts with 17 medico-legal authors having considered the question in the same period. Berner (1867) 25–26.

63 See Kessler (1884); Oppenheim (1892); Heimberger (1899); v Lilienthal (1899); Schmidt (1900).

64 Mittermaier (1819b) 346.

65 Ibid. 355.

different standard, indeed the *Carolina's* approach was regarded as inappropriate not for the lower standard it was taken as implying, but rather because of the changes in the understanding of '*Arzt*'. The '*Arzt*' of the *Carolina* was not to be compared with, '…those medical practitioners who have been examined and licensed by the state', in contemporary nineteenth-century life and in whom absolute trust ought to be placed.[66] For such practitioners, safety from the reaches of the criminal law was to be found, '…in the application of the common skill required by the practice'.[67] Given the relatively un-standardised nature of medical practice in *Prussia* before the 1825 curriculum reforms, one wonders what *Mittermaier* thought as the decades progressed if he was already willing, in the 1810s, to credit the university-educated practitioner with such indulgence. Further, he stressed the uncertainties of medical science: it lacked a fixed body of infallible rules, it was only possible to look to the establishment of practitioners' actual behaviour, a clearly sociological standard.[68] This argument would become familiar in the medico-legal arguments seeking to define a *Kunstfehler*, albeit the direction of influence is unclear. Rather liability might arise from practicing drunk; abandoning a patient having taken them on and not arranging proper substitute care; using unqualified assistants, or, quackishly, going beyond the agreed surgical operation.[69]

*Geiß* later took a narrower position, arguing that criminal liability would only result where an orthodox practitioner had culpably failed to treat a patient by, for instance, claiming that it was too late to attend when timely attendance would have saved them; suffered a personal fault such as drunkenness or administered the incorrect drug.[70] Short of these moral failings, he was less generous. Although for the first of his three examples he drew explicitly on the '*unfleiss*' of the *Carolina* as justifying this,[71] the '*unkunst*' could, it seems, be discarded. Reading the relevant Roman sources, considered in later chapters, as only discussing the criminal liability of quacks,[72] he rejected liability for merely negligent injury.[73] If it were otherwise, one would risk medical practitioners shying from heroic treatments and progress would be impeded. He did, however, acknowledge that the trend of legislation and even medico-legal thought seemed to be against him, pointing resignedly to the equation of the

66 Mittermaier (1819b) 355.
67 Ibid. 356.
68 Ibid. 356.
69 Ibid. 356–357.
70 Geiß (1838) 586–587.
71 Ibid. 586, n 31.
72 Ibid. 585.
73 Ibid. 587–588.

breach of an occupational duty with gross negligence in art 67 of *Feuerbach's Strafgesetzbuch*, which suggested that the standard may have been perceived as less indulgent in practice.

### *(iv) Mid-century codifications and scholarship*

*Geiß* was, in fact, in sync with a similarly indulgent approach towards the congruence of criminal liability and orthodox practice found in the later *Strafgesetzbuch für das Grossherzogtum Baden* 1845. There, § 543, a provision primarily intended to provide a ban from practice, included a specific limitation for a *Kunstfehler*:

> *'Ist die Tödtung oder Körperverletzung Folge eines bloßen auf irriger Ansicht beruhigenden, Kunstfehlers, so wird der Angeschuldigte, in so fern er innerhalb der Gränzen seiner kunstberechtigung gehandelt hat, von keiner Strafe getroffen.'*

Whilst it was apparently possible for a practitioner to be liable for neglect of his occupation, for instance through being late to attend a patient, criminal liability could not attach to injury, which resulted from behaviour that was merely ignorant.[74] The latter was the province of disciplinary proceedings.[75] Rather, criminal responsibility would only attach where a practitioner had been aware that his practice lacked the necessary skill.[76]

The 1851 *Preussisches Strafgesetzbuch* also embraced criminal liability for merely negligent conduct.[77] As to the standard set, it dispensed with the explicit requirement of gross negligence, but had also eschewed mere negligence. *Beseler's* commentary on the code suggested, that negligent homicide would generally require something close to advertent negligence,[78] and, citing the case of medical practitioners and apothecaries, that only gross breaches of an occupational duty should suffice to ground liability.[79] The breach itself, was, it seems, no longer considered gross *per se.*

*Mittermaier* returned to the subject in 1853. Both *Geiß's* views, and the protection against liability for *Kunstfehlers* in Baden's *Strafgesetzbuch* were commended,[80] and he was critical of the fact that the *PStGB* lacked any guidance as to how a judge should assess whether something was a *Kunstfehler* or not;

74 Thilo (1845) 433.
75 Ibid. 433. The same argument was later rehearsed by *Berner*, see Berner (1867) 24.
76 Thilo (1845) 433.
77 Beseler (1851) 47–50.
78 Ibid. 50.
79 Ibid. 364, describing it as requiring, '...an exceedingly high degree of negligence'.
80 Mittermaier (1853) 1–5.

albeit § 202 *PStGB* contained such guidance for builders.[81] Rather he relied on opinions from various cases, all reported in the medico-legal press, concerning medical liability. In all of them the opinion was, in line with the prevailing trend elaborated in the previous chapter, determinative of the question of fault. He approved recent uncited cases as requiring gross negligence or obvious inattention from the practitioner.[82] Interestingly, he decried the language of the *Kunstfehler* as inapposite given its manifold definitions in the medico-legal literature, but retained an approach that would reflect the settled, later understanding of the term as focusing on what was, in essence, customary[83] within orthodox medical practice, whilst allowing that such practice could change over time.[84] Indeed this seems to have been given a wide reading such that, upon qualification, each practitioner was, themselves, said to be the best judge of what should be done in any given situation.[85]

Whilst *Geiß* had relied on the old Roman rule, *culpa enim est, immiscere se rei ad se non pertinenti*, for both quacks and those more orthodox practitioners such as practical surgeons and apothecaries who strayed into, 'medicine in the narrower sense',[86] *Mittermaier* was happy to restrict it only to quackery.[87] As such, the unauthorised practitioner could not rely on the, '…less harsh assessment of a *Kunstfehler* […] which can be used in connection with a legitimate medical practitioner'.[88] A meaningful distinction here between *Geiß* and *Mittermaier* may be found in that the latter regarded certain parts of the para-medical marketplace as providing a useful service and was keen to protect them.[89]

In 1858 *Mittermaier* returned to the topic again, focusing on the relationship between the court and expert evidence.[90] He noted the 1855 case of *Dr Krieger* who had subjected a child with dropsy to a spirit bath and, in the process, caused them to suffer burns. The child later died. In the subsequent prosecution, despite having been condemned for not following a safer method of using such a bath

81 Mittermaier (1853) 7. The relevant part of § 202 read '…*welche bei der Ausführung eines Baues wider die allgemein anerkannten Regeln der Baukunst dergestalt gehandelt hat*'.

82 Mittermaier (1853) 32. This was supported in due course by *Kalisch* in his response to *Casper's* wider definition of a *Kunstfehler*. See Kalisch (1860).

83 Mittermaier (1853) 180–181. He lists various examples of what he means but was unable to point to any such use by the courts.

84 Ibid. 183.

85 Ibid. 184.

86 Geiß (1838) 585–586.

87 Mittermaier (1853) 174–175.

88 Ibid. 175.

89 Ibid. 177. *Mittermaier* suggested that for these practitioners a disciplinary sanction was the more appropriate route to punishment, at 178.

90 Ibid. 3.

by the experts at first instance, one of the opinions on appeal noted that a similar practice was in use in Berlin and, in due course, he was exonerated by the concurring opinion of the *Obermedicinalcollegium*.[91] *Mittermaier* reported the relative paucity of criminal negligence actions against medical practitioners, explaining this as being the result of either a disinclination on the part of the prosecutor to support such cases (possibly having taken heed of medical demands that an opinion ought always be sought as a preliminary step before opening any prosecution), or, on the grounds that the courts did not think practitioners exhibited culpable behaviour.[92] Again he separated the indulgent position in such cases from the more rigorous application of the law to cases rooted in '*Nachlässigkeit*' or rash, foolhardy treatment.[93] As for a general rule here, he noted the attempts to formulate a standard in the medico-legal literature but was, as *Berner* had been above, critical of adopting *Casper's* suggestion. *Casper* had argued that a practitioner would not be liable unless they had done something that the predominant majority of practitioners in that position would not have done and this latter course of action met with the approval of the predominant majority of all medical teachers and authors.[94] Not only, *Mittermaier* countered, was a majority hard to find on any question, there was insufficient guidance as to the geography of any such majority, ought a Prussian practitioner, who had learned better practice abroad, be bound by his, in comparison, backwards native brethren?[95]

### *(v) A retreat from indulgence*

A shift away from this indulgent stance can be identified following the *PStGB*. The idea that there could be no criminal liability for merely unskilled practice was posited by *Berner* in 1867. First, he insisted a, '...lack of skill is not negligence', on the basis that one could not be liable merely for, a 'failure of the intellect', only for, a 'failure in acting'.[96] Secondly, echoing *Mittermaier's* position, a wide margin of discretion had to be afforded to orthodox practitioners who had undergone approved training. *Berner* regarded neither ground as capable of rational analysis. The examinations for licensure were necessarily limited in their scope and did not proceed under the fiction that the licensed practitioner knew how to deal with all possible situations. Rather, it was for the

91 Mittermaier (1853) 11–12.
92 Ibid. 12.
93 Ibid. 16.
94 Ibid. 16.
95 Ibid. 17. As he pithily noted: 'If *Casper's* view was practicable the world would be condemned to a standstill.'
96 Berner (1867) 28–29.

licensed practitioner to demonstrate in every single case that he possessed the required knowledge and skill,[97] and where he did not, the nature of the duty he had undertaken in practice indeed rendered such errors criminally culpable.[98] He rejected the argument that medicine could not be constrained to a fixed set of rules for fear that progress would be stunted. Indeed, despite the manifold conditions that could present, it was the absence of any general rules that characterised not orthodox practice but charlatanry.[99] Centuries of medical practice could provide an equitable and judicious standard for what could be expected in any given situation and, as long as the goal was the health of the patient and not 'mere experiment', medical progress would not be hindered.[100] Predictably, the role of the expert opinion was key in revealing whether the required standard had been met but, *Berner* stressed, the final decision lay with the, 'now properly informed judge' who, pointing to the numerous cases reported by *Casper*, felt themselves up to the task.[101] He felt that lessons could be learned from the preceding codifications and argued that liability for a *Kunstfehler* should be limited, drawing on article 67 of *Feuerbach's Strafgesetzbuch*, to situations where there was existing practice against which to judge the defendant's behaviour. Equally, he was disparaging of the prosecutorial discretion allowed to the public prosecutor in cases of medical injury in the absence of any request. It could be assumed that the patient would be too grateful to press charges and in lieu of that, the public interest in doing so was not compelling enough.[102]

### 3. The *Reichsstrafgesetzbuch* 1871

#### (A) The triumph of general rules

The contrast between the splintered civil law, examined in the following chapters, and the criminal law became stark with the arrival of the *Reichsstrafgesetzbuch* (*RStGB*) in January 1872.[103] The text drew heavily on the

97 Berner (1867) 29.

98 Ibid. 30.

99 Ibid. 30. This point was drawn on by *Ortloff* in 1888 as supporting the adoption of *Virchow's* definition of a *Kunstfehler*.

100 Ibid. 31.

101 Ibid. 32.

102 Ibid. 33. See also similar sentiments from the medical perspective: Oesterlen (1882) 600–601, *Oesterlen* suggested a preliminary expert opinion be secured from a faculty or medical college as to whether there was an answerable case.

103 Wetzell (2014) 2. *Wetzell* notes the swift passage of the *Gerichtsverfassungsgesetz* (1877) and the *Strafprozessordnung* (1877) as the complementary parts of this initial stage of codification; Schmidt (1995) § 297, 343

provisions of the *PStGB*,[104] and the 1867 *Strafgesetzbuch für den Norddeutschen Bund*, indeed many provisions were taken straight from the latter. The *RStGB* reflected their generalist approach to liability over objections from medical practitioners such as *Virchow*, who had previously warned of the uncertain scope of application of such general provisions to medical practitioners. As discussed in the previous chapter, he had recommended that two lines be added to § 198 *PStGB*, or its equivalents, to ensure that medical practitioners would only be liable due to committing a *Kunstfehler* as he defined it.[105]

The *RStGB* instead retained broad provisions on negligent killing (§ 222) and negligent bodily injury (§ 230) that offered no special rule concerning liability for medical error:

> '*§ 222*
> '*Wer durch Fahrlässigkeit den Tod eines Menschen verursacht, wird mit Gefängniß bis zu drei Jahren bestraft. Wenn der Thäter zu der Aufmerksamkeit, welche er aus den Augen setzte, vermöge seines Amtes, Berufes oder Gewerbes besonders verpflichtet war, so kann die Strafe bis auf fünf Jahre Gefängniß erhöht werden.*'
>
> '*§ 230*
> *Wer durch Fahrlässigkeit die Körperverletzung eines Anderen verursacht, wird mit Geldstrafe bis zu dreihundert Thalern oder mit Gefängniß bis zu zwei Jahren bestraft. War der Thäter zu der Aufmerksamkeit, welche er aus den Augen setzte, vermöge seines Amtes, Berufes oder Gewerbes besonders verpflichtet, so kann die Strafe auf drei Jahre Gefängniß erhöht werden.*'

Although a fine was possible, the second sentence of each paragraph provided that the attendant prison term could be raised (to five and three years respectively) where the defendant was obligated to take care because of his office, calling or trade and had failed to do so. Furthermore, § 232 (1) *RStGB* ensured that the prosecution of intentional or negligent bodily injury (the former provided for by § 223 *RStGB*) was not dependant on a request by the victim, where it arose as the result of the breach of such a duty related to the defendant's office, calling or trade. Orthodox practitioners lamented this development in the years following,[106] and, as late as 1888, were demanding that an action should only begin after a preliminary, medically-overseen expert opinion had vetted it.[107] In a key shift in the criminal law's regulatory power, there was no equivalent provision to § 199 *PStGB* barring unorthodox practice.

104 Riegger (2007) 70.
105 Virchow (1879) 514–516.
106 *Aerztliches Vereinsblatt* (1894) 573.
107 Deneke (1888) 260–265.

## (B) Compensation and the *Reichsstrafgesetzbuch*

A single set of facts may, of course, have generally grounded both civil and criminal liability under the various criminal codes examined above.[108] § 231(1) *RStGB* allowed the victim of a bodily injury to claim up to two thousand thalers (ultimately six thousand marks following the currency conversion in 1876) in the form of a fine (*Buße*) alongside the criminal sentence.[109] Such an award, per § 231 (2), barred further claims for compensation.[110] The *PStGB* had lacked any such mechanism, with § 6 *PStGB* simply noting that the right to compensation (*Schadenersatz*) was independent of any punishment; indeed *Windscheid* certainly regarded the fine as a new concept.[111] The idea had been the subject of considerable discussion amongst criminal scholars in a relatively short period following 1871, with argument centred on whether it was a purely punitive,[112] compensatory,[113] or mixed award.[114] Discussing the otherwise settled compensatory nature of damages for civil claims regarding personal injury in the late nineteenth century, *Gerber* noted that the old quasi-penal wrongs of the Roman and old Germanic systems had been largely been dispensed with in the modern codifications, including the then second draft of the forthcoming *BGB*.[115] The basis for calculating a fine was free assessment by the judge. In that sense, although formally separated from the civil law, *Gerber* regarded the award as having the same effect as the older law.[116] This point regarding the calculation of the award was a key criticism, for the judge was not required to consider evidence as to the extent of the harm, or indeed whether there had been harm at

108 Gerber (1850) 375, 'A delict can, at first, lead to a claim for compensation, then also to the payment of a criminal fine.' This was naturally different to the black letter confusion discussed above surrounding claims that, '…simultaneously provided for compensation and punishment': Windscheid (1865) § 326, 215–216.

109 A similar provision could be found in § 188 dealing with claims based on copyright.

110 Gerber (1895) 438.

111 Predictably, *Windscheid's* treatment appears, as a second footnote to the same section, in the first edition following the *RStGB*: Windscheid (1879) § 326, 249 n 11. *Windscheid* noted the use of the term in other Imperial statutes of the period as well. These are listed in Stobbe (1885) § 200.

112 Flesch (1876) 290.

113 Dochow (1875).

114 Flesch (1876) 278; *Windscheid* made a similar point, Windscheid (1879) § 326, 249 n 11. A later view saw the fine as a form of settlement sum: Weinrich (1902) 128 f.

115 Gerber (1895) § 199, 374; § 258, 438. On the other hand, referring to § 231 *RStGB*: 'A fine, which has been introduced by some of the new Criminal Codes is more important.'

116 Gerber (1895) § 258, 438.

all before allowing or dismissing a claim for a fine.[117] This was criticised as an unacceptable degree of uncertainty for the victim,[118] and spoke to the criminal element of the concept for *Windscheid.*[119] For others, the importance of fines simply stood in for a claim for compensation.[120] That said, the *Reichsstrafprozessordnung* (*StPO*) 1877 rendered the claim actively intransmissible,[121] and required the plaintiff to specify the sum.[122] That *Gerber's* discussion appears for the first time in the 1895 17$^{th}$ edition of his text and was not present beforehand may suggest that the argument over the nature of a fine in the criminal law scholarship, was prompted by the impending enactment of the *BGB*.

As to the procedural interplay of both claims, the majority of scholars appeared to deny that a previously successful criminal prosecution could be used as a ground without more but were content to permit the investigatory files to be used in support of the civil case.[123] In practice the answer appeared to vary depending on the region; some courts and regional legislation stressed the independence of any later civil investigation from the earlier criminal findings;[124] some were content to let the criminal findings stand until evidence to the contrary was produced;[125] and some regions, such as *Prussia*, required fresh

117 Weinrich (1902) 123, discussing *RG 18.03.1880.*

118 Flesch (1876).

119 Windscheid (1879) § 326, 249 n 11. Elsewhere, he described it as a compensatory measure albeit with '...a peculiar form', see Windscheid (1879) § 455, 752 n 19 although he appeared less ready to characterise it when discussing § 188 *RStGB* and *inuria*, § 472, 821 n 7a.

120 Stobbe (1885) § 200, 385. *Stobbe* neatly summarised the current state of the debate amongst criminal and intellectual property scholars, agreeing with *Kohler*, one of the latter, who described a fine as, '...compensation and only compensation for the bodily or psychiatric harm to the injured party'. *Stobbe* appears to compare the admittedly arbitrary assessment by a judge favourably to the fixed nature of damages in earlier legal systems.

121 § 444 (4) *StPO.*

122 § 445 *StPO.* This went unmentioned by *Stobbe, Gerber* and *Windscheid* suggesting that its use as a control mechanism operated to set a maximum from which a judge could feel free to depart rather than binding the judge to the sum specified.

123 Schäffer (1854) 11. He listed eleven leading criminal scholars, *Mittermaier* amongst them

124 Ibid. 14. See also Beseler (1851) § 6, 81. *Beseler* noted the point of the section was to ensure that a criminal finding was not prejudicial to any later civil action for compensation calling it 'absolutely acceptable' and noting that a similar provision was to be found in article 10 of the *Rheinisches Strafgesetzbuch.*

125 Simon (1856) 272, discussing the rule to that effect provided in § 46 of the Hanoverian *Strafprocessordnung* 1850. *Simon* himself was in favour of independence because of the differing procedural and bases of the criminal and the civil law.

evidence before such findings could be challenged.[126] The *Reichszivilprocessordnung* (*ZPO*) 1877 certainly envisaged the potential for influence by criminal proceedings on a civil case, § 140 permitting the suspension of an action until any relevant criminal proceedings were completed.[127] Nevertheless, the relatively high sums that could be recovered, allied to the potential advantage of having the state prosecutor mount a patient's case, in effect, on their behalf, would have rendered this a considerably less expensive route to recovering compensation than pursuit of a civil action.

### (C) Medical error in the *Reichsstrafgesetzbuch*

The happenstance that the *RStGB* overlapped with the existence of the *Reichsgericht* provides a greater clarity than was previously available as to the law in practice here. A further feature of the *RStGB* was the availability of prosecutorial discretion without the need for a complaint by the injured party, a situation lamented in the medical press.[128]

#### *(i) An objective standard*

The requirement in § § 222 and 230 *RStGB* that death or bodily injury be caused negligently was understood to mean negligence *simpliciter*, it did not depend on demonstrating the degree of negligence, be it gross or minor.[129] That said, the governing academic opinion viewed the accused's subjective intelligence, capabilities and appreciation of the risks of their behaviour as the key focus of whether they had been negligent,[130] albeit would suffice to foresee the death or bodily injury as a normal consequence of their actions.[131] When applied to medical practitioners, however, the increased sentences provided for in § § 222

126 Simon (1856) 272–273.

127 § 140 *ZPO* '*Das Gericht kann, wenn sich im Laufe eines Rechtsstreits der Verdacht einer strafbaren Handlung ergiebt, deren Ermittelung auf die Entscheidung von Einfluß ist, die Aussetzung der Verhandlung bis zur Erledigung des Strafverfahrens anordnen.*'

128 *Aerztliches Vereinsblatt* (1894) 573; § 232: '*Die Verfolgung leichter vorsätzlicher, sowie aller durch Fahrlässigkeit verursachter Körperverletzungen tritt nur auf Antrag ein, insofern nicht die Körperverletzung mit Übertretung einer Amts-, Berufs- oder Gewerbspflicht begangen worden ist.*'; *RG 25.10.1881* RGSt 5, 74.

129 Oppenhoff (1872) § 59, 142; § 222, 385. Bruck (1885) § 32, 77. See § 31, 76–77 noting that such distinctions had been present in *Feuerbach's* code and the Hanoverian code.

130 Ibid. § 59, 142; Bruck (1885) § 26, 68. As *Bruck* noted, the minority view preferred the judge to assess a 'average degree of insight and prudence'. He was critical of this as presenting the judge with too uncertain a task, § 27, 69–70.

131 Bruck (1885) § 15, 43.

(2) and 230 (2) *RStGB* by reason of the defendant's failure to demonstrate, '*...der Aufmerksamkeit, welche er aus den Augen setzte, vermöge seines Amtes, Berufes oder Gewerbes besonders verpflichtet war*', imposed an objective standard against which the behaviour of such defendants would be measured.[132] In doing so it created an exception to the focus on the defendant's subjective capabilities. Far from qualification providing immutable proof of the necessary skills and knowledge, it had become an ever-changing standard against which a trained practitioner would be measured and with which they would be expected to keep up.[133]

Moreover, despite their, by now long, absence from any statutory text, the old definitions of the *Carolina*, in particular the relevance they gave to medically assessed standards of conduct, also continued to retain their interpretive influence even in this late period, with one commentator noting that medical negligence in the broader sense of applying to all those involved in medical practice could be broken down into practice that was either ignorant ('*unfleiss*') or unskilled ('*unkunst*'/'*Kunstfehler*').[134] The former was understood as the passive omission to meet the standards of medical practice whilst the latter involved their active transgression.[135] This echoed the earlier continuation of the relevance of these terms in unpacking the *PStGB's* application to medical practitioners. Indeed, *Berner* had adopted the distinction in 1867 albeit was not necessary to formally plead one category or the other.[136]

Yet during the parliamentary discussions regarding the *RStGB*, all attempts to create a lesser offence for medical errors had been rejected by a large majority;[137] it was clear that transgressing the professionally accepted boundaries of medical practice now could, but was not the only way to, ground liability for medical error, broadly conceived.[138] Nevertheless, there remained, at least in some scholarship, a feeling that the criminalisation of negligent medical practice should allow for the non-culpable taking of extreme risks in the face of a fatal illness, even if the result remained death for the patient.[139]

132 Ehrenzweig (1892) 56. See also, *RG* 25.10.1881 RGSt 5, 77.

133 Bruck (1885) § 33, 81.

134 Frank (1901) § 222, 277 putting several *Reichsgericht* decisions into each respective category. See also Bruck (1885) § 33, 82 n 1.

135 Frank (1901) § 222, 277; *Riegger* adopts this reading of *Frank* at 71.

136 Berner (1867) 23; 32.

137 Oppenhoff (1872) § 222, 387.

138 Hälschner (1884) 27, n 3.

139 Bruck (1885) § 29, 73–74.

### (ii) *The impact of the Gewerbeordnung 1869*

This apparent broadening of the potential scope of liability may be explained by the impact of the *Gewerbeordnung* 1869, with § § 222 (2) and 230 (2) *RStGB* coming to be read as covering unorthodox practitioners and quacks who held themselves out as being qualified for practice or having suitable skill to offer treatment.[140] In a decision from 1877, reported from one of the *Königlichen Obertribunal in Strafsachen*, the court held that such an interpretation was in line with the reasoning behind § 230 and indeed noted that the accused, a practitioner advertising himself as '*medicus non approbatus*' who had poorly set a leg, mounted no defence to this reading of said section.[141]

Furthermore, to mollify the impact of the *Gewerbeordnung* 1869, and the necessarily more liberal approach to healthcare provision, criminal liability was tightened,[142] deploying § 222 *RStGB* in quasi-regulatory fashion.[143] Thus, taking on practice knowing that one was not qualified to do so would be regarded as culpable negligence.[144] The effects of this approach can be seen in the same decision from 1877 discussed above. There, culpable negligence could be identified in the accused having taken on treatment of a child, '...in the face of his inadequate anatomical and surgical knowledge, rather than calling for a qualified practitioner'.[145] Although the mere practice of medicine without having undergone a scientific, academic education remained not, itself, capable of grounding a charge of criminal negligence,[146] the *Reichsgericht* adopted much of the same reasoning. In 1881 the court held that the sharpened liabilities of § § 222 (2) and 230 *RStGB* would, in principle, apply to those engaged in paramedical occupations such as female midwifery (*Hebamme*).[147]

This was confirmed in an 1882 *Reichsgericht* decision; the standard to be applied in all cases was that of the orthodox medical practitioner: '...whomsoever practices medicine as their trade, must make good infringements against recognised rules of medicine just like an examined and licensed medical

140 Hälschner (1884) 27; Frank, (1901) § 222, 277; Riegger 71; Oppenhoff, 1901 § 222, 525 f. See *RG 03.07.1884* RGSt 6, 505; Bruck (1885) § 33, 82.

141 Oppenhoff (1877) 654, decision of *17.10 1877.*

142 Oppenhoff (1872) § 222, 387; 1901, 526.

143 Bruck (1885) § 33 79–80.

144 Bruck (1885) § 33, 82; Frank (1901) § 222, 277; Riegger (2007) 71; *RG 12.04.1882* RRGSt 4, 313. This reflected the earlier approach in *Feuerbach's StGB*, which, per article 66, had held those who practiced without authorisation from the state to have been grossly negligent in doing so if harm resulted.

145 Oppenhoff (1877) 656, discussing *RG 17.10.1877*

146 Oppenhoff, 1901, § 222, 526, citing *RG 26.10.1893.*

147 *RG 25.10.1881* RGSt 5, 74.

practitioner'.[148] There, the defendant *Kurpfuscher* applied heated compresses to the patient's injured arms, a treatment, regarded as 'incorrect and inappropriate' by the expert evidence.[149] A similar approach was taken where a quack barber injured his patient in the course of a cupping therapy and was held liable under § 230 *RStGB*.[150] Given the defendant was practicing as a trade,[151] the relevant standard to be applied was to be found in the higher duty of care imposed by those sections. The standards of orthodox medical practice ('...as an examined and licensed medical practitioner', as the court put it)[152] were thus decisive. Indeed the court noted the need to protect the population from unregulated medical practice as revealed in the preparatory documents for the *Reichsstrafgesetzbuch*. This stance had two important consequences.

First, as emphasised in a later decision, the regulatory distinction between licensed practice and, commonly unorthodox, unlicensed practice was removed as far as criminal liability was concerned. There, either the defendant was a midwife (*Hebamme*) with the required certification,[153] or, without the required certification, was practicing quackery and in either case they would be held to the practice of orthodox practitioners.[154]

Secondly, the court confirmed that the standard that was expected from orthodox practitioners in the first place was that of the state of the medical art, compliance with the 'recognised rules of medical practice'.[155] It was this feature of the decision in particular that appears to have doomed the defendant, their chosen treatment being deemed as, '...plainly dangerous according to the standards of modern science'.[156] Other ways of stating the same test could be identified in the cases. In one decision from 1880,[157] a practitioner had been called to help with a difficult delivery and, having broken first one of its arms and then its jaw in an unsuccessful attempt to free a trapped child, incorrectly presumed the child to be dead and so delivered it using, amongst other things, a hook through one eye. The child succumbed to the resulting injuries. The court in *Neustettin* declared him guilty under § 222 *RStGB* by reason that his

148 *RG 12.04.1882* RRGSt 4, 313.
149 *RG 12.04.1882* RRGSt 4, 313.
150 *RG 03.10.1884* (1890) 53 Vierteljahrsschrift für gerichtliche und öffentliche Medicin 371.
151 *RG 12.04.1882* RRGSt 4, 314.
152 *RG 12.04.1882* RRGSt 4, 314.
153 § 30 Gewerbeordnung 1869.
154 *RG 14.01.1887* RGSt 15, 182.
155 '...contrary to the recognised rules of medical practice, *according to the current state of the scholarship...*' *RG 12.04.1882* RRGSt 4, 313 (emphasis added).
156 *RG 12.04.1882* RRGSt 4, 314.
157 *RG 08.06.1880* RGSt 1, 446.

presumption that the child was dead was a, '...gross infringement of the rules of medical science'.[158] There was no suggestion that the use of 'gross' had been intended as a term of art and the *Reichsgericht* did not correct the phrasing in upholding the decision. In their words, the negligence of the defendant was in, '...the assumption that the same scientifically unjustified indications suggested the death of the child and that, thus, led to its dismemberment'.[159] Again, in framing the applicable standard, both courts had laid stress on the scholarship to which, in effect, orthodox practitioners were the gatekeepers.

Finally, a decision from 1888 relied on the evidence that the defendant unorthodox practitioner, a bookbinder with a side business in medical care, had caused the death of a child suffering from diphtheria through his failure to meet the standards of 'appropriate medical treatment'.[160] A similar case was later reported concerning an orthodox practitioner whose negligence, in failing to diagnose a breech birth, had led to the death of his pregnant patient.[161] In all these cases, regardless of the way the standard was articulated, it was linked to the practice of what orthodox practitioners accepted as proper, largely reflecting in substance, if not in name, the internally developed conception of the *Kunstfehler* explored in the previous chapter.[162]

### *(iii) Antisepsis as a recognised rule*

Where practice was uncodified, the importance of the expert opinion was clear.[163] The *Reichsgericht* considered the standard of care expected from an orthodox practitioner in such a situation head on in 1884. There, an orthodox medical practitioner was charged with negligent homicide for failing to have adopted measures such as antiseptic bandaging which would, it was claimed, have protected the patient's wound against infection.[164] The question of whether the continued use of lint and salves over antisepsis could be regarded as a *Kunstfehler* had been raised in the medical press four years earlier. The violent shift in medical practice that *Lister's* discovery had occasioned,[165] naturally

158 *RG 08.06.1880* RGSt 1, 446.

159 *RG 08.06.1880* RGSt 1, 449.

160 *RG 18.09.1888* RRGSt 10, 493.

161 *Aerztliche Sachverständigen-Zeitung* (1896) 516.

162 Ehrenzweig (1892) 51.

163 Where practice was codified these could be drawn on directly by the courts, see *RG 25.10.1881* RGSt 5, 74; Ministry for Medical Affairs (1878); Ministry for Medical Affairs (1892). Each contained the text of the state instructions for midwives as an appendix.

164 Ehrenzweig (1892) 57, *Ehrenzweig* notes that antiseptic played a particularly special role in many surgical claims.

165 Lister (1867).

prompted the question how doing something that had long been acceptable could be regarded as negligent. Yet, the 1881 *Deutsche Ärztetag* had adopted the platform that it was the duty of every practitioner to use such measures.[166] The *Reichsgericht* was, in due course, called to consider whether a practitioner's personal preference as to the method of treatment could exculpate him. The evidence on which they did so was not elaborated in the relevant case report but was given extensive coverage in the medical press, permitting a clear view of the progress of a single case to the *Reichsgericht* and the use of multiple expert opinions to clarify the medical view of the defendant's behaviour. The case stemmed from an incident in 1882 where a workman, *H*, was stabbed at a public meeting, suffering a serious but, as the *Landgericht* later stressed,[167] not life-threatening injury. He first sought medical attention from a barber-surgeon, who recommended another, orthodox practitioner be called, a *Dr N*. *H* received treatment from *N*, who, it transpired, had not undertaken any antiseptic measures. *H* perished some days later.[168] An opinion requested by the prosecutor found that *N* must have known that the wound was penetrative, and that he had incorrectly diagnosed it. His failure to diagnose and treat accordingly – he had applied lint, a cold poultice and a sticking plaster – was regarded by the *Gerichtarzt's* opinion as a gross infringement of the fundamentals of modern surgery and, as such, an absence of the, '…regard to which he was beholden by reason of his calling'.[169] *N* protested that the finding failed to respect his discretion to choose the method of treatment, noting antisepsis was subject to energetic protests, and was not officially mandated.[170] The prosecutor thus requested a further opinion from the *Medicinal-Comité*. That opinion was damning. Having failed to properly examine the wound, he had not shown the necessary care in using antisepsis and closing it. The question having been put in these terms by the prosecutor,[171] they found that these actions infringed the recognised rules of medical practice.[172] As to a practitioner's discretion, whilst it was clear that practitioners were not bound to a single method, they could not behave indiscriminately. *N* was sentenced to fourteen days of imprisonment; the court's reasoning is worth quoting in full:[173]

166 Although contemporary medical literature on the *Kunstfehler* certainly seems to have regarded it as such, see Krähe (1984) 101–103.

167 *Aerztliches Vereinsblatt* (1885) 45.

168 Ibid. 36.

169 Ibid. 37–38.

170 Ibid. 39.

171 Ibid. 39.

172 Ibid. 41.

173 Ibid. 45.

> 'This procedure is considered, with good reason, to no longer be a contested rule of medical practice, rather, having been tested through experience, as a recognised axiom of modern medical science. Such rules must be followed by a medical practitioner in practice; he cannot ignore them either by reason of his ignorance or misunderstanding, nor may he protect himself by calling on the supposed freedom of scholarship, which might allow him to cling to a contrary view. In so far as possible, he must aim for the level of the scholarship, so that he obtains knowledge of those rules, which are questionable and can monitor them.'

The defendant appealed to the *Reichsgericht*. The argument that there could be no fault in his having adopted his own method, 'tested over long years of practice', in contrast to antiseptic, which was, he maintained, still an experimental practice, was given short shrift.[174] The *Landgericht* had taken it as proven that antiseptic was, '...no longer at the stage of an experiment [...] but rather a rule of medical practice which, with reason, was no longer contested'. No flaw could thus be detected in the finding that, '...the practicing medical practitioner must be conscious of the level of the scholarship so that he can take account of the rules, if he omits to do this, then he must bear the burden of his negligence.'[175] *Ehrenzweig* later noted that there had been opposition by some medico-legal authors to regarding the use of antiseptic as a fundamental part of good practice as it might unnecessarily burden practitioners in the hinterlands who had no practical access to it.[176] He suggested that the failure to use such measures might not lead to criminal prosecution depending on the context of the practice.

### 4. Conclusions

*Laufs* and *Eichener* explain the eventual absence of specialist criminal liability in the codifications of this era as being, in part, because the specific approach of the *Carolina* was seen as irrelevant, particularly for orthodox practice.[177] The natural law influence on the drafting baulked at replicating the, by then, '...grey, murky and medieval' form of the *Carolina*.[178] They argue that the absence of a modernised version of article 134 *Carolina* was in keeping with the increased

174 *RG 03.07.1884* RRGSt 6, 507.

175 *RG 03.07.1884* RRGSt 6, 507–508. See also *RG 04.06.1883* RRGSt 5, 403. See also Haebler (1898) 370. There an orthodox practitioner was imprisoned and fined for negligently causing the death of a child, having poked his ear with a hair pin to remove a seed.

176 Ehrenzweig (1892) 58–59.

177 Laufs/Eichener (1991) 90–91. They note the rather startling fact that *Benedikt Carpzow* (1595–1666), a renowned criminal jurist of the era, listed § 134 *Carolina* under headings for *Kurpfuscher* rather than *Medicus* in the index to his *Opus decisionum illustrium saxonicarum* (1660).

178 Laufs/Eichener (1991) 92.

respect for, and trust in, the professionally controlled standards that the state licensure enacted in the nineteenth century;[179] it had simply become increasingly unthinkable that an orthodox practitioner could be charged with a criminal offence. Evidential difficulties and the privileged position of orthodox practitioners diminished the relevance of criminal law.[180] Certainly medical authors in the final years of the nineteenth century thought that: 'Negligence that the medical practitioner commits in the course of the practice of his medical art and science is no different from every other negligence.'[181]

Yet there are nuances that do not so easily fit that narrative. If the shape of the relevant statutory provisions had moved from specificity to generality, it is unclear that the standard of care had followed or developed much at all. Despite the suggestions that article 134 *Carolina* imposed a standard higher than simple negligence, by the nineteenth century the standard of care settled on simple negligence, a fact that confused some contemporary civil law scholars.[182] In fact, all efforts to render it formally harder to sue a medical practitioner, to require gross rather than simple fault, had been resisted by the legislator, despite the persistent arguments by contemporary scholars that *culpa lata* was indeed more appropriate. At a stroke, the prevailing view amongst medico-legal authors that criminal liability would only attach to grossly negligent conduct had been disabused.[183] The underlying rationale of these authors in many cases was the desire to ensure that practitioners were not dissuaded from breaking new medical ground. The focus of the law was less on risking besmirching a practitioner's honour than on their role as steward of a set of skills intended to benefit all. There was at no point any suggestion that the criminal law truly countenanced a *formal* indulgence towards medical practice and, where rules were specific, it was seldom to the practitioner's advantage.

The idea of indulgence towards practitioners in the informal application of the law is easier to evidence. To be sure, orthodox practitioners *were* privileged in that their performance was, in effect, measured against the opinion of experts drawn on by the court. From the *Fall Horn* through to the *Reichsgericht*, the role of expert evidence appeared decisive of a practitioner's fault. But engagement as court advisors, as the *Carolina* demonstrates, was hardly novel. The conceptual and institutional overlap between the courts, who required expert evidence, and

179 Laufs/Eichener (1991) 94, n 96.

180 Ibid. 94–95.

181 *Aerztliches Vereinsblatt* (1896) 445.

182 Zimmermann (1873) 227–228, taking the sharpened liability of § § 222 and 230 as imposing liability for *culpa lata* and thus bolstering his claim that the civil law shared a similar standard.

183 Ehrenzweig (1892) 68.

orthodox practitioners themselves, who over the course of the nineteenth century had developed a readily transferrable concept and discourse on error, permitted medical practitioners to police themselves. Yet the 1884 *Reichsgericht* decision discussed above demonstrated that an orthodox practitioner could not rest on their laurels and licensure did not absolve a practitioner of the need to stay up to date with the *currently* accepted standard of medical practice and scholarship.

Finally, what is particularly striking in this era is the continuation of the quasi-regulatory tradition of the *Carolina* in the law of the nineteenth century. This can be identified in two features of the law. First, the overlap between the criminal and disciplinary spheres provided for in the continued availability of a ban from practice under some of the earlier codes. The *PStGB* 1851 appears to mark the break between the two realms in that regard with questions of licensure and the right to practice becoming, properly, tools of the emerging disciplinary apparatus rather than the criminal law. Secondly, the fact that the logic of the *Gewerbeordnung* 1869, that medicine was a trade open to all, was dismissed, given the absence of a successor to § 199 *PStGB* in the *RStGB*. Unorthodox practitioners were judged against the standards of their orthodox, scientific brethren. Thus, whilst the relevance of expert evidence increased as courts adopted the language of the medical discourse, the criminal law retained a degree of specificity to practitioners' disadvantage and, through its quasi-regulatory application and refusal of a more indulgent standard of fault, was well placed to control injurious medical error in this era. Having established a foundation of the nature of medical practice and practitioners and the role of the criminal law, the following chapters consider how medical error was handled by the civil law.

Chapter 3

# Medical Error and Contract Law

'…first out of humanity'[1]

We now turn to the civil law and begin by considering how a contractual analysis was deployed to categorise the practitioner-patient relationship and the effect this had on claims concerning medical error. As much of the German law here was strongly influenced by a view of the Roman law, our analysis begins, necessarily, with a brief consideration of the law in that much earlier period. We consider both the nature of medicine and medical practice in *Rome* then unpack how these various types of practice caused persistent difficulty in categorising the practitioner-patient relationship. It will be shown that, far from suggesting a static, monolithic relationship between the law and practice, the Roman law likely evolved over time towards a more liberal approach to contracting for medical care. We then address the same doctrinal discussion as it took place in the nineteenth-century German scholarship. Here, having often taken the Roman law, incorrectly, as adopting a static view of the relationship between law and medical practice, often to defend the view that medical practice was a higher calling, the same process was played out again against the backdrop of contemporary medical practice established in chapter one. We will consider the extent to which medical error was specifically visible in contemporary sources as a topic for separate analysis, or, instead, fell to be considered as part of the general run of the doctrinal rules. Here we discover that there was very little by way of specific treatment of the legal problems surrounding injurious medical practice outside of a lengthy exchange between two late-century judges, *Zimmermann* and *Hefke*, each writing in their extra-judicial capacity. Whether in the general or specific literature, we find that the process of reconciling Roman legal structures with German medical practice was confusing and opaque, and one which relied on the construction of a variously idealised or realistic gestalt for contemporary medical practice. The discussion of the contractual relationship between practitioner and patient was driven by one's choice between these two competing models, confirming the importance of the sociological and regulatory standing of medical practitioners and the long,

1 Zimmermann (1873) 228.

restrictive reach of the Roman view of labour. Often where, as in the case of the legislation during this period, a fresh start could be made, a considerably clearer legal view of medical practice emerges. Finally, we consider the impact that the various possible options had on the approach to the formal standard for, and, if any, the actual assessment in practice of, fault. Here, we find, within the general literature, that the emerging consensus around the relationship being categorised as some form of simple service contract, matched increasing acceptance of the standard being one of simple fault, with suggestions in the case law that, as with the criminal law, the *Kunstfehler* provided the underpinning logic for analysing medical error in practice. Whilst this latter point also emerges from the exchange between *Zimmermann* and *Hefke* – whatever the standard, both agreed that it was tied to expert evidence as to the commonality of the practice – much of their disagreement hinged on the former's insistence that the standard remained, in this period, gross fault whilst the latter vigorously defended the use of a simple fault standard.

## 1. The Roman inheritance

### (A) Roman medicine and medical provision

While there had been a long-standing tradition of medical study and learning in Greece, this was not the case in Roman life.[2] There we find two main sources of medical knowledge, a home-grown tradition of folk remedies based on, '...herbs, chants, prayers and charms',[3] which saw medicine as part of the authority and knowledge of the *paterfamilias*,[4] and the imported expertise of Hellenistic medicine from Greece. The former eschewed formal learning in favour of medical knowledge as transmitted by non-medical men in encyclopaedias and general handbooks.[5] In contrast the latter was distinctly more intellectual, often based on a theoretical underpinning, focused study and eventual specialism.[6] As is to be expected in a pre-modern era, both magic and religion overlapped closely, in particular tending towards this in the countryside.[7] Attempts were eventually made to distinguish, at least for the

2 Edelstein (1966); Nutton (1995a) 11.
3 Nutton (1995b) 39.
4 Scarborough (1970) 296, 297. A common example can be found in Cato, *De agri cultura*, if one credits cabbages as a universal remedy.
5 Nutton (1995b) 40. Nutton (1992) 35, The tradition was '...domestic, practical medicine marked by a strong chauvinism'.
6 Nutton (1995a) 11–35. Nutton (1992) 15–35
7 Nutton (1995b) 40; Nutton (1984) 1, 8–9; Nutton (1992) 56 noting the long survival of magical / folk remedies.

purposes of provincial salaries, the more orthodox from the non-orthodox, using the absence of magic ritual as the yardstick.[8] Following the abortive efforts of *Archagathus* around 219 BC,[9] the influence of the Hellenistic model in *Rome* increased under *Caesar* and *Augustus* through slavery, immigration and the eventual incentive of citizenship.[10] By the time of *Celsus* (c AD 30), the two traditions had, to an extent, merged,[11] and in the person of *Galen*, the Roman Empire would realise its own *Hippocrates*.[12]

In contrast to practice in Greece, few natural born citizens muddied their hands with medicine.[13] The actual practice of medicine, provided mainly by *servi*, *liberti*, *peregrini* and to a lesser extent *ingenui*,[14] was left to a largely unregulated mixture of those with some sort of training, those whose expertise was based on experience and those who were simply mountebanks.[15] The latter could easily avoid detection through a combination of urban anonymity and a necessarily highly mobile practice.[16] There was no 'profession', and the urban patient faced a bewildering range of options with choice diminishing in the countryside.[17] As to where one received healthcare, it was often a domestic experience.[18] Outside the army or extensive properties, where one might find a *valetudinaria* in which slaves would be cared for,[19] a precursor to the modern hospital, offering care to all,[20] was unknown until the influence of Christianity in the fourth century.[21]

8 D.50.13.1.3. *Below* noted the likely post-classical nature of this text, Below (1953) 5.

9 Pliny, 29.6. *Nutton* cautions that Archagathus, '...was not the first doctor active in Rome [...] but the first to practice as a civic doctor in true Hellenistic fashion', Nutton (1981) 9, 18.

10 Ibid. 18; Scarborough, (1970) 297.

11 Scarborough (1970) 296.

12 Heldrich (1940) 141.

13 Scarborough, (1970) 299; Below (1953) 20. Scarborough (1969) 113; Nutton (1992).

14 Below (1953) 6–21, suggesting that the weight fell mainly on the first two categories; Nutton (1992) 39–40.

15 Galen's work reveals, '...the extreme fluidity of any line separating a layman from a *medicus*' Nutton, (1990) 256. *Scarborough* notes that, 'Quackery was rife on all levels of society', Scarborough (1969) 97.

16 Galen XIV; Nutton (1971) 63.

17 Nutton (1990) 244; Nutton (1992) 53.

18 Nutton (1995b) 52.

19 Ibid. 49–50.

20 Ibid. 49–51 notes that some care was available at the temple of Asclepius in the Tiber

21 Nutton (1984) 9; Harig (1971) 179.

22 Nutton (1995b) 45; Nutton (1971) 52, 55.

Despite many centres of medical learning a practitioner's training was never evidenced by any officially recognised certification.[22] Nor was medical training compulsory for medical practice.[23] Public reputation, personal recommendation and even interrogation by the prospective patient sufficed.[24] Even where the state chose to involve itself in regulating practice, it focused on 'civic obligations and taxation, not medical care'.[25] A practitioner willing to attest their own medical skill was, from 40 BC, able to benefit from the grant of immunity from taxes and liturgies.[26] Originally, there was no limit to the number of practitioners who could benefit thusly, but a *numerus clausus* between five and ten per city was eventually established by *Antoninus Pius* beyond *Rome* itself.[27] From a quality control perspective, however, the process of attestation, requiring only an oath before lay magistrates rather than perhaps a body of respected medical practitioners, did not inspire confidence.[28] Moves towards enshrining a hierarchy amongst practitioners can be seen in the establishment in 368 AD of a college of civic medical practitioners (*archiatri*)[29] for *Rome* by *Valentinian* and the increasing use of grades to differentiate the crowded medical marketplace.[30] Nevertheless, through suspicion about standards of care and reliance on lower class practitioners, the Roman world did not generally accord medicine a high degree of respect.[31]

23 Nutton (1992) 54–55. The choice between a woman who may have received some measure of training and the common figure of the barmaid-midwife is indicative.

24 *Galen* regarded personal interrogation of a practitioner's knowledge of *Hippocrates* and their record (and willingness) of offering a prognosis as good guides. See Nutton (1990) 245.

25 Nutton (1995b) 45.

26 Below (1953) 22–34

27 D.27.1.6.2; Below (1953) 34. On the fiction that *Rome* was itself the 'patria' of all citizens the immunities were extended to encompass any liabilities a practitioner may have had in their original place of residence. Nutton (1981) 19; D.27.1.6.11.

28 Scarborough (1970) 301; Nutton (1971) 52, 55. Nutton (1995b) 46. Although D.50.9.1 suggests that appointment was based on fulfilling a requirement of *probitas morum* and *peritia artis*, the decision as to whether this was satisfied lay in the hands of the town decurions and would likely have been judged by the relative success or otherwise of their practice rather than by the acceptance of fellow practitioners, Nutton (1971) 54; Below (1953) 40–44; Nutton (1992) 53.

29 Although the term itself was first given to *Nero's* personal physician, Ritter v Rittershain (1875) 28.

30 Nutton stresses the uniquely Roman nature of the college with the normal system of a *numerus clausus* remaining the case outside of the city. Nutton (1981) 19; Nutton (1984) 11.

31 Nutton (1995b) 41, 'In short, the practice of medicine was far from being a high-status occupation.'

## (B) Roman medicine and the law

Turning to the Roman law on medical liability, there were no special rules relating to medical error. The *medicus* was absent from the Twelve Tables, as a direct concern,[32] which is, perhaps, surprising given the specific nature of the other provisions.[33] Aside from the midwife, there was no visible legal distinction between types of practitioner.[34] Rather, their diverse social standing would likely have accounted for any difference in legal treatment. Although both the practitioner and their fees were present as examples in many texts,[35] few dealt directly with the assessment of fault, or what, precisely, was the relevant contractual relationship. What laws there were did not give the impression that unregulated membership of the medical fraternity would, at least, be checked by their rigorous application.[36]

### *(i) The Roman contractual schema*

Any analysis must begin from the peculiar concurrence of Roman medical practice and law that focused the available actions not on the recovery of damages for personal injury, but rather the resulting economic losses resulting from harm suffered by those in your *potestas*. Furthermore, outside contract, a personal action in delict was largely absent given the practice of medicine by the *paterfamilias* within the household could not result in liability;[37] we are left to divine the treatment of the *medicus* within the liability regime. This 'failure of the legal imagination' lends the resulting Roman law its distinct shape.[38]

Outside the family where, in the vast majority of cases, care was private, liability would be, as *Proculus* suggested in D.9.2.7.8, '*vel ex locato vel ex lege aquilia*'. Focusing on contract, precisely whom this would be concluded with depended on the status of both practitioner and patient. Additionally, although '*vel ex locato*' suggests some form of the contract for paid hire, *locatio conductio*, this cannot be assumed to have been the case for all practitioners. Particularly

32 Watson (1988) 65; Köbler (2006) 157, 160; This is not to say that a *medicus* could not be subject to the general provisions in the XII Tables for bodily injury, see Riegger (2007) 40; *Heldrich* gives the crown for the first jurist to consider medical matters to *Alfenus Varus* in D.38.1.26, Heldrich (1940) 141.

33 Ibbetson (2003) 481.

34 Heldrich (1940) 151–152. The disciplines were in fact often practiced together, Ritter v Rittershain (1875) 31.

35 Heldrich (1940) 157; D.13.7.8 for example.

36 Ritter v Rittershain (1875) 32.

37 Watson (1988) 67.

38 Ibid. 78. The failure here, '...was massive, but it is very understandable' given the nature of Roman medicine and social mores.

where they were an *ingenui*, the situation is ambiguous. *Daube* posits that had the contract been 'a recognised type' there would have been more juristic interest in the subject but offers the 'general difficulty of suing a doctor' as a plausible reason why interest may have been lacking.[39] The uncertainty of the contractual analysis stemmed from the exclusion of certain activities, classically *artes liberales*,[40] from *locatio conductio.*[41] Whether medicine was locatable was intimately related to a practitioner's status, their learning and the supposed inestimability of medical practice.[42] Any argument that medicine was beyond the standard services contract must otherwise account for the income that private practitioners could earn.[43] For medical practice by slaves or freedmen the situation was, in theory, straightforward as any contract was between the patient and the relevant master or *paterfamilias*, sidestepping discussions regarding *artes liberales*.[44] For freeborn practitioners, whose relevance increased over time, with only 'meagre and ambiguous' evidence,[45] and the legal sources reflecting medical practice at various stages of development, a clear answer eludes us, but three positions can be identified:

First, that the practice of medicine was not regarded as, or analogous to, an *ars liberalis* and thus there was no difficulty with the use of *locatio conductio* regardless of the status of the practitioner.[46] *Heldrich* relied on a selection of texts, which – although none note it directly – can be read as suggesting that *locatio conductio* was always the appropriate relationship.[47]

39 Daube (1955) 180.

40 Although the term itself is unknown to the Roman legal sources, with *Heldrich* opining that it emerges first in 1700 in a work by *Johannes Adolf Berger*. Furthermore, there was little consensus as to what it meant. See Heldrich (1940) 142–143 and Silber (1940) 161.

41 Kaser (1971) 569, lists *artes liberales*, doctors, architects and surveyors as examples of activities that became regarded as unsuitable for location.

42 Loewenfeld (1887) 420; Heldrich (1940) 144 was critical of the application of *Loewenfeld's* sources to medicine, 145–146.

43 Heldrich (1940) 147. The disadvantage to this monetary incentive was the attraction it provided for charlatans and quacks, Ritter v Rittershain (1875) 32; Scarborough (1970) 299; Below (1953) 61–81; D.9.2.7, noting the recoverability of physician's fees.

44 Heldrich (1940) 153; Below (1953) 56, 109; For freedman-practitioner *locatio conductio operarum*. With slave-practitioners their status as both a thing and a person created a nominative ambiguity as to the correct form of the contract with *locati servi* or *locatio conductio rei* both valid options, Buckland (2007) 504.

45 Daube (1955) 180.

46 Heldrich (1940) 157; Silber (1940) 161.

47 Heldrich (1940) 150 f discussing the granting of an *actio in factum* in D.19.5.1.27, see also Below (1953) 82. This would be superfluous if there was also the *actio mandata directa* available. *Below* goes on (at 88–99) to criticise reliance on this

Secondly, that medicine was always regarded as, or analogous to, an *ars liberalis*. This accounts for *Ulpian's* categorisation of medicine alongside *artes liberales* in other contexts;[48] it applied to learned practitioners of all standings. A minority restricted this to freeborn practitioners.[49] Of that latter, *Loewenfeld* argued that the contractual action in D.9.2.7.8 concerned surgical treatment by a slave and as such could be distinguished as it did not concern 'learned' medicine.[50] Although that view leaves the *medicus* outside *locatio conductio*, a contractual analysis could tenuously be rescued with *mandatum*.[51] Whilst formally gratuitous, the development of the *cognitio extraordinaria* permitted an *honorarium*, preserving the supposed higher status of medicine but accounting for money changing hands for medical services.[52]

Thirdly, that the categorisation of medicine amongst *operae liberales* changed with the social standing of the practitioner and the sophistication of their practice.[53] This view discriminates between *servi*, *liberti*, and the *ingenui*.[54] For

fragment; D.38.1.25.2 suggests that hire is an appropriate relationship between a physician and third parties.

48 D.50.13.1.pr; 1; 2; 3; D.50.9.4.2; Against this view, see Heldrich (1940) 149, stressing the fact that *Ulpian* only ever saw medicine as closey related to the *artes liberales* yet in D.50.13.1.pr grants them the *extraordinara* for their fees, a contradiction which, along with the following passages on midwives and specialists suggests interpolation (supported by *Below*, albeit drawing the contrary conclusion). If the text is true, they read it as simply a focus on the 'new' procedure without suggesting that this had supplanted the existing contractual scheme for regarding the nature of the relevant claim being discussed, Below (1953) 149.

49 Heldrich (1940) 144. Citing Loewenfeld (1887) 365, as the key text but he was critical of the application of *Loewenfeld's* analysis of the '*artes liberales*' to medicine.

50 Loewenfeld (1887) 365, 420. *Heldrich*, noting that in neither the era of *Proculus* nor *Ulpian* was any legal distinction between the two types of practice visible, remained unconvinced, Heldrich (1940) 151; *Below* also rejected this distinction, with further references citing CIL 6,3986 and the 'slave doctor' reading of the text on the basis that the patient is a slave and the action is not being brought against a master or patron, Below (1953) 85, 87; *Watson* supports a reading of D.9.2.7.8 as involving a slave given the contractual allusion, Watson (1988) 75.

51 Below (1953) 82–84 and Watson (1988) 77–78 are rightly critical of this view given the utter absence of any text describing the relationship as such.

52 Kaser (1971) 577–578; Watson (1988) 78; A key difference was that as the contract was nominally gratuitous, the mandatory could not claim withholding of payment as a ground for non-performance, Buckland (2007) 515.

53 *Kaser* noted the relevance for any analysis of *locatio conductio* of the changing social context of work, Kaser (1971) 568. *Loewenfeld* regarded apparently less cerebral practitioners, such as surgeons, as appropriate for *locatio conductio*. Loewenfeld (1887) 420.

54 Heldrich (1940) 142.

*ingenui*, one view is that whilst they might have been able to locate their services in earlier times,[55] by the Byzantine era they had graduated beyond that grubby world and had to rely on *mandatum* and the *cognitio extrodinaria*.[56] *Below* presents an alternative view of the *ingenui*: that in the classical period *locatio conductio* would have been regarded as inappropriate but the introduction of the *archiatri* had, by the time the compilers approached the classical sources, inured them towards the practice of medicine and they were thus open to *locatio conductio*.[57] He stresses differences in the social standing of medical practice in post-classical times to claim that '*vel ex locato vel*' in D.9.7.8 is an interpolation, demonstrating that there was no contractual relationship in classical times.[58] By contrast, he relies on the *cognitio extrodinaria* for *ingenui*-practitioners, without the underlying need for *mandatum*, to account for payment.[59]

The fluidity of medical practice this third view permited is the most attractive of the three models but the final picture is still murky. As to the consequences, if we set aside talk of *mandatum*, the main effect of medicine's supposed status as non-locatable was that there could be no contract between *ingenui*-practitioners and freeborn patients, and, alongside the slow demise of slavery and the *Lex Aquilia's* focus on property damage, those patients were left without any action for injurious treatment.[60]

### *(ii) Fault and scope of recovery*

The success of any action, required the harm be caused intentionally or negligently.[61] Although originally a practitioner acting under *mandatum* would only have been liable for *dolus*, by the classical era the standard of liability had been adjusted to match that of *locatio conductio*,[62] with the promisor in both situations expected to act as a *bonus paterfamilias.* As to the scope of recovery, if the action was in *locatio conductio* the conductor could sue to avoid having to pay

55 Kaser (1971) 569 noted that sophists, doctors and architects were not originally excluded from *locatio.*

56 Heldrich (1940) 150, argued that the categorisation of medicine as a 'free art' was a development of Byzantine law.

57 Below (1953) 98. He rejected entirely the use of *mandatum* in the absence of *locatio conductio* in classical times and relies solely on the *cognitio extrodinaria* to recover an agreed fee, at 108.

58 Below (1953) 87–88. He also found it suspicious that *Proculus* would have been discussing a contractual action in a commentary on the *Lex Aquilia*.

59 Below (1953) 108.

60 Watson (1988) 78–79. The slave's master, as we will see, retained their action under the *Lex Aquilia*.

61 Supported by *Proculus*, D.9.2.7.8; Noted by Kehr (1972) 33.

62 Zimmermann (1996) 425–426.

the fees based on the unskilled treatment, a course unnecessary in *mandatum*. Under either form of *locatio conductio* the entirety of any resulting economic losses could be recovered.[63] If the claim was brought using the *cognitio extraordinaria* or an *actio in factum*, the judge was given the freedom to assess the recoverable losses themselves.

## 2. Nineteenth-century Germany

The sources of civil law in the nineteenth-century Germany were manifold and make clearly stating the law, even post-1871, a tricky task.[64] What is at least clearer is that that much of the relevant law had its roots in the modernised Roman law rather than the Germanic sources, although this is not to say the latter should be ignored.[65] The jurists of this period were forced, by choice, to grapple with the tensions present in the classical Roman law. The relevant civil law treatment of medical practitioners was mostly general in character. To the extent that there was anything specific to medical practitioners, it was in the interpretation or application of those rules in practice. Whilst for practitioners internal debate was focused on defining and regulating medical error, rarely considering the legal bases of the relationship, for most lawyers the focus was categorisation, often based on the social standing of medical practice, with the fault standard following on from that.

### (A) Legislation and academic commentary

The Roman inheritance, so intimately connected as it was with the social status of the medical practitioner and a division between forms of labour, did not translate well into readily applicable rules for a later iteration of healthcare, and the resulting confusion was visible in the *gemeines Recht*, with scholars struggling to identify the proper categorisation of liability for medical error and, accordingly, the content of that liability.[66] As in classical *Rome*, the focus was on payment with only a few commentators considering the ramifications of injurious practice. Greater clarity was found in legislation and we begin with the most influential of these statutes before moving to consider the surrounding

63 Below (1953) 120, noting the great flexibility of the 'bona fide' nature of the contract.

64 As *Mittermaier* drolly lamented: 'For the majority of German legal relations there is no general source of law', Mittermaier (1892) 5.

65 Puchta (1838) 1, 'For private law particularly, Roman law has [...] the greatest import.'; Wieacker (1995) 301 ff; Rückert (2013a) 708, 722 ff.

66 Hegener (1925) 10–11; Zimmermann (1873) 222.

academic commentary.[67] This literature may be broken into two groupings: the general commentaries, often Pandectist but with some relevant work from Germanist scholars in addition, and a much smaller number of more specific works which dealt explicitly, and at relative length, with the legal categorisation of the practitioner-patient relationship. Each will be addressed in turn.

### *(i) Legislation*

Whilst the various regional codifications in the German territories drew on the preceding *ius commune* to an extent, they often represented a marked development on it. The run of their writ relegated the relevance of the *gemeines Recht* to a subsidiary, supplementary body of rules. This was particularly the case where they drew on the developed natural law, an increasingly substantial counterweight to Romanist analysis,[68] which apparently tended to do away with the 'confusion and controversy of obsolete problems'.[69] The nature of the contractual relationship between a medical practitioner and their patient, superimposed as it was onto a hierarchy of forms of labour, was one such problem from Roman law that had, seemingly, become obsolete.[70] These codes largely ignored the complications of the Roman law here in favour of a simple contract for services, which could form the basis of the legal relationship without excluding any form of labour. The *Codex Maximilianus Bavaricus civilis* 1756 (often simply called the *Bayerisches Landrecht*) made no distinction within *Miethecontracte* (although there were some such as smiths and metalworkers who were banned from the contract altogether)[71] but it appeared to bar both lawyers and medical practitioners ('*Arzt oder Medicus*') from contracting their services.[72] In the case of the

67 See generally the excellent historical introduction in Rückert (2013a).

68 This influence was more visible in the Prussian *Allgemeines Landrecht* (*ALR*) of 1794, the *Badisches Landrecht* of 1809 (being in effect a German version of the repealed *Code civil*) and the Austrian *Allgemeines Bürgerliches Gesetzbuch* (*ABGB*) of 1811. The Bavarian *Codex Maximilianus Bavaricus civilis* of 1756 was less naturalistic, albeit as *Wieacker* notes not entirely without natural law influence, and reflected a distinctly greater *ius commune* feel. See Stein (2000) 111–113; Wieacker (1995) 260–269.

69 Wieacker (1995) 260 discussing the *Codex Maximilianus Bavaricus civilis*.

70 A similar survey to what follows can be found in Hirte (1996) 150 f.

71 See *Codex Maximilianus Bavaricus civilis* IV, 6. § 2 notes that '*Ist regulariter Niemand hievon ausgeschlossen, der nicht ein besonderes Verbot wider sich hat.*' Indeed, these particular restrictions, which had originally been aimed at those making noise in the vicinity of more contemplative occupations such as teachers or councillors had lapsed over the course of the nineteenth century. See Danzer (1894) 246, § 2.

72 *Codex Maximilianus Bavaricus civilis* IV, 1 § 12.

former this was restricted to contracts *quotam litis* but, as to the latter, the acknowledgment that it could cover contracts concerning medicine (*'um der Gesundheit'* in the relevant provision) suggests a broader bar than the old Roman rule that a contract agreed in the throes of malady was not enforceable.[73] Reflecting practice in the *gemeines Recht*, examined below, this view was undermined by the fact that medical practitioners were absent from the treatment of mandate (*Vollmacht*) and that, at least in later years, there was scope for using the state tariffs as a guide to remuneration for medical practitioners.[74] *v Kreittmayr's* annotations, as draftsman, suggested that practice in *Bavaria* hewed closed to that of the *gemeines Recht* and recognised only an innominate contract between practitioner and patient.[75]

In due course the Prussian *Allgemeines Landrecht* 1794 (*ALR*) broke wholly with the Roman tradition and explicitly abandoned the distinction without any restrictions;[76] instead drawing a broad distinction between contracts for services and contracts for work.[77] Within the former there was a further division placing craftsmen (*Handwerker*) and artisans (*Künstler*) in a shared category,[78] and subjecting them to a higher degree of liability than the contrasting category shared by manual and day labourers, on the basis of their having a better rationalised, free-standing corpus of recognised practice to which they could be held.[79] The *ALR* eschewed any special provisions designed for those who would previously have been designated as *operae liberales*.[80] This practice was followed in the heavily naturalistic *Badisches Landrecht* and the *ABGB*.[81] Even where

73 C.3 *de professoribus et medicus* (10,52).

74 Referring to IV, 1 § 12 one commentator notes that whilst remuneration was left for the agreement of the parties, it could, in some cases, be fixed by the central authorities, Danzer (1894) 246, § 2

75 Bauridl (1874) 343.

76 Anders/Gehle (2001) 3, noting that any similarity to the old law of *locatio conductio* was, '...only discernible at the margins'. They argued that this reflected a fundamental change in outlook following increases in industrialisation which helped narrow the gap between 'higher' and 'lower' occupations.

77 Fischer (1887) §§ 76–77, 431 ff.

78 *ALR* I II § 920, *'Was vorstehend von gemeinen Handarbeitern verordnet ist, findet in der Regel auch alsdann statt, wenn Werkmeister oder Künstler zur Verrichtung einer gewissen Arbeit gedungen werden.'*

79 *ALR* I II § 921 *'Doch sind diese die Arbeit nach den Regeln ihrer Kunst zu verrichten, und dabey auch für ein geringes Versehen zu haften schuldig.'* Förster/Eccius (1887) § 138, 268.

80 Förster/s (1887) § 138, 269.

81 *ABGB* § 1151 set out the basic rule: *'Wenn jemand sich zur Dienstleistung oder Verfertigung eines Werkes gegen einen gewissen Lohn im Gelde verpflichtet, so entsteht ein Lohnvertrag.'* This was elaborated in § 1163, *'Die hier aufgestellten Vorschriften gelten auch von Rechtsfreunden, Aerzten und Wundärzten, Factoren, Provisoren,*

codification was largely Pandectist in structure, as was the case of the *Sächsisches Bürgerliches Gesetzbuch* (*SBGB*, 1863),[82] the old Roman distinctions were abandoned for a *Dienstvertrag* capable of enclosing all forms of labour.[83] The promise of reward for performance was sufficient to incorporate all occupations under one contract.[84]

In the continued absence of a general German civil code there were a raft of attempted codifications late in the nineteenth century, of which the *SBGB* was the only one to have survived to term. Two of these abortive pieces of legislation are worth noting: the draft civil code for *Bayern*, which appeared between 1861 and 1864, and the so-called *Dresdner Entwurf* of 1866, which was an attempt to codify the law of obligations within the crumbling German Confederation, and would go on, in due course, to form the basis for the corresponding parts of the *BGB*.[85] In each case a unitary model of *Dienstvertrag* was adopted, if never enacted.[86]

### (ii) *Pandectist scholarship*

Turning to contemporary academic commentary on the *gemeines Recht,* we are faced with a different view of the law, one predominantly rooted in, and constrained by, the classical Roman law. As to the presence of medical error as a topic in these texts, it is notably general, often appearing as an adjunct to discussion of the broader, abstract legal categories. This allowed questions of fault in the context of medical error to be subordinated to broader arguments within contract law.

*Künstlern, Lieferanten und anderen Personen*, welche sich für ihre Bemühungen einen Gehalt, eine Bestallung, oder sonst eine Belohnung ausdrücklich oder stillschweigend ausbedungen haben, insofern hierüber keine besondern Vorschriften bestehen.' (emphasis added).

82 Wieacker (1995) 367, although as *Wieacker* notes it was not quite as Pandectist as some legal historians have intimated.

83 See §§ 1229 ff *SGB* pp § 1230: '*Die Dienste können in körperlicher Kraftanwendung oder in Leistungen bestehen, welche eine besondere Sachkenntniß, eine Kunstfertigkeit oder wissenschaftliche Bildung erfordern*'; Wengler / Brachmann (1878) 502 § 1230 n 5.

84 Siebenhaar (1872) 644 f discussing § 1230 *SBGB*; Siebenhaar (1869) 286, discussing the *Motive* for the code.

85 Wieacker (1995) 366–367.

86 Draft Bayern civil code Art 484; *Dresdner Entwurf* Art 615; Anders / (2001) 3–4.

### (a) Distinguishing forms of labour

Pandectist scholarship – although it generally recognised a basic structure of both *locatio conductio operarum* (often called *Dienstmiethe*) and *locatio conductio operis* (often called *Werkmiethe*)[87] – adhered to a Roman division within the former between *operae liberales*,[88] which could not be the object of contracts for hire ('*Miethvertrages*'),[89] and lower forms of labour (*operae illiberales, locari solitae, aber honestae)*, which could, until nearly the end of the century.[90] Some emphasised the inestimability of such work given its communitarian nature;[91] or that it required scientific knowledge, true craftsmanship or a particular mental facility;[92] or all of the above.[93] The resonance between these characteristics and the occupational aspirations of orthodox practitioners was clear, and the persistence of the distinction, particularly as it applied to medical practitioners, was supported by the tendency to view the Roman rules as a single, rational body of text rather than, as suggested above, likely representing a muddled process of medical-historical and legal-historical development centred on the status of the practitioner.[94] Clarifying a contractual basis was particularly problematic given the stickiness of this division between the types of occupation, with medicine characterised as inestimable. Two contractual bases thus emerged: a minority who focused on mandate and, those who, willing to abandon Roman distinctions altogether, embraced some version of *Dienstmiethe*. For the minority, the close connection between mandate (*Mandat*) and the *operae liberales* could be

87 Tillmanns (2007) 14; Rudorff (1853) § 365, 524; For completeness *locatio conductio rei* was also often addressed, going by the modernised name '*Sachmiethe*', Windscheid (1870) § 399, 454–455. See generally Hirte (1996) 149–150 for the disputed nature of these terms in nineteenth-century Germany.

88 Puchta (1855) § 365, 232–233, noting that any occupation, '…which would be brought into disrepute if they were treated as being the subject of a market price, cannot be the subject of a *locatio conductio*'. *Hirte* notes this definition alongside the requirement of a scientific education, Hirte (1996) 150. See also Windscheid (1870) § 404, 473, occupations, '…which alone or predominantly require unrestricted intellectual activity'. At a later point, he noted that the Romans had not applied *Dienstmiethe* to medical practitioners.

89 Seuffert (1852) § 332, 210–11.

90 Anders/(2001) 3, citing *RG 4.11.1886* RGZ 18, 173; See, for example, Glück (1816) § 1048, 315; Unterholzner (1840) § 504, 344; Sintenis (1847) § 113, 561 n 8; Seuffert (1852) § 332 210–11; Dahn (1878) 156; Brinz (1882) § 332, 762.

91 Glück (1816) § 1048, 315; Dernburg (1886) § 115, 303. As *Dernburg* there poetically put it '…a medical practitioner stands in the service of humanity'.

92 Seuffert (1852) § 332 211.

93 Bauridl (1874) 325.

94 An example of this may be found in *Zimmermann's* ready treatment of the *actio utilis* given to a freeman in D.9.2.13.pr. as analogous to the action for injury to a slave, Zimmermann (1873) 225.

maintained using the *cognitio extraordinaria* or *actio praescriptis verbis.*[95] *Dernburg* was alone in claiming that the relationship remained, in 1886, a full *Mandat.*[96] In his schema, as in some others,[97] the service at the heart of that contract had to occur at the behest of the employer. Thus, higher callings, unsusceptible as they were to such control, remained excluded.[98]

### (b) The emerging consensus

The solution for some was to sculpt an innominate '*Arztvertrag*'.[99] Others dealt with medical practitioners simply as an exception alongside *Dienstmiethe* without tackling anything other than payment.[100] But some, such as *Seuffert* and *Windscheid*, were more honest in recognising that the situation was *sui generis.*[101] *Unterholzner* provided an early example, noting that although one could not speak of location or conduction in these situations there was, nevertheless, a 'binding reciprocal obligation'.[102] Prefiguring *Windscheid*, *Sintenis* also adopted a *sui generis* contract for service.[103] *Windscheid's* original position in 1866, maintained until 1873, revolved around rights to termination.[104] His footnoted grumbling – that to regard the relationship as *Mandat* was in ignorance of modern economic and social mores – demonstrated the extent to which modern function risked subordination to ancient form; as does the fact that it was a

95 Brinz (1882) § 334, 772 n 10, noting the *cognitio* as a development of mandate. On the *actio praescriptis verbis*, see D.19.5.22; Glück (1816) 315 n 41; Puchta (1838) § 310, 339 n(p); maintained later in Rudorff (1853) § 315, 466 and Schirmer (1877); Unterholzner (1840) § 504, 344; Seuffert (1852) § 332,210–11, § 334, 214; Arndts (1855) § 314, 461; v Vangerow (1869) § 650, 467 who simply quotes verbatim D.50.13.1 and 19.5.1.22; Vering (1875) § 204, 500–501

96 Dernburg (1886) § 115, 303.

97 Brinz (1882) § 332, 762.

98 Dernburg (1886) § 112, 295 citing *Brinz*, above.

99 Hegener (1925) 11. As he put it, it was a, '...*sui generis* contract, which was regarded partly as an analogy to mandate, partly according to the rules of innominate contracts'.

100 Glück (1816) § 1048, 315; Unterholzner (1840) § 521, 373; Seuffert (1852) § 334, 215; Vering (1875) § 204, 500; v Vangerow (1869) § 650, 467.

101 Seuffert (1852) § 334, 214; Windscheid (1866) § 404 130; See also the earlier example in Unterholzner (1840) § 514, 358; See also v Vangerow (1875).

102 Unterholzner (1840) § 521, 372.

103 Sintenis (1847) § 119, 685, 691–2; Rudorff (1853) § 315, 466. An alternative phrasing was given by *Sintenis* as '...customary and conventional', Sintenis, (1886) § 120, 684. Schäffer (1850) 1 and Pfeiffer (1844) 156 are replete with summaries of these cases before the courts, albeit many deal with alimony and lodgers or journeymen's accommodation; Unterholzner (1840) § 521, 375; Arndts (1865) § 314, 507, repeated in subsequent editions.

104 Windscheid (1866) § 404, 131 n 3.

footnote to his preferred one:[105] Where there was no right to freely terminate, *Windscheid* stressed that the resulting contract was, simply, the same as it would be were the contract a recognised contract for services.[106] Whilst ostensibly accepting the division between forms of labour, he simultaneously belittled it, and emphasised that the idea of earning money from one's mental acuity was no longer a stain on one's honour.[107] By the fourth edition in 1875, and onwards, his focus was entirely on this *Dienstmiethe*-analogous innominate contract.[108]

Other contemporaries, disdainful of ersatz solutions, claimed the contract was *Dienstmiethe* proper; abandoning any restriction on suitable occupations. The service contract had received little by way of extended academic analysis beyond Pandectist texts, but by the time it did, enthusiasm for the distinction was clearly flagging. In 1874 *Dankwardt* had advanced beyond *Windscheid* in stating that the requirement of a particular form of labour was explicitly, '…of no more practical worth'.[109] In 1886, the effect of *Windscheid's* position could be seen before the *Reichsgericht*. There, the court noted that the development of other forms of service contracts rendered the terminological distinction between forms of labour irrelevant.[110] Writing in 1888, *Wendt* had put it simply: 'The modern world considers medical practitioners, lawyers, teachers, surveyors etc as *operae locari solitae*; they practice their service no longer *beneficii loco* but rather through synallagmatic contracts…'.[111] Widespread payment tariffs certainly made a mockery of stubborn insistence that such work was inestimable.[112] By contrast, although medicine's status as a free trade after 1869 might have proven influential, it received little attention.[113] Looking back on this period *Hirte* is

105 Windscheid (1866) § 404, 131 n 3.

106 Ibid., § 404, 131. Windscheid preferred to retain the overarching term *Miethvertrag* and was dealing with situations which would be, but for the absence of payment in money or being the wrong sort of *operae*, regarded either as suitable for *Sachmiethe* or *Dienstmiethe*.

107 Windscheid (1866) § 404, 131 n 3.

108 Windscheid (1879) § 404, 521 n 3. His about face influenced by Dankwardt (1874) 308.

109 Dankwardt (1874) 311. See also, Dankwardt (1875) § 317, 239, 'It is no longer necessary that the service is *operae locari solitae*.' See also Rückert (2013a) 724–725.

110 *RG 04.11.1886* RGZ 18,175. The case concerned a Prussian state railway official suing his employer for injury sustained during his employment.

111 Wendt (1888) § 260, 628; See also Förster/Eccius (1892) § 141, 310, describing the distinction as 'antiquated'.

112 As one example, see Fischer (1887) discussing the *Edikt* of *21.06.1815* which regulated medical costs in *Prussia*.

113 Although *Zimmermann* did allude to its importance, Zimmermann (1873) 223; See also Unterholzner (1840) § 521, 375 n(r), 'Our payment tariffs for medical practitioners and lawyers are established.'

correct to describe support for *Dienstmiethe* as probably dominant in the literature, but this was only the case during the final decades of the century.[114] Thus, the dominant approach to the practitioner-patient contract became a modernised form of *locatio conductio*, described by some as *Dienstmiethe*, an implied contract by others;[115] by some to be an ersatz *Miethvertrag*,[116] a 'contract for service...which has the shape of a hire contract',[117] or simply, finally, to have 'no particular designation'.[118] But, as we will see below, this choice had an important corollary effect on the formal standard of fault for questions of medical error.

### *(iii) Germanist scholarship*

Late Pandectist willingness to erode traditional Roman categories may have been influenced in part by the forward-looking position taken in contemporary Germanist scholarship.[119] These scholars sought to preserve the traces of the older customary rules that had developed concurrently with the received Roman rules, but often as a subsidiary or adjunct to them.[120] There were German roots for analogous contracts here in the old feudal claim to *Frohnen* (socage),[121] and the *Gesindevertrag*, a consensual contract covering servants and household help.[122] The latter, in particular, formed a natural home for the development of a general contract for services as the medieval hangover of binding oneself to a family was jettisoned.[123]

Romanised accretions ignored, there was no normative basis for bifurcating contracts based on a worker's status. To the extent that any distinction remained,

114 Hirte (1996) 151.

115 Arndts (1855) §314, 461 (cribbing heavily from Puchta) on the basis of D.19.5.22; D.4.1.

116 Windscheid (1866) §404 131; Dankwardt (1874) 310.

117 Brinz (1882) §334, 772 n 10.

118 Seuffert (1852) §334, 214.

119 *Wieacker* characterises the Germanists being of a 'practical bent' when it came to their analysis, at least in the first half of the century, Wieacker (1995) 319 f.

120 Mittermaier (1843) §292, 53 noting that the *gemeines Recht* had clung closely to the Roman law and anything that native law could add was as exceptions to, or derivations from, it. Similar sentiments could be found in the work of arch-Germanist *Georg Beseler*, see Beseler (1853) 342.

121 Danz (1799) 188; Mittermaier (1824) §246, 226; Eichhorn (1845) §248, 617 f.

122 Stobbe (1885) §187 pp 270.

123 Compare Mittermaier (1824) §175, 174 with later editions where the contract is regarded as being decided in line with contracts concerning services. See Mittermaier (1843) §294, 59 f; For a complete picture of the historical development of the *Dienstvertrag* see v Gierke (1917) §199, 590 f.

by the middle of the century, it was often visible in a frequently two-fold division into separate, but, crucially, largely identical, contracts. These were given various names, with the clearest designation to be found in *Bluntschli's* classification: the '*Lohndienstvertrag*', dealing broadly with manual labour and, reserved for liberal occupations, the '*Freidienstvertrag*'.[124] The close, contemporary relationship of this literature to its Pandectist counterpart supports the plausibility of its influence, if oblique, on Pandectist developments.[125]

### (B) *Zimmermann* and *Hefke*'s exchange

Although there was little specific legal literature on the subject, what there was is revealing for the divisive arguments it presents. The two central pieces of scholarship are both articles rather than commentaries, albeit one of them is extensive. The first, and the shorter, was published in the *Archiv für Civilistische Praxis*, then, as now, the leading journal for civil law scholarship, in 1873 by *Zimmermann* a judge in *Gießen*.[126] Whilst he acknowledged that the practitioner-patient relationship was an old problem, the impetus behind his choice to examine the subject was the recent *Gewerbeordnung* 1869 and the formal transition of medicine to a trade; a reminder of the importance of the medical narrative examined in chapter one for the concomitant legal analysis.[127] As an indication of the relative paucity of specific treatments of the subject by legal rather than medico-legal sources, *Zimmermann* notes that he was unable to source the older literature on the subject referring to two works from 1794 and 1814 respectively.[128] These proved unavailable to *Hefke* as well.[129]

The second article was by *Hefke*, a judge in *Oldenburg*, in the *Archiv für praktische Rechtswissenschaft*.[130] Whilst published in 1886, the article, and the accompanying appendix considering the liability of the *mensor* in Roman law, were in fact written in 1879.[131] As it seems largely to have been inspired by *Zimmermann's* piece they provide the best view into the on-going arguments

124 Bluntschli (1854) § 126, 56–60. Medical practitioners are listed as falling within the latter; Stobbe (1893) 446. See the extensive pull-out 'map' of contract provided there; Gerber (1895) § 210, 357, who noted, 'The law of service contracts is overwhelmingly of a modern form: The medieval German rules, no less than the Roman ones, are obsolete.'

125 Matthiaß (1910) § 122, 323, reflecting Bluntschli (1854) 56–57.

126 Zimmermann (1873) 222.

127 Ibid. 223.

128 Ibid. 223, n 1.

129 Hefke (1886a) 55.

130 Ibid. 1–69, 113–152.

131 Hefke (1886b) 168.

about the practitioner-patient relationship. Indeed, *Hefke* targeted *Zimmermann* directly as the latter, rather than the Pandectists who shared his views, offered something more than a mere assertion of his position.[132] The structure in each is, broadly speaking, the reverse of that adopted in this study. Each author appeared to work backwards from what they regarded as the proper standard of liability towards the attendant categorisation that justified that position. Following the appearance of each they are cited in the respective next subsequent editions of *Windscheid* as opposing views on the point and, thus, may be regarded as the leading specialist literature on the subject in the late nineteenth century.

The key difference between the two authors was their approach to the detailed treatment of the various classes of medical practitioner that abounded in *Rome* as set out above. Whilst they both distinguished between species of practitioner, their respective interpretation of those relationships and their chosen analogy to the world of Imperial Germany took each in a very different direction. As we have seen, failure to make such distinctions, or focusing on a narrow conception of the medical practitioner as presented in the Digest and other sources, was apt to provide a misleading basis for the contemporary law and the same pattern is repeated here with a fresh twist. As such, there is clear water between the two authors and it is only *Hefke's* article that need seriously detain us in this chapter, *Zimmermann's* conclusion will be considered in the following chapter. *Hefke* rejected *Zimmermann's* approach and the similar approaches to be found in some of the Pandectist scholarship. His basis for this, to put it briefly, was that they all eschewed the use of contract law altogether.[133]

### *(i) Zimmermann's rejection of Roman orthodoxy*

For *Zimmermann*, despite conceding that Ulpian – in D.9.2.7.8 – suggested that Roman law adopted a contractual relationship grounded in *locatio conductio* for some class of practitioners, the medical market place was mixed and D.19.5.26.1, concerning the use of the *actio praescriptis verbis* rather than a *locatio conductio*, suggested that that contractual approach was not universal.[134] Emphasising the non-contractual approach to claiming fees that Ulpian adopted for more homogeneously learned occupations such as teachers, when *Zimmermann* considered the social standing of the contemporary orthodox medical practi-

132 Hefke (1886a) 3.

133 He lists *Sintenis, Wetzell, Puchta, Vering, Hänel and Mommsen* as being conspirators in rejecting the relevance of the contractual analysis he presented, Hefke (1886a) 3.

134 Zimmermann (1873) 223–224.

tioner it was sufficient to prompt a move away from Ulpian's view of medical practitioners.[135]

The internal organisational process that German orthodox practice was undergoing, underpinned by the scientific, university-based nature of medical education in the Germany of the era led him to conclude that contract was an inappropriate model for medical services. Although he conceded that medical fees were regulated by published tariffs this was not suggestive of the full civil law contract that *locatio conductio* would imply, rather merely a legal response along the lines of *actio in factum praescriptis verbis*;[136] the common rhetoric of payment taking the form of a *Honorar* rather than a *Lohn* was deployed. He went on to categorise the practitioner-patient relationship as one based on trust,[137] but avoided the pitfall of suggesting that mandate was the correct analogy by noting that a practitioner was not carrying out the *patient's* business by treating them and indeed could not just arbitrarily treat a patient.[138] Finally, emphasising the version of the Hippocratic oath then in use at German universities – which talked down any contractual claim for payment – and the fact that civil servants did not stand in a contractual relationship with the citizenry,[139] he concluded that the relationship was not suitable for reduction to contract. Practitioners had, in effect, educated themselves out of contractual bondage and fundamentally practiced their art, '…first, out of humanity', clearly lifting them above common tradesmen.[140] His preferred delictual analogy will be explored in the following chapter.

### *(ii) Hefke's defence of contract*

*Hefke* was scathing of *Zimmermann*'s position and those who shared it. The absence of much contemporary evidence from legal life to support *Zimmermann's* claim appeared telling, to *Hefke*, as the exercise in academic interpretation that it was. This is not to say that *Hefke* had much stronger evidence on his side. Again, as with the general commentaries, the approach was skewed by any view taken of the sociological position of medical practice in nineteenth-century life. As far as *Hefke* was concerned, the trappings of orthodox practice in the shape of the oath were of little relevance to the private law categorisation of the

135 Zimmermann (1873) 225.
136 Ibid. 226.
137 Ibid. 226.
138 Ibid. 226.
139 Ibid. 230.
140 Ibid. 228.

relationship.[141] The same was said of such rhetorical frivolities as reliance on the 'humanity', or otherwise, of medical practice. Seemingly without requiring citation of wider sources, the old categorisation of occupations as *illiberales* and *liberales* was thought to have '...not the least worth anymore'.[142] The crux of *Hefke's* position, then, was recognition that the contemporary law ought not to be bound by the strictures of the Roman model, but rather that only the parts of the Roman law that caused the most limited complications should be adopted.[143] For *Hefke*, this involved a rejection of both the idea of an innominate contract reliant on the *actio praescriptis verbis* or the *extraordinaria cognitio*, or the use of *Mandat*.

The former, despite its supporters, explored above, was, in *Hefke's* view, fundamentally a subsidiary action intended to fill gaps in the *Roman* legal system. It was never intended to play a central role, as the growth of *stipulatio* evidenced, and ought only to be applied in contemporary German life where there was no known contract, or analogy to such a contract.[144] He stressed that there was no indication in Justinian's *Corpus* that an *actio praescriptis verbis* was ever deployed to allow a claim for compensation on the basis of poor performance by a medical practitioner.[145] Finally, if the Romans had done so, the patient would have been in the unenviable position of – in the absence of a claim for *damnum inuria datum* – lacking any sort of action where they had not yet handed over payment, and indeed the practitioner could, it seemed, declaim any liability by refusing the payment![146] The latter idea, using *Mandat*, was given even shorter shrift; post-classical attempts to create a non-gratuitous form of *Mandat* only served to remove the key distinction between it and *Dienstmiethe*. *Hefke* argued that one had to avoid the nomenclature of a given Roman tool or accept its basic principles as authoritative.[147] Tellingly, and predictably, having denied any relevancy to the old distinction between forms of labour, *Mandat* was ultimately irrelevant as it was simply not the case that medical practitioners in Imperial Germany intended their work to be gratuitous. Indeed, he claimed, according to both the leading scholarship, and practice, the contract between practitioner and patient was non-gratuitous, thus ruling out the use of *Mandat*.[148]

141 Hefke (1886a) 3.
142 Ibid. 4, 66, n 81.
143 Ibid. 29–30.
144 Ibid. 11–17.
145 Ibid. 17.
146 Ibid. 24–25.
147 Ibid. 41.
148 Ibid. 43–44. *Hefke* cites *Windscheid* § 404 as single-handedly comprising the leading doctrine.

*Hefke* placed the central weight of his argument on *Dienstmiethe* and modern ideas of hiring services, but hedged his position by noting that the practitioner-patient relationship was properly to be classified as *Dienstmiethe* or at least as a contract which was analogous to it and whose fundamentals ought to be drawn from that named contract.[149] He acknowledged the mixed medical marketplace in *Rome*, which had originally allowed some, but not all, medical practitioners to locate their services, arguing that it was to this former class, represented by a *libertini* practitioner (in contrast to *ingenui*, freeborn practitioners who were barred from locating their services), that Ulpian was referring in D.9.2.7.8.[150] *Hefke* contended that the *extraordinaria cognitio* would then have been the only tool used to provide a basis for compensation of loss caused through poor practice for the class of practitioners whose work could not be located.[151] In time, however, as the boundaries between classes of persons weakened, the *extraordinaria* came to be used by *libertini* instead of the *actio locati*, with patients eventually being allowed to choose between the *actio conducti* and the *extraordinaria* where the practitioner was a freedman.[152] As such, he sought to reconcile *Ulpian's* apparent divergences in D.9.2.7.8 and D.50.13.1, and stressed that the increasing absurdities of distinguishing between the legal remedy available on the basis of the person of the practitioner left that distinction ripe to be discarded. Indeed, he claimed, the growth of the *extraordinaria cognitio* was the visible in the absence of *Miethe* and any distinction between *ingenui* and *libertini* practitioners in the post-classical sources.[153]

The banal quintessence of the Roman law for *Hefke* was simply that where a practitioner's services were *operae locari solet* it was possible to apply *locatio conductio.*[154] From that basis it was a short step to identify *Dienstmiethe* as the correct contemporary legal analysis for Imperial Germany provided one could, as *Hefke* did, disregard any distinctions between forms of labour.[155] The contemporary meaning of *operae locari solet* had become those services, which were given economic value. On that basis there were no services, least of all medical practice given the local fee tables, which could be regarded as *non solitae* and thus the concept lost all coherence and relevance.[156]

149 Hefke (1886a) 44.
150 Ibid. 66–68.
151 Ibid. 118–9.
152 Ibid. 123.
153 Ibid. 126–128. According to *Hefke* this explains the absence of D.9.2.7.8's '*vel ex locato*' from the Institutes 4.3.7.
154 Ibid. 131.
155 Ibid. 135.
156 Ibid. 131–132.

### *(iii) Court practice*

It is characteristic of each article that the focus of argument was on the modern interpretation given to the Roman law sources, and their contemporary reading by many of the Pandectist works discussed above. However, *Zimmermann* did explicitly draw on a small number of cases before the *Hofgericht* in *Gießen* decided between 1853 and 1871, whilst *Hefke*, without citing them, or indeed discussing them even in outline, did claim, in an endnote, that the article and its explanatory appendix owed their existence to several cases that he had dealt with or come across in practice.[157] and his work contained citations to cases reported in *Seuffert's Archiv.* At any rate, the use of these cases by *Zimmermann* had more to do with the standard of care and the appropriate level of visitation than the categorisation of the relationship. Given the unreported nature of many lower court decisions, and the general focus of much of the literature on the Roman sources rather than practical daily legal life, it is no surprise to see cases reflected, if only anecdotally, in the scholarly writings of a judge. The fact that *Hefke* could cite relevant cases from the *Seuffert's Archiv* suggested that while the level of cases may be low, there was certainly enough to bolster a reading of the bare Roman sources.

Ultimately neither article offered a definitive answer as to the categorisation of the medical relationship in practice, each was polemic. But they do reinforce the perception drawn from the generalist literature canvassed above that there were a range of options available, that the discussion was fierce and on-going throughout the late nineteenth century, and that the outcome depended on one's reading of the Roman sources and the resulting analogies, if any, that could be drawn to one's view of contemporary medical practice. In sum, the contractual analysis, may have been more of a practical problem where the practitioner wanted to enforce payment rather than providing the patient with an action but it played a key role in determining the standard of care expected from a practitioner.

## 3. Contractual standards of fault

We now consider how the various approaches to categorising the practitioner-patient relationship as some species of contractual relationship impacted on the standard of fault that would be applied to it. Except for the minority who supported mandate, the emerging Pandectist consensus supported a simple fault standard as the vestiges of gross fault were discarded in theory and in practice. Furthermore, a clear sense that unpacking this abstract standard in practice

157 Hefke (1886b) 168.

required reliance on expert medical evidence and the internal occupational logic of the *Kunstfehler* emerged in the relevant civil law during this period. We first consider mandate, before turning to the more overt service contract models.

### (A) Mandate

By far the minority position amongst the possible iterations of the practitioner-patient contractual relationship, the historical, but understandable, confusion over the standard of liability in Roman law persisted into Pandectist writing. In pre-classical Roman law the mandatary (*mandatarius*) would have been liable originally only for *dolus*.[158] But as the gratuitous nature of the engagement broke down, they may have come to be liable for *culpa lata* or even *culpa levis* as well,[159] perhaps even as early as the classical period.[160] Amongst Pandectist authors then, it is too much to hope for that a clear picture would emerge. Some supported a model of *Mandat* that could encompass medical practitioners and endorsed the view that the mandatary would be liable for *dolus* and *culpa*,[161] others, that they would be liable instead to compensate the mandator for every error ('*Verschuldung*') in the course of performing his mandate.[162] As to the former, as *Zimmermann* noted in the late nineteenth century, however, the fact that *culpa* was susceptible to multiple meanings in Roman law did not necessarily mean that this was restricted to meaning *culpa lata*. As to the latter, *Dernburg's* adoption of this liberal position on the standard of liability, not an uncommon stance for the period,[163] demonstrated that the practical difference between his restrictive approach to *Dientmiethe* and the more catholic view of the value of labour taken by the majority of scholars was perhaps not as large as might, at first blush, appear; at least when it came to the question of the standard of care. The party providing the services under such a contract would have, likewise, been liable to the same degree.[164] His justification was that the old Roman view – rooted in the approach to depositees – that those such as

158 D.17.1.29.pr.

159 D.17.1.8.10; D.50.17.23; D.17.1.22.11; Thomas (1976) 307; Zimmermann (1996) 429.

160 Zimmermann (1996) 428. *Zimmermann* notes that in the modern gratuitous form of the contract available in the *BGB*, liability for *culpa* could still be established through the fiction of an implied promise to exercise skill and care, 429.

161 Brinz (1882) § 334, 778.

162 Dernburg (1886) § 116, 304. '*Verschuldung*' here encompassed *dolus, culpa lata* and *culpa levis*, § 37, 98.

163 Glück (1814) 261, 303; Sintenis (1847) 574; Mommsen (1855) 364–365; Windscheid (1887) § 410, 570.

164 Dernburg (1886) § 111, 292; § 112, 295.

mandataries who took on an obligation solely in interests of another party had their liability restricted accordingly, had been abandoned.[165] Hence the mandatary could be indeed liable for every error even though he went, formally speaking, unremunerated.[166]

In any case, the practical relevance of *Mandat* appears limited as there is only one reported case suggesting that, rather than a *Dienstmiethe*, a contract analogous to mandate was suitable for a medical practitioner and patient.[167] Furthermore the preponderance of scholarly opinion suggests that it was a minority position.

### (B) *Dienstmiethe* and analogous contracts

As we have seen, the leading view amongst Pandectist authors in the late nineteenth century was that the contract was either a *Dienstmiethe* or an innominate analogous contract sharing many, if not all, of the features of a *Dienstmiethe*. A shared feature of these variants within the *Dienstmiethe* model was that liability was, as it was even for those who denied its applicability to medical practitioners for whatever reason,[168] based on simple negligence.[169] The obligation that would arise under the contract, at least when it was applied to medical practitioners, was to treat the patient not to cure them.[170] In contrast to the more restrictive model outlined below, *Hefke* described the scope of the duty under this model as being liability for '*omnis culpa*'.[171] Given the skilled nature of medical practice, the most relevant type of fault took the form of liability for failure to meet the standard required of a skilled practitioner: *imperitia culpae adnumeratur.*[172] Such a standard arose as an implication of

165 Dernburg (1886) § 37, 100; Mommsen (1855) 392 f.

166 Dernburg (1886) § 37, 100.

167 Decision of the *Hofgericht Gießen 11.04.1871*. Discussed but not reported in full by *Zimmermann* in Zimmermann (1873) 234. The case concerned the right of a University Professor practicing as a *Hausarzt* who had been engaged for the year for 20 fl to end the contract and claim for the tariff fees due for his subsequent treatments.

168 Glück (1816) § 1054, 411; Brinz (1882) § 332, 763; Dernburg (1886) § 111, 290.

169 Unterholzner (1840) § 521, 376. *Unterholzner* suggested that the practitioner would be liable under the ersatz-*locatio conductio* for minor fault.

170 Sintenis (1861) § 119 679 n 2; Windscheid (1875) § 404, 516 n 8; Hefke (1886a) 36, '...merely for careful medical treatment'.

171 Hefke (1886a) 139.

172 D.50.17.132; Zimmermann (1996) 386. See also *OAG Lübeck 25.11.1865*, Seuffert's Archiv 20, 343 confirming the view that *imperitia* was regarded as a form of *culpa*. In that case, discussed in the text following, *culpa levis*.

taking on the treatment of the patient,[173] and was based on what it was, objectively, that the patient could expect from them.[174]

### (i) *Academic and judicial opinion*

The use of *imperitia* when it came to the formerly non-locatable forms of labour can be found explicitly from the first edition of *Windscheid's Lehrbuch* onwards, with later authors also adopting it.[175] Having relied on D.19.2.9.5 to supply the relevant standard for *Dienstmiethe* proper,[176] he described the standard as being that degree of skill and expertise, '...which one is expected to acquire in the medical arts through customary effort and diligence'.[177] The *Oberappellationsgericht (OAG) Lübeck*, in a decision that came too late for inclusion in that edition of *Windscheid* but made its way into later editions,[178] suggested the application of a flexible objective standard drawn from the practice of the respective skill or trade when it came to assessing fault.[179] There, a blacksmith, accused of not knowing the effective measures to take while shoeing wild horses, was held not to have breached his contract by reason of *imperitia* as it had not been shown that he had failed to do that, '...which in the same case would have been done by the most careful blacksmith in *Frankfurt*', as the court stressed, '...the *peritia* of an *artifex* is not to be regarded as an absolute standard'.[180] Returning to medical practitioners *Hefke* described the standard in his own words as requiring, '...*summam diligentiam* and such expertise and care, which one presumes from a medical practitioner', but noted his preference for *Windscheid's* formulation.[181] Fault thus depended neither on the individual characteristics of the practitioner nor, without more, simply on the result their services had affected.[182] The realisation that *Dienstmiethe* could encompass all forms of remunerated labour had removed any concerns about concurrently applying the normal rules regarding contractual diligence.[183]

173 Hefke (1886a) 148 n 145; 151–152.
174 Windscheid (1875) § 404, 515.
175 Dankwardt (1875) § 31, 248; Wendt (1888) § 260, 628.
176 Windscheid (1866) § 401, 120 n 3.
177 Ibid. § 404, 132 n 4.
178 Windscheid (1873) § 404, 475 n 4.
179 *OAG Lübeck 25.11.1865* Seuffert's Archiv 20, 343.
180 *OAG Lübeck 25.11.1865* Seuffert's Archiv 20, 343.
181 Hefke (1886a) 139, 150. Others phrased it in a similar fashion: see Sintenis (1861) § 119 679 n 2, '...it must be judged only from his standpoint and that of the respective field to which he belongs'.
182 Sintenis (1861) § 119 679 n 2.
183 Dankwardt (1875) § 31, 248; Wendt (1888) § 260, 628.

*Windscheid's* specific link to the state of the medical art suggested a standard that was flexible as medicine developed. *Hefke*, likewise, rejected *Zimmermann's* claim that the absence of a fixed body of medical rules made the assessment of whether the practitioner had been at fault both overly difficult and indeed risked stagnating medical progress.[184] *Hefke* also dismissed any relevance for the practitioners' oath. It had not been relevant as a rhetorical device to allow medical practitioners to raise themselves out of the grubby world of remunerated services, nor was it relevant to the standard of liability expected; in any case, such oaths were not incompatible with a contractual liability for '*omnis culpa*'.[185]

As to how one was to assess whether a defendant had failed to meet the required standard, whilst *Windscheid* was silent, *Hefke* was admirably clear. The question, '…is one that lies outside jurisprudence and therefore in individual cases depends on the answer of the experts'.[186] That said, it was one that would, in any case, require, as *Windscheid* had suggested, consideration of the, '…current status of medical scholarship'.[187] Yet there were cases in which having medical opinion on your side did not always win the day, albeit not on the question of fault. In a decision from the *OAG Lübeck* in 1856, the court was not convinced that the majority of medical opinion – so the defendant practitioner claimed – being against the idea that secondary syphilis could cause infection in others, barred a finding of causation between the defendant practitioner entrusting a wet nurse with an infected child and the subsequent infection of the child and her family. That the events followed in such close succession was sufficient.[188]

The *Dienstmiethe* analysis of the practitioner-patient relationship, and with it the normalised standard of liability *Windscheid* and *Hefke* presumed, had received support in a decision of the *OAG Oldenburg*, reported in 1875.[189] The case was decided on the basis of the *Landrecht* but the court noted that this did not differ in any way from the *gemeines Recht*. There, an apothecary who had long experience moonlighting as a vet, treated the plaintiff's horse to no avail; it worsened and died. The plaintiff sued for compensation on the basis that the defendant had negligently punctured the horse's stomach muscles, or that he had stimulated an existing puncture making it worse, or, finally, that he had

184 Hefke (1886a) 7.

185 Ibid. 3–4, 5–6.

186 Ibid. 149, citing Ulpian in D.46.3.31 '*Inter artifices longa differentia est et ingenii et naturae et doctrinae et institutionis*.'

187 Ibid. 7.

188 *OAG Lübeck* (1862) 4 Kritische Vierteljahresschrift für Gesetzgebung und Rechtswissenschaft 137.

189 *OAG Oldenburg 22.02.1875* Seuffert's Archiv 31, 297.

neglected to apply appropriate materials to abate the horse's injury. At first instance the claim had been put that he had grossly violated, '...the care of an ordinary, licensed vet'. This was altered on appeal to claim that he lacked the knowledge and capability, '...which one, through customary effort and diligence, may be expected to acquire in the practice of veterinary medicine'.[190] The *OAG* rejected the defendant's appeal against that second point and in addition discussed the appropriate approach to the liability of medical practitioners at uncommon length.

To start with, any comparison between the *Mensor* and the *medicus* in Roman law, which as we shall detail in the following chapter was *Zimmermann's* preferred approach, was rejected. On the basis of D.9.2.7.8 the liability of the latter was, on either of the bases there enumerated, one that could encompass *culpa levis.*[191] In light of the prevailing view of their services and, in particular, its estimability, the view that the modern approach was based on *Dienstmiethe*, and its attendant standard of liability, was preferred.[192] Careful consideration of the circumstances was required to understand the obligation that had been undertaken but generally it was one of, '...competence and skill of an average sort'. Regard must be taken of the fact that the rules of a skill or science were often contested and subject to change, and their application required a degree of subjective discretion or leeway. Finally, said the court, given the inherent uncertainty in many situations, mistakes were possible by even a careful expert despite taking care.[193] As such, mistakes would lead to a duty to compensate only where they revealed, '...an infringement against the generally accepted principles of the respective skill', echoing the *Kunstfehler* as defined in *Virchow's* terms, and that this would not have occurred had the expert practiced with the requisite degree of care.[194]

### *(ii) Codifications*

A similar result followed on from the tendency of civil codes in the latter part of the eighteenth and the earlier part of the nineteenth century to abandon the restriction on a medical practitioner sealing a bilateral contract for their services. The removal of the *operae liberales / illiberales* distinction in *Prussia* resulted in a medical practitioner, no different to any other skilled person, being liable for minor fault as long as they, in line with I XI 8 § 921 *ALR*, followed the rules of

190 *OAG Oldenburg 22.02.1875* Seuffert's Archiv 31, 298.
191 The court additionally relied on D.19.2.9.5. and D.1.18.6.7.
192 *OAG Oldenburg 22.02.1875* Seuffert's Archiv 31, 299.
193 Ibid. 299–300.
194 Ibid. 300.

their '*Kunst*'.[195] Had the other party explicitly specified a manner in which the work had to be done, failure to do so would be regarded as a moderate fault.[196] These rules had been enshrined in the *ALR*,[197] and drew on the tripartite schema of negligence, objectively viewed,[198] that the code had enacted, providing for gross, moderate and minor forms.[199] The first was equated with *dolus*, the second with what could have been avoided with customary degree of attention,[200] whilst the third was a cypher for *culpa levissima*.[201] As to recovery, whilst the degree of fault with which the contractual obligation was negligently performed would ordinarily vary the scope of interest the hirer could recover, in the case of skilled occupations such as medicine, the whole interest was always recoverable regardless of the degree of fault exhibited.[202] Whilst the *Sächsisches Bürgerliches Gesetzbuch* (*SBGB*) on the other hand provided a contractual liability only for both gross and minor negligence,[203] and in § 1237 had clarified that the obligation was performance of the task undertaken, not the guarantee of a result,[204] minor fault here imposed a *culpa levis* standard,[205] a degree of care 'which an ordinarily aware *paterfamilias* would demonstrate'.[206] Recovery under the *SBGB* will be discussed in greater detail in the following chapter.

## 4. Conclusions

*Rückert* posits the question whether a history of contractual labour in German law exists at all, or whether it is simply borne on the whim of the political and social mores.[207] Here, it is clear that doctrine played a significant role in shaping

195 I XI § 921 *ALR*, '*Doch sind diese die Arbeit nach den Regeln ihrer Kunst zu verrichten, und dabey auch für ein geringes Versehen zu haften schuldig.*'
196 Förster/Eccius (1887) § 138, 268; cited by Zimmermann (1873) 229; See also Fischer (1887) §§ 76 432.
197 I XI §§ 920–924 *ALR*.
198 Deutsch (1963) 14.
199 I III §§ 18–23 *ALR*. Förster/Eccius (1873) § 27, 146–149; Schermaier (2007) 1112.
200 This was further linked to a *bonus paterfamilias* standard in II 18 § 275 *ALR*; Deutsch (1963) 14 n 45.
201 Jansen (2009) 17, noting however the later rejection of a distinction between *culpa levis* and *culpa levissima* in Pandectist scholarship, see also Deutsch (1963) 13.
202 I V §§ 285–289.
203 §§ 1236, 728, 121, 122 *SBGB*; Siebenhaar (1872) § 394, 645; § 74, 122.
204 Siebenhaar (1869).
205 Siebenhaar (1864) 151 noting that the standard was one of the, '…good or diligent *paterfamilias*'.
206 §§ 122 *SBGB*.
207 Rückert (2013a) 815–816.

the discussion of the practitioner-patient relationship, if not necessarily the law in practice, well into the late nineteenth century, and lagged behind the social changes that had, by then, long taken root. Our survey of the possible contractual bases that were available for an action against a practitioner because of their injurious practice supports the following conclusions: The nineteenth century witnessed an increasing trend towards allowing a medical practitioner to seal a simple remunerated service contract with their patient. This process was set within an extended quagmire of discussion, which attempted to reconcile the Roman scheme with a different type of medical practitioner and practice. As we have seen in chapter one, the process of self-organisation undertaken by orthodox medical practitioners, who remained the focus of many of the legal discussions, was a slow and often interrupted one, ongoing well into the late nineteenth century. It is not surprising to find then that many of the legal arguments stemmed from an author's basic assessment of the sociological nature of medical practitioners. Despite the fevered and competitive nature of medical practice in late nineteenth-century Germany, in many cases there seemed to be an apparently irreconcilable dichotomy on the part of legal authors between the idea that a practitioner aimed to earn money from their practice and the deeply ingrained cultural image of the noble, selfless healer. In the absence of a clear and authoritative source for the civil law there continued to be a pluralist approach amongst authors towards categorising the practitioner-patient relationship, a problem rooted in the emphasis put on reconciling the Roman model with modern German practice. This model, incoherent as it is, was a significant formant of legal life in the nineteenth century as that incoherency was cast onto a very different model of medical practice. The tension between the two was only reconciled late on in the century, with the law lagging considerably behind social practice in coming to recognise the status of medical treatment as a possible subject of a simple service contract. With this emerging consensus, the connected question of the fault standard was, likewise, settled. Finding a natural home within the Roman idea of *imperitia*, fault came to be conceived as a failure to meet the standard required from fellow practitioners in the same situation. This provided a ready home for the logic of the *Kunstfehler* and blocked the path to imposing a formally higher requirement for actionable medical error in law. Nevertheless the inherited confusion of the Roman law damned nineteenth-century contract law to a confused and opaque approach to medical error, retarding the development of a specific legal treatment of the subject and, thus, ultimately weakening it against the encroachment of extra-legal influences on the subject, a weakness the medical discourse was well-placed to exploit.

Chapter 4

# Medical Error and the Law of Delict

'...just like jurists, theologians, philologists, and philosophers'[1]

In this chapter, we consider the relevance of the law of delict and the *sui generis*, quasi-delictual approach advocated by *Zimmermann* based on the *actio in factum contra mensorem qui falsum modum dixerit,* granted against the surveyor who incorrectly measured a plot of land (hereafter *actio contra mensorem*). As in the previous chapter, we begin with the Roman inheritance before turning to the law in nineteenth-century Germany. The picture that emerges here is that, again, a restrictive view of delictual recovery – which depended from the original Roman law – slowly gave way to a more inclusive approach to the scope of recovery available in delict. Again, whilst the academic discussion lagged behind, contemporary legislation and court practice were at the forefront of creating this recognisably modern approach. Unlike the difficulties we have seen with contractual categorisation, the social standing of a medical practitioner did not have as clear an impact on the formation or relevance of the general delictual rules, this being far more the case with *Zimmermann's* approach. Rather, the problem was one of the *general* approach to the law of delict, not a particular one based on a given view of medical practice. We then turn to consider the analysis of fault and its assessment where the defendant relied on a delictual claim. In a clear parallel with the contractual practice, the nineteenth century saw – apart from *Zimmermann's* approach, which we consider separately – an increasing emphasis on simple fault assessed with reference to expert medical practice in the form of *imperitia*. Finally, we consider the approach toward assessing fault as it concerned unorthodox practice, where, increasingly, merely taking on medical practice itself, came to be framed as sufficiently culpable to ground a claim.

## 1. The Roman delictual inheritance

Compared to the law of contract, the Roman law of delict supplied relatively less contested ground. For a start the action for *inuria* was of limited use, beyond perhaps falsely informing others that a person suffered an embarrassing disease,

1 Zimmermann (1873) 225–256.

given the requirement of intention.[2] Where the patient was a slave, the *Lex Aquilia* provided a focal point.[3] The provisions of the first chapter covered the unlawful killing (*occidere*) of a slave, while the third chapter applied to unlawful injury caused through burning (*urere*), breaking, (*frangere*) or tearing apart (*rumpere*) property. Although narrower at first, the statute was broadened in important ways.[4] The original interpretation of the relevant verbs in each chapter evolved into a wider reading, which saw *occidere* encompass less direct situations such as administering poison.[5] In the third chapter, *rumpere* came to be understood as *corrumpere*, ballooning to encompass all forms of bodily injury that might result from medical error.[6] Over time, the *Lex* also permitted recovery for harm caused to a son in *potestas*, and, probably later, an *actio utilis* for the injury (but not death) of a freeman,[7] but the likely Justinianic nature of that development is important in that it confirms contractual recovery as the main route for many such patients seeking recovery.[8] Indeed, for those who could not then afford to pay for care, a route to compensation appeared closed altogether.[9] Alongside any actions available from *locatio conductio* or under the *Lex*, *Below's* reading of D.19.5.26.1 suggests compensation could be recovered from a practitioner with an *actio in factum*. In keeping with his position, this would have been of use where the practitioner was an *ingenui* or where the patient was freeborn, and thus the *Lex* irrelevant.[10]

As to the fault standard required, as in any claim under *locatio conductio*, the practitioner was expected to act as a *bonus paterfamilias* although the delictual action required merely *culpa levissima*. The analysis of *culpa* was approached casuistically,[11] with the behaviour of the defendant measured objectively against the behaviour of the relevant group, in our case medical practitioners;[12] but the absence of serious regulation made that malleable in practice. Within the *Lex* this came to encompass the originally separate requirement that the loss be

2 There is evidence that it could be awarded to a person whose mind had been 'alienated' by drugs or other means. *Labeo* D.50.13.3.pr; *Watson*, noting that this requirement meant, '...there was not fertile soil here for the growth of medical malpractice'. See Watson (1983) 71.

3 Watson (1983) 74, stressing the *Lex* as the, 'original and prime context for medical malpractice'.

4 Buckland (2007) 587.

5 Hausmaninger (1996) 14–15; D.9.2.7.6.9.pr.

6 Ibid. 16–18.

7 D.9.2.13.pr.

8 Zimmermann (1996) 1016; Riegger (2007) 42–44.

9 Heldrich (1940) 156–157.

10 Below (1953) 118.

11 Zimmermann (1996) 1008.

12 Hausmaninger (1996) 27.

caused wrongfully (*inuria*).[13] For those who held themselves out as having a particular skill or expertise, liability for *imperitia* would apply in either head of claim.[14] Using the wrong drug or inadequate post-operative care were noted as specific examples of *culpa*.[15] Whether there was a particular distinction between more and less orthodox practitioners is unclear, but there are suggestions that this classification occasionally mattered.[16]

As to what might be recovered, the practical utility of delict, each chapter of the *Lex* carried a different penalty, referenced to the historic highest value of the thing. Although narrow, by the classical era both ascertainable *lucrum cessans* and *damnum emergens* (for instance the cost of additional restorative medical care) were included.[17] Away from the various economic losses that might be recovered, the Roman law offered little solace in terms of non-pecuniary losses. The inestimability of a freeman's body (*liberum corpus nullam recipit aestimationem*)[18] disinclined Roman law towards compensating scarring or disfigurement during treatment.[19]

## 2. Nineteenth-century Germany

Turning to the law of delict in nineteenth-century Germany, we find somewhat more solid analytical ground in that there were fewer iterations of the relevant rules than was the case with contract in that period, but this was undercut by the absence of much discussion about how these applied specifically to medical error. A medical practitioner may, of course, have been made the subject of a delictual action in the right circumstances. One of the advantages for the patient was that the necessary relationship could arise without the worries over payment and undertaking that obsessed contract law. Indeed, the social status of the practitioner, important as it may have been to the level of skill demanded from them, was, refreshingly, irrelevant to the potential raising of a delictual action.

13 Zimmermann (1996) 1006–1007.

14 D.9.2.8.1; D.19.2.9.5; I.4.3.7: *Imperitia quoque culpae adnumeratur, veluti si medicus ideo servum tuum occiderit, quod eum male secuerit aut perperam ei medicamentum dederit*, Birks / McLeod (1987) 125; D.9.2.8.pr; D.1.18.6.7 (*…ita quod per imperitiam comisit*).

15 D.9.2.8; Echoed in Justinian's Institutes I.4.3.6.

16 D.50.13.1.3. This is of more than speculative interest as a successful claim that the plaintiff's slave had been negligent in submitting to care in the first place would operate as a successful defence for the whole of a delictual claim, see Zimmermann (1996) 1011–1012 discussing the more familiar barber-shop / playground example.

17 Zimmermann (1996) 961 ff.

18 D.9.3.7.

19 Below (1953) 121; D.9.1.3; D.9.3.7.

Furthermore, although the twentieth-century German law was characterised by a necessary flexibility in its law of contract,[20] this was less so the case in the nineteenth century.[21] That left the delictual action to play an important role where the party suffering loss was not in a contractual relationship with the practitioner or the contractual analysis failed altogether. However, as with contract law, the Roman roots of this area were deep and, as we have seen in the classical Roman law, the core action in the *Lex Aquilia* was bounded by several restrictions. Only by overcoming these restrictions could the nineteenth-century German law offer patients' this additional route.

### (A) The crumbling mask of the *Lex Aquilia*

The general picture of development here is easy to state: Under the assault of successive generations of scholarly writing, in particular that of the Dutch natural law school and the scholars of the *usus modernus Pandectarum* in the seventeenth and eighteenth centuries,[22] alongside attendant pressure from litigants, the structure provided for delictual liability by the *Lex Aquilia*, and the diverse fragmentary delicts that rounded out the Roman law, had been slowly collapsing, with generalised principles of fault liability emerging from beneath the old Roman mask.[23] This was perhaps best captured in the legislation of the era. Thus, in the period before the *BGB*, a modernised version of the *Lex Aquilia*, whether ossified in regional codification, part of the *gemeines Recht*, or, an interpretive device for the more naturalistic codifications, provided the intellectual framework around which a claim could be constructed. These combined developments gave patients of this era a considerably stronger residual action which could, if needs be, deal with the core liability problems created by medical error without the encumbrances that had proved so restrictive in the Roman law.[24]

The first, key step in this process had been the abandonment of a restriction against bringing an action for harm to oneself. The body had, by the nineteenth century, long since become estimable in delict.[25] In addition, by the seventeenth century, the action had been broadened to include a claim by dependents where a person had been killed.[26] By the end of the nineteenth century the action had

20 Markesinis (1987).
21 Pennitz (2008) 275–283.
22 Gordley (2006) 160 ff.
23 Zimmermann (1996) 1018.
24 Glück (1808) § 700, 321–322.
25 Gerber (1895) 65. This argument was based on D.9.2.13 pr.
26 Zimmermann (1996) 1024–1026.

further expanded to include the award of damages for pain and suffering (*Schmerzensgeld*) thus closing an odd lacuna that had long seen such damages awarded by way of fixed tariffs in the Germanic customary law.[27] The second step, albeit a slower and more opaque process within the *gemeines Recht*, was confirmation of the non-penal nature of the modern action, exorcising the old Roman confusion and allowing clear analytical distance to be put between the criminal law and the nascent rules in delict.[28] The latter now calculated loss on a strictly compensatory basis.[29] Finally, partly as a consequence of this recasting of the Aquilian action, recognition of its passive transmissibility ensured that the death of a practitioner would not outrun a claim for compensation.[30] It should be noted that in line with the long-standing German approach to the concurrency of obligations, delict could cumulate alongside a contractual claim.[31] The importance of the law in practice ought not be underestimated in this process, for it was successive generations of legal practitioners who had established the reality of this expansion beyond the old, long-since-out-dated Roman boundaries on liability.[32]

We will examine the sources of the relevant delictual rules, as in the preceding chapter, in the legislation of the era and in the *gemeines Recht* viewed through the work of the Pandectists. Again, brief mention will be made of the relevant Germanist works. The picture that emerges is one of a confusing, scholarly retrenchment of the Roman position in the face of legislative and, increasingly, judicial acceptance of a broader principle for the recovery of negligently-inflicted loss.

## (B) Legislation

Despite the numerous codifications during the nineteenth century there was no specific, statutory delictual action that explicitly purported to regulate the practitioner-patient relationship. To the extent that the codes would avail a patient, the solution was to be found by applying the general rules.

The *Codex Maximilianus Bavaricus Civilis* 1757 had adopted a broad, general liability intended to offer considerably greater protection than the classical *Lex Aquilia*, in the fault-based action of IV 16 § 6.[33] Others had also successfully

27 Zimmermann (1996) 1026.

28 Ibid. 1020.

29 Ernst (2001) 342.

30 Zimmermann (1996) 1021–1022.

31 Jansen (2009) 16; Glück (1808) § 705, 384–385; Hefke (1886c) 361. *Hefke*, at 361–362, suggests that the choice lay in the hands of the judge and not the parties.

32 Zimmermann (1996) 1031.

33 Ebert (2004) 105.

enacted a true general principle of fault liability shorn of any of the old, Aquilian restrictions, and, in several Germanic jurisdictions, the prevailing tendency had been to mimic the French practice with a similarly broadly drafted clause. This was perhaps best exemplified by § 1382 of the *Badisches Landrecht* 1810, but may also be seen in I 6 §§ 8 and 10 of the *Allgemeines Landrecht* and § 1295 (1) of the *Allgemeines Bürgerliches Gesetzbuch* in *Prussia* and *Austria* respectively. Later codifications such as the *Sächsisches Bürgerliches Gesetzbuch*, which drew heavily on the Austrian code,[34] demonstrated a similar tendency towards a broad general clause for delictual liability in § 116. It was indicative of the break with the prevailing *ius commune* that many of these codifications provided for the recovery of *Schmerzensgeld* in the event of personal injury.[35] Even the so-called *Dresdner Entwurf* of a civil code for the German *Bund* in 1866, whilst it had steered a middle ground by providing specific provisions for the various Roman delicts, had, in articles 211 and 212, contained a general liability for negligent harm.[36]

### (C) *Gemeines Recht*

Although based on the regional codifications of the period, the doctrinal analysis of delictual liability in the *gemeines Recht* might be thought to have undergone a similar process of evolution towards a single broad principle of delictual recovery, this was, in fact, not the case in the latter half of the nineteenth century. For many scholars of this period the unstructured nature of a broad principle of fault liability was, similarly, not to be commended. Instead, there was a noticeable return to the limited nature of the classical Aquilian action in scholarly writing,[37] even to the point of undoing the medieval accretions.[38] This is telling of the era in that, as we shall see, it was the *gemeines Recht* that received most attention from legal scholars rather than the regional codifications. The latter largely hewed to the shape of the former, and it was that body of scholarship which provided the *fons et origio* of the twentieth-century law, not, as one might otherwise have thought, the statutory authority of the preceding regional codifications. That said, it is perhaps not surprising to find that a group of scholars bent on using the distilled essence of the classical Roman law to guide the development of the contemporary German law may have been more willing

34 Ernst (2001) 341 n 1.
35 I 6 §§ 112 f *ALR*; § 1325 *ABGB*; § 1489 *Sächsisches BGB*.
36 Ernst (2001) 344; Mossler (2001) 365–366.
37 Jansen (2009) 100.
38 Ernst (2001) 343.

to focus on the historical *Lex Aquilia* than how it stood in nineteenth-century legal life.

### *(i) Germanist views of delict*

Germanist literature had little to say regarding the law of delict. As in the law of contract, this was a topic which had long been the purview of the 'foreign' Romanised law. The old customary laws had, ironically perhaps, suffered the same fate as pre-classical Roman law in that a system of tariffs and fixed penalties,[39] which shared a penal character with the classical Aquilian action, had been superseded by a more flexible, open-textured system for compensating losses.[40] As such there was little of interest that a Germanist could offer the discussion when it came to delictual recovery for personal injury in the nineteenth century, and the pattern of potential influence between the old customary rules and the Romanised, contractual rules, is not repeated here.[41] That is not to say that, given the long-running development of the *usus modernus*, in the German-speaking lands there was not a certain degree of pride that could be taken from developments towards the sort of broad principles contained in the regional codifications as being German in character, but this requires us to understand the 'German' character of these rules as fundamentally Roman, albeit cultivated in a German context.[42] Nevertheless, there were occasional attempts to rationalise the nineteenth-century expansion of the Aquilian action as being supplemented by older principles drawn from the Germanic law.[43]

### *(ii) Pandectist views of delict*

In an era often defined by structure rather than content,[44] it is unsurprising that the treatment of delict by Pandectist authors frequently followed the fragmented nature of the Roman law of delict, rather than modernised contours that had been developed in the preceding century.[45] This suggests that the various ways in

39 v Savigny (1853) 316;

40 Bluntschli (1854) § 110, 1; Glück (1808) § 702, 341. See generally Ebert (2004) 14 ff.

41 For an outline of the modern relevance of actions rooted in the old German law, see Gengler (1854) 771 ff.

42 Stobbe (1885) § 200, 375.

43 Bluntschli (1854) § 110, 2; Gerber (1895) § 258, 436 pointing to the development of liability for the merely unlawful conduct of a principal and for children as resurrected *German* ideas.

44 *Ernst* notes the emphasis on the Roman *structure* amongst Pandectists: Ernst (2001) 343.

45 Puchta (1838) 432 f; Dahn (1878) 172 f; Vering (1875) § 204 ff; Vering (1887) § 208 ff.

which the Aquilian action had been previously, or elsewhere, extended might also be subject to reconsideration and indeed this was a discussion that was, '...particularly disputed by contemporary legal scholars'.[46] The fact that modern developments were often simply, and shortly, canvassed at the end of a Romanesque structure reinforced the perception that the classical Roman law in all its forms had regained the analytical centre ground.[47] Of the leading Pandectists, *Windscheid* was one of the few who attempted to meld the contemporary shape of the action with the classical structures that had birthed it.[48]

The most basic extension of the *usus modernus pandectarum* – the removal of the old *nulla corporis liberi aestimatio fieri potest* rule – and its application to personal injury and death went largely uncontested;[49] likewise the passive transmissibility of the action.[50] However, this was not the case with the other modern extensions. One notable feature of the *gemeines Recht* was the extent to which the compensatory nature of a delictual claim, axiomatic to modern eyes, continued to be muddled with punishment thus blurring the line between the criminal law and private law. This confusion was an unfortunate hangover from the rather odd measure of damages that could be recovered under the *Lex Aquilia* in Roman times, which could see the plaintiff wildly overcompensated, and the several liability that resulted amongst multiple defendants.[51] In addition, the idea of awarding damages for pain and suffering (*Schmerzensgeld*), a key distinction from what could be recovered with a contractual claim, was often misunderstood, despite a long history in the *usus modernus pandectarum*,[52] as involving a punitive aspect,[53] an idea with particularly strong resonance for Germanists.[54] Indeed as *Windscheid* noted, delictual claims for compensation could be said to have an inherently punitive nature given their disregard for the

46 Glück (1808) § 705, 382.

47 Glück (1808) § 705, 382 is indicative of this sort of approach; Bilstein (1994) 19.

48 Windscheid (1866) § 455; Sintenis (1847) § 125.

49 Unterholzner (1840) § 676, 700–701; Gerber (1895) § 258, 435; Windscheid (1866) § 455 297; Hefke (1886c) 221. But not always, see Glück (1808) § 702, 340–341; Sintenis (1847) § 125, 773.

50 Glück (1808) § 702, 341; Dernburg (1886) § 133, 344.

51 Zimmermann (1996) 973.

52 Ebert (2004) 193.

53 Puchta (1838) § 387 n(h) comparing what he called the arbitrary financial penalty of *Schmerzensgeld* under the Aquilian action to the provisions of article 20 *Carolina*; Brinz (1857) § 120, 520; See also Windscheid (1866) § 455, 302–303, who regarded *Schmerzensgeld* as, in reality, punishment. He did concede that this was contested, at 303, n 33.

54 Gengler (1854) 774 n 4.

economic state of the defendant.[55] Despite having long been under attack,[56] the idea that private law had a role in punishing wrongs was still 'vividly alive' in the Pandectist scholarship of the nineteenth century.[57] The principle was often identified where an author, as noted above, made little to no effort to do anything other than restate the classical Roman position without regard for the intervening centuries,[58] and could be rationalised as part of the most practical and important institutions that were recognised by the modern law.[59] Such a result required the finesse of a distinction between delicts that still justified the punitive approach of the Roman law, such as *inuria* (*Injurie*), and those that did not. Although he maintained the modern relevance of punitive damages for this former group, *v Savigny* was content to note that the focus of the modern Aquilian action on pure compensation was not to be doubted.[60] Others such as *Glück* maintained that, as a delict, the action had a necessary penal element but was not a 'purely penal claim'; rather it was a mixed action supplying both compensation and punishment.[61] Often drawing on *v Savigny*, other Pandectist authors regularly confirmed the evolved, non-penal nature of the action.[62] For these authors, *Mommsen's* 1855 elaboration of his '*Differenztheorie*' had provided the compelling intellectual basis on which the law of delict could be confined to a purely compensatory role.[63] The codification and sophistication of criminal law in the same period appears to have provided a complementary justification for doing so by filling the lacuna that had existed from the point of view of the Roman public law.[64] Yet the idea of private law accepting some role in punishing wrongs remained in the scholarship until the very end of the

55 Windscheid (1866) § 327, 219.

56 Zimmermann (1996) 1019–1020.

57 Jansen (2009) 96.

58 Puchta (1838) § 387, 432. The author's text remains unchanged in subsequent editions, see Rudorff (1863) § 388, 571; v Vangerow (1869) § 681, 597.

59 v Savigny (1853) 330.

60 v Savigny (1853) 312; Glück (1808) § 705, 384 describing the modern form of action in practice as, '…pure compensation'; Sintenis (1847) § 125, 771 n 1; 773 n 17 simply dismissing the penal calculation of damages under chapters 1 and 3 of the *Lex Aquilia* as no longer practical.

61 Glück (1808) § 703, 351; Brinz (1857) § 118, 514.

62 Blume (1852) 281, noting the break with the Roman law and describing the existence of quasi-penal actions as '…only an extraordinary addition to compensation'; Gerber (1855) § 165, 401–402; Dahn (1878) 171, who noted the penal character had long since disappeared; Stobbe (1885) 374.

63 Jansen (2009) 96.

64 Blume (1852) 281 f; Gerber (1895) 438. He suggested that it had been replaced with fines regulated by the criminal code; *Windscheid* explicitly referenced the *Reichstrafgesetzbuch* in later editions, see Windscheid (1887) § 455, 753; Hefke (1886c) 364; Stobbe (1885) 374; Diwald (1905) § 24, 33.

century.[65] It was, as *v Savigny* had noted nearly half a century earlier, capable of giving rise to '…very varied doubts and disputes' amongst the Pandectist authors.[66]

This stood in stark contrast to the approach taken by the courts, who, despite a tendency by some to draw analogies from the criminal law or the old Germanic rules,[67] had generally neither accepted nor applied the idea of a punitive role for private law in this period,[68] nor had they evidenced any difficulty in assessing *Schmerzensgeld* as a compensatory measure of loss when they chose to award it.[69] In fact, this point was taken as understood by writers later in the century[70] and was, eventually, conceded by *Windscheid* in later editions.[71] The fact that his earlier stance had been criticised by the infant *Reichsgericht* in 1882, when it had seized the chance to make clear that a claim for *Schmerzensgeld* was a civil claim, may have helped refresh his outlook on the question.[72] Equally, the picture was different in the codified regions. There, the argument that delict had a purely compensatory role was, predictably, considerably easier to make where it concerned the application of the naturalised law, as in *Prussia*.[73]

Despite grudging acceptance of the extended boundaries of the modern Aquilian action, a feature of the Pandectist scholarship, again in contrast to the legislation of the era, was a refusal to recognise a streamlined basis for the Aquilian action as a general liability for fault. This position can be attributed partly to the structure of Pandectist analysis and partly to normative concerns about the scope of liability.

As noted above, the overall shape of the Roman law of delicts often provided the structural basis for analysis. If a broad principle of liability based merely on fault was recognised, that structure would have been placed under intolerable pressure as the re-purposed Aquilian action would have undermined the other more limited liabilities within that structure. No effort had been made, nor the result sought, to establish a unified law of delict.[74] Normatively there was much

65 Jansen (2009) 96.
66 v Savigny (1853) 301.
67 Ebert (2004) 195.
68 Jansen (2009) 97–98; Ernst (2001) 342.
69 Glück (1808) § 705, 388, although he notes that there was an opposing view in the literature, n 60; Sintenis (1847) § 125, 774.
70 Dernburg (1886) § 132, 343 f.
71 Windscheid (1887) § 455, 755.
72 *RG 17.11.1882*, RGZ 8, 117 f
73 Evelt (1854) 318; Eccius (1896) § 151, 500 ff.
74 Ernst (2001) 343–344, describing their reluctance to do so as 'striking'.

disdain, particularly in the latter half of the century,[75] for the potentially broad scope of liability that would result if liability were based on fault without any other controlling device.[76] As in the twentieth century, the potential creation of broad liability for economic losses stood foremost amongst the fears. For many, such control was to be found in the idea of illegality or wrongfulness (*Widerrechtlichkeit*). As *Windscheid* noted, a claim would only arise where the defendant had no legal right to have behaved as they did, *and* had been at fault.[77] An injurious act was then taken to be illicit in and of itself in the absence of a justification.[78] This sort of reasoning might be taken to suggest a broad undermining of the supposedly limited scope of delictual liability, and, alongside *Windscheid's* apparent insistence to the contrary, is indicative of the 'cloudy inconsistencies' that abounded as to the underlying rationale for delictual liability.[79] Indeed this nineteenth-century focus on illegality had been prefigured even in the supposedly broad basis of liability in the *usus modernus pandectarum* through a focus on the particular rights and interests – coinciding heavily with those protected by the various Roman delicts – which were protected by it.[80]

### (D) *Zimmermann's* sui generis approach

Moving away from the core of contemporary delict – an emerging consensus on a general rule for recovery of negligently inflicted harm – one consequence of many Pandectists' somewhat ad hoc contractual solution outlined in the previous chapter was an attempt to breathe life into an alternative way of providing the patient with an action for injurious harm; one that had certainly been overlooked by the Romans themselves it is worth noting: the *actio contra mensorem*. This was possible because a restricted view of the implied innominate contract for payment only permitted a procedural claim for the enforcement of some measure of payment.[81] That was not, in the view of many scholars, a material claim grounded in a bilateral contract between the parties.[82] This applied equally for those who took the view that mandate required the mandatee to act as proxy for the mandator and, as such, was an inappropriate description of the practitioner-patient relationship in any situation except where,

75 Ernst (2001) 348–349.
76 v Ihering (1861) 12; Ernst (2001) 349.
77 Windscheid (1866) § 455, 298.
78 Ernst (2001) 348.
79 Ibid. 347–8.
80 Ibid. 345.
81 Wetzell (1878) 63–64.
82 Zimmermann (1873) 226, notes that the innominate contract was in fact merely an *actio in factum praescriptis verbis*.

perhaps, both parties were practitioners themselves.[83] Those of this ilk also tended to view any other contractual analysis as flawed on the basis of the exclusion of *operae liberales* from *Dienstmiethe* and, again, were then reliant on other types of action to fully explain the relationship.[84] As demonstrated above, the general law of delict could, in the expanded Aquilian action, provide the basis for a claim regarding injury caused by medical error, but the *sui generis* solution of the *actio contra mensorem* proved attractive to some both for the apparent accuracy of the sociological analogy it required and, equally if not more so, for the high bar to liability for medical errors that it would have established.

Categorising the *actio contra mensorem* is, admittedly, challenging. Its placement in Book XI of the Digest offers no aid, for that book lies in between more solidly delictual or contractual subjects and the fact that Book XI contains a ragbag of actions concerning runaway slaves, gamblers and funeral matters suggests miscellany over categorisation. Considering the *argimensor* commanded a less contentious position amongst liberal occupations in *Rome* than medical practitioners,[85] an analogy to service contracts is perhaps stretching too far, but the situation certainly seems much closer to mandate. Viewed thus it could be rationalised, as with the development of a claim for the mandatee's *honorarium*,[86] as providing protection for the mandator and specifying the required standard of care. Nevertheless, many Pandectists explicitly designated the action as a delict where they gave it a category at all, and, for simplicity, we treat it as such here.[87] Indeed, as the leading advocate of this approach, *Zimmermann* regarded the exchange of monies as only incidental to the foundation of the action, suggesting that he viewed it as quasi-delictual at the very least.[88]

As briefly set out in the previous chapter, *Zimmermann* had rejected the modern, flexible view of contract law espoused by the likes of *Windscheid* and *Hefke* that recognised either an innominate contract analogous to *Dienstmiethe* or the full contract itself. His basis for doing so was the unsuitability of contract

83 Wetzell (1878) 63–64. *Sintenis* makes a similar argument but was doing so to highlight the availability of the innominate contractual solution, Sintenis (1847) § 113, 561 n 8.

84 Wetzell (1878) 64. *Wetzell* was primarily discussing the relationship of a lawyer with their client but noted the analogy to medical practitioners, stating that such occupations were performed '…as a courtesy ("*beneficii loco*")', cited on this point by Hirte (1996) 151.

85 Zimmermann (1996) 388, 413 f.

86 Indeed, D.11.6.1.pr explicitly designates the remuneration given to the *agrimensor* as an *honorarium*.

87 Mommsen (1855) 399; Brinz (1857) § 117, 510; v Vangerow (1869) § 700, 630; Vering (1887) § 213, 592.

88 Zimmermann (1873) 226, '…irrespective of any promised or provided honorarium'.

law for the highly-regarded services of a medical practitioner. In seeking to categorise the practitioner-patient relationship then, he instead took the contemporary model of orthodox practice in nineteenth-century Germany and, looking back into Roman law, sought to identify what he saw as the better analogy of a situation where the Roman law had provided for the extra-contractual liability of a person with unique skills. He found what he was looking for in the person of the *agrimensor* (*Feldmesser*). His view was, predictably, coloured by the emphasis he placed on the status and position of orthodox medical practice in contemporary German society. Orthodox medical practice was predicated, as we have seen, on a university-based 'scholarly education'; it deserved to be respected, '...just like jurists, theologians, philologists, and philosophers.'[89] The continued practice of payment by means of an honorarium (*Ehrensold*), even where this was regulated by legislative decree as in the regional tariffs, and the ritualised oath sworn at university, made categorisation within service contracts – in *Zimmermann's* view only relevant to '...day workers, manual labourers or farmhands' – unsuitable.[90] Finally, even if these sociological features were insufficient to complete the analogy, like the *agrimensor* the medical practitioner's art was practised for the good of the community rather than personal interest.[91] As such, the *actio contra mensorem* was the correct analogy for dealing with the liability of a medical practitioner.[92] It is worth noting that the practical bifurcation of medical practice between orthodox and unorthodox practice served in *Zimmermann's* eyes not only as one of the factors to promote the orthodox practitioner out of the grubby world of contracting for their services, but also to relegate into it those unorthodox practitioners (*Heildiener*) who did not train at university or take any oath regarding the grand aspirations of their practice.[93]

Other authors had explicitly canvassed the relevance of the *actio contra mensorem* to the legal analysis of a skilled party's liability in this period, particularly – inevitably – its application to surveyors.[94] *Hefke* excoriated six other jurists of the era for sharing *Zimmermann's* approach but, unlike *Zimmermann*, not citing any evidence to support their position. Yet closer study of these six reveals a split as to why the action was being drawn on at all. For some the *actio contra mensorem* was simply evidence of the absence of a full contractual

89 Zimmermann (1873) 225–256.

90 Ibid. 226.

91 Ibid. 226.

92 D.11.6, *Si mensor falsum modum dixerit...*

93 Zimmermann (1873) 226–227.

94 Glück (1809) §765, 385. The modern relevance of the action for surveyors (*Gelehrten*) '...suffered no doubt', but *Glück* certainly did not suggest anything broader.

route and was cited for its support of the idea that any payment took the form of an *honorarium*.[95] For others, the primary lure was the raised standard for liability with which the action was associated,[96] for one, it was both.[97] However, at least one scholar, writing later on the basis of *Zimmermann's* views, found the sociological analogy between the Roman *agrimensor* and the German *'Arzt'* convincing and was willing to deny the applicability of any recognised service contract, to rely on an innominate contract enforced by an *actio praescriptis verbis* to cover payment and, importantly, deploy the *actio contra mensorem* to delineate the practitioner's potential liability for poor practice.[98]

Regardless of one's views on whether the practitioner-patient relationship could be comprehended by some species of contract, *Zimmermann's* solution was not without its critics. *Wendt* disparagingly described the continued citation of this title as relevant to legal, medical or indeed, and perhaps surprisingly, surveying practice as, '…a piece of purely antiquated jurisprudence'. His argument, refuting *Glück's* positive endorsement regarding surveyors seventy-nine years earlier (ironically by drawing upon the same logic), was based on the fact that surveyors (as in the case of lawyers and medical practitioners) had long been capable of sealing a contract for their services and to rely on an action predicated on the absence of contract, '…dispensed with all truth, except for Roman law.'[99] As we shall see below, the main attraction of the *actio contra mensorem* for *Zimmermann* was the alternate fault standard that action supplied, *culpa lata*, in contrast to that available in any general delictual action, *culpa levis*. In short, as with the contractual contortions, a particular view of medical practice was here, again, being deployed to make it harder for a patient to successfully recover damages from a medical practitioner.

95 Vering (1887) § 204, 571.

96 Hänel (1833) § 52; Mommsen (1855) 399; Sintenis (1861) § 101, 339 n 60 for whom the action could be used as the basis of liability for those whose work required the application of, '…an art or science' generally. 'The extension from *mensor* to other artists and learned occupations presents no difficulties.' See Bauridl (1874) 325 for a similar use; Puchta (1863) § 267, 410 n (s).

97 Wetzell (1878) 63–64.

98 Bauridl (1874) 330. *Hefke* does not cite *Bauridl's* work, perhaps not surprising given its appearance in a southern regional circular rather than a national journal which might have appeared in *Oldenburg* where *Hefke* was based at the time of writing.

99 Wendt (1888) § 260, 629.

### 3. Delictual standards of fault

Turning to the core of the law of delict we find a high degree of overlap between the approach here and that found with *Dienstmiethe* in the previous chapter. This is not surprising given the era's emphasis on fault as the decisive factor in establishing liability and the natural home that thinking also found in the development of the *Lex Aquilia*.[100] Simply put, fault could be understood either in the wider sense of intention or the narrower sense of inadvertence.[101] Of relevance here was the fact that *imperitia*, certainly in Roman law, had been discussed in the context of the *Lex Aquilia* as much as it was in *locatio conductio*, locating a natural home for discussions of how the fault of a skilled defendant could be rationalised.[102] Furthermore, there was evidence in practice that from the patient's perspective, delict clearly did provide a residual form of protection from negligent harm and the possibility of compensation where there was either no contractual relationship,[103] or, likely in the form of an *actio in factum*,[104] an implied contract that only enforced payment of a customary sum for the services rendered.[105]

#### (A) Academic writing

Few scholars discussed the delictual nature of any claim against a medical practitioner, but the few that did suggested there was less, but not no, discussion as to the standard to be applied in delict compared to that seen in more contractual claims. Writing in 1838, *Hepp* had drawn a parallel between the liability of the medical practitioner in Roman law not only for shoddy practice but also for unskillfulness, *imperitia*, and the schema in article 134 *Carolina*: '*unfleiß*' paralleled *culpa* and '*unkunst*' *imperitia*.[106] It will be recalled that *Mittermaier* had rejected these forms of liability for simple, mere *culpa* on the basis that the licensed practitioners of contemporary life bore no relation to those of 1532 who had required that broad measure of sanction.[107] *Hepp* countered that it could not be assumed that mere academic examination

100 Bilstein (1994) 19.

101 Sintenis (1847) § 125, 772.

102 Zimmermann (1996) 1009; I.4.2.7.

103 *OAG Lübeck*, (1862) 4 Kritische Vierteljahresschrift für Gesetzgebung und Rechtswissenschaft 137. There, the action concerned a practitioner against whom an action in delict was maintained for infecting a wet nurse and her family by not explaining that a child he had placed in her care was syphilitic.

104 Mommsen (1855) 399 describing the *actio contra mensorem* as such.

105 Arndts (1855) § 314, 461.

106 Hepp (1838) 28–29.

107 Mittermaier (1819b) 355.

imparted the necessary wisdom and skill; it was unclear why a dilettante (*Stümper*) could be allowed to bamboozle the patient at the cost of their life. Yet, confusingly and idiosyncratically,[108] he regarded it as too much for the law to expect them to withdraw from practice where the patient had entrusted their health to them. *Imperitia* was not based on the want of skill, for then, he claimed, one would have to allow all those who did not have such skills to escape liability. To do otherwise would be to penalise the blind for their blindness. Rather it was based on advertent contravention of the law, and the imputation of fault, whether in civil or criminal law, was justified as the practitioner had foreseen the risk and acted nevertheless.[109]

Emphasising how *culpa levis* focused on the behaviour of what the *bonus paterfamilias* would have done in the circumstances, *Mommsen* stressed that the standard of fault was a flexible one that would require more or less from the defendant depending on the exigencies of the situation.[110] As such, when it came to those who undertook an activity requiring greater skill, it would be an actionable *culpa* to fall short of the skill required; that is to say, liability was based on *imperitia* as usually understood.[111] Indeed despite his support for the limited use of the *actio contra mensorem* for occupations that held the required respected position in contemporary German life, when it came to medical practitioners he conceded that the broad scope of the *actio legis Aquiliae* rather undermined any effect this would have on restricting liability; the latter would always overreach the former.[112] Others had simply noted the fact that an Aquilian action could be had against a medical practitioner who caused injury by their negligent conduct without linking the standard of liability to *imperitia.*[113]

It fell to *Hefke* to offer the only extended, specific analysis of the point in the latter part of the century, and, then, only in order to support his contractual position. Having dealt with fault in that contractual context, he wished to demonstrate that the *gemeines Recht* took no different an approach to the liability of a medical practitioner '*per se*', that is to say, in delict.[114] He argued that it was plainly obvious that the medical practitioner would be liable for '*omnis culpa*' in contract.[115] The Roman sources had made clear that a medical practitioner

108 Hefke (1886a) 146.

109 Hepp (1838) 30–31.

110 Mommsen (1855) 364–365.

111 Ibid. 365–366, relying on I.4.3.7, D.1.18.7.8 and D.19.2.9.5.

112 Ibid. 400–401. This can be contrasted with his other chosen example of liability for giving a legal opinion, which apparently would not have been so undermined.

113 Arnold (1853) 578.

114 In contrast to the medical practitioner as a contractual debtor for services, Hefke (1886a) 139.

115 Hefke (1886a) 139.

would also be liable in delict by reason of *imperitia*.[116] He rejected *Zimmermann's* interpretation of *Ulpian's* fragment in D.1.18.6.7, discussed below, arguing that the choice of '*decipere*', '*imperitia*' and '*humana fragilitas*', all pointed to *culpa levis* rather than *culpa lata*. In particular, he argued that, whilst *imperitia* may have other meanings, the presence of the other two terms and the absence of any explicit mention of *culpa lata*, as was the case in D.11.6.1.1 – the basis of the *actio contra mensorem* – was indicative of the lower not the higher standard.[117] Indeed, the fact that for medical practitioners there was not, as there had been for the *mensor*, a special rule suggested that the liability was no different from that of every other skilled defendant.[118]

In due course *Hefke* defined *imperitia* as applied to medical practitioners as, '...the absence of that knowledge and skill which may be expected or presumed, and therefore demanded, from average medical practitioners or experts respectively'.[119] This, he regarded, correctly, both as reflecting the leading academic view of the day,[120] and being in line with the contractual standard under D.19.2.9.5.[121] Thus the standard was, as in *Dienstmiethe*, and in line with the general approach of the *Reichsgericht*,[122] an objective one measured against the knowledge and skills of the average practitioner.[123] The same standard was said by *Hefke* to apply in situations where a medical practitioner took on care of the poor, who could not, then, offer any remuneration on which a contract could be grounded. There, *Hefke* was of the opinion that, despite the fact the treatment was a mere *donatio*, a medical practitioner would still remain liable for *omnis culpa* in the same fashion as under a service contract but, oddly, cited D.1.18.6.7 as the basis for this rather than suggesting a delictual claim, which, by his own logic, would have been available, in theory, to the aggrieved patient.[124] Finally, when it came to the scope of recovery in delict under the *gemeines Recht* there was, with the exception of the slippery question of the basis for an award of damages for pain and suffering,[125] uncontested acceptance that in cases of death

116 He relied on D.9.2.6.7.8, I.4.3.6, I.4.3.7 and D.9.2.52.pr, arguing that the '*inscientia*' in the latter was the same as '*imperitia*' in the Institutes.

117 Hefke (1886a) 143. A similar argument was used by *Mommsen* to delineate when *dolus* and *culpa* (understood to then mean *culpa levis*) could be distinguished from one another, see Mommsen (1855) 359.

118 Hefke (1886a) 146.

119 Ibid. 148–149.

120 Hasse (1838) 94; Windscheid (1875) § 404, 515 n 4.

121 Hefke (1886a) 149.

122 Bilstein (1994) 53 f.

123 Hefke (1886c) 368–9; Deutsch (1963) 10, 12; Bilstein (1994) 53 n 277.

124 Hefke (1886a) 135.

125 Gengler (1854) 774.

or personal injury the plaintiff, or their dependants could recover all material damage including medical costs, lost earnings and funeral costs.[126]

### (B) Codifications

The relevant codifications of the era had enshrined a modernised, broad form of Aquilian liability in their provisions on delict. At the heart of this, despite a degree of retrenchment, was the principle of liability based on fault; a characteristic shared by all. Where a system adopted a bipartite approach to fault, this sometimes contrasted a *culpa levis* standard with intention, as in the Austrian *Allgemeines Bürgerliches Gesetzbuch.*[127] Indeed, despite its heterodox choice of subjective fault for the majority of defendants, the *ABGB* imposed an objective standard on those who practiced an 'office, art, trade or craft'.[128] In the case of the Saxon Civil Code (1863) negligence, defined in § 121, was broken down further in § 122 which provided for both minor and gross negligence. The former corresponding to failure to show care commensurate with 'a prudently careful *paterfamilias*', the latter was irrelevant for delict. In any case, damages for personal injury, whether by delictual or contractual means, would include, per § 1489, medical costs, damages for pain and suffering and, where the injury created an incapacity, loss of future earnings. Where the injury was fatal, a claim could be maintained by the heir for medical costs and examination as well as the funeral costs.[129] Finally, the intricate tripartite arrangement of negligence in the *Allgemeines Landrecht,* noted above in the context of *Dienstmiethe* and also visible in the *Bayerische Landrecht,*[130] tied the scope of delictual recovery to the defendant's degree of fault,[131] a mechanism unknown to the classical *Aquilian* action.[132] For instance when it came to personal injury, minor negligence would allow only recovery of the medical costs, moderate negligence allowed the recovery of lost earning capacity in addition,[133] and gross negligence both all the profits that would ordinarily have been expected and, where the injured party

126 Bilstein (1994) 22.

127 Förster/Eccius (1873) § 27, 145. See § 1294 AGBG.

128 § 1299 *ABGB* § 1299.

129 § 1491 *SBGB.*

130 Deutsch (1963) 14 n 49.

131 Förster/Eccius (1873) 560–561. This is likely to have been more relevant to cases of property damage than personal injury as discussion of scope involved various permutations of the value and potential profit to be had from the plaintiff's damaged property.

132 Kiefer (1989) 146; Förster/Eccius (1873) 551.

133 As *Förster* put it elsewhere, the pertaining state of the plaintiff upon their injury, Förster (1892) § 151, 493; I 6 *ALR* §§ 115, 117.

was a person of higher standing an award of damages for pain and suffering no less than half, but no greater than double, the medical costs.[134] Regarding death, the deceased's widow and children (and in some cases dependants) could maintain a claim, which similarly varied in scope with the degree of fault.[135]

### (C) Fault and the *actio contra mensorem*

As was not unknown amongst nineteenth-century German legal scholars, in thrall, in principle, to the Roman law, a scholar might first decide on a desired outcome and then reason towards a compatible result. For our subject, this was most obviously the case with *Zimmermann's* use of the *actio contra mensorem.*[136] As noted, this was based, in part, on the drawing of an apparently more convincing analogy between the role of the nineteenth-century orthodox practitioner,[137] and the high regard in which the Roman *mensor* was held.[138] But just as clearly visible was a desire to ensure that nineteenth-century medical practitioners were not exposed to an overly broad liability. This could be achieved given the supposedly more indulgent standard of care imposed by the *actio contra mensorem*.

Bolstered by the belief that *Ulpian*, in D.1.18.6.7, had been using '*imperitia*' as a synonym for *culpa lata*,[139] *Zimmermann* began by stressing that the *Carolina*, in article 134, provided liability only in the form of gross fault, carelessness or unskillfulness (read conjunctively) and the *RStGB* in §§ 222 and 230 had provided for the same. As such, '…it was not possible that a claim for mere *culpa levis* could be levelled against a medical practitioner.' It would not do to have the criminal law undercut by the civil law.[140] An odd claim to make,

134 I VI §§ 112–114 *ALR*. Förster (1873) § 151, 457–459. *Förster* noted that these provisions had a root in the court practice surrounding § 20 *Carolina.*

135 Förster (1892) § 151, 490–492.

136 Zimmermann (1873) 229 n 18; See also Wetzell (1878) § 8 58 f.

137 *Zimmermann's* emphasis on the university-based nature of medical practice suggests a singular focus on orthodox rather than unorthodox practice.

138 Indeed, some jurists of the age saw it as the vehicle for a *Sonderweg* applicable to experts of all varieties, Sintenis (1861) 101, 339 n 60 but as was often pointed out, this did not reconcile with his liberal interpretation of *Dienstmiethe*, see § 119 679 n 2; Wetzell (1878) § 8 58 f. For a more restrained position, which limited its use to those occupations that fell outside *Dienstmiethe*, see Puchta (1838) § 258, 278.

139 Zimmermann (1873) 224; D.1.18.6.7: *Sicuti medico imputari eventus mortalitatis non debet, ita quod per imperitiam commisit, imputari ei debet: praetextu humanae fragilitatis delictum decipientis in periculo homines innoxium esse non debet.*

140 Zimmermann (1873) 227–228. This assumption that the criminal law required gross negligence on the part of the practitioner, whilst clearly visible in the jurisprudence of the *Carolina* was, as we have seen, less clearly the case in the

perhaps, given the absence of any necessary doctrinal link between the criminal and the civil standards of fault, but one that was, certainly in the case of the *RStGB* – at least by the 1880s – incorrect. Having placed so much reliance on the sociological trappings of orthodox practice, *Zimmermann* was then remarkably quick to dismiss the unhelpful influence these might have to lower the relevant standard of liability. To the argument that practitioners ought then to be held to their goal, commonly stated in their oath or in the relevant local guidelines of providing the 'highest care', *Zimmermann* cannily replied that these superlatives were addressed to the nation and thus defined that relationship not the one between practitioner and patient.[141] Likewise, he emphasised the public law nature of the *Gewerbeordnung* 1869 in order to explain that the status of medicine as a free trade did nothing to alter the *social* standing of the licensed practitioner, much less equate their liability with that of the unlicensed one.[142] Indeed, by way of conclusion, *Zimmermann* drew on the university education of the orthodox medical practitioner as a way of demonstrating a further supportive analogy to the liability of state officials. Such officials, he argued, had a similar scientific education and nor could they, at least at that stage,[143] be the subject of service contract. Choosing as an example the liability of a judge – which was restricted to *culpa lata* – medical liability must, he claimed, be likewise.

The underpinning importance, for *Zimmermann's* argument, of the strong relationship between licensed practice and quasi-public, remunerated practice was clear.[144] *Zimmermann* took all the above, allied to his rhetoric of medical practice's beneficial and selfless nature, as perfecting the analogy to the *mensor*; and with it a baseline standard of *culpa lata* for medical liability. In Roman law, the *mensor* and his customer fell outside the mutual protection afforded by *locatio conductio* but, nevertheless, an action was granted on the negligence, and *culpa lata* or *dolus*, of the surveyor depending on whether payment had been taken or not.[145] The high threshold for liability that the *actio contra mensorem* was taken as providing for the nineteenth-century medical practitioner was

*RStGB. Zimmermann's* stance can be attributed to its coming so soon after the code's enactment and his reliance on *Mittermaier* and *Berner's* mid-century texts advocating gross negligence.

141 Zimmermann (1873) 229.

142 As noted above, *Zimmermann* seemed content with lesser practitioners being able to avail themselves of *Dienstmiethe* and, by his logic, a less protective formal standard of care.

143 *RG 4.11.1886* RGZ 18, 173, 175.

144 Zimmermann (1873) 230.

145 D.11.6.1.1, *Sed et si mercedem accepit, non omnem culpam eum praestare propter verba edicti: utique enim scit praetor et mercede eos intervenire.*

central to *Zimmermann's* advocacy of it and was intimately tied to the high status he attached to the gratuitous provision of one's skills for the benefit of another.

Having established the standard he thought most appropriately encapsulated orthodox medical practice, *Zimmermann* provided further insight, albeit confusingly, into how this worked in practice. He achieved this partly through doctrinal analysis, but also by detailing several cases that had been heard before his court in *Gießen*. Although he noted that when it came to medical science there was no generally accepted codex,[146] he was willing to assert – not unfairly – that there were substances, which were known to be poisonous when given in large doses.[147] The administration of such a dose could thus be regarded, *per se*, as gross carelessness. *Culpa lata* it seemed (although he was just as happy to call it *imperitia*) should be understood as it was in the criminal law: 'Ignorance of that, which all licensed practitioners must know.'[148] He completed the Carolingian schema by noting that a practitioner ought not practice frivolously (which he equated with *luxuria*).[149]

*Bauridl*, who was generally supportive of *Zimmermann's* position as reflecting not only the *gemeines Recht* but also the *Landrecht* in *Bayern* at the time of his writing in 1874, confirmed that the obligation placed on a medical practitioner was not one that went so far as to require a guarantee of cure.[150] Echoing the notion that medicine lacked a codex, he drew on *Henke's* medico-legal work, which suggested both that such an absence of fixed rules was a position supported by the law, as it did not wish to bind a medical practitioner's hands at the bedside, and, also, that as the standard of liability from a medical perspective – drawing on the internal discussions canvassed in chapter one – supposedly focused only on *dolus* or *culpa lata*, the standard applied by the civil law ought to be no different.[151] Furthermore he suggested that the assessment of

146 Zimmermann (1873) 230. A similar line to that taken by *Mittermaier* in 1853 and reflecting most medico-legal texts up to *Virchow*.

147 An example that had been given around the same time by *Virchow*, Virchow (1879) 519.

148 Zimmermann (1873) 231. What it was that licensed practitioners ought to know was then said to be ascertainable from regulatory documents such as the *Bekanntmachung, betreffend die Prüfung der Ärzte, Zahnärzte, Thierärzte und Apotheker* of 25th September 1869, (1869) 34 Bundesgesetzblatt des Norddeutschen Bundes Band, 635.

149 Zimmermann (1873) 231.

150 Bauridl (1874) 340. He noted, at 343, that *Zimmermann's* interpretation of the standard of liability reflected that of the great draughtsman *v Kreittmayr's* Annotation to the *Bayerische Landrecht*. He did not, however, accept the analogy to the liability of a judge as being helpful or indeed relevant to discussing medical liability, at 339.

151 Bauridl (1874) 329–30. Drawing on Henke (1821) 609–612.

fault for any skilled defendant was an absolute standard linked not to individual capability but rather the, 'dominating field of knowledge'.[152] This, he noted, '...obviously cannot be decided by a layman, rather it can only be confirmed by a medical practitioner as a non-partisan specialist.'[153] Thus, the decision was still left in the hands of experts and, indeed, was designed to be coterminous with their own, internal conception of medical error.

Amongst the cases from the *Hofgericht* in *Gießen*, *Zimmermann* discussed two, which dealt explicitly with issues of medical error and orthodox practice. In the first, the defendant claimed that the practitioner had, '...through irresponsible and senseless treatment', caused his thumb to be stiff and useless and, indeed, that after removing a splinter of bone, the plaintiff had declared the treatment failed. The plaintiff contended that it had not been shown how he should have behaved differently and that, given the seriousness of the injury, the choices had been amputation or stiffness, the latter of which he had settled on. The court accepted the case against him and he appealed on the basis that there had been no proof of 'gross fault or lack of skill'. The appeal court ruled in his favour. The plaintiff had to show more precisely how the treatment had been irresponsible or lackadaisical and had failed to do so. Although the court did not directly address the standard of liability, *Zimmermann* noted that the legal expert evidence had approached the question on the basis that an orthodox practitioner was only liable for 'gross fault'.[154] In the second, the patient claimed that the practitioner, a University Professor practicing as an eye specialist, had caused him to have cataracts following an operation for calluses, which had, scrofulitically, set his humours out of order. The court found for the practitioner, holding that all that had been agreed was, as had been carried out correctly, a cataracts operation.[155]

Aside from these hints as to the standard of liability, it is particularly striking that in both instances the discussion about the practitioner's fault was framed by the context of an action by the practitioner to recover their fees. It was, in other words, a rejoinder by the defendant *patient* seeking damages against the plaintiff *practitioner*, who demanded payment; a reversal of the archetypal twentieth-century state of affairs. *Bauridl* reported a similar case from 1840 in which the appeal court of Middle Franconia enforced the payment of a surgeon's bill as the defendant had failed to demonstrate how the treatment, which he had claimed involved excessive materials (which was to say the bill was not to his liking), had

152 Bauridl (1874) 340 citing (albeit they disagreed as to the *standard* of fault required) Sintenis (1861) § 119 679 n 2.

153 Bauridl (1874) 341.

154 Zimmermann (1873) 231–232.

155 Ibid. 233–234.

been inappropriate and had, as was necessary, contravened the 'rules of practice'.[156] A practitioner having to sue for their fees was not a situation limited to cases where there had been negligent injury in the process and nor was it limited to suing only the recalcitrant patient.[157]

In summing up his position, *Zimmermann* stated that, flowing from the *actio contra mensorem*, the standard of liability was that of *culpa lata*, of which the following were examples: abandonment without convincing grounds of a patient whose treatment had been undertaken;[158] use of incorrect chemical abbreviations or providing the weight of medicines using abbreviations and causing errors harmful to the patient, and, '…if he contravenes the generally accepted rules of medical practice through ignorance, lack of skill or absence of attention or care.'[159] This latter reflects the standard given by *Henke* that was cited by *Bauridl* and, as such, mirrors the approach in the criminal law: breaching the occupational duty – described in terms readily commensurate in practice with the *Kunstfehler* – was, itself, *culpa lata*.[160]

There were, ultimately, however, clear difficulties in basing the approach on the *actio contra mensorem*. First there was contemporary judicial authority from the *OAG Lübeck* that the action was merely subsidiary and was only available in so far as damages were not recoverable under another action.[161] Secondly, *Hefke*, amongst others,[162] disputed that the *actio contra mensorem* still had liability for

156 Bauridl (1874) 328, 340.

157 Arnold (1853) 578. *Arnold* reports a case where, the healed patient having refused to pay, a surgeon sued the person who had wrongfully injured them. He sought to claim not only his fees but also his legal fees from having to bring the case. The court allowed the first but denied the second, noting that they had not, on proper analysis, been caused by the defendant's actions, citing *OAGE 28.03.1845* 1109 42/43. (Likely the *Munich OAG* but he noted in the preface that the citations are to the case numbers for his fellow judges more than for other readers for whom it would merely be of interest that there were decisions to cite.)

158 There, the practitioner moving to a new house was a suitable excuse, as was a personal hindrance such as illness, a patient's failure to follow prescribed instructions, or the patient's loss of confidence in the practitioner, Zimmermann (1873) 238.

159 Zimmermann (1873) 237–238. As an example of the latter he gave prescribing greater than the generally accepted maximum dose of a dangerous substance.

160 Bauridl (1874) 341.

161 Basing themselves on D.11.6.3.2 and D.11.6.3.3. See also Glück (1809) 380. *Glück* pointed to the fact that when it came to remunerated services, a relationship of *locatio conductio* often ruled out the *actio contra mensorem*.

162 Windscheid (1875) § 404 n 4, 515. Having, as had medical practitioners, lost the sense that it was beneath them to work for money, or non-altruistically, the basis for the higher standard of liability '…falls away in the modern day.'

*culpa lata* at its heart and instead argued that the modern *mensor* was now liable for '*omnis culpa*'.[163] Indeed, the *OAG Lübeck* had also stressed that the prevailing view was now that a claim for *culpa levis* would be allowed if the defendant had been remunerated, blurring the boundary considerably with *Dienstmiethe*.[164] This view was confirmed in a subsequent decision of the *OAG Oldenburg* reviewing the literature.[165] Finally, the practical difficulty of an action with true roots in the *actio contra mensorem* was that this would have risked a potentially indeterminate range of plaintiffs given the action's availability to anyone who had an interest in the provision of an accurate measurement, or, analogously, medical treatment.[166] Indeed, had the analogy been pursued, the flexible approach taken by the classical jurists to the action's application would at least have left it well-placed to deal with the liability of untrained practitioners who engaged in providing medical services as well as more orthodox practitioners,[167] and, equally, would have provided a non-delegable liability for the fault of a person the practitioner engaged in their own stead.[168]

Yet, despite its nature as an outlier amongst the scholarly texts of the age, and its rejection in court,[169] the publication of his article in such a highly regarded journal, *Zimmermann's* own experience as a judge, *Bauridl's* endorsement of it as reflecting not merely the position of the *gemeines Recht* but also of the *Landrecht* in *Bayern*, and its support in the medico-legal literature, mean this view cannot so easily be ignored, and the absence of a definitive ruling on the categorisation of the medical practitioner permits the conclusion that his view reflected at least part of the situation in nineteenth-century practice.

### 4. Unorthodox practice

So far, this chapter has focused, mainly, on the law as it concerned orthodox practitioners. This final part considers the – sociological if not formally legal – category of unorthodox practitioners. To what extent was their liability affected by the various doctrinal approaches, if at all? There was – in practice if not in scholarly theory – no difficulty with such a practitioner sealing a contract for their services, and they were certainly as vulnerable to a delictual liability as their

163 Unterholzner (1840) § 521, 376; Hefke (1886b) 153.

164 *OAG Lübeck 31.10.1870* Seuffert's Archiv 25, 187–188. See also Glück (1809) 385; Windscheid (1875) § 404 n 4, 515 noting that this had been the case in the post-classical Roman law.

165 *OAG Oldenburg 22.02.1875* Seuffert's Archiv 31, 299.

166 D.11.6.3.1.

167 D.11.6.7.2.

168 D.11.6.2.1.

169 *OAG Oldenburg 22.02.1875* Seuffert's Archiv 31, 297.

licensed, orthodox brethren. But for those who sought to rely on the higher social standing of medicine to rule out a contractual analysis, unorthodox practitioners, and thus the extra-contractual scheme to which they were relegated, were potentially problematic. Understanding how fault was analysed for such practitioners and the extent, if any, to which it differed, based on their standing, to that of the orthodox practitioner, demonstrates the degree to which the law privileged one over the other.

It is certainly clear that Pandectist authors regarded *culpa* as supplying an abstract, objective standard of conduct expected in each situation.[170] The key question then was whether there was a separate standard of care applied in practice to the average unorthodox practitioner. It was not absurd to suggest that the law could recognise the reality of these distinctions in the medical marketplace. There had been a passing suggestion in the early literature that in assessing whether the defendant had been negligent, their location may have been relevant as a repository of local mores and customs.[171] But later authors cautioned against the dangers of allowing such logic to undermine the mores of the wider population.[172] Indeed, although there are few civil cases to draw on, and unorthodox practice did not often feature in scholarly discussions about medical liability, it seems likely that the standard expected from such medical practitioners was, in reality, likely that of orthodox medical practice.

Discussing delict, *Arnold* had suggested in 1844 that a quack (the fantastically designated '*Nichtarzt*') would have been liable in delict for the harm suffered by their patient on the basis that taking on the practice of a, '…science, which he did not himself possess', would itself be regarded as *culpa*.[173] Neither previous success at a procedure, nor being called upon to provide it would exculpate an unorthodox practitioner.[174] *Mommsen* had taken a similar, albeit generalised, position with regard to liability for a skilled activity; the justification for liability lay in the fact, '…that the obligor had set himself to the task despite lacking the skill.'[175] *Hepp* had deployed similar logic to rebut *Mittermaier's* insistence on a *culpa lata* standard for orthodox practice.[176] What the argument lacked in failing to acknowledge the reality of medical provision, it made up for in reflecting the

170 Mommsen (1855) 364; Deutsch (1963) 14.

171 Hasse (1838) 103–104.

172 Mommsen (1855) 365 n 5.

173 Arnold (1853) 578. Cited by Bauridl (1874) 342.

174 Arnold (1853) 579. Citing a decision from 1845 where a cartman had allowed an unorthodox practitioner, who had presented himself as a 'horse and medical expert' to administer a drink to his sick horse. The horse died and the practitioner was held liable, *OAGE 08.02.1845*, 259 41/42.

175 Mommsen (1855) 366. See also Hasse (1838) 93.

176 Hepp (1838) 29.

approach of § 199 *PStGB* – albeit without the safety valve of not penalising such practitioners where a licensed practitioner was, in fact, unavailable – which had treated remunerated quackery as, without more, an offence. What is further striking about this approach to fault is that not only was it a clear parallel to the position in the criminal law, but that, certainly in later editions of his work, *Arnold* was citing a collection of civil decisions in support of his claim, suggesting that this was more than mere academic argument.[177] *Zimmermann* had gone so far as to suggest, in line with D.11.6.1.1, that where the patient chose a less qualified or experienced practitioner they themselves would be to blame for any resulting harm.[178] In time, *Bauridl* offered a more nuanced variant. He endorsed *Arnold's* approach to *culpa* as, '…scarcely without fail, correct', where the patient thought they were getting a legitimate medical practitioner, but distinguished it from the position where the *patient* knew that their healthcare provider was a charlatan and entrusted their wellbeing to him or her nevertheless. There, the patient stood *in pari turpitudine*, and was as much the author of their own destruction.[179]

A somewhat contrasting position was adopted by the *OAG Oldenburg* in the 1875 decision that *Hefke* relied on, and suggested instead that the fault would lie in failing to meet the standard of an orthodox practitioner, not merely undertaking unorthodox practice. There, the defendant had been a licensed apothecary who had, in addition and without license, practiced as a vet. The decision is therefore notable in that it deals not only with unlicensed practice, but rather with dabbling by a licensed practitioner beyond his authorised remit. There, the reasoning of the court below, that the defendant's *culpa* lay in not having the requisite certification, had been rejected: 'Both, holder of a concession or not, are, in principle, not to be differentiated.'[180] It was understandable that, given the prevailing view that a scientific education was necessary for the practice of medicine, the standard of a 'prudent medical practitioner' could only be demanded from someone who had undergone that training. But this did not mean the unlicensed practitioner could offer a lower standard and, in this, the court appears to have rejected a separate standard for unorthodox practice. Acknowledging that the skill of unlicensed practitioners sufficed in many cases, the question was whether in any given situation their skill would suffice. It was for the unorthodox practitioner to assess this themselves and, if they had any

177 Arnold (1853) 578–579 citing, at 579 n 1: Hufnagel (1846) 409, this has proven unavailable.

178 Zimmermann (1873) 228.

179 Bauridl (1874) 342–343.

180 *OAG Oldenburg 22.02.1875* Seuffert's Archiv 31, 300.

doubts, to refrain. The correct standard in that case had been to ask what would be expected from a, '...veterinarian of the customary (average) type'.[181] This appears to have been the same approach taken in a later case, which focused on the incorrect use of cocaine as an anaesthetic by a natural healer who offered dentistry services, in the course of which, he killed a young girl.[182] It was not impossible then for the unorthodox practitioner to escape civil liability, but they practiced at their own risk and, as in the criminal law, appeared to be held to the standard of their orthodox brethren.

## 5. Conclusions

*Watson* was correct that the lack of a delictual remedy for injured freeborn patients was a failure of the imagination in classical Roman law.[183] He suggests that the social context of medical practice overwhelmed the chance for delictual remedies to be used to create such an action. This is an important point. It suggests that the iteration of legal rules may be heavily influenced by the context in which they were created. Roman law failed to develop as Roman medicine did, but perhaps this would have been different had medical practice itself been more coherent. Nevertheless, as with the law of contract, this Roman model was a significant formant of legal life in the nineteenth century. It characterised nineteenth-century German law and, in so doing, weakened it against the encroachment of extra-legal influences as it was left for the contextual application of general rules to admit any form, if desired at all, of specialised rules for medical error.

Yet the role of a delictual claim in contemporary German life was, in keeping with the general development of the law of delict in this era, of far greater relevance than it would have been for much of the Roman period. The eventual shucking off of the myriad restrictions on bringing an action, and the extension of the damages recoverable to encompass the patient's pain and suffering in the form of *Schmerzensgeld*, would have provided an attractive route to those few who could afford to bring a civil action, offering as it did a broader scope of recovery than in contract. Yet the emergence of this clear, generalised pattern for delictual recovery in nineteenth-century Germany was a haphazard process, retarded considerably by the purist approach to the Roman sources, and of uncertain value to many outside the various legislative pockets where such a rule, in principle, pertained. Whilst the approach to fault matched that of the

181 *OAG Oldenburg 22.02.1875* Seuffert's Archiv 31, 297.

182 *Aerztliches Vereinsblatt* (1896) 447.

183 Watson (1988) 79.

emerging contractual consensus, which is to say simple fault assessed against expert evidence of orthodox medical practice, this did not go entirely uncontested. Indeed, although the various available civil actions, whether contractual or delictual, might concur, this was not enough to dissuade hardy souls such as *Zimmermann* and *Bauridl* from advocating or – to take their evidence from practice at face value – reflecting in their writing a solution, which, in repurposing the *actio contra mensorem*, was to be applauded more for the ingenuity of its treatment of the Roman sources than for its likely accuracy. That the more indulgent standard of care that lay at the heart of that claim played a large part in convincing *Zimmermann* to adopt this as his preferred scholarly rationale of the practitioner-patient relationship suggests, as seen in the criminal law of this period, a continuing preference by some for a position that would have placed the practitioner at a significant advantage. This may be leavened by the finding that, even for *Zimmermann*, it appears that a *Kunstfehler* would have satisfied this standard, but the rhetorical overlap with the internal, medical view of error remains. As to unorthodox practice, we again find that the civil law here appears to have followed the position of the criminal law in that the standard of the orthodox practitioner was, in practice, determinative of the standard for the various para-medical, unorthodox practitioners who continued to play a large role in the medical marketplace.

Chapter 5

# Medical Error and the BGB

'Medical liability is no new invention [...]; and its present-day form deserves no reproach'[1]

'Juridical and medical thinking differ greatly from one another'[2]

## 1. Introduction

In this chapter, we look at the further development of the law relating to medical error in the years between 1900 and 1945. This period is bounded at one end by the coming into effect, in 1900, of the first comprehensive civil law code for Imperial Germany, the *Bürgerliches Gesetzbuch* (*BGB*) and, at the other, by the suspension of the national legal system, and the abolition of the *Reichsgericht* in 1945. It has been established in the previous chapters that medical error was the subject of vigorous discussion in both legal and medical circles during the nineteenth century. That trend continued during this period. However, whereas the legal literature was relatively sparse and often touched on medical error in passing or as a topic defined by the general approach to an area of the law, the early twentieth century saw an explosion in the number of scholarly works directly concerned with medical error and the legal analysis of myriad aspects of medical practice.[3] These begin to appear remarkably quickly following the enactment of the *BGB* and, in some cases such as *Rabel's* 1904 work *'Die Haftpflicht des Arztes'*, or *Ebermayer's* 1924 volume *'Arzt und Patient in der Rechtsprechung'*, were authored by the leading legal minds of the day.[4]

1 Rabel (1904) 4.

2 König/Kostlin (1937) 23.

3 Writing in 1903, *Kollbrunner* noted that despite *Zimmermann's* statement in 1873 that the nature of medical liability had received little discussion in the legal literature it had been subject to a kaleidoscopic range of analyses since then, see Kollbrunner (1903).

4 Although less well-known to later generations, *Ebermayer* had been a judge of the *Reichsgericht*, and, at the time of publication, was the *Oberreichsanwalt* to that court and, as such, one of the senior-most legal practitioners in the country.

A single or simple explanation for this is unclear, but the fact that the *BGB* offered, for the first time, a brilliant clarity of doctrinal foundation, in comparison to the confusion of the previous century, provides a plausible explanation for why a range of legal problems could now be discussed repeatedly and at such length. But this explanation ought not to be oversimplified and it seems unlikely that the mere emergence of a fixed, unified model of the civil law accounts for the rapid change in the nature and extent of the legal literature. It was in the period covered by this chapter that the social and regulatory groundwork of orthodox medical practitioners in seeking to secure their place as the dominant providers of healthcare began to take hold. The practice of orthodox medicine came, more and more, to involve new advances and technologies, and the shift to hospital-based care was cemented, often increasing the invasive nature of the medical treatment possible. These developments in medical practice, alongside the firm foundation of the *BGB*, prompted a greater need for legal analysis of the practitioner-patient relationship in all its guises. Certainly, the number of cases appears to have rocketed and, as always, a healthy market for practising lawyers was closely tied to the presence of extended scholarly treatment. The large number of litigated cases is visible in the many commentaries on the *BGB*, which emerged during this period, albeit they offered little by way of systematisation in comparison to their modern equivalent.[5]

The form medical liability took in the *BGB* may have been general rather than specific, but a remarkably abundant specific literature appeared during the early twentieth century.[6] As discussed below, there was not yet a coherent enough body of rules to suggest a freestanding '*Arztrecht*', but the volume of literature that medical error generated in this pre-1945 period is, given the tendency to treat medical error as a problem born from the relationship between the post-war legal structures and medical practice, surprising, and much of it will form the subject of this chapter. Yet what is striking in much of it is the urgency with which it reflects an increasing number of claims for medical error along with the perception, common to twenty-first-century lawyers, that this represented an immediate threat to good medical practice.[7] Equally, as the century progressed, there appear fewer cases where the basis for the argument over appropriate

5 Strohal (1928) 955, 1732–1734; Kober/Engelmann/Geiler (1929) 1790–1791; Keidel (1931) 123, 372; Soergel (1931) 947–948; Lobe/Oegg/Schliewen/Seuffarth (1934) 261–263; Palandt (1939) 775–776; Soergel (1939) 569–571.

6 *Rümelin* noted that there, '…exists a considerable literature concerning medical responsibility for *Kunstfehlers*', Rümelin (1913) 6.

7 Representative examples may be found in Rapmund/Dietrich (1913) 173; Haberland (1932) 3304; and Bremer (1934) 1.

practice was, in reality, a counterclaim aimed at avoiding the bill.[8] Few offered any attempt at an explanation as to why that might be the case. The increasing rigour of medical, particularly surgical, treatment, which blossomed in this period, alongside the clarity of the available legal tools and a social shift towards litigation rather than gratitude regardless of result, offer plausible factors for this process.[9]

Similarly evident, albeit difficult to mark, was a shift away from the criminal law as both a common tool for dealing with the negligence of orthodox medical practitioners,[10] and as a fount for legal analysis of the problem. Although the analysis of civil fault under the *BGB* drew on the rationalisation that had taken place under the *StGB*, this gave way to freestanding analysis of the civil law as the concepts of fault in each area diverged more clearly,[11] even if this was often overlooked by medical practitioners.[12] The criminal law remained relevant for the analysis of unorthodox liability and the many attempts at reform of the *StGB* saw fruitless efforts to enact a privilege for orthodox medical practitioners (*'Berufsrecht'* or sometimes *'Eigenmacht'*) designed to limit the burgeoning field of consent-based liability;[13] equally, greater control over prosecutorial discretion was provided late on in the period.[14] It was suggested that in many cases a criminal prosecution preceded civil proceedings, '…in order to save costs',[15] and that a fine, the award of which ruled out a future civil claim, was only sought where the plaintiff had no desire to try for a higher sum in the civil courts.[16] But, whilst the continued availability of criminal fines might have limited the attractiveness of a civil claim at first,[17] the sums awarded for immaterial harm, aided by the concurrency of the obligations in delict and contract,[18] quickly outstripped the criminal law's 6,000M limit.[19] It was, however, a risk to do so, as successful criminal prosecution was no guarantee of a civil sanction.[20] There was generally little discussion of the potential use of § 823 (2) *BGB* in conjunction with the various relevant *'Schutzgesetze'* of the *StGB*, suggesting that this was an

8 Rabel (1904) 21; Hübner / Warneyer (1939) 169.
9 König / Kostlin (1937) 44.
10 Hübner / Warneyer (1939) 170.
11 Schermaier (2007) 1144–1145.
12 Rümelin (1913) 10–11.
13 Riegger (2007) 97–105, 119–120.
14 Ibid., noting the changes to § 232 *StGB*.
15 Rapmund / Dietrich (1913) 173.
16 Joachim / Korn (1911) 368, suggesting that often the patient did not claim a fine.
17 Rabel (1904) 5.
18 Rümelin (1913) 37 n 1.
19 Hübner / Drost (1955) 21–22.
20 Joachim / Korn (1911) 368.

infrequently used route to compensation for medical injury.[21] The *StGB* thus went unaltered during the period that saw it joined by the *BGB*, but the relevance of the criminal law was undermined by the high degree of protection given by the *BGB* to interests in the body. Provisions of the *StGB*, which had no counterpart in the civil law such as the duty of secrecy (*Schweigepflicht*, § 300 *StGB*) or supplying a false medical certificate, § 278 *StGB*, were, however, more likely to benefit from the interface provided by § 823 (2) *BGB*.[22] In short, insofar as it concerned medical error, the criminal law was of decreasing relevance in comparison to the civil throughout this period.

This chapter now examines four topics: First, the effect that the *BGB* had on the categorisation and doctrinal analysis of an action for medical error, in particular the various contractual actions that might arise with the increased prevalence of insurance practice. Secondly, we will examine the analysis of fault under the *BGB*. Here we take advantage of the large rise in the number of reported decisions to detail the extent of liability for medical error and the increasing dislocation between legal and medical conceptions of error, each examined in the previous chapters, as the decades passed. Following the initial continuity of the relevance of medical conceptions of error, it will be established that the courts increasingly moved, often in the face of scholarly criticism, to decouple a finding of fault from the idea of a *Kunstfehler*; in effect, unwilling to defer to the expert view. As part of this process, we, thirdly, look in detail at two case studies, which focus on specific examples of common liability-generating situations from this period: liability based on X-rays and diathermy, and for retained foreign bodies. Both these situations allow us to analyse how the courts dealt with the increasing availability of technology and the impact of medical advances in this period. Finally, we consider the impact of the Nazi regime on the development of the law following the seizure of power in 1933.

The picture that emerges from this period is increasing control exercised by judges over what constituted appropriate medical practice. The high degree of control over the contours of liability enjoyed by orthodox practitioners came under assault on a number of fronts. The concept of a *Kunstfehler* as inherently tied to a sociological, medically-defined form of behaviour gradually yielded as courts increasingly asserted their own competence to examine and critique accepted practice. The key question then becomes what, if anything, was it that they put in its place as a guiding rationale, and what explains this position?

21 Rabel (1904) 5–6 mentions this without examples.

22 Bremer (1934) 14; König/Kostlin (1937) 8–9.

## 2. Categorising medical error in the *BGB*

In this part, we examine the changes heralded by the coming into force of the *BGB* in January 1900. This was the first time that a unified civil law had been established for the whole of the Empire and, at a stroke, created a new foundation for the civil law relationship between medical practitioner and patient. The basic model enacted by the *BGB* as it stood in 1900 remained, as with the law of obligations generally, unchanged until 2002, with further changes specific to our subject finally following in 2013.[23]

The *BGB* confirmed the fundamental nature of medical liability as a form of liability governed by general provisions.[24] Liability for medical error was, and until the enactment of the *Patientenrechtegesetz* in 2013 would remain, governed by the general rules on liability, nominally applicable to any and all defendants.[25] A mark of this is discernible in the literature of the period given '*Arztrecht*', or similar terms such as '*Arzthaftung*' or the perhaps broader '*Medizinrecht*' – any of which might suggest that the law was being developed as a coherent, free-standing body of interpretive rules – were not yet in common usage.[26] The titles of *Rabel's* or *Ebermayer's* respective works were more demonstrative of contemporary thought although *Köbler* is wrong to suggest that the term was absent from the literature before 1938.[27]

The relevant part of the code itself was largely, although – following the protests which emerged when the first draft was made public in 1887 – not entirely, the product of the Pandectist scholarship of the nineteenth century discussed in the preceding chapters and the positivism which defined the late nineteenth century.[28] Whilst it was drafted by committee, *Windscheid*, whose textbook had become the repository of a century's worth of Pandectist effort, was a member of the First Commission and his influence – additionally present through the inclusion of a number of respected practitioners on the Commission – was instrumental in drafting the *BGB*'s law of obligations.[29] The influence of these weighty intellectual forerunners lent the substance of the German law of obligations in the twentieth century its characteristic quality and also, generally, accounted for the dogmatic (in)elegance of the style in which the *BGB* was written.[30] This was perhaps most notable in the highly abstracted manner of the

23 Riegger (2007) 97; Katzenmeier (2002) 85 f; Stauch (2015).
24 Weinrich (1902) 34.
25 Köbler (2009) 168.
26 Ibid. 170.
27 For example, see, Joachim / Korn (1911).
28 Wieacker (1995) 371–374.
29 Wieacker (1995) 374–375.
30 Wieacker (1995) 373, 375.

provisions, and the division of the code into a preceding General Part, collecting those conceptual elements common to multiple areas, followed by books dealing with the specific legal relationships.[31]

### (A) *Arbeitsverträge* in the *BGB*

The immediate contribution of the *BGB* to medical liability was the availability of a single, defined contractual regime to govern the provision of services by medical practitioners. On the basis of the foregoing chapters it was clear that, certainly at a theoretical level, the *gemeines Recht* had been particularly opaque in this regard, and that a scholar's opinion hinged largely on their view of medical practice and practitioners. These differences of opinion over the social standing of medical practice could now, at least, be measured with reference to the fixed point of the code.[32] In the relevant part, the drafters opted for a broad category of '*Arbeitsverträge*' within which there was a simple division between a contract to produce work (*Werkvertrag*) and a service contract (*Dienstvertrag*). The latter was defined in § 611 *BGB* as follows:

> *'Vertragstypische Pflichten beim Dienstvertrag.*
> *(1) Durch den Dienstvertrag wird derjenige, welcher Dienste zusagt, zur Leistung der versprochenen Dienste, der andere Theil zur Gewährung der vereinbarten Vergütung verpflichtet.*
>
> *(2) Gegenstand des Dienstvertrags können Dienste jeder Art sein.'*

This instantly undermined the position of those who had sought to maintain a distinction in contract law between the so-called liberal and illiberal or higher and lower forms of labour. § 611 (2) *BGB* explicitly abolished the distinction that had so plagued the discussion in the nineteenth-century literature; any form of labour, and thus all forms of remunerated medical practice, could now, theoretically, be encompassed under this modern, German form of *locatio conductio operarum*. This was aided in part by the fact that the model of mandate (*Auftrag*) adopted in the *BGB* focused on an unremunerated relationship, thus firming up that formerly contested boundary.[33] As such, mandate was relevant where a practitioner was offering treatment individually and out of charity with no expectation of payment, but the literature of the era assumed that this was an exceptional case. As *Hellwig* observed, whilst in common speech the practitioner

31 Wieacker (1995) 376–377, 385.

32 See generally Rückert (2013b), noting, at 831, the radically egalitarian and general model provided by § 611 *BGB* – whereby *locatio conductio* was, in effect, universalised – in comparison with the two centuries that had preceded it.

33 Hegener (1925) 13, 16

might say that, '…he was mandated to come to his patients', this was no reflection of the legal conception of the relationship.[34] The formal justification given for this was, as *Windscheid* had noted since 1866, and contemporary regional codifications had demonstrated,[35] that the modern conditions of society and enterprise no longer lent themselves to such a distinction between forms of contract.[36] Indeed as one commentator emphasised, the fact that even some Honour Courts had, by the turn of the century, come to consider the absence of any sort of remuneration (*Entgelt*) for the efforts of a practitioner as an affront to their honour, suggested the lofty aims of orthodox medical practice were considered by practitioners themselves as reconcilable with earning a living.[37]

The point had not gone uncontested in the drafting process. *Loewenfeld*, commenting on the first – ultimately unchanged – draft of § 611 *BGB*, had been fiercely critical of equating all forms of service. Whilst concerned with so-called liberal callings generally, he held fast, in particular, to the idea that orthodox medicine was an uncertain and noble practice carried out in the service of humanity rather than with the aim of making a living.[38] This view of medical practice apparently ruled out the use of *locatio conductio operarum* as the patient was unable to specify the service, which a medical practitioner ought to perform. As he noted, '…the medical practitioner – and thus is there no distinction between modern and Roman medicine – directs the patient, and is not directed by them.'[39] Equally, and despite the *Gewerbeordnung* 1869, which, he noted, orthodox practitioners were by then openly protesting, the equation at private law of all forms of medical practice as 'services of every type' was neither in the interests of practitioners nor patients. Medical practice was, regardless of its public law categorisation, an *ars liberalis* defined by its scientific underpinning, and the draft threatened to undermine that entirely.[40]

Nevertheless, the draft went unaltered in that respect and medical practitioners were, finally, permitted to engage in a contract for remunerated services without fear of debate.[41] Indeed, in a further recognition of existing practice, a number of provisions recognised the relevance of tariffs or simply 'customary compensation' as guides for the amount of remuneration due under these

34 Joachim/Korn (1911) 340; Hellwig (1905) 16.

35 Anders/Gehle (2001) 4.

36 Hegener (1925) 11, noting that this had been relied on, in part, in the drafting of the *BGB*, see Mugdan (1899) § 456.

37 Hegener (1925) 12.

38 Löwenfeld (1890) 893–894.

39 Ibid. 894.

40 Ibid. 913–914.

41 Rückert (2013b) 843–845, 862.

contracts where there was nothing to suggest otherwise.[42] Substantial numbers of regional tariffs, or provisions for the prices to be fixed by the state ministries, continued to govern the payment of practitioners well into the twentieth century.[43] Alongside the adoption of the will-based model of contract familiar from the nineteenth century, the classification of the relationship between medical practitioner and patient in normal circumstances as a contract remained clear.[44] With the characteristically unadorned model of contract as agreement reflected in the *BGB*, no formality was required to found the contractual relationship, but in practice it would spring into existence upon agreement, evidenced through explicit or implicit conduct by the practitioner, or their assistants,[45] to treat the patient.[46] It was insufficient that the patient was merely in the waiting room, or that the practitioner had just hung their sign outside the building, or advertised in the papers;[47] in all but exceptional cases, a practitioner could not be forced to contract their services. Such cases were regulated by § 360 (1) 10 *StGB* dealing generally with a citizen's failure to offer necessary aid in the event of an accident, although it bears remembering that the Honour Courts saw fit to police such omissions as well.[48]

Despite the generality of the provisions in the *BGB*, there were several issues specific to the contractual analysis of medical practice that received detailed treatment for the first time in the initial decades of the twentieth century, as legal analysis of the practitioner-patient relationship offered an extended, contextualised, specific approach within the associated scholarship. The absence of '*Arztvertrag*' – like '*Arztrecht*' – from the first two editions of the *Grimms' Deutsches Wörterbuch* suggested that it had not been recognised as a freestanding topic for doctrinal analysis.[49] Yet, as part of the raft of new literature dedicated to the subject of medical liability, scholarship dedicated to the '*Arztvertrag*' began to appear as early as 1905.[50] Writing in 1925, *Hegener*, who confined himself to orthodox practitioners,[51] argued that the abrupt, albeit foreshadowed, shift to abandoning a distinction between the forms of labour had caused difficulties

42 § 612 (2) *BGB*.

43 See the 18 schemes listed in Hegener (1925) 40.

44 Rabel (1904) 5–6.

45 Hegener (1925) 29.

46 Flügge (1903) 59–60; Rabel (1904) 6; Bremer (1934) 8.

47 Hegener (1925) 28.

48 Bremer (1934) 8.

49 Köbler (2009) 168–169.

50 Ibid. 170. The earliest example he cites was a dissertation (which has proven unavailable for this work), Teufel (1919), but there was also Meyer (1905). However, the trend was not universal, see Hellwig (1905) 15 f.

51 Hegener (1925) 8.

with the contractual analysis as this distinctly un-Roman view of society had to be reconciled with the overtly Roman logic of the *BGB's* law of obligations.[52] Furthermore, he argued, the neutral view of the law as to the moral worth of a contractual task created an additional incongruity, which was particularly challenging for the legal analysis of the patient–practitioner relationship.[53]

### (i) Settling the contractual debate

Reminiscent of the confusion the Pandectists had laboured under, which precise type of contract to actually apply to the practitioner-patient relationship remained, at least at first, the subject of much debate.[54] Early authors, such as *Flügge* in 1903[55] and *Rabel*, in 1904,[56] were certainly of the opinion that, as far as treatment was concerned, the question was beyond doubt (as the latter put it) and clearly fell to be analysed as a service contract on the basis, shared by many other contemporaries,[57] that the underlying bifurcation of the obligations assumed under a service contract and a contract for work made the latter unsuitable. Under the former, as § 611 (1) made clear, the contractual debtor was only obliged to perform the agreed service rather than achieve a specific result; under the latter it was expected that the promised work would indeed be produced, that a specific result would, indeed, be achieved.[58] As in the *gemeines Recht*, the assumption remained that a medical practitioner did not agree to the latter concerning the obligation to treat their patient. But this understanding of the distinction between the two forms of contract was, at least at first, not universally accepted and at least two main lines of counter-argument were advanced in favour of viewing the practitioner-patient relationship as a contract for work, particularly where the author sought to establish a different way of distinguishing the obligation owed. The first, adopted by *Lotmar*, sought to divide the contracts depending on whether there had been an agreement to pay based on time or the work achieved. The latter, more appropriate for most forms of medical treatment, corresponded with a contract for work.[59] The second, adopted by *Rümelin*, preferred to focus on who bore the risk within the

52 Hegener (1925) 11.
53 Ibid. 12–13.
54 Bremer (1934) 2, describing it as 'highly contested'.
55 Flügge (1903) 64.
56 Rabel (1904) 76.
57 Hegener (1925) 14.
58 Markesinis / Unberath / Johnston (2006) 528.
59 Hegener (1925) 14. *Lotmar's* view was heavily contested, see Joachim / Korn (1911) 348.

contract.[60] A third view, advanced by *Enneccerus* and *Lehman* amongst others, adopted a middle ground and preferred to see the contractual obligations as mixed on the basis that some of the duties undertaken by a practitioner were susceptible to analysis as having promised a specific result.[61] Finally, some scholars including earlier editions of the influential *Staudinger* commentary, had even gone so far as to suggest that the particular power relationship between practitioner and patient meant that both forms of contract were inappropriate as it was inappropriate to say that the former submitted to the latter's instructions, and that, instead, a *sui generis* contract ought to be constructed to encompass it.[62]

In such a way, a form of the old division between higher and lower forms of labour would have been retained and, for some, would have required an inquiry into whether the treatment offered was of a higher (performing a complicated operation) or lower (a dentist fixing a patient's crown) nature with the contractual obligation differing as required.[63] This was not an entirely unrealistic view of matters and is one that has won greater support over time: Not all medical activities are equally uncertain or best conceived of as requiring a mix of art and science to tackle. Where a matter was not reliant on such an application of the defendant practitioner's talents there was no reason why the obligation could not be categorised as a contract for work and the case would have been particularly strong where the duty undertaken concerned non-clinical matters or, with advances in medical technology, the provision of prosthetics,[64] or the like.[65] *Bremer*, for instance, supported the default choice of a service contract but was of the opinion that matters such as the supply of a medical certificate or the carrying out of an autopsy were susceptible to analysis as a contract for work.[66] *Hegener's* opinion, confirmed a decade later by *Bremer*,[67] that a service contract was the dominant view by 1925 vindicated *Rabel's* earlier certainty,[68] and had, by then, been reflected in the case law.[69] But this categorisation was ultimately as much to do with broader contractual dogma about the nature of the obligation assumed than necessarily the juridical conception of medical treatment itself.

60 Hegener (1925) 15.
61 Bremer (1934) 2–3.
62 See Bacharach (1915) 819; Bremer (1934) 3, noting that *Nipperdey*, Staudinger's new overseer, jettisoned the suggestion from later editions.
63 Joachim/Korn (1911) 348; Hegener (1925) 19; König/Kostlin (1937) 5.
64 König/Kostlin (1937) 5.
65 Hübner/Drost (1955) 4, pondering dentistry.
66 Bremer (1934) 6–7.
67 Ibid. 2.
68 Hegener (1925) 12, 21. This remained the default position post-war as well, see Hübner/Drost (1955) 4.
69 Bremer (1934) 2; *RG 01.03.1912* (1912) 41 JW 528; *RG 28.03.1930* RGZ 128, 121.

The debate confirmed a view of medical treatment as a special, and uncertain skill,[70] which could not be guaranteed, indeed this view ossified in legal practice, but also had important corollary effects on the nature of a practitioner's liability as well as associated matters such as the limitation period (considerably longer at 30 years in the case of a *Dienstvertrag*) and parties' respective termination rights, which differed accordingly.[71]

### (ii) The patient as a third party

Further issues flowed from the somewhat complicated schema required to encompass the patient, medical practitioner, institution and insurer. Thus, for a private patient the contract for medical care formed during a consultation with a practitioner, orthodox or otherwise, was simple enough to understand once it was accepted that it would, short of something exceptional (and foolishly unselfish on the part of the practitioner), be regarded as a service contract.[72] In the minority of situations where the patient was unconscious or, say, suffering a fit in the street, and hence unable to offer the necessary corresponding declaration of will, the provisions of the *BGB* concerning *negotiorum gestio* (§§ 677 ff *BGB*) offered a clear way of framing the basis for liability.[73]

Beyond this, the flexibility of German contract law regarding the protection that a contract between A and B might offer to C (found in § 328 *BGB*), came to deal with common situations such as the treatment of children or wives, where the patient was not themselves a party to the contract, and was often used to circumvent the use of *negotiorum gestio* where there was a suitable party to contract on behalf of the patient. In such circumstances, the contract between the parent or spouse and the practitioner might be regarded as stretching to cover the care received by the respective patient. But, despite the assumption of some scholars,[74] this was not an immediate given of the codified law. In 1914, the *Reichsgericht* had denied that there was any contractual protection afforded to a child whose parents contracted for medical care. There, the practitioner summoned to deal with the plaintiff's son, who was suffering a severe nosebleed, had, it was claimed, operated so poorly that two further operations were required to fix the original bungled job leaving the child disfigured.[75] The

70 Hellwig (1905) 17.

71 Giesen (1988) 12.

72 Hübner/Drost (1955) 4; Katzenmeier (2002) 94.

73 Flügge (1903) 62; Rabel (1904); Bremer (1934) 24–25; König/Kostlin (1937) 6; Hübner/Drost (1955) 6.

74 Rabel (1904) 6, who noted that, '…is, naturally, also the rule if a father gets his child treated.'

75 *RG 19.06.1914* RGZ 85, 183.

court was clear that the contract was between the parent and the practitioner, not the child, having neither been made in the child's name, nor through the parent acting as the child's agent in that respect. This position was later abandoned in a decision in 1936.[76] There, the practitioner was at fault in poorly setting a child's fractured elbow with the result that over 60% of the limb's function was lost.[77] A claim for damages on the basis of the child's contractual claim was allowed given that § 823 *BGB* was satisfied despite the fact that, as the court acknowledged, when making the relevant contract with a practitioner, the parents did not, as a matter of course, stress that they were doing so on the child's behalf.[78] The circumstances and aim of the contract's formation, viewed objectively, would indeed support such an analysis.[79]

But the way citizens accessed healthcare complicated the analysis of the legal relationship between practitioner and patient as the model of contract focused on by Pandectist authors diverged from the context in which most treatment occurred. Two situations were commonly addressed: first, where the patient relied on their insurance-fund for access to healthcare; secondly, where a practitioner was appointed as a household practitioner (*Hausarzt*).[80] When it came to the question of whether the third-party patient (there, say the contracting party's servant) had any claim in their own right, the latter situation was unproblematic. The contract was clearly a service contract,[81] and it was made for the benefit of the relevant third parties in the household.[82] More often the problem was rather termination rights and calculation of payment for what was, in effect, an aleatory contract.[83] In each case the continued applicability of a contractual analysis for the practitioner-patient relationship depended on the flexible approach to the rights of a third-party adopted, in principle, in the *BGB*.

In the former, contracts would have been in place between the insurance fund and the patient (encompassing, increasingly, their family members in addition). Thanks to the relational abstraction that the institutionalisation of insurance practice provided, there was no immediate, direct contractual relationship between the patient and the practitioner treating them. Rather, the only direct claim either had was against the fund for, respectively, treatment or payment for

76 Hübner/Drost (1955) 5.
77 *RG 29.09.1936* RGZ 152, 175.
78 *RG 29.09.1936* RGZ 152, 176.
79 *RG 29.09.1936* RGZ 152, 177.
80 Flügge (1903) 63, describing these two situations as 'countless' and 'numerous' respectively; Hegener (1925) 75 f.
81 Joachim/Korn (1911) 351.
82 Flügge (1903) 80; Hegener (1925) 77.
83 Hellwig (1905) 28; Joachim/Korn (1911) 351.

treatment given.[84] The restricted choice of practitioner that was a feature of the nineteenth-century insurance schemes changed in the first decade of the twentieth century as the various efforts of, and strikes organised by, the *Hartmann-Bund*, a popular medical trade union, won a measure of freedom of choice for both patients, and practitioners.[85] In this process they created the four-way set of relationships that pertains in German healthcare to this day. A nexus comprised of the patient, the practitioner (or, often, the hospital), an insurance fund and the relevant insurance-fund practitioners association replaced the direct relationship between practitioner and patient.[86] It was not immediately obvious from this situation that a contractual analysis was to be preferred. As the healthcare reforms of the 1880s began to bite, it had originally been the view that the state insurance funds owed only what was essentially a public law, welfare-based duty towards their subscribers.[87] This was predicated on the inherently public rather than private nature of the subscriber's claims against their insurer, confirmed by the comprehensive social welfare scheme enacted by the *Reichsversicherungsordnung* 1911. As a result, this created a range of views in the literature as to how best, if at all, the practitioner-patient relationship could be founded on a contractual claim. Some, such as *Meyer*, relying on the quasi-public law relationship between the fund and the practitioner, denied any contractual claim between practitioner and patient entirely, or argued that the patient's only recourse for a practitioner's poor treatment was against the fund itself.[88] Even those, such as *Hegener*, who preferred to see some sort of contractual relationship between practitioner and patient preferred to regard it as a direct, bilateral contract, whose contents was the same as that between the fund and the practitioner; '… if the medical practitioner commits a wrong, he is burdened merely with duties, without providing corresponding rights.'[89] These views were, ultimately, rejected by the courts, who preferred *Hellwig's* analysis that the patient was to be afforded third party rights under the contract between the fund and the practitioner.[90] Analysing the patient's relationship within this scheme, the *Reichsgericht* confirmed that both the contractual relationship between a fund-practitioner and the patient's insurance fund, and that between the insurance fund and the receiving hospital were sufficient to ground a

84 Hegener (1925) 81.
85 Labisch (1997) 45.
86 Katzenmeier (2002) 94.
87 Hegener (1925) 80–81; Ebermayer (1924) 95 and König/Kostlin (1937) 4, describing it as an 'public law duty of care'.
88 Hegener (1925) 85, citing Meyer (1905) 20.
89 Ibid. 85.
90 Hellwig (1905) 28; Rabel (1904) 6.

contractual action between the patient and the practitioner or the operator of the hospital on the basis of § 328 (2) *BGB*.[91] The underlying purpose of such contracts, being as it was to provide for the care of the subscribing patient, sufficed to justify reading in this extension, and to provide the patient with a basis for any action, which was fundamentally regarded as being based on the private law.[92] Thus the potential contractual black hole that the party who had suffered the loss had no action, was avoided.[93]

Beyond treatment in a practitioner's own consultancy, an inherent feature of German healthcare was the possibility that the receiving hospital would not always be responsible for all aspects of the treatment. Two variants would become common: The hospital might provide merely the ancillary services such as accommodation and nourishment, or both such services *and* medical care. The latter, the so-called '*totaler Krankenhausvertrag*', focused liability on the hospital itself. In the case of the former, a so-called '*aufgespaltener Arzt-Krankenhausvertrag*', a claim might be taken against the treating practitioner, under a separate contractual action, or the hospital itself, depending on the cause of the patient's injury. This arrangement could cause difficulties for the patient in identifying whose door their claim ought be brought to,[94] but in the majority of cases involving hospital-based care, a patient reliant on their insurance scheme for access to healthcare would by treated under a '*totaler Krankenhausvertrag*'. Although this language to describe the various possible contractual schemes appeared in scholarly writing by the 1950s,[95] it was largely absent in the literature beforehand and indeed the tendency, at least up to the 1930s,[96] to focus on household practitioners before insurance practitioners reflected, in passing, a continuing focus on private practice that had characterised the nineteenth-century scholarship.

### (iii) The scope of the '*Arztvertrag*'

Here we consider the nature of the obligation that the contractual analyses outlined above would place on a practitioner. Given the accepted distinction between a service contract and a contract for work, the core obligation under-

91 *RG 27.09.1915* RGZ 165, 106; *RG 04.06.1915* (1915) 44 JW 916; Ebermayer (1924) 94.

92 *RG 01.6.1915* (1915) 44 JW 916.

93 Ebermayer (1924) 94–95.

94 Laufs (1977) 12.

95 Hübner/Drost (1955) 8.

96 The problems caused by a *Hausarztvertrag* appear absent from the literature at least from 1937 onwards, see König/Kostlin (1937); Hübner/Drost (1955).

taken by the practitioner was simply to apply their skills, according to the *lex artis*,[97] in trying to heal the patient rather than achieve a cure.[98] Echoing the language earlier adopted by *Oppenheim*,[99] authors summarised a practitioner's duty as being 'healing, alleviation or improvement' or a variant thereof.[100] Yet there were, at least formally, difficulties in linking negligent performance of that obligation to the contract under which it was owed.

The law of contract as laid down in the *BGB* was, despite intentions, hardly perfect and revealed one of the drawbacks of relying on the Pandectist view of the law of obligations. On its face, the code provided for only two ways in which a contract could be breached, impossibility of performance and delayed performance.[101] Certainly where the performance was initially impossible, the former did not appear to cause much trouble; practitioners were not in the habit of promising objectively impossible treatment.[102] More likely however were situations of intervening impossibility, which blended into situations where performance was delayed. Performance in these cases often meant a pre-arranged visit to the patient, and the myriad emergencies that might arise with other patients or sickness on the part of the practitioner themselves suggested that, in practice, a practitioner would be able to avoid a claim on the basis that they had not caused the situation.[103] Nevertheless, there was an expectation, based on the duty to perform in good faith per § 242 *BGB*,[104] that a practitioner would notify the patient of their inability to attend, with failure to do so resulting in liability for any harm thus caused.[105] Equally, where the details and timing of a consultation had not been fixed earlier, it was suggested that the requirement of performance in good faith allowed a broad discretion on the part of the practitioner as to how to proceed.[106]

97 Joachim / Korn (1911) 352–353, '…payment does not depend on the consequence of the service performed. It suffices that they could and should have been able to succeed in accordance with the rules or medical practice and scholarship (*lex artis*).'

98 König / Kostlin (1937) 5.

99 Oppenheim (1892) 21 f.

100 Joachim / Korn (1911) 352, 371; Rabel (1904) 36.

101 Zimmermann (1996) 810–814.

102 Bremer (1934) 9.

103 Ibid. 10, noting that, regarding liability for delay, there was division in the literature as to whether the requirement of issuing the defaulting debtor with a warning (*Mahnung*) applied to medical practitioners.

104 Hegener (1925) 33; Bremer (1934) 10. *Bremer* regarded it as highly unlikely that a case could be maintained for delay in performance, noting that such cases were only very seldom seen.

105 Joachim / Korn (1911) 362.

106 Hegener (1925) 35.

More likely, and given considerably greater attention in the literature, were situations where a practitioner had simply performed negligently. In response to this gap in the legal architecture of the *BGB* the *Reichsgericht* undertook the swift development of liability based on merely defective performance. Despite the inelegant suggestion to treat § 276 *BGB*,[107] examined in greater detail in the following parts, as a basis for liability in and of itself, this was ultimately achieved on the basis of a theory advanced by *Staub* and provided a remedy of damages for the negligent violation of a contractual duty provided there was no other remedy available.[108] § 276 *BGB* was, as originally intended, relegated to describing when an obligation would be breached, not providing the source of it, an interpretation attributed to *Mommsen's* misreading of the Roman sources.[109]

The remedy for injury flowing from the breach of a service contract between practitioner and patient could be found in § 280 (1) which clarified that the breach of a duty, whether contractual or otherwise, could sound in damages. Although, in line with the emphasis on contractual performance adopted in the *BGB*, doing so was possible, particularly where a practitioner had agreed to provide medicaments as well as treatment and it was common to simply accept damages in lieu of performance.[110] § 249 (1) *BGB* provided that such awards were intended to put the plaintiff in the position they would have been in had the breach not occurred.

### (B) The role of delict

Whilst the nature of German healthcare, alongside the flexibility of contractual doctrine, ensured that a contractual model of healthcare endured, there was, naturally, an alternative route to compensation in the form of general delictual liability. Again, nothing was specifically provided for medical practitioners.[111] In this section we consider the delictual actions open firstly to private patients, and, secondly, the special regime established for public institutions such as university clinics. Delict was useful in that it provided patients whose contract was with the institution rather than their practitioner (albeit that the practitioner, as agent of the institution was carrying out the treatment) a residual action where, for whatever reason, a claim against the institution itself was unavailable, and, equally, an action encompassing a claim for damages for pain and suffering.[112]

107 Bremer (1934) 12.
108 Dannemann (1993) 31.
109 Wieacker (1995) 412.
110 Rabel (1904) 20.
111 Flügge (1903) 84.
112 Ebermayer (1924) 97.

### (i) Private patients and wrongfulness

The *BGB* provided several different delictual claims for negligent medical treatment, primarily through the 'mini-general clause'[113] of § 823 *BGB* and § 826 *BGB*. The former, given its general application to persons in all situations, was of greater importance in practice. It provided two relevant bases for liability:

> *'§ 823 Schadenersatzpflicht*
> *(1) Wer vorsätzlich oder fahrlässig das Leben, den Körper, die Gesundheit, die Freiheit, das Eigentum oder ein sonstiges Recht eines anderen widerrechtlich verletzt, ist dem anderen zum Ersatz des daraus entstehenden Schadens verpflichtet.*
>
> *(2) Die gleiche Verpflichtung trifft denjenigen, welcher gegen ein den Schutz eines anderen bezweckendes Gesetz verstößt. Ist nach dem Inhalt des Gesetzes ein Verstoß gegen dieses auch ohne Verschulden möglich, so tritt die Ersatzpflicht nur im Falle des Verschuldens ein.'*

§ 823 (1) *BGB* was the central provision intended to deal with negligently inflicted harm. It eschewed the broad, general clause of the earlier Prussian and French codes and, rather, created a distinct phenotype.[114] A claim would succeed where the plaintiff could demonstrate that one of the (albeit non-exhaustive) enumerated list of protected interests had been wrongfully (*'widerrechtlich'*) infringed by the defendant's intentional or negligent (*'fahrlässig'*) conduct. The third requirement, of negligent behaviour, will be considered below, but, certainly, the first requirement was not difficult to satisfy where a claim concerned medical treatment.[115] In line with the familiar European scheme of offering greater protection to bodily interests, the inclusion of the body and health amongst the enumerated protected interests oriented § 823 (1) *BGB* towards the types of interest most readily infringed by negligent medical treatment. Furthermore, supported by the pre-1900 decisions of the *Reichsgericht*, the legal conception of what constituted an injury to the patient's body or health was, predictably, very broad, encompassing merely transitory interference or the aggravation of an existing condition.[116]

The second requirement, that the conduct must be wrongful, has proven to be one of the paragraph's most distinctive characteristics and accounts for the interrelationship of §§ 823 and 826 BGB.[117] Whilst it has resulted in rivers of ink being spilt over how wrongfulness is best to be assessed, or at least meaningfully

113 Markesinis/Unberath (2002) 69.
114 See Brüggemeier (2006) 14.
115 Flügge (1903) 84–85; König/Kostlin (1937) 7.
116 Rümelin (1913) 29; König Kostlin (1937) 7; *RG 20.05.1889* RGSt 19, 226–227.
117 Deutsch Ahrens (2002) 39.

so,[118] as in the *gemeines Recht* there was surprisingly little attention given to the question of how to assess a medical practitioner's wrongfulness in this era.

There are two explanations for the relative lack of consideration given to the assessment of wrongfulness here. First, despite the different methods developed during the twentieth century for assessing whether conduct was wrongful, wrongfulness was, at its core, intended to ensure that the defendant had violated a legal norm in the absence of any excuse for doing so. Under the approach prevalent before 1950,[119] the so-called *'erfolgsbezogene Rechtswidrigkeit'*,[120] the injurious result of medical error would be obvious. Where, as would be the case with the archetypal medical error cases, the wrong complained of was a direct interference with the patient's bodily integrity, such wrongfulness could be presumed given the importance of the interests concerned.[121] The practitioner would then be left in the impossible position of, in effect, having to demonstrate justification in the sense that the patient had consented to their negligent treatment; this – certainly to modern eyes – absurdity, supported by some,[122] was explicitly rejected by the *Reichsgericht* in a decision from 1911, which held that a patient could not provide valid consent for negligent medical treatment.[123] As *Flügge* had earlier put it the, '...patient's consent is the boundary for penalising the medical practitioner; within these boundaries, however, the practitioner must ensure the care required is applied to every endeavour.'[124]

Secondly, when it came to medical error, much of the groundwork to operate § 823 (1) *BGB* had, unwittingly, already been done. The *'Körperverletzungsdoktrin'*, the root of the idea that every non-consensual medical intervention was, *per se*, a criminal injury and which emerged from the *Reichsgericht's* celebrated 1894 *Hamburger Fall* decision, was readily embraced. This ensured that treatment carried out without consent was viewed, inherently, as a wrongful interference with the patient's bodily integrity. In cases involving negligent failure to disclose a risk, the analysis was thus easier, as the very nature of the wrong confirmed the wrongful nature of the interference and prevented any justification being provided. The importance then of the initial rejection of a 'medical right' or 'right of intervention' as part of that process was clear: consent was the only mechanism by which a practitioner acquired justification for their conduct.

118 Markesinis/Unberath (2002) 79.
119 Markesinis/Unberath (2002) 80; visible in Flügge (1903) 85 and Rapmund/Dietrich (1913) 177 n4.
120 Deutsch/Ahrens (2002) 41.
121 Flügge (1903) 84; accepted as settled case law by *Hilger*, Hilger (1951) 69.
122 Fromherz (1912) 28.
123 *RG 14.03.1911* Seuffert's Archiv 67, 101; König/Kostlin (1937) 7; Nor was there a medical right to intervene, Katzenmeier (2002)112; Rümelin (1913) 26, 29–30.
124 Flügge (1903) 70.

Even following the modern approach of assessing the behaviour of the defendant rather than the result (the so-called '*Handlungsunrecht*'), the defendant's behaviour is assessed against an objective duty of care (*allgemeine Sorgfaltspflicht*). Thus, the fact that fault is assessed objectively, reduces the gap between conduct that is unlawful, and that which is negligent to nothing, instead prompting subtle consideration of whether the law imposes a duty in the first place. Indeed, *Markesinis* notes that there are few situations in which the theories really lead to differing results but in that it demonstrates the persistence of arguments as to what obligation was imposed by law, rather than by voluntary assumption under a contract, the topic is worth consideration in this early period.[125]

There were those who were prepared to aggressively defend against the idea that the law imposed a general duty on medical practitioners not to cause harm through negligent practice, in effect challenging the idea that wrongfulness could be presumed when it came to negligent, but consensual, treatment. *Fromherz* argued that where the claim concerned injurious treatment there could only be a contractual action as demonstrating the unlawfulness required to mount a claim in delict was impossible. It was simply not to be presumed that such conduct was unlawful for the purposes of a claim in delict. As he put it:[126]

> 'The medical practitioner crystallises no general risk, nor breaches a general duty of care if he omits a timely diagnosis or treats a patient, whose consent for such treatment has been secured, in a manner that turns out to be negligent, or evidences a *Kunstfehler*.'

This contrasted with the approach taken by other scholars of the era. *Rabel* appears to have conceived of wrongfulness in a manner broad enough to suggest he thought that medical practice *was* defined by several general duties. It was, as he put, it a general requirement for both contractual and delictual liability that the conduct had to be wrongful in the sense that it infringed a legal duty placed on the practitioner. He then went on to outline the most important of these in a factual rather than legal sense.[127] Amongst his list of the eleven most important duties were offering aid, securing valid consent, appropriately skilful treatment and secrecy, the third of which would clearly have provided a rationale for the wrongful conduct required in § 823(1) *BGB*. Similarly, *Rapmund* and *Dietrich*, in their widely-published handbook, suggested that justification such as to nullify the wrongful nature of a practitioner's conduct could be found within the confines of any contractual obligation.[128] As with *Rabel*, this would have ensured that breach of the obligation to treat *lege artis* could not be rescued

125 Markesinis / Unberath (2002) 81–82.

126 Fromherz (1912) 456–457.

127 Rabel (1904) 9.

128 Rapmund / Dietrich (1913) 177 n 4.

by trying to demonstrate that the patient had consented to a dubious treatment. Furthermore, in a seminal 1911 decision, the *Reichsgericht* had confirmed that there was a general duty on the medical practitioner to avoid *Kunstfehlers.*[129] Although the question was not discussed in any of the literature, it seems likely that this rationale would have put paid to the claim of an unorthodox practitioner that the patient understood the unorthodox nature of their treatment.

§ 823 (2) *BGB* provided a delictual claim where the defendant had negligently breached a '*Schutzgesetz*', regardless of whether the statute specified a requirement for negligence or not. Certainly, in this pre-1945 period, it proved to be of considerably less significance to negligent medical practice than § 823 (1), there being few recognised statutes with relevance to medical practice,[130] but it did provide a ready way of linking a successful criminal claim with a corresponding delictual one.[131]

### (ii) University and municipal hospitals

Delict certainly played a key role for one important iteration of the practitioner-patient relationship that was clarified with the advent of the *BGB*: where treatment was undertaken based on a relationship grounded in public rather than private law. This would have been the case where the patient was treated by the district physician (*Kreisarzt*) or accepted for treatment at a university or municipal hospital, not as a private patient,[132] and the medical practitioners were state officials rather than private practitioners.[133] A contractual analysis failed in these situations.[134] Treatment was instead based on the public welfare duty owed by the institution.[135] Equally, in other situations, the *Reichsgericht* accepted that a contractual analysis was impossible, such as where the patient

129 *RG 14.03.1911.*
130 König/Kostlin (1937) 8.
131 Rabel (1904) 5.
132 König/Kostlin (1937) 13.
133 Rabel (1904) 57. Status as a *Beamter* revolved around the public law nature, if any, of the post, Bremer (1934) 43.
134 Bremer (1934) 43; Ebermayer (1930) 109.
135 Bremer (1934) 45; Hübner/Drost (1955) 10. The content of this duty was malleable and had a mixed nature. For instance, despite earlier restrictive decisions (see *OLG Stuttgart 26.10.1909*) in *RG 08.01.1926* RGZ 112, 290, the *Reichsgericht* held that the public law duty could allow claims based on §§ 278 and 844 *BGB*, but excluded damages for pain and suffering; Contra Rümelin (1913) 65 f, who was happy to declaim both the application of § 278 BGB and the availability of damages for pain and suffering in an action against a public welfare institution.

was brought to the hospital by the police or was being treated as part of a public health initiative.[136]

In these circumstances, the practitioner's liability was restricted to a delictual claim against them in their role as a civil servant. The advent of the *BGB* heralded a broad shift in this liability away from the regional administrative regimes of the nineteenth century, towards a model governed by private law.[137] The key provision was the special delictual regime created in § 839 (1) *BGB* which established the liability of officials for breaches of their official duties:

> *'(1) Verletzt ein Beamter vorsätzlich oder fahrlässig die ihm einem Dritten gegenüber obliegende Amtspflicht, so hat er dem Dritten den daraus entstehenden Schaden zu ersetzen. Fällt dem Beamten nur Fahrlässigkeit zur Last, so kann er nur dann in Anspruch genommen werden, wenn der Verletzte nicht auf andere Weise Ersatz zu erlangen vermag.'*

Unlike § 823 (1) *BGB* the scope of liability was broader in that it was not restricted to particular types of interest. Rather, the various official duties owed by a given official served to delineate the paragraph's ambit;[138] although the plaintiff was still required to demonstrate the negligence of the *Beamter.* A further substantial difference could be identified in that liability for negligently caused harm under § 839 (1) *BGB* was subsidiary to any other available remedy. Nevertheless, whilst the *BGB* thus clarified a single basis for liability, it did nothing to unify the degree to which medical practice in any given state was, indeed, carried out by the state. This continued discrepancy led *Rabel* to the 'very radical view' that § 839 (1) *BGB* should be applied analogously to the contractual relationship between private practitioners and their patients. It would be absurd, he argued, if there was a substantial difference in the scope of liability between two medical practitioners simply because one was a civil servant and the other a private practitioner, a situation, he noted, which would alter as one moved from state to state.[139] Furthermore, the heavy burden of caring for a large number of public patients in such institutions would leave officials with an alarming risk of liability compared to their private counterparts given that such administrative duties as ensuring a daily visit for each patient could prove challenging in busy but understaffed institutions.[140] Others noted the potentially broader scope of

136 König/Kostlin (1937) 4, citing *RG 26.11.1929* RGZ 126, 253.

137 Rümelin (1913) 75.

138 *Deutsch*, noting its potentially open breadth, compared it to § 823 (2) *BGB* in nature, Deutsch/Ahrens (2002) 156.

139 Rabel (1904) 58; And, indeed, it did, Joachim/Korn (1911) 113 f. Although the position was changed somewhat by the *Beamtengesetze* of 30.06.1933 and 26.01.1937 respectively, the position of University medical professors, and municipal practitioners remained unaltered, see Bremer (1934) 44.

140 Rabel (1904) 59. Precisely this duty was later adopted by *Ebermayer* as the sort of duty, which, as required by § 839 (1) BGB created an individual responsibility to

liability for omissions.[141] His fears were not unjustifiable as § 839 *BGB* established primarily a *personal* liability for the official, and given their liability was based merely on the negligent breach of an official duty it had clear potential to be broader than a private practitioner's.

A different extreme position was adopted by *Rümelin*, again based on his underlying view about the nature of medical treatment. Although he acknowledged that, in general, a claim might be brought against the state to nullify the personal liability of an official,[142] he sought to distinguish medical practitioners from other sorts of civil servant. As they could not be made the subject of coercive rules (*Zwangsmaßregeln*), he did not accept that when a medical practitioner carried out an operation, it could be considered part of the exercise of official authority; as he saw it, the patient's consent was the foundation of the practitioner's conduct in a way that distinguished itself from other officials whose public function was the very premise of their conduct.[143] Thus, the direct claim against the state possible under §§ 31 and 89 *BGB* was rejected.[144] Furthermore, such was the public law nature of the relationship between the patient and the institution that it sufficed to oust any private law analysis entirely. As such, there could be no vicarious action against the state either, and so the practitioner would be left as the sole target of liability.[145] In practice, neither *Rabel* nor *Rümelin's* arguments won much support, although *Rümelin* could point to one decision in which a court had denied both the direct and vicarious liability of the state, instead holding two practitioners at a state hospital personally liable under § 839 (1) *BGB*. There, in *OLG Stuttgart 26.10.1909*, the two defendant practitioners, who had treated the plaintiff at a public hospital, were unable to shift their liability to the state under § 31 *BGB* as they were not regarded as falling within 'constitutional' for the purposes of the section.[146] The decision post-dated *Rabel's* work but, to an extent, it retrospectively vindicated his fears in that the narrow view of who was a 'agent of the state' saddled the practitioners with liability on the basis of §§ 823 and 839 *BGB*.[147] That decision was roundly criticised by later scholars, with *Bremer* stressing that *Rümelin's* view would have created an unsatisfactory exception to the detriment of public medical practitioners when compared to their fellow civil servants whose

the plaintiff rather than a broad, intangible duty owed to all members of society, see Bremer (1934) 44 n 7.

141 Rümelin (1913) 39.

142 Ibid. 40.

143 Ibid. 69–70.

144 Ibid. 67.

145 Ibid. 74.

146 Ebermayer (1930) 110.

147 Ebermayer (1924) 95

negligence would be, in effect, transferred to the state.[148] Indeed, eventually, the *Reichsgericht* addressed the point in a similarly critical fashion.[149] Yet each approach, using the underlying similarity of the medical practitioner's task to synergise a hybrid form of liability for all manner of practitioners, privileging public practice so much that any contractual analysis disintegrated in the name of protecting the vital research function of such establishments, demonstrated the continued importance, and malleability of what medical practice meant in the eyes of the legal scholars analysing it.

In due course, the liability of state officials was *de facto* substituted for the liability of the State by article 131 of the *Weimarer Reichsverfassung* (*WRV*) 1919, which provided a single regime rather than, as had been the case previously, leaving it up to individual states to enact a rule.[150] This reduced the danger any given public practitioner might find themselves in:[151]

> *'Verletzt ein Beamter in Ausübung der ihm anvertrauten öffentlichen Gewalt die ihm einem Dritten gegenüber obliegende Amtspflicht, so trifft die Verantwortlichkeit grundsätzlich den Staat oder die Körperschaft, in deren Dienste der Beamte steht. Der Rückgriff gegen den Beamten bleibt vorbehalten. Der ordentliche Rechtsweg darf nicht ausgeschlossen werden.'*

Despite *Rümelin's* position, adopted before the enactment of the constitution, there was settled case law to the effect that carrying out the state's welfare duties, including the provision of healthcare, did fall within the understanding of 'public authority' in article 131 (1) *WRV*.[152] This provided a form of action to which the personal liability under § 839 (1) *BGB* would indeed be subsidiary,[153] and ensured that medical practitioners were neither an exception amongst fellow civil servants nor left, as a result, with the heavy burden of a personal liability.

Thus, the action had a different quality to that ordinarily available to a private patient under § 823 (1) *BGB* and, after 1919, an easier ultimate target. The state, in effect, took over the potential personal liability of the practitioner and indeed the *Kammergericht*, in a 1929 decision, confirmed that the only available action for harm caused by the negligence of a university surgical professor was that against the state using § 839 (1) *BGB*,[154] confirming that their practice fell within

148 Bremer (1934) 45; Hegener (1925) 87–88; *RG 30.10.1906* RGZ 64, 232. See Rümelin (1913) 54–55, noting that the *Reichsgericht* seemed happy to draw a distinction between the types of patient in a manner he was seeking to avoid.

149 *RG 08.01.1926* RGZ 112, 293.

150 The *Reichsverfassung* 1871 contained no similar provision.

151 König/Kostlin (1937) 13–14.

152 Bremer (1934) 45 n 14; Hilger (1951) 76–77.

153 Bremer (1934) 44.

154 *KG 05.01.1929* (1929) 58 JW 2287; Bremer (1934) 45.

the notion of public authority.[155] The court particularly stressed that the aims of such an institution being to provide research, teaching and development for practitioners, justified this rejection of the ordinary private law relationship, although this met with mixed views in the scholarship.[156]

### (C) Concurrency and recoverable damages

As is clear from the preceding, there were several different ways in which a claim might be put depending on the nature of the institution and the patient; a contractual action based on the free and willing agreement of each party, and a broader, general obligation in delict imposed by the state on all.[157] In this section we will consider the main advantages of one action over another, in particular the differences in the scope of damages recoverable under each.

The *BGB* further clarified the scope of the respective remedies. § 249 *BGB* spoke of restoring the position of the plaintiff whether contingent on a contractual or tortious breach.[158] In that regard, § 253 *BGB* restricted the availability of damages for pain and suffering to those cases specified by the law; § 847 (1) *BGB* restricted this to delict over contract. This appeared to give the patient a significant practical benefit where they could prove a delictual action.[159] But matters were not that straightforward. Although the second half of the twentieth century saw a widespread acceptance of the concurrence of liability in delict and contract such that German courts rarely emphasised any persisting differences,[160] the first half of the century saw a broad range of views as to whether one action restricted another.

As to the contract–delict overlap, however, for some scholars, the former would always trump or limit the latter as, in effect, a *lex specialis*.[161] There was scant literature which directly considered the question as it related to medical practitioners, often subsuming it within broader consideration of the law of obligations, but one such specific piece appeared in 1912. There, *Fromherz* ultimately restricted the patient to a claim in contract unless they had suffered injury as a result of the failure to secure the patient's consent.[162] He was

155 Ebermayer (1930) 111.

156 Some agreed, König/Kostlin (1937) 13; Hübner/Drost (1955) 10; others did not, Ebermayer (1930) 110.

157 Katzenmeier, 79–80.

158 Rabel (1904) 20; Bremer (1934) 51.

159 Bremer (1934) 40.

160 Giesen (1988) 36.

161 Bremer (1934) 40, discussing *Hellwig* and *Siber*; Contra Rümelin (1913) 35, suggesting that this position had long been under pressure.

162 Fromherz (1912) 443.

influenced by contemporary case-law of the *Reichsgericht*, which had suggested that the plaintiff could indeed be restricted to a claim in contract where the injury flowed, properly viewed, from a breach of the specific contractual duty rather than the more general delictual one.[163] Admittedly this was an uncertain science,[164] but naturally prompted one to divine what the obligation imposed by the respective bases was. He relied on his esoteric approach to wrongfulness in the law of delict based on a selective reading of the seminal *Reichsgericht* decision *RG 14.03.1911*, which was otherwise understood as permitting concurrent claims. *Fromherz's* mistake was to assume that the *Reichgericht's* statement concerning the patient's consent nullifying the otherwise wrongful nature of the *Kunstfehler* as regards a claim in delict, could be understood as suggesting that the patient could consent to negligent treatment *per se*, rather than the risks inherent in the operation.[165] From this basis he maintained that, unless the claim involved the absence of consent, if it were merely for negligent treatment, then it had to be brought in contract rather than delict as the latter, where the patient consented to the treatment, imposed no general duty to refrain from behaving negligently. As he put it:[166]

> 'As it concerns *Kunstfehlers* in the course of medical treatment, a practitioner is consequently liable primarily only by reason of contractual principles, only in specific exceptional cases are they liable in delict and, thus, for damages for pain and suffering.'

Increasingly, however, where there was a contract, there was thought to be no difference in the obligations assumed under each head of liability. This position had certainly been visible in the earlier literature – with *Rabel* seemingly assuming that the nature of the obligation made no difference to the context[167] – and amongst *Fromherz's* direct contemporaries.[168] By 1934, nearly all academic commentary concurred on the point.[169] The tide of argument was aided by the fact that the *Reichsgericht* settled on a strong preference for the concurrency of claims, allowing the defendant a choice as to how they framed their action, and rejected the *de facto* use of contract to dilute the general duty to refrain from physically injuring others. The generally recognised duty to refrain from physically injuring

163 See *RG 03.12.1907* RGZ 67,182; Fromherz (1912) 443–444 n 9.
164 Fromherz (1912) 446.
165 Ibid. 455.
166 Ibid. 457.
167 Rabel (1904) 8 n 3; Zitelmann (1908) 9; Rümelin (1913) 25 n 3.
168 Rümelin (1913) 28.
169 Hegener (1925) 64; Bremer (1934) 42, citing numerous authors; Hübner/Drost (1955) 18–19.

others did not differ depending on the basis of the obligation,[170] a view taken as the leading opinion by at least 1934.[171] In two decisions from 1911, the *Reichsgericht* stressed that by reason of their calling, the duties owed by a medical practitioner were, in essence, equivalent whether under a contract or in delict, and that if they were unlawfully infringed and caused injury to the protected interests set out in § 823 (1) *BGB*, then a claim would stretch to the additional recovery of damages for pain and suffering.[172] Where the actions overlapped and one was satisfied, this would satisfy the other; where they did not, only one action would remain. Certainly, the burgeoning number of cases suggests that such issues seldom prevented a successful claim for such damages. Indeed, the basis for *Fromherz's* jeremiad were two decisions from the *OLG Karlsruhe* from 1904 and 1909 in which the court had indeed awarded damages for pain and suffering.[173]

The availability of such damages through a delictual claim was of more than merely theoretical interest.[174] Practically, it was often this head of damage, broad and flexible as it was, that accounted for the trend of increasingly large sums being awarded, so much so that the *Reichsgericht* emphasised a need to protect medical practitioners from unreasonable claims for damages for pain and suffering.[175] In the *Reichsgericht's* seminal decision in *RG 14.03.1911* the young patient, having claimed 45,000M, received 14,000M for her reduced marriage prospects following her disfiguration at the hands of the negligent practitioner.[176] Some noted a trend towards 1940 of increasingly large awards,[177] with one *Reichsgericht* decision confirming the lower court's award of 50,000M. That decision was fiercely criticised by *Wussow* in 1943 as having been taken 'without thought'. He suggested that the normal sum should be 4,000M with 12,000M in exceptional cases, but *Hübner* and *Drost*, unbothered by the size of the award, and willing to constrain *Wussow's* fears to their wartime context, were later supportive of the decision as having properly accounted for the common factors the courts took account of.[178] In any case, the quantum and basis for damages for pain and suffering could move with the mores. In 1929, the loss of

170 *RG 19.06.1914* RGZ 85, 183. There, the court explicitly rejected *Fromherz's* interpretation in a case concerning a *Kunstfehler* claim based on § 823 BGB by the third-party child; see also *RG 13.10.1919* RGZ 88, 433.

171 Bremer (1934) 41–42.

172 Ebermayer (1924) 84–85. See also *RG 14.03.1911*, Rümelin (1913) 27 n 2.

173 Fromherz (1912) 435.

174 Bremer (1934) 54.

175 Rümelin (1913) 28.

176 Rapmund / Dietrich (1913) 180 n 1, *RG 14.03.1911*; Rabel (1904) 20.

177 Hübner / Drost (1955) 21.

178 Hübner / Drost (1955) 21–22.

the patient's teeth was not to be regarded as a disfigurement given that artificial teeth were unremarkable in daily life, whilst with the advent of X-rays, damages for lost fertility were said to have been a particularly fecund source of damages.[179] Equally, there was evidence of a countervailing tendency of courts in the Nazi era to award lower, sometimes derisory sums as compensation for personal injury, despite the headline figures noted above.[180]

The bifurcation of recoverable damages made the content of the obligation imposed by the law of delict a key battleground in the scope of a medical practitioner's liability. As in the nineteenth century, the external observer's conception of what medical practice entailed played a large role in determining this. For *Fromherz*, the medical practitioner was no different to the man on the Charlottenburg omnibus, and cases concerning the concurrence of duties owed to houseguests seemed a natural, and thus liability-limiting analogy. For many others such as *Rabel*, *Rümelin*, *Hegener* and the *Reichsgericht* itself, it was *precisely* the particularly intimate, trust-based nature of the occupation, and the potentially devastating consequences of the practitioner's negligence, that explained the duplication of the duties owed in both contract and delict.[181] It would neither do to say a medical practitioner was only concerned about their patient's body and health by reason of a contract to that effect, nor, as *Fromherz* had asserted, that there was no general '*Verkehrspflicht*' to provide careful treatment.[182] Indeed, *Rümelin*, with one eye on unorthodox practitioners, explicitly tied the availability of damages for pain and suffering to the provision of an adequate degree of protection for injured patients.[183] To a degree, this particularistic view of medical practice was no doubt fuelled by the contemporaneous efforts of orthodox practitioners to enforce a binding set of occupational norms. Built on an internalised set of ethical principles, these bound a practitioner whether there was a contract or not. In this sense, as the courts moved to narrow the gap between the contractual and the delictual duties, the scope of a practitioner's legal duty came, in practice, to be closely aligned to the core duties imposed by the Honour Courts.

179 *OLG Frankfurt a.M. 25.01.1929* (1929) 58 JW 2289; Bremer (1934) 54.

180 Bloemertz (1984) 13, noting the award of 300M for the loss of a leg.

181 *RG 14.03.1911* (1911) 40 JW 449; Rabel (1904) 8; Rümelin (1913) 34; Hegener (1925) 64; König/Kostlin (1937) 7. The same rhetoric was used to explain the scope of the public law duty towards charitable patients, see RGZ 112, 290.

182 Rümelin (1913) 34.

183 Rümelin (1913) 37.

## 3. Fault and medical error in the *BGB*

Having mapped out the changes in the way actions for medical error were categorised in the *BGB* and how that categorisation operated in practice in the previous part, we turn to consider the standard of liability imposed by the *BGB*. As noted in the chapter's introduction, this period is rich in relevant materials and decisions. This allows us to sketch a considerably thicker account of the law in practice. We will consider two issues in this part. First, what was the fault standard adopted by the *BGB*? Secondly, how did that relate to or change the legal understanding of what constituted a *Kunstfehler*? In considering the latter, we will unpack an analytical, interpretive shift in the application of the *Kunstfehler*; identify pressure on its scope of application; the role that therapeutic freedom within particular medical groupings played in justifying this interpretive shift; and the question of how the law dealt with unorthodox practice.

### (A) § 276 *BGB*

Justified by the drafters of the *BGB* on economic and socio-political grounds, rather than the manifold, often Kantian, arguments in the legal literature,[184] fault remained central to liability as conceived in the *BGB*.[185] When it came to the breach of an obligation then, simply put, unless an alternative was specified, which in many cases it was,[186] the code provided a default standard in § 276 *BGB* of liability for intention or negligence. Cases of intentional injury by a medical practitioner remained rare;[187] the same could not be said for injury through negligence:[188]

> '*§ 276 Verantwortlichkeit des Schuldners*
> *(1) Der Schuldner hat, sofern nicht ein anderes bestimmt ist, Vorsatz und Fahrlässigkeit zu vertreten. Fahrlässig handelt, wer die im Verkehr erforderliche Sorgfalt außer Acht läßt. Die Vorschriften der §§ 827, 828 finden Anwendung.*
>
> *(2) Die Haftung wegen Vorsatzes kann dem Schuldner nicht im voraus erlassen werden.*'

In practice, and despite the considerably different requirement for each action in the *BGB*, the fact that both the contractual claim based on a service contract and the delictual claims in §§ 823 (1), (2) and 839 *BGB* required proof of the defendant's fault, removed any difference between the standard of care in the

184 Katzenmeier (2002) 154.
185 Zimmermann (1996) 1035.
186 Markesinis/Unberath (2002) 379–380.
187 Bremer (1934) 12; Hübner/Warneyer (1939) 170–171; Hilger (1951) 32. However, see *OLG Colmar 20.02.1914*, Ebermayer (1924) 84, for the use of § 826 BGB against a dentist who had removed all the patient's teeth.
188 Mansfeld (1915) 334, 337; Bremer (1934) 13.

two types of actions that may have existed in the *gemeines Recht*. Rather, this focused both contractual and delictual claims for medical error through the prism of § 276 *BGB* ensuring that the default standard of care imposed through either a contractual or delictual action were coincident.[189] Indeed the natural resonance of the law of delict with the foremost interests infringed by medical error, and the channelling of both forms of liability through § 276 *BGB*, largely aligned the actions in practice.[190] A final, but key feature was that the definition of negligence in § 276 *BGB* enshrined a simple fault standard.[191] Thus, the degree of fault was not relevant to the existence of liability in a contractual or delictual action, but it could be taken into account for the purposes of an award of *Schmerzensgeld*.[192]

As to what fault actually meant in practice, § 276 *BGB*, although commendable for fixing a statutory definition, was somewhat ambiguous:[193] '*Fahrlässig handelt, wer die im Verkehr erforderliche Sorgfalt außer Acht läßt.*' Fault was defined as a failure to show the required care ('*erforderliche Sorgfalt*'), but by what reference was that gnomic catchall to be measured?[194] The drafting committee, set on retaining the axiomatic place of the broad fault principle that had emerged from the *gemeines Recht*,[195] had gone through a number of variants before arriving at this formula discarding both 'the care of a prudent *paterfamilias*' and the 'care customary in the circumstance' along the way.[196] The former had been denounced in part due to its unsuitability for occupational groups and fears that it would tend towards the broader standard of the Roman *bonus paterfamilas*.[197] Thus it could not be said from the text alone whether § 276 *BGB* was intended to be applied in a purely objective fashion – although the preparatory materials suggested this had been the drafters' aim[198] – or, indeed, whether it properly captured the fault principle central to much of the *gemeines Recht* if it was![199] The resulting, and enduring, scholarly discussion, centred on

189 Hegener (1925) 61.
190 Katzenmeier, 81–82, noting the objectivisation of fault in particular.
191 Rümelin (1913) 9; Schermaier (2007) 1156; Markesinis / Unberath / Johnston (2006) 153; This simple fault standard was often contrasted with France, Rabel (1904) 74–75; Rümelin (1913) 7–8.
192 Hilger, 80; RGZ 136 393, *07.04.1932*.
193 Walter (2004) 14–15, 49.
194 Ibid. 50.
195 Katzenmeier (2002)150–151.
196 Endemann (1903) 639 n 2; Deutsch / Ahrens (2002) 59; Schermaier (2007) 1133, 1135; Walter (2004) 15–17; König / Kostlin (1937) 49.
197 Schermaier (2007) 1136.
198 Jansen (2009) 117 n 151.
199 Schermaier (2007) 1136–1137, 1144.

how to reconcile an objective interpretation of the standard of fault imposed in § 276 *BGB* with the idea of fault as a moral failure.[200] Often some version of a compromise was struck, with an objective standard being tailored to the defendant's concrete person or circumstances.[201] Drawing on the *gemeines Recht*, objectivists increasingly focussed on grouping defendants according to their field of activity ('*Verkehrskreis*') and applying the standard of care generally expected from people in that cohort.[202] This lent itself naturally to skilled groupings, the oldest and most important category,[203] where the technical or special nature of the defendant's activities required the court to focus on a particular set of actors,[204] alongside sex, age, health and education as other potential factors.[205] This position was closest to the settled, general practice of the *Reichsgericht*, which came to treat § 276 *BGB* as setting just such an objective standard, tailored to the defendant's field of activity.[206] Thus an identical standard would be expected of people in the same situation regardless of personal idiosyncrasies.[207] With the broad, but hardly total,[208] acceptance of fault as denoting the failure to satisfy an objective standard rather than a personal failing, the more subjective elements of Pandectist thought were rejected, and the relationship between behaviour and liability changed.[209] As such, § 276 *BGB* was to be applied in a normative, iterative fashion, which provided considerable scope for social change to help determine judicial expectations of the care required in the circumstances.[210]

Despite the fierce nature of the wider debate in this period,[211] in the literature on medical liability it was universally accepted that the definition of negligence offered in § 276 *BGB* spoke to an objective standard, albeit it was often expressed in slightly different ways.[212] Frequent stress was put on the need to tailor the

200 Walter (2004) 18 ff; Jansen (2009) 117.
201 Deutsch (1963) 22 f.
202 Ibid. (1963) 30–32.
203 Ibid. 40, 34.
204 Walter (2004) 65–66.
205 Deutsch (1963) 34; Walter (2004) 65, 79 f.
206 Ibid. 38; Schermaier (2007) 1149; Walter (2004) 34–35.
207 Ibid. 38, noting that sex was downplayed.
208 Katzenmeier (2002) 162; Jansen (2009) 118.
209 Katzenmeier (2002) 160–161.
210 Deutsch / Ahrens (2002) 60; Katzenmeier (2002)161–162.
211 Rümelin (1913) 7, describing it as a 'lively argument'.
212 The *Reichsgericht* had adopted 'prudent' as its adjective of choice, Katzenmeier (2002) 160 n 69; In line with this it was commonly reflected in the literature, see Flügge (1903) 70, 'a prudent medical practitioner in the practice of his calling'; Rabel (1904) 11, 'the behaviour demanded from every prudent medical practitioner'. He equated this with the abstract figure of the 'average medical practitioner'; Joachim / Korn (1911) 353, 'Thus, he is bound to apply all the rules of

standard to the situation in which the treatment had been given,[213] but not, as some noted, the practitioner's age or sex.[214] The *Reichsgericht* repeatedly described the standard as being the 'care of a prudent medical practitioner'.[215] Gone from both discourses was any discussion of the standard as one of gross negligence,[216] but there was a continued rhetoric of medicine's importance, with *Rümelin* stressing the role of medicine's social utility as an important informal influence on constructing the standard to be applied, bearing in mind that it would be preferable to the 'doubtful utility' of a formal gross negligence standard.[217]

In the era of the *BGB*, gross negligence as a formal fault standard was, for our purposes here, restricted by § 680 *BGB* to claims based on *Geschäftsführung ohne Auftrag*, which replaced § 276 *BGB* in cases of 'imminent danger': § 680 *BGB*: '*Bezweckt die Geschäftsführung die Abwendung einer dem Geschäftsherrn drohenden dringenden Gefahr, so hat der Geschäftsführer nur Vorsatz und grobe Fahrlässigkeit zu vertreten.*' *Rabel* had contested this as superfluous given that, at least as applied to medical practitioners, the pressing circumstances of a medical emergency could be accommodated within § 276 *BGB* as an extenuating circumstance, accounted for in constructing the degree of care required in the circumstances.[218] Equally, there were suggestions that given the ordinarily threatening situations where the practitioner-patient relationship was classified as a *negotiorum gestio*, § 680 *BGB* made it scarcely possible to maintain a successful action against a practitioner, a likelihood borne out in the absence of such actions in practice.[219]

### (B) The *Kunstfehler* and *'erforderliche Sorgfalt'*

As has been seen in the preceding section, there was, in practice, no fixed single standard of care imposed by § 276 *BGB*. Rather, the standard would have to be

medical practice and scholarship insofar as he stands able'; Rapmund / Dietrich (1913) 177 n 5; Rümelin (1913) 11, 'a competent medical practitioner; Ebermayer (1930) 91, 'the average standard of prudent companions in the calling'; Bremer (1934) 13–14, 'a prudent "average practitioner" in the same circumstances'; König / Kostlin (1937) 47; Hilger (1951) 33, 'like a prudent and conscientious colleague'; *RG 15.02.1919* RGZ 95, 16.

213 Rabel (1904) 7; Rümelin (1913) 9–10; Ebermayer (1930) 91; König / Kostlin (1937) 47.

214 Rabel (1904) 11–12, 81–82, citing numerous general treatises on obligations; Rümelin (1913) 11–12; Bremer (1934) 13.

215 Bremer (1934) 13; (1912) 41 JW 529.

216 Although it occasionally resurfaced amongst practitioners, Rümelin (1913) 14.

217 Rümelin (1913) 13.

218 Rabel (1904) 7, 80. Emphasising labour in particular.

219 Bremer (1934) 28; Hilger (1951) 88.

tailored to the defendant at hand, and the circumstances in which they found themselves. Of course, those claiming a particular skill, such as medical practitioners, warranted to their patient that they had such aptitude.[220] This was one of the most important duties undertaken,[221] and subsequent failure to demonstrate that skill could easily ground liability,[222] whether there was a contractual relationship or not.[223] The readily identifiable contours of orthodox medical practice presented a clear body of praxis from which an account of what those skills were could be drawn.[224] This kept the issue of the role of accepted medical practice in defining the required standard of care itself at the forefront of much of the law in practice. Practically speaking, a *Kunstfehler* was, unsurprisingly given its intimate connection to errors in treatment, often noted as the most likely cause of medical liability.[225] But, on the precise relevance of occupational conduct to whether a practitioner was at fault, the *BGB* had been silent. In this section, we examine this question as it relates to the *Kunstfehler* as reborn in the nineteenth century. In short, whose opinion defined a given behaviour as required ('*erforderlich*') in the circumstances?

We will do this by looking at four aspects of legal analysis as it pertained to the *Kunstfehler* in this era. First, what was the relationship between the definition of fault in § 276 *BGB* and the concept of the *Kunstfehler*? Secondly, what was the scope of medical behaviour regarded as susceptible to analysis as a *Kunstfehler*? Thirdly, how did German law deal with the problem of divergence between medical experts as to the correct approach to take in defining accepted medical practice? Here we will see that, in wrestling with these questions, the deeply sociological model of fault present in the nineteenth century, gradually began to give way to a more ethical model of fault as courts increasingly felt capable of judging medical behaviour, broadly conceived, regardless of practitioners' opinion. In consequence, the understanding and utility of the *Kunstfehler* came under sustained pressure from both courts and scholars. A final sub-section will consider the approach to unorthodox practitioners in this era.

220 Endemann (1903) 639–640; Bremer (1934) 12.
221 Rabel (1904) vii, 36 f.
222 Ebermayer (1924) 86–87.
223 *RG 04.07.1916*, reported in Ebermayer (1930) 136.
224 Deutsch (1963) 32–33.
225 Rabel (1904) 36; Ebermayer (1930) 88–89.

### (i) The changing interpretation of the *Kunstfehler*

It was clear by the late nineteenth century that the term *Kunstfehler* had come to be used generally as a synonym for medical error by both lawyers and medical practitioners.[226] As to its doctrinal relevance, it supplied, in effect, the fault analysis required for a successful action. Turning to the early twentieth century, although numerous scholars stressed the extra-legal nature of the concept, '...the "*Kunstfehler*" is no legal concept, rather it is a concept which is used in medical science',[227] or the fact that the expert evidence on which it was based remained, 'only an aid to the judge' and was not, itself binding,[228] they nevertheless retained it as an organising construct, rather demonstrating its power as an informal interpretive device for analysing medical error in practice. For many, a *Kunstfehler* remained, following *Virchow*, the breach of 'recognised rules of medical practice',[229] and the *Reichsgericht's* retention of the concept, if only as diminishing grist for its analytical mill, drove its continued scholarly embrace. The court itself defined a *Kunstfehler* as an 'infringement of the principles of medical science',[230] with other, similar formulations also appearing.[231] In any case, the underlying ideas were congruent with *Virchow's* definition in associating it with a failure to comply with generally accepted forms of medical behaviour.[232] This might suggest a continuation of the largely sociological approach to fault of the nineteenth century but that approach increasingly came under pressure in this period.

The question of exactly what role the *Kunstfehler* played in legal doctrine came to the fore as the era's increased number of decisions, alongside a burgeoning scholarship and a clarified structure for civil liability, focused more attention on it. There were two approaches in the literature, one of which was, by a considerable margin, the dominant view. *Rümelin*, who was happy to use the term '*Kunstfehler*' as a direct synonym for lack of 'required care',[233] and who

226 Katzenmeier (2002) 273; Indeed, the term continued to appear in the early twentieth century as a synonym for occupational error generally, Endemann (1903) 640 n 6, who equated it with *imperitia*. See also Bremer (1934) 12.

227 Bremer (1934) 11; Rümelin (1913) 14; Hegener (1925) 69; Ebermayer (1930) 89; Hilger (1951) 36.

228 Mansfeld (1915) 337; Ebermayer (1932) 3305

229 Mansfeld (1915) 335; Hegener (1925) 69, 'widespread view'.

230 *RG 14.03.1911* Seuffert's Archiv 67, 102; Hegener (1925) 69.

231 *RG 04.07.1916*, '...the generally recognised rules of medical scholarship', Ebermayer (1930) 136; *RG 22.03.1932* 8 HRR 1932, 1828. '...recognised rules of scholarship'; *RG 08.02.1934* 10 HRR 1934, 786, '...an infringement of the rules of medical practice.'

232 Hilger (1951) 36.

233 Rümelin (1913) 2.

acknowledged the continued role of medical practice in the developing legal literature on the subject,[234] was the first to identify the nature of the problem explicitly.[235] There were two broad ways of viewing the relevance of a *Kunstfehler* for legal practice. Simply put, it was either an objective concept, and thus designated any and all failures to provide 'appropriate treatment', or, it was a subjective concept, which only identified '*negligent* inappropriate treatment'.[236] This lens provides a useful way of unpacking the various approaches adopted by the courts and other scholars.

As to what the actual answer was, differing views abounded in this era and they seldom clearly distinguished between these two basic conceptions. Supporters of a purely objective interpretation were few. Yet although most practitioners, and indeed the *Reichsgericht*, came to regard it more subjectively,[237] there were varying degrees within the broad categorisation of objective, which blurred the edges of *Rümelin's* simple dichotomy. We will examine these in turn, before looking in more detail at the developing position of the *Reichsgericht* itself, but it should be understood that the ultimate importance of how the concept was viewed lay in the fact that it stood to open up an analytical space for the courts to assert a greater degree of control over whether there ought to be liability in any given case, regardless of whether the plaintiff could demonstrate that the defendant had breached a generally accepted rule of medical practice. In short, it opened the door to courts plainly challenging medical expertise.

Certainly, some scholars did view the *Kunstfehler* as a purely objective concept. At its most extreme, this objectivist view was used as the basis for suggesting a radical realignment of liability for medical practitioners. In 1932, *Haberland* argued that the concept of a *Kunstfehler*, tied, as it seemed to be, to medical judgment, provided blanket protection to practitioners whose negligence had obviously injured the patient.[238] Given that judges were incapable of assessing medical matters for themselves, they would, he argued, focus solely on the conclusions of the medical experts as to whether they regarded the defendant's behaviour as evidencing a *Kunstfehler* or not. If not, liability was avoided. Amongst his examples was a situation where the patient, suffering from two kidney stones that had been identified by X-ray, underwent an operation during which only one was removed. Here, he argued, there was clearly a mistake, yet, it

234 Rümelin (1913) 6, referring to *Rabel*, *Hellwig* and *Zitelmann's* work.

235 See also Hilger (1951) 36 ff.

236 Rümelin (1913) 16, emphasis added.

237 Drawing on some of the early case law (*RG 01.03.1912* RGZ 78, 432), *Rümelin* described this as the customary view, Rümelin (1913) 16, but given the multiple opposing views that emerged, even within the court, this is of limited validity.

238 Haberland (1932) 3304.

was said, no *Kunstfehler* according to the expert opinion. Furthermore, he reported cases where a practitioner had been called before an Honour Council for disciplining on the basis that he had, in an opinion, designated a fellow practitioner's behaviour as a *Kunstfehler*. This, *Haberland* claimed, created pressure on such experts to the detriment of patients and the law, although that suspicion was contested by *Ebermayer*, who reasoned that the court oath undertaken by all expert witnesses was sufficient to protect against such action on the part of an Honour Court.[239] *Haberland's* preferred solution was to redefine a *Kunstfehler* as any injury caused by incorrect treatment by a practitioner even in the absence of negligence on the part of the defendant;[240] in effect, instituting a form of strict liability for medical injury so as to avoid the dangers, as he saw it, of under-compensation and the denial of the patient's rights.[241]

*Haberland's* approach was fiercely criticised in the literature for potentially suffocating practitioners with an overly broad liability, risking the reputation of the occupation and undermining the public's trust,[242] as well as undermining the primacy of fault-based liability within the *BGB*.[243] That it was so resoundingly rejected, failing to find support in either practice or scholarship, evidenced the shift in this period away from seeking to enshrine the primacy of medical standards as the decisive factor for medical liability.

The more frequently adopted, and certainly less radical, scholarly position allowed that a *Kunstfehler* could exist objectively, separate from a finding of fault, but only where it was defined in *Virchow's* familiar terms. As the era of the *BGB* began, and despite the acknowledgement that the basis for liability lay in demonstrating fault,[244] *Rabel* regarded '*die im Verkehr erforderliche Sorgfalt*' simply as being congruent with a *Kunstfehler*, judged, as it was, by the relevant expert witnesses. For the judge themselves to decide on the 'golden sweet spot' of what conduct was required from a medical practitioner would be a 'transgression of juristic competence'.[245] Indeed, where a decision was 'incorrect' (in the sense that a practitioner was thus unduly held liable), he regarded that as being solely the fault of the relevant experts, not the court,[246] suggesting an

239 Ebermayer (1932) 3305

240 Haberland (1932) 3304; Hilger (1951) 36.

241 Haberland (1932) 3304.

242 Goldhahn / Hartmann (1937) 4; König / Kostlin (1937) 43 with further references; Hilger (1951) 37.

243 Straßmann (1932) 3305; König / Kostlin (1937) 43; Hübner / Warneyer (1939) 171.

244 Rabel (1904) 37.

245 Ibid. 38–39.

246 Ibid. 39. Other contemporary commentary elevated the interpretation of 'required care' as meaning compliance with 'all the rules of medical practice and scholarship', Joachim / Korn (1911) 353.

entirely passive role for judges in scrutinising accepted practice.[247] In one early decision under the *BGB*, the *Reichsgericht* went so far as to suggest that infringement against the accepted rules of medical practice would, without more, demonstrate the failure to provide the required care, a position distinguished from *Haberland* only in its fidelity to *Virchow's* phrasing.[248]

In contrast to *Haberland's* solipsistic approach, most scholars shifted towards a quasi-objective position, holding that whilst a *Kunstfehler* was indeed a free-standing concept, it only coincidentally overlapped with legal notions of fault. As *Ebermayer* – by then the leading commentator in this area[249] – put it, directly rebutting *Haberland*, a *Kunstfehler* was such, '…whether it was free from fault, or the result of negligence or intention.'[250] Yet he immediately stressed the importance, when it came to the question of whether there might be civil liability for a *Kunstfehler*, of the analytically separate question whether the defendant was *also* at fault.[251] Other academic advocates of this quasi-objective position emphasised that the practical result was that a *Kunstfehler* could be, but was not always, coterminous with fault on the part of the practitioner.[252] Certainly this view was visible in decisions of the *Reichsgericht* which, whilst recognising the *Kunstfehler* as an inherent analytical part of assessing medical liability, began to stress that there was indeed space between the *Kunstfehler* and the legal concept of fault. In one case from May 1931, the court noted that:[253]

> '…the concept of the *Kunstfehler* often overlaps with negligence. Yet the terms do not entirely coincide: not every *Kunstfehler* is a fault, and not every fault is a *Kunstfehler*.'

247 This view was not restricted to *Rabel* or this early period, see Goldhahn/Hartmann (1937) 2.

248 *RG 14.03.1911* Seuffert's Archiv 67, 101.

249 Kahl (1930) 1545, described him as, '…long the leader and master in medico-legal disputes and controversies.' *Ebermayer* had originally written a series of reports on medico-legal issues during the 1910s in the *Deutsche Medizinische Wochenschrift*, before collecting and expanding these into his first monograph in 1923. This was followed in quick succession by numerous subsequent editions before an attempt at a more synoptic and theoretical treatment of the topic in his widely cited 1930 work.

250 Ebermayer (1932) 3305.

251 Ibid. 3305; *Hilger* thus misread *Ebermayer* as there supporting a fully objective notion of the *Kunstfehler* without qualification, Hilger (1951) 38. Indeed, a focus on fault over the relevance of a *Kunstfehler* may be identified in his earlier work, see Ebermayer (1924) 81, 90. The importance of fault was made explicit before his 1932 exchange with *Haberland*, see Ebermayer (1930) 90

252 Bremer (1934) 11–12, 15; Hübner/Warneyer (1939) 171; *RG 22.03.1932* 8 HRR 1932, 1828, '…a medical practitioner normally only behaves culpably if he strays from the recognised rules of scholarship.'

253 *RG. 12.05.1931*, Hübner/Warneyer (1939) 153–154, emphasis added.

And again in 1934:[254]

> '…according to the case law of the *Reichsgericht*, the concept of the *Kunstfehler* in no way corresponds with medical fault; it is entirely possible that there may be a retrospective finding of a *Kunstfehler*, that is to say, an objective violation of a rule of medical practice, without, at the same time, this leading to the conclusion that the medical practitioner was at fault in the circumstances.'

Even where the *Reichsgericht* appeared to acknowledge a quasi-objective view of the *Kunstfehler*, by the 1930s this was increasingly done in the process of carving out conceptual space for courts to find a medical practitioner at fault regardless of whether the plaintiff could prove a *Kunstfehler*. Although, as noted above, it had often been presumed that in most cases where the plaintiff could prove a *Kunstfehler* this would likely lead to a finding of fault, it was not until that May 1931 decision that the *Reichsgericht* made clear that the reverse of that logic did not follow. There the *Reichsgericht* upheld the lower court's finding of fault despite the expert witnesses' evidence that the defendant had not committed a *Kunstfehler*.[255] That decision, although only briefly reported, was used as the foundation in later decisions, which confirmed the rule: even in absence of a *Kunstfehler* there could still be finding of fault sufficient to satisfy § 276 (2) *BGB* and ground liability.[256]

What explains this rather inelegant position? Most likely a combination of reflexive reliance on the analyses inherited from the nineteenth century alongside the increased importance of the disciplinary regimes overseen by the Honour Courts in the early twentieth century. Certainly the latter, and thus the continued use of the term by medical practitioners themselves, would have left legal scholars – at least those, like *Ebermayer*, focused on expounding the practical law regarding medical practice as a whole – and courts unable to entirely deny the existence of the concept.[257] Yet many increasingly sought to stress the importance of the court's own assessment of whether the defendant practitioner's conduct manifested fault as a separate, but now key, consideration for the question of liability.[258] One attraction of the quasi-objective approach might have been the unenacted suggestion that where it could be shown that the practitioner had breached a generally accepted rule of medical practice, the

254 *RG 23.02.1934*, Hübner/Warneyer (1939) 40–41. See also, *RG 08.02.1934* 10 HRR 1934, 786.

255 *RG 12.05.1931* 7 HRR 1931, 1748.

256 *RG 12.10.1934* (1935) 64 JW 115, repeated verbatim in *RG 21.06.1940* (1940) DR 1949.

257 See, for instance, *Ebermayer's* nascent attempt at typology with '*Kunstfehler* in a narrower sense', Ebermayer (1930) 89.

258 Ebermayer (1932) 3305.

burden of proof regarding fault, ordinarily on the plaintiff in both contractual and delictual claims,[259] might shift and require the defendant to explain why, despite this, there had been no failure to demonstrate the care required in the circumstances.[260]

The continued presence of some objective view of the *Kunstfehler*, whatever its relevance to liability, confirmed its acceptance by courts and scholars as a necessary part of the analysis. But, as the increasing emphasis on its merely coincidental congruence with the degree of care required by § 276 (2) *BGB* demonstrated, it in no way signalled acceptance of the *Kunstfehler* as the decisive yardstick for medical fault. Increasingly, those who adopted a more subjective approach were bolder in openly collapsing what had long been a concept rooted in medical views of what constituted appropriate medical conduct into a purely legal one.

The beginnings of the subjective approach can be seen in a 1911 decision of the *Reichsgericht*.[261] There, the patient had been treated with galvano-caustic therapy for a swollen sebaceous cyst on her face and claimed in delict for the non-pecuniary loss flowing from her resulting disfigurement. In line with the expert evidence, the lower court found that there had been a *Kunstfehler* in that the treatment itself had been incorrect for the condition and that, furthermore, it had been incorrectly performed leading to burns and scarring. That this amounted to a *negligent* breach of the practitioner's general undertaking to avoid *Kunstfehler* was sufficient to ground liability, and the case was later taken to have emphasised the need for this consideration alongside the question of whether there had simply been a *Kunstfehler* as far as the medical experts were concerned.[262]

A definitive, and oft-cited,[263] dictum followed in 1912, when the *Reichsgericht*, in *RG 01.03.1912*, emphasised that it was permissible for even the most skilled and careful medical practitioner to make a mistake without attracting the censure of the law, again reinforcing the notion that liability could not be founded simply on evidence of a *Kunstfehler*, as understood by medical practitioners:[264]

259 Rabel (1904) 22; Hübner / Drost (1955) 24 ff, noting the general reluctance of the *Reichsgericht* to apply the doctrine of *prima-facie Beweis* to medical cases; *RG 01.03.1912* Seuffert's Archiv 74, 435; Franzki (1982) 57–61.

260 *RG 08.02.1934* 10 HRR 1934, 786.

261 *RG 14.03.1911* Seuffert's Archiv 67, 101.

262 Hilger (1951) 38, incorrectly took the decision as supporting a subjective point of view despite the absence of any assertion by the court that a *negligent* failure to comply with accepted rules was required.

263 Mansfeld (1915) 334, 337; Ebermayer (1924) 81.

264 *RG 01.03.1912* RGZ 78, 435.

> 'The appeal correctly states that the most careful medical practitioner does not operate with the safety of a machine, that despite all the skill and care of the operator, a nick, a cut or a stitch can fail, even where the medical practitioner concerned routinely succeeds.'

Not every mistake could be equated with fault and attention had to be given to the fact that the patient's constitution and own idiosyncrasies might cause difficulties for even the most careful of practitioners.[265] In that decision, the patient underwent an unsuccessful operation for exostosis in their ear canal which resulted in splinters of bone remaining on the eardrum. This lead to a further two operations resulting, eventually, in paralysis of the facial nerves. The bill having been refused, the practitioner sued and was met with a counterclaim for damages on the basis of a *Kunstfehler* during the first operation. The *Reichsgericht* condemned the decision of the *Kammergericht*, upholding the counterclaim, that the defendant could discharge their burden of proof by showing simply that operations of this sort usually occurred without such harm occurring. It was not for the practitioner to explain whereby the harm had resulted.[266] To require such positive evidence on their part would create a burden on practitioners that was self-evidently too great. As to any perceived unfairness of forcing the patient to adduce evidence of negligence, the court noted that expert witnesses were often capable of identifying fault where appropriate.[267] On this view, a *Kunstfehler* was only relevant in that it might provide evidence of fault rather than suggesting liability could result from a failure to comply with accepted medical behaviour without more.[268] Increasingly, in other decisions and scholarly analyses,[269] emphasis was put on the need to conceptualise the claim as a '...culpable infringement against the rules of medical practice.'[270]

Such was the trend towards the subjective view of the *Kunstfehler*, some scholars began to call for the abandonment of the term altogether. In their widely cited 1937 monograph, *König* and *Köstlin* noted that the myriad interpretations, which had arisen in recent decades simply demonstrated that there was no single, defining interpretation of the concept.[271] Those in evidence ran the gamut, as we have seen, from *Haberland's* expansive understanding

265 Bremer (1934) 14.

266 *RG 01.03.1912* RGZ 78, 435.

267 *RG 01.03.1912* RGZ 78, 435–436.

268 Bremer (1934) 11–12.

269 *RG 03.05.1921* RGZ 102, 231; Ebermayer (1930) 89–90; Bremer (1934) 12.

270 *RG 08.02.1934* 10 HRR 1934, 786; *OLG Königsberg 14.09.1934* 11 HRR 1935, 721. See also Ebermayer (1924) 90, '...a blameworthy incorrect treatment, a so-called *Kunstfehler*.'

271 König/Kostlin (1937) 43.

through to those which, in effect, subsumed it within a court-driven analysis of fault. Indeed some authors,[272] including at least one prominent commentary in the period,[273] simply used the term *Kunstfehler* to refer generally to any sort of negligence associated with medical practice, a usage which, as *König* and *Kostlin* noted, rendered the concept so broad that, '...no specific idea of the *Kunstfehler*, delimited by negligence, exists anymore.'[274] They placed blame for the confusion, which had resulted amongst lawyers, on the fact that there was an unresolved tension in *Virchow's* original example of what constituted a *Kunstfehler*. As they read it, the example of a practitioner who had, during surgery, injured the patient's bowel and then, without dealing with that injury, reintroduced it to the abdomen, conflated two different sorts of wrong.[275] The reintroduction of the injured bowel into the abdomen was clearly an infringement of the generally recognised rules of practice.[276] But an injury to the bowel itself might result, even where a medical practitioner had shown the highest degree of diligence. The former then, was a *Kunstfehler*, while the latter was not, in that it hung on the question of the level of care and attention demanded from the surgeon rather than whether he had breached an accepted rule of medical practice.[277] Failure to adequately distinguish these different analyses had only led to confusion as, if both were to be regarded as a *Kunstfehler*, then *Virchow's* definition was no more precise than using the term, as *Staudinger* was, to refer to a medical practitioner's general duty to avoid causing negligent injury.[278] Rejecting the optimism of earlier scholars for a general definition,[279] and trying to rescue the core of *Virchow's* by then long-standing work from a subjective interpretation, which would have seen it fully subsumed within the logic of the law,[280] *König* and *Kostlin* instead suggested that as it only seemed to be creating confusion and misunderstanding amongst lawyers, the concept of the *Kunstfehler* ought to be abandoned,[281] in favour of recognising a specific basis for liability where a medical practitioner had infringed, '...fundamental therapeutic rules of the science.'[282] Defined thus, space remained within medical liability for an

272 Ebermayer (1924) 80.
273 Staudinger (1929) § 611 V I d; König (1933) 165.
274 König/Kostlin (1937) 44.
275 Ibid. 44. The genesis of this analysis can be found in *König's* earlier work, König (1933) 161.
276 König/Kostlin (1937) 44; König (1933) 164.
277 König (1933) 164.
278 König/Kostlin (1937) 44–45.
279 Rumelin 16 n 1.
280 König (1933) 164.
281 König/Kostlin (1937) 47.
282 Ibid. 67.

objective analysis of accepted medical practice, which subsumed any separate analysis of fault. Nevertheless, they immediately acknowledged the difficulty in identifying anything more than a very small core set of rules that could be so analysed,[283] and suggested nothing to circumvent the problem of accepted approaches shifting over time, or how such rules might be constructed beyond the more readily investigated academic discourse of university-based practice.[284]

Although there was little wider enthusiasm for their suggestion, their willingness to abandon the term '*Kunstfehler*' altogether demonstrates the pressure that the received analysis was coming under throughout this period. That the corollary to their suggested re-categorisation was that, outside of cases to do with a fundamental therapeutic rule, courts were free to police medical behaviour under the rubric of fault, shows the increasing importance, and acceptance, in this era, of the courts' own encapsulation of the questions underpinning assessment of medical behaviour.

As this sub-section demonstrates, the jurisprudence of the *Reichsgericht* as it concerned the *Kunstfehler* – other than continuing to treat with the term itself – reflected the emerging split in the surrounding scholarship. Ultimately, the line between those who adopted a subjective approach and those who preferred to see the *Kunstfehler* as quasi-objective was thin, given both acknowledged the possibility that the medical view of the defendant's behaviour could, in at least some cases, be less relevant than the legal view. That the *Kunstfehler* often overlapped with fault is no surprise,[285] but this could only have been on the basis of their analytical separation, support for which may be derived from the critical response to *Haberland's* suggested elevation of the *Kunstfehler* to the sole decisive concept. But the fact that both courts and commentators increasingly viewed a *Kunstfehler* as arising where the defendant had *negligently* breached an accepted rule revealed a key conceptual shift in the analysis, fuelled by the fact that the extra-legal nature of the concept was increasingly under pressure as courts and legal scholars focused a considerably greater degree of attention on medical liability. This shift was characterised in the 1931 confirmation by the *Reichsgericht* that a court could find the defendant at fault despite the absence of a finding that they had committed a *Kunstfehler*.

The gradual rejection of a formalised concept of *accepted* medical behaviour and the emergence of an informal, iterative approach to *acceptable* medical behaviour leaves open the question of how the courts actually dealt with

283 König/Kostlin (1937) 46.

284 Ibid. 72–74.

285 See *RGZ 08.02.1934* 10 HRR 1934, 786 where the court noted that a *Kunstfehler*, '...regularly represents fault on the part of the actor.'

assessing medical error in this period and whether that actually led to different outcomes in practice. It is to this that we now turn, considering the scope of the *Kunstfehler* analysis, how it operated where there were differing opinions as to the nature of accepted medical practice and it's relevance to unorthodox practitioners.

### (ii) Scope of application

As analytical space emerged between the concepts of fault and the *Kunstfehler*, a further key question began to emerge. Given that, in practice, the *Kunstfehler* was an influential element of assessing whether a medical practitioner was at fault, the question of precisely what sort of activities it applied to then became a key preliminary filter on judicial control over the fault analysis. In short, what medical behaviours were medical enough so as to focus the question of fault on accepted practice? Here *Virchow's* analysis offered no initial guide itself, focusing mainly as it did on the risks posed by tying a legal standard to the ever-shifting state of medical norms and drawing, for his example, on conduct that was more obviously medical: performing surgery.[286] Away from that end of the spectrum of medical behaviours, however, it was less clear where the line ought to be drawn; if surgery was at one end, more mundane matters were to be found at the other. Where a patient injured themselves by tripping in an unlighted passage on route to the bathroom following a consultation,[287] or when a patient who had been administered a local anaesthetic for an operation on their callouses, having been told to lie still on the consulting table whilst the practitioner left them alone momentarily, fell off and injured themselves,[288] there was, it seemed, little need for the courts to address themselves to the question of accepted practice in deciding whether the practitioner had been at fault. Indeed, where a medical practitioner failed to correctly annotate a prescription, resulting in the patient dying from a grossly excessive dose of novocaine, the *Reichsgericht* did not feel the need to analyse the question of fault in terms of a *Kunstfehler*.[289] If the ability to rely on the logic of the *Kunstfehler* was tied to behaviours, which were intrinsically, rather than merely incidentally, medical, then as the practice of orthodox medicine took on an increasingly scientific and technological flavour during the course of the early twentieth century, increasingly large parts of medical behaviour risked becoming less susceptible to analysis along these lines.

286 This analysis was not universally accepted, Hilger (1951) 42.

287 Rabel (1904) 56, discussing *RG 23.02.1900* (1900) 29 JW 302. See also *RG 05.07.1930* (1931) 60 JW 1466, cited by Hilger (1951) 40.

288 Hilger (1951) 40.

289 *RG 27.09.1929* RGZ 125, 374.

Particularly as it concerned questions of diagnosis and administration of treatment, the increasing replacement or at least augmentation of an intuitive assessment by the practitioner themselves, which had been the focus of nineteenth-century medical practice, with greater technical powers to comprehend the patient's pathology – as the bedroom was replaced by the laboratory – patients and courts were able to more clearly understand what was known and, as we will see, what was knowable when it came to medical treatment.

This question of delineating the precise scope of application of the *Kunstfehler* when it came to medical behaviours did not clearly emerge in the literature until comparatively late.[290] If anything, it may be identified as a matter of deduction from the cases and, even then, it is certainly not clear that courts reasoned openly along these lines. But, as *Hilger* noted, a line had to be drawn clearly somewhere otherwise it would be impossible to differentiate a *Kunstfehler* from the overarching concept of negligence, in essence confirming the fully subjective view discussed above and significantly diminishing medical influence over the legal analysis of the standard of care.[291] Understanding in what areas of medical behaviour the courts were willing to supplant discussion in terms of a *Kunstfehler* with their own analysis is thus a useful way of gauging not simply how aggressively the German courts in this period were willing to police medical behaviour themselves but rather also to suggest, where that was the case, why?

Alongside the general increase in decisions concerning medical practitioners in this era, the doctrinal genesis of the question can be found in discussion within the German literature of a decision of the Swiss *Bundesgericht* from 1904, which concerned the scope of the *Kunstfehler's* application. There, a bandage was left inside the patient following an operation.[292] In assessing whether the practitioner was at fault, and finding that he was not, the *Bundesgericht* rejected the relevance of the *Kunstfehler*, noting that the question did not depend on the assessment of the practitioner's expertise and skill, rather, it hung simply on whether he had, in forgetting to remove the bandage, demonstrated the required attention of any careful person of normal skill and ability in the circumstance.[293]

Arriving too late for discussion in *Rabel's* monograph of the same year,[294] it was *Rümelin* whose commentary on the case was picked up by later authors. Relying on both the roots of the concept in the use of '*unkunst*' in the *Carolina*,

290 Hilger (1951) 39–45.

291 Hilger (1951) 44.

292 *SBG 03.06.1904*, *Karrer v Bircher*, Entscheidungen des Schweizerischen Bundesgerichts (1904, vol 30) 304.

293 Goldhahn / Hartmann (1937) 102.

294 *Rabel* added a short appendix to his bibliography noting that *Kollbrunner's* thesis (Kollbrunner (1903)) on the Swiss law had arrived too late for inclusion, Rabel (1904) 87.

and – perhaps tellingly of the potential for confusion here – on its linguistic usage in everyday life,[295] *Rümelin* emphasised that a *Kunstfehler* was best understood as a '...failure of medical expertise.'[296] Extensively citing the text of the Swiss decision in his footnotes,[297] he distinguished cases where expert evidence and a *Kunstfehler*-based analysis was relevant (focusing on '...inadequate knowledge, inadequate ability') and cases where the root of the complaint was not concerned with medical expertise, and that approach was, thus, irrelevant.[298] Yet he immediately acknowledged that this did not provide for a clear analysis in all cases.[299] This much was clear from the very examples that he had used to demonstrate the second category. There was, he claimed, no need to rely on the analytical device of the *Kunstfehler* where a practitioner had forgotten that he had promised particular treatment; where his earlier treatment had made further measures necessary; or when, in the heat of the moment, he administered the wrong drug.[300] Indeed *Rümelin* had challenged the *Bundesgericht's* decision not to treat the matter as a question of whether the defendant's behaviour in that case evidenced a *Kunstfehler.* He felt that there should clearly be a rule of practice requiring the practitioner, or their assistant during surgery, to count the bandages used. Failure to do so would thus always be regarded as a *Kunstfehler.*[301]

Many later scholars in the period adopted a similarly rough distinction between areas where fault was discussed in terms of the *Kunstfehler* and areas where it was not, even if no clear test emerged to clearly distinguish one from the other. The former was often generically, and predictably, described as being associated with the exercise of expertise with no further finesse attempted.[302] One enduring, if no more illuminating, approach was *Ebermayer's* 1930 description of the core situations intended to be covered by the *Kunstfehler* as '*Kunstfehler* in a narrower sense'.[303] This approach was absent in his earlier, more narrative works and is indicative of his greater attempts with that later work to provide an analytical framework for the law. Again harking back to the *Carolina*

295 Rümelin (1913) 14.

296 Ibid. 14. *Hegener* later stressed *Rümelin's* clear influence by Roman law and the law of the *gemeines Recht*, Hegener (1925) 69.

297 Rümelin (1913) 15 n 2.

298 Ibid. 14–15.

299 Ibid. 16.

300 Ibid. 15.

301 Ibid. 15 n 2; Goldhahn / Hartmann (1937) 103.

302 Joachim / Korn (1911) 352–353; Rümelin (1913) 15, '...in connection with the quality of expertise' had become by the time *Hilger* was writing simply, '...for certain injurious behaviours', Hilger (1951) 36.

303 Ebermayer (1930) 89.

– and cribbing heavily from *Rümelin*[304] – he stressed that the concept was intended to cover failures of medical expertise.[305] *Bremer* later divided cases into those which required evidence of intention or failure to comply with the accepted rule and those, designated '*Kunstfehler* in a broader sense',[306] which by contrast required only evidence of the practitioner's carelessness.[307] Despite this, as with his peers, he offered no taxonomy of situations that might arise in practice and into which category they would fall.[308] *Ebermayer*, having set up the distinction, declined entirely to focus on anything other than '*Kunstfehler* in a narrower sense', the outcome of liability in both sorts of cases being the same.[309] This emphasis on more clearly linking the *Kunstfehler* analysis to a specific *medical* error became a feature of much of the literature in this era,[310] but no greater clarity as to what that actually meant was achieved and rather must be identified deductively from the courts' approach in myriad different settings, if at all.

A *Kunstfehler*, in the narrower sense, could certainly arise during the diagnosis of the patient's illness,[311] but the most common reported forum remained harm caused by errors during a chosen treatment itself.[312] Whilst there were clearly large parts of providing treatment that involved the exercise of *medical* skills, and so were, in theory, susceptible to analysis in such terms, a restrictive approach to matters on which a *Kunstfehler*-based analysis could be considered relevant left outwith it a broad range of closely related medical behaviours such that it undermined the degree of control medical practitioners had over the courts' assessment of fault. That there was some sense that simply because the defendant was a medical practitioner the analysis of fault did not always require consid-

304 Ebermayer (1930) 89.

305 Ibid. 89.

306 Ibid. 90.

307 Bremer (1934) 12. *Bremer* relied equally on *Rümelin's* analysis to identify the gist of what the *Kunstfehler* was restricted to, Bremer (1934) 11.

308 Ibid. 12–14. Indeed, *Bremer* eschewed any attempt to organise cases of liability, reasoning that their myriad factual settings rendered such efforts pointless.

309 Ebermayer (1930) 89.

310 Hilger (1951) 41. *Hilger's* own definition, at 45, drew heavily on *Rümelin's* linkage of the *Kunstfehler* to a failure in medical skills or knowledge. Evidencing it's sheer inutility, however, he concluded, at 42, that *Virchow's* own example of reintroducing the damaged bowel was in fact nothing to do with the exercise of medical skills or knowledge at all.

311 Bremer (1934) 16; König/Kostlin (1937) 58 f, see also, at 46, their suggestion that diagnosis was one area where there might be clearly established rules of medical practice; Hübner/Warneyer (1939) 26 f. Also see below (X-rays), which often concerned both diagnosis and treatment.

312 Bremer (1934) 18; Hübner/Warneyer (1939) 172; Hilger (1951) 46–47.

eration of accepted medical practice is perhaps trite; there was nothing uniquely *medical* about a road traffic accident caused by a medical practitioner over any other competent adult driver.[313] But the failure of both the courts and the surrounding scholarship to accurately identify when this was the case, the predictable risk of using an extra-legal concept, which, as *Rümelin* had observed, lacked 'sharp boundaries',[314] to shape the contours of the law, provided a liminal space where the courts could deny the relevance of such an analytical approach precisely *despite* the fact that the details of a given case were a closer analogy to surgery than to a car accident.

### (iii) Therapeutic freedom and the problem of pluralism

Alongside the emergence of a contest over what matters were, truly, medical, the increased amount of focus on medical error in this period cast into sharper relief the issue of whether there was, in any given case, a relevant generally accepted practice on which to draw. This turned attention to the question of how the courts should deal with disagreements in the medical discourse. However doctrinally limited, the crux of relying on the contours of accepted medical practice to delineate fault in any case is how a system deals with situations where there was clear division over which of a number of options was 'accepted', or indeed simply where there was not yet any sort of general practice at all. The approach adopted by the German courts reveals a degree of ambivalence about this problem. In some situations where the answer from the medical discourse was disputed, the courts were wary of being seen to overstep their authority by picking sides; in others, it was precisely this ambiguity which prompted courts to assert their right to disregard the opaque or unsettled nature of the medical discourse.

There was a lone suggestion that where a matter was obvious ('*augenfällig*') the court could decide whether there had been an infringement against such rules for itself without hearing further evidence,[315] equally, there were those who thought that the court had no business in any circumstance choosing between competing schools of thought where the expert evidence diverged.[316] Nevertheless, the process of accessing what, if anything, was generally accepted

313 Ebermayer (1924) 92–93, discussing *RG 10.01.1916*; Ebermayer (1930) 141–142, additionally discussing *Bayerisches Oberstes Landesgericht* (*BayObLG*) *18.02.1913*, which had indeed attempted to engage the standard of care expected of a practitioner in their medical practice as the relevant standard for a road accident caused by the practitioner on route to their patient for the purposes of § 230 (2) *StGB*.

314 Rümelin (1913) 14.

315 Bremer (1934) 11.

316 Hegener (1925) 66; Rabel (1904) 38–39.

in the relevant medical practice remained bound to the provision of expert evidence.[317] The general shift in this period towards both greater judicial control of proceedings and the free assessment of evidence would clearly have provided judges with sufficient procedural justification to take a decision in these circumstances. But it should be stressed that the close association of orthodox medical practice with the state, and the fact that a judge was under no procedural obligation to call for more than one expert opinion,[318] did provide the necessary conditions for a less pluralistic view of medical practice to be advanced to the court in practice and thus it is, perhaps, surprising then to see the question being given such consideration. Indeed, in light of the perceived dangers of trusting a single expert with the role of pronouncing on whether practice was accepted or not, *Rümelin* revived cautious support for instead appointing an independent board, or according opinions given from the medical colleges and faculties particular weight beyond their *de facto* role as the institutional repository of medical expertise.[319] As we shall see in this subsection, German courts did not advance a particularly clear analysis, but, rather, at some times exploited the uncertainty of medical practice to assert their own judgement, and at other times permitted the plurality of medical approaches to shield a practitioner from liability.

A persistent feature of the continued use of the *Kunstfehler* as an organising construct was the refrain, aired in the previous century as well,[320] that there were, in fact, no 'generally recognised rules' at all; medical practice was constantly evolving and practitioners required protection from being held to static, potentially retrograde, standards.[321] So much so that, as noted above, some, such as *König* and *Kostlin* called for the abandonment of the term, and its baggage, altogether in anything other than the very small amount of cases where

317 Flügge (1903) 70; Kollbrunner (1903) 101; Hegener (1925) 66; Bremer (1934) 11.

318 § 404 (1) *ZPO*; Dwyer (2008) 195–196.

319 Rümelin (1913) 17–18 n 1. Similar plans surfaced elsewhere in the period as well, see *Kollbrunner's* report of the Austrian Medical Chamber's petition to the state in 1902 that no action should be brought unless the Chamber had previously signed off on a supportive opinion as well as similar contemporary suggestions in France and Germany, Kollbrunner (1903) 102 n 1. Others complained that the system too readily held a regular practitioner to the standards of a specialist given the propensity of the latter to set the bar too high, Goldhahn / Hartmann (1937) 3.

320 See the discussion of *Mittermaier's* scholarship in chapter two.

321 Hegener (1925) 69; Hildebrand (1925) 32–33; Ebermayer (1930) 89; Bremer (1934) 11; König / Kostlin (1937) 46, 'If the court defines a particular therapy, every practitioner will beware, even if he believes differently, against deviating from the "court-approved" therapy.'

a clear, unified practice could be identified.[322] Where there was no accepted practice they argued – adopting a view shared by many others – a practitioner should be able to choose another method without fear of sanction;[323] fundamentally, these disputes were best left to medical practitioners, not the courts.[324] The therapeutic freedom of a medical practitioner was regarded as central to practice,[325] and doubt as to what the accepted rule was in any given situation should, it was thought, fall in favour of the practitioner.[326]

Yet this, often alarmist, position was frequently muddied by the converse fear that such an approach to fault risked allowing any practitioner, whether orthodox holdout or quack, to justify their own personal view of the 'correct' approach to the patient's diagnosis and treatment. As *Rabel* noted, one could not simply hold, conservatively, to what one had been taught originally; equally, there was some unknown boundary when it came to new and untried methods.[327] A similar desire to check the scope of therapeutic freedom appeared in other works throughout this period;[328] but what this meant in practice was harder to identify. Certainly, the case of the holdout (*Querkopf*)[329] was the more straightforward of the two; we will examine the approach to unorthodox practitioners in the following sub-section. Building on the *Reichsgericht's* 1884 decision, treated as authoritative by early twentieth-century scholars,[330] the courts regarded the duty to remain up to date as a central part of medical practice,[331] and *Mittermaier's* earlier claim that merely holding the necessary

322 König/Kostlin (1937) 46; *Hildebrand*, similarly sceptical of widespread rules in medical practice, nevertheless also suggested that there was a small core of basic principles, which a practitioner was expected to satisfy; stopping bleeding from a patient's artery was his chosen example, Hildebrand (1925) 33.

323 Rümelin (1913) 18; Ebermayer (1930) 89.

324 Hegener (1925) 66; Hildebrand (1925) 32; König/Kostlin (1937) 46.

325 König/Kostlin (1937) 67.

326 Rümelin (1913) 18; Hildebrand (1925) 33. Such an attitude perhaps explains why *Rabel* stressed the need for experts called before the court to be honest about there being a contrary opinion in the medical discourse, Rabel (1904) 39; König/Kostlin (1937) 55, later suggested that in fact the problem was that experts too often resorted to reporting a 'theoretical, academic account' rather than the reality of what happened in practice.

327 Rabel (1904) 38. See also *Goldhahn* and *Hartmann*'s commentary on *RG 04.07.1916*, noting that the defendant's actions, whilst not considered a breach of any accepted practice at the time, had become such by the 1930s. There, he had failed to cut a deep enough incision to relieve an infected finger, leading to the loss of the arm, Goldhahn/Hartmann (1937) 75.

328 Ebermayer (1930) 89; König/Kostlin (1937) 67–69.

329 Rümelin (1913) 17.

330 Rabel (1904) 38 n 1.

331 Joachim/Korn (1911) 353–354; Bremer (1934) 14 n 26; *RG 07.01.1938* (1938) 67 JW 2203.

state license was sufficient to justify whatever choice of treatment the practitioner saw fit to adopt was now rejected out of hand.[332] Courts expected practitioners to develop their practice and one could neither hold to clearly outmoded forms of treatment,[333] nor take on treatment which was beyond one's capacity.[334] There was a suggestion that more senior and specialist practitioners were less likely to deliver more careful, conservative reports in contrast to their bolder, grubbied-by-daily-practice brethren.[335] One was not required easily to give up on long-held, proven methods,[336] but where there was no reason for choosing an obviously more dangerous treatment, a finding of fault was likely to result. In *OLG Stuttgart 12.07.1929*,[337] an orthodox practitioner had removed two benign warts from his patient's hand using quicksilver. On the basis that there was no expert willing to support this, 'remarkable "treatment"', and indeed not even a suggestion in the broader literature that this was to be favoured over the many other less dangerous treatments available, the court regarded this as a paradigmatic *Kunstfehler.*[338]

Where a course of action was supported by a minority of divergent opinions as to the 'correct' approach, despite the emphasis in the scholarship on the need to protect space for novel approaches, the German courts were, in some situations, as willing to treat such disagreement as the very reason for the court to intervene in the assessment, as they were to follow the academic lead. Particularly if a subjective view of the *Kunstfehler* was taken, then the law had greater need to be clear about how to deal with medical pluralism.

Certainly, *Ebermayer's* early work suggests that the courts were happy to deny a *Kunstfehler* where the commonly undertaken treatment carried as yet unknown risks which damaged the patient,[339] or where the defendant could demonstrate that there was a significant body which supported his approach: A 1917 decision of the *OLG Hamburg* held, in agreement with the expert opinion, that there had been no *Kunstfehler* where a practitioner had adopted a functional rather than static treatment for a broken wrist. Given the high number of bones

332 Rümelin (1913) 17.

333 *OLG Celle 19.01.1912*, cited in Ebermayer (1924) 85 and then repeated in Ebermayer (1930); Bremer (1934) 15 noting that liability would result where the old practice was in direct contravention of the new; König/Kostlin (1937) 68.

334 *RG 07.01.1938* (1938) 67 JW 2203.

335 Goldhahn/Hartmann (1937) 3.

336 König/Kostlin (1937) 67.

337 5 HRR 1929, 1909.

338 Hilger (1951) 51–52.

339 Ebermayer (1924) 87, reporting *RG 04.05.1920* concerning a 0.6g dose of arsphenamine, which caused the patient to lose their hearing; Hübner/Warneyer (1939) 172.

in the wrist, it could not be said that the static method would succeed in avoiding loss of functionality and stiffness. As such, a functional approach, was permissible.[340] As the court noted, it was no infringement against generally recognised rules because it was:[341]

> '...a method [...] which qualified supporters of medical scholarship, academic tutors and respected medical practitioners adopt and teach in universities and learned journals.'

There was little clarity as to the weight of evidence necessary to demonstrate that a defendant's behaviour was in line with the accepted rules and a reduction in the number of opinions concerning *Kunstfehlers* published in the medical press in this period compared to those discussed earlier makes it difficult to assess beyond the text of the decisions themselves. Certainly it was possible that competing expert opinions might appear before the court and in one such case *Ebermayer* was critical, noting the likely resulting disutility of a claim for damages, of a 1929 decision from the *OLG Celle*. There, a practitioner escaped liability on the basis that a single expert's testimony in his favour suggested *a priori* that he had not breached an accepted rule of medical practice.[342] That decision may be contrasted with a later one from the *OLG Karlsruhe*, where it was held *not* sufficient as proof of fault to simply show that a notable professor would have regarded a different treatment as better in the circumstances.[343]

There was a rhetorical tendency in some of the literature to note that liability was often avoided by adopting the majority approach in any given situation.[344] Indeed, it was not always clear, as had been the tenor of the discussion during the drafting process of § 276 *BGB*, that the required standard of conduct was not, in practice, equated with the customary standard of care,[345] particularly likely where the medical view was unified. In *RG 16.10.1934*, discussed further below, the *Reichsgericht*, noting three expert opinions to the effect that no-one in the defendant's position would have behaved differently, emphasised that, as to what care was required in a given medical situation, '...experience of practice, here

340 Ebermayer (1924) 87, discussing *OLG Hamburg 31.03.1917*; Goldhahn/Hartmann (1937) 169–170.

341 König/Kostlin (1937) 70.

342 Ebermayer (1930) 104, discussing *OLG Celle 11.01.1929*.

343 König/Kostlin (1937) 68, discussing *OLG Karlsruhe 31.05.1935* (2 W 82 35). *König*, at 71, was himself critical of *Ebermayer's* alarmist stance but only where, in line with his broader theory, such questions concerned fundamental therapeutic rules rather than the (apparently) less certain sort of rules that *Ebermayer's* case concerned.

344 Hilger (1951) 33–34.

345 König/Kostlin (1937) 49.

medical practice, must also be considered.'[346] Remitting the decision on procedural grounds, they explained that the lower courts could not simply disregard evidence that medical practice was contrary to their suggested standard without giving a reason for doing so.[347]

As noted above, the 1930s were marked by increasing emphasis from the *Reichsgericht* on the irrelevancy of the *Kunstfehler* and accepted practice in some situations, and this approach gained particular ground in the context of disagreements as to what accepted practice actually was. The decision of the *Reichsgericht* in *RG 12.05.1931* can be seen as laying the foundation for the courts to better independently sculpt the scope of medical liability. There,[348] the defendant had severely burned the patient's surrounding skin in the course of radiation therapy to treat benign prostatic hyperplasia. Due to the state of the art at the time, there were no established protocols for the dosage and the defendant appeared to have adopted the more aggressive protocol used for prostate cancer. Given the absence of, 'recognised, [...] fixed dosage standards', neither of the two experts felt it possible to say that the defendant was at fault by reason of having committed a *Kunstfehler.*[349] Nevertheless, both concurred that the defendant had breached his duty of care as a practitioner undertaking such treatment not to injure the patient's skin. This provided the court at first instance with all that was required to hold that the defendant had been at fault in so behaving, a finding which the *Reichsgericht*, although describing it as short,[350] nevertheless supported as sufficient. Yet that decision was, in essence, merely declaratory and, in relying heavily on the expert evidence in any case, did not necessarily herald a particularly broad development. The logical extension was for the court itself to define the contours of liability in certain situations, contrary to the views of medical experts, and this is precisely what it began, if infrequently, to do.

As the court emphasised in *RG 12.10.1934*, albeit tersely, this approach – of the court setting the standard itself – would be more easily justified where a case did not concern rules which were generally accepted in practice.[351] There, the patient's fractured femur was treated, in line with the then accepted approach, with a traction bandage. Healing progressed well, but the patient began repeatedly complaining of pain in their leg. Despite the fracture healing well,

346 *RG 16.10.1934* (1935) 64 JW 274.

347 Ibid.

348 *RG 12.05.1931* 7 HRR 1931, 1748. A fuller version of the facts is given in Hübner/Warneyer (1939) 153–154.

349 *RG 12.05.1931* 7 HRR 1931, 1748.

350 Ibid.

351 *RG 12.10.1934* (1935) 64 JW 115.

the practitioner did not remove the bandage earlier than was usual, notwithstanding repeated complaints about pain from the patient. It transpired the bandage had caused a pressure sore. The expert opinion in the case made clear that the treatment did not evidence any *Kunstfehler*, nor did there seem to be any evidence that there was any disagreement in the literature, nevertheless, the *Reichsgericht*, correcting the mistaken assumption of the lower court that where there was no *Kunstfehler* in a medical situation there could be no fault, held that the practitioner had been at fault and was liable.[352] Now, where the court was unconvinced that there was a sufficiently clear body of rules in medical practice, they were more willing to critically appraise medical behaviour themselves rather than, as was the hope in the earlier scholarly literature, remain respectfully disengaged.[353]

As the courts populated this newly excavated degree of control over medical behaviour, they allowed themselves considerable room for manoeuvre. As above, there was very little attempt to more precisely define in what circumstances a disagreement in the surrounding medical literature was sufficient to shift the discussion outside of a *Kunstfehler*-based analysis, nor, conversely, at what point a particular practice became a generally accepted rule. They did, however, give direction as to the abstract standard of care expected in such situations, suggesting that in cases of uncertainty, practitioners were expected to act conservatively in the patient's interests rather than heroically. In a 1922 decision, where the patient had been misdiagnosed as a result of the practitioner's choice to omit particular tests, the *Reichsgericht* noted that, given the importance of the interests involved for the patient, they could:[354]

> '...demand, that in constructing a clinical presentation, everything, including remote possibilities for injury and rare manifestations of risk, which are, nevertheless, understood within the scholarship, are weighed in [the practitioner's] considerations.'

In 1932, in the context of a disagreement in the medical discourse, the *Reichsgericht* repeated this rigorous position on the standard of care expected from practitioners. There, a patient suffering from osseous tuberculosis had been admitted to hospital for treatment where, he claimed, he contracted a secondary infection of erysipelas from a patient housed only a few beds away in the ward when a nurse had successively changed their dressings.[355] The *OLG Hamburg* had been unwilling to find the supervising practitioner at fault on the basis of an

352 Goldhahn / Hartmann (1937) 148–149.

353 *RG 21.06.1940* (1940) DR 1949.

354 *RG 22.12.1922* (1923) 52 JW 603.

355 *RG 22.03.1932* 8 HRR 1932, 1828, the case was widely reported in medical journals, Goldhahn / Hartmann (1937) 173.

expert opinion which had supported the treatment of patients with open wounds next to patients with ersypriel, shingles and the like. On appeal, the patient argued that the expert opinion in fact revealed there was an ongoing dispute in the medical discourse over that point and that as long as this was the case and as long as an isolation-based approach was supported by some distinguished practitioners, then in practice, '…on grounds of great caution',[356] he ought to have been isolated. The *Reichsgericht* accepted this argument, noting that the appointment of the expert by the *OLG Hamburg* was not decisive, the real question being not whether a patient would be treated according to one practice or another, but rather how best to protect patients against infection.[357] As such, it was right that a practitioner was required to show, in the words of the *Reichsgericht*, great caution and isolate such patients where the discourse was unclear and there was not another pressing reason to justify a lower standard of care.[358]

Having begun to undermine the dominance of the *Kunstfehler* in assessing medical fault before the courts, practitioners feared that the courts might then impose an overly rigorous standard of care, divorced from the realities of everyday practice. Indeed, such fears were increasingly familiar in the literature towards the end of the period covered,[359] and such was the obvious potential for this that the *Reichsgericht* itself began to openly warn of an over-extension of the standard of care owed in medical practice. In *RG 07.01.1938* the court heard an appeal from a practitioner who had been held liable for failure to debride the plaintiff locksmith's injury, a 4-centimetre wound which was contaminated with axle grease.[360] The court stressed that if, at the time of treatment, there had been a uniform view that debridement was necessary in proper practice, then there would no doubt have been a *Kunstfehler* at hand and, accordingly, fault.[361] Yet, this was not the case. Opinions in both medical practice and literature conflicted, as had been emphasised in the expert opinion, and it was upon this footing that the lower court had based its finding of fault. Yet as the *Reichsgericht* noted, the expert, *Prof X*, had reported that bleeding wounds suffered in industrial accidents and those contaminated with oil, metal and emery, were, in practice, less prone

356 *RG 22.03.1932* 8 HRR 1932, 1828.

357 Goldhahn / Hartmann (1937) 174.

358 *RG 22.03.1932* 8 HRR 1932, 1828. The court suggested that spatial and economic reasons might be particularly relevant to the latter.

359 Ebermayer (1930) 137; König / Kostlin (1937) 49–50, 55; Kallfelz (1938) 2204, 2205; Goldhahn / Hartmann (1937) 149, wondered what level of care was required to avoid liability if, as was clear from *RG 12.10.1934*, compliance with accepted practice was not sufficient; Hilger (1951) 34, 34 n 65.

360 *RG 07.01.1938* (1938) 67 JW 2203.

361 *RG 07.01.1938* (1938) 67 JW 2204.

to infection. Experience in the first world war had shown, by contrast, that seeping wounds contaminated with clothing or dirt were much more likely to lead to infection and thus required debridement. Furthermore, all experts on the subject of debridement were of the view that patients with wounds such as the plaintiff's uniformly rejected the procedure, a fact the court considered formidable.[362] On this basis, the *Reichsgericht* felt that the lower court's finding of fault, in contrast as it had itself highlighted, to the expert opinion, could not be supported. Considering the industrial character of the area from which the case emanated, to hold that primary debridement of industrial wounds was necessary, '...must be seen as an over extension of the duty of care'. Nor could fault be found in the fact that the defendant had not applied a prophylactic antiseptic wash to the fresh wound as it was not yet scientifically clear that this actually reduced the incidence of infection over the sterilised bandage the defendant had administered.[363]

As with *RG 16.10.1934*, noted above, it is possible to see these cases as simply situations where the lower court either misread the expert opinion as revealing disagreement in the medical discourse or insufficiently justified their contrary position. Certainly, towards the end of the 1930s the *Reichsgericht* repeated its earlier assertion, that customary care was insufficient to escape a finding of fault. As the court noted in 1938, although custom might satisfy the level of care required under § 276 BGB, this was merely coincidence.[364] There, the court noted that when it came to putting in place safety measures to guard against patients harming themselves whilst undergoing medical treatment, each case had to be decided on its own merit. In particular:[365]

> 'It is, however, no overextension of the concept of care, if measures are demanded through which, as common sense would indicate, the incident would have been avoided.'

In *RG 08.03.1940*, the court provided one of its strongest statements regarding patients' rights in this period. There,[366] the defendant, fearing, incorrectly, that a growth was malign, had removed the whole of the patient's breast rather than, as agreed, the growth itself. Although the case ultimately turned on failure to secure consent, there was consideration of whether there had been fault in assuming malignancy and omitting an investigatory procedure. The *Reichsgericht* emphasised that, to avoid unnecessarily stretching the concept of fault, courts ought to investigate what the usual medical response was in a given case, and

362 *RG 07.01.1938* (1938) 67 JW 2204.
363 Ibid.
364 *RG 04.02.1938* (1938) 67 JW 1246.
365 Ibid.
366 *RG 08.03.1940* RGZ 163, 129.

where the answer was unanimous to provide a reason for departing from that. Nevertheless, this evidence would be no answer to the court finding that a practitioner had, in fact, failed to demonstrate the care required in the situation.[367]

### (iv) Unorthodox Practitioners

In the early twentieth century, a number of states had further regulated unorthodox practice at the local level,[368] but the redoubt of the *Kurierfreiheit*, the notion that medical practice was in theory open to anyone, remained unbowed. Necessarily then, given the nature of the medical marketplace,[369] the courts in this period further developed their approach towards the liability of unorthodox practitioners as much as they did their university-trained brethren. As noted above, the existence of the charlatan[370] alongside the orthodox hold-out was often used in arguments about the need for a qualification to the idea of therapeutic freedom – the former often eliciting greater fear than the latter[371] – and was said to be one of the reasons for supporting an objective idea of fault in medical practice.[372] *Rümelin* reported that cases hinging on accepted practice had been rare up to 1913,[373] but that such cases were more prevalent, '…in the fight against homeopathy and, if needs be, against quackery.'[374] This is not surprising given that we have seen the standard of care in the nineteenth century used as one method by which the courts could, in the absence of being able to rely on public law tools, protect the population against less than scrupulous medical services. Here, however, a different approach was taken, with the courts veering between attempts to similarly use the law to protect patients, whilst at the same time acknowledging the pluralist nature of the medical marketplace. Of course, the potential difficulties here were not just

367 *RG 08.03.1940* RGZ 163, 134.
368 Joachim/Korn (1911) 336 f.
369 A discussion in the *Reichstag* in January 1927 had revealed little inclination to abolish the, by then longstanding, *Kurierfreiheit*, Melies (1929) 8 n 1.
370 *Melies*' exhaustive review of the contemporary literature served to demonstrate that none of the posited definitions in law of '*Kurpfuscherei*' were apt to reflect the reality of the marketplace, Melies (1929) 11–24; Joachim/Korn (1911) 330, conceding that their definition was, at best, a sociological one.
371 In particular, see Ebermayer (1930) 89.
372 Rabel (1904) 12–13. *Rabel* regarded the decision in *RG 12.04.1882*, concerning criminal fault in taking on treatment that a quack knew was beyond them, as authoritative.
373 This was no longer the case by 1925 it seems, Hegener (1925) 66.
374 Rümelin (1913) 19. Bohne (1933) 1775 f, suggesting that actions for quackery were a rising problem in the era.

restricted to obvious charlatans. Given the continued popularity of alternative therapies, the law had to also deal with practitioners who, whilst licensed, chose to practice these alternatives instead. Much of the law here concerned criminal rather than civil claims but it is instructive nevertheless.[375]

Thus, on the one hand, in 1910, the *Reichsgericht* held that a disclaimer of liability for negligent injury, which an unorthodox practitioner (there a bone-setter) had agreed with his patient, was enforceable in that it did not offend against good morals.[376] Indeed a number of commentators noted that a patient who had willingly chosen an unorthodox practitioner might have their damages reduced in accordance with § 254 *BGB*.[377] On the other, in 1912 the court held that a licensed practitioner who offered alternative therapy for syphilis could not plead their own good faith belief in the efficacy of those natural methods over the proven orthodox treatments of which they were aware;[378] it was necessary to give regard to the state of orthodox practice.[379] Continuing the theme, in *RG 18.01.1929* the court held that a practitioner of naturopathic medicine had been at fault in failing to adopt the, by then, accepted practice of testing a syphilitic patient for spirochetes.[380] One could not ignore the dominant view of the university-based tradition in which he had trained simply because he based himself on a contrary practice.[381] Equally, it could not be said that the patient had, in choosing to go to such a practitioner, turned down the chance to be

375 Melies (1929) 1–8, describing the criminal law as the natural home for this topic; similarly, König/Kostlin (1937) 71–72.

376 Ebermayer (1924) 92, considered this a questionable privilege for quacks. *Rabel* (and before him, *Gossler* on the basis that it would do damage to the necessary trust between practitioner and patient) had earlier doubted that such a disclaimer was enforceable regardless of the standing of the practitioner, Rabel (1904) 68–69; Gossler (1814) 9. Contra, Bremer (1934) 55; *Rümelin*, not citing the case, thought similarly for orthodox practitioners, Rümelin (1913) 20–21; *Korn*, argued that as, in practice, most cases involved gross negligence on the part of the practitioner (mere *culpa levis* being of apparently 'minimal practical importance'), this could not be excluded as to do so would undermine the relationship and was, in any case, likely contrary to acceptable practice, Korn (1912) 43; See also Kollbrunner (1903) 87–89.

377 Rabel (1904) 15; Bremer (1934) 55–56; Hübner/Drost (1955) 26–28. An emphasis on the correlate duties of the patient was a common feature of this period, Mansfeld (1915) 334, 340.

378 Ebermayer (1924) 124, reporting *RG 25.06.1912* which he appears to have overlooked in his earlier works; Joachim/Korn (1911) 334, noting that this had earlier been a particular problem with possible prosecutions. See also *RG 15.07.1908* (1908) 37 JW 579 where the court rejected the argument that the practitioner had any faith in his ability to cure dropsy.

379 König/Kostlin (1937) 73.

380 Ibid.

381 Ibid.

treated according to the precepts of the more scientific and scholarly tradition.[382]

Yet over the course of the 1930s, this approach gave way to an equivalency of treatment between the different forms of medicine with emphasis thus shifting to the patient's knowledge of what they were submitting to,[383] rather than necessarily holding alternative practitioners to be at fault merely because there may have been more efficacious orthodox treatments available. In a 1931 decision concerning the criminal liability of an unlicensed practitioner under § 222 *StGB* the *Reichsgericht* confirmed that the *Kunstfehler* analysis was divorced from a particular strand of medical knowledge.[384] Despite its roots in orthodox medicine, it's application was not locked to university-based *Schulmedizin* as traditionally understood. Rather, the logic of the *Kunstfehler* analysis would apply to the defendant practitioner's own body of knowledge without discrimination. A focus on *Schulmedizin* to help identify what the generally accepted rules of practice were did not, without more, require a court to consider what practitioners of that university-based tradition had to say in the matter.[385] A practitioner was not negligent in diverging from their own orthodoxy simply because others, either within their school of medicine or without, would have acted differently.[386] There, the unlicensed practitioner opted to treat the patient 'conservatively' (seemingly consisting of rubbing butter onto the patient)[387] following a bout of acute peritonitis (suggesting appendicitis) rather than, as was the leading view in orthodox practice, to operate within 48 hours.[388] Not only, it appeared, was it in principle (if not in always in practice as we have seen) inappropriate for the courts to interfere with the medical discourse, this discourse was apparently broad enough to encompass the various quasi- and para-medical fields that populated the medical market in this period.[389] Indeed in remitting the case, the *Reichsgericht* noted that the effect of the *Kurierfreiheit*

382 Ebermayer (1930) 89–90.

383 *OLG Hamburg 03.04.1928*; König/Kostlin (1937) 74. *König* suggested that there might be an exception to the otherwise safety of an unorthodox practitioner who had fully informed his patient of the alternatives where there was a case in the public interest (epidemics or sexually-transmitted diseases) for the application of *Schulmedizin*; *RG 29.02.1932* (1933) 62 JW 2062.

384 *RG 01.12.1931* RGSt 67, 12; Hübner/Warneyer (1939) 171. See also *RG 08.07.1930* RGSt 62, 26, (1931) 60 JW 1483, where a builder homeopathist of 40 years' experience was not at fault despite not using the diphtheria vaccine on a patient labouring under that illness; *RG 06.12.1929* (1930) 59 JW 1595.

385 *RG 01.12.1931* RGSt 67, 16; Hübner/Warneyer (1939) 171.

386 Hübner/Warneyer (1939) 172; König/Kostlin (1937) 72.

387 *RG* 01.12.1931 RGSt 67, 13.

388 Hübner/Warneyer (1939) 172.

389 König/Kostlin (1937) 72.

and the restrictions in the *Gewerbeordnung* 1869 (§§ 29, 147) were such as to render the German law different to the law of most other civilised nations: 'Most states have simply passed a law that permits registered medical practitioners alone to practice medicine.'[390] Those who felt, as many scholars did, that this risked significant harm to the population, were met with the *Reichsgericht's* stinging response that it was for the legislator to restrict the privileges afforded to unlicensed practice if they felt it necessary.[391] This led to the spectacle of calling for expert evidence from disciplines which lacked any overarching occupational structure and, as *RG 01.12.1931* demonstrated, could result in some odd bedfellows.[392] As a decision of the *LG Frankfurt* subsequently put it:[393]

> 'The court sees no reason to intervene in the persistent scholarly argument between practitioners of the homeopathic inclination and those of the university-based tradition.'

*König* suggested that the decision in *RG 18.01.1929* would operate as a check on the equivalency of orthodox and unorthodox practice,[394] but there is scant evidence that the courts were willing to extend the duty to scrutinise one's own practice beyond those licensed practitioners who offered alternative therapies,[395] and even then, courts seemed unwilling to hold that a particular orthodox treatment was to be preferred. In a decision from 1937, the *Reichsgericht* confirmed that a licensed practitioner offering homeopathy was not at fault despite having correctly diagnosed his patients with diphtheria and, nevertheless, having chosen homeopathic treatment rather than the then widely accepted allopathic serum.[396] The court did, however, impose a duty, which was said to bite harder on unorthodox practitioners, to inform the patient about the state of their health and the malady they were suffering in order to allow the patient the opportunity to adopt a different course,[397] and it remained the case

390 *RG 01.12.1931* RGSt 67, 22. See also Melies (1929) 2.

391 *RG 01.12.1931* RGSt 67, 25

392 Given 'conservative' supporters spanned both licensed and unlicensed practice the defendant had the benefit of a university professor, *Prof Dr K*, supporting his approach, *RG 01.12.1931* RGSt 67, 27.

393 König/Kostlin (1937) 72, discussing *LG Frankfurt a.M. 27.03.1934* (O 436 32). See also *RG 19.03.1937* (1937) 66 JW 3087.

394 König/Kostlin (1937) 73.

395 In *RG 19.03.1937* (1937) 66 JW 3087, referring to *RG 08.07.1930* the court, at 3089, noted that this was more likely to be the case where it was clear '...that as it concerns a particular illness, a particular measure is particularly effective.'

396 *RG 19.03.1937* (1937) 66 JW 3089. See also *RG 15.01.1937* 14 HRR 1938, 857; Hilger (1951) 50–51.

397 *RG 29.02.1932* (1933) 62 JW 2062; *RG 19.03.1937* (1937) 66 JW 3087.

for both orthodox[398] and unorthodox[399] practitioners alike that taking on a task beyond your level of competence was negligent.

Given the nature of the marketplace in this period and, post-1935, the emphasis placed by the Nazi state on the need to respect medical pluralism, it is perhaps unsurprising that the courts took a broad view of the defendant practitioner's right to be able to rely on their own body of accepted knowledge.[400] But this also demonstrated the flexibility of the *Kunstfehler* analysis. It was all too easily moulded into a broader reaching concept than had previously been the case, and certainly one that had not been intended by its progenitors and supporters. The assumption flowing from the late nineteenth-century cases, that orthodox medicine operated as a benchmark against which other forms of practice had to measure themselves, had been almost entirely reversed, certainly in the case of an unlicensed practitioner. Yet it sits oddly with the more assertive approach, outlined above, which was almost entirely concerned with orthodox practitioners, and we find none of the rhetoric of the vulnerable patient here. What was required would, it appears, vary not with the underlying medical nature of the act, but rather because of the willingly chosen schema of knowledge on which it was based.

### 4. The *Kunstfehler*, medical advances and patient safety

The previous parts have mapped out the conceptual changes in the approach to medical error in this period. We have seen how courts and scholars increasingly reinterpreted the *Kunstfehler* so as to allow space for the courts themselves to assess whether particular medical behaviours were negligent. By way of example, in this part we look at the approach taken by the courts in two particular fact patterns: The first is the use of X-rays (*Röntgen* rays) and radiation-based therapies such as diathermy. The second is the failure to remove objects from inside the

398 *RG 07.01.1938* (1938) 67 JW 2203.

399 *RG 15.07.1908* (1908) 37 JW 579; *RG 10.04.1905* RGSt 38, 34. *König* suggested that equivalency would tend towards a stronger duty on unorthodox practitioners to transfer complicated surgical cases to an orthodox practitioner, König / Kostlin (1937) 73–74. This had been floated, if not applied, in *RG 01.12.1931* RGSt 67, 24–25. See also, Bohne (1933) 1775 f.

400 Berufsordnung für die deutschen Ärzte 1937 § 4: '*Der Arzt hat die Pflicht, sich fortzubilden* und ohne Voreingenommenheit für oder gegen eine bestimmte Richtung in der Heilkunde *sich mit allen wichtigen Heilverfahren vertraut zu machen. Bei jedem Krankheitsfall muß der Arzt bestrebt sein, auf einfachstem Wege den bester Heilerfolg zu erzielen.*' (emphasis added). See also *RG 16.06.1936*, (1938) 67 JW 2204 where the court discussed, if also rejected, the changing nature of the medical 'occupation rank' in light of the *RÄO* 1935, which thus required balancing the health of the patient and that of the '*Volk*'.

body during surgery. These two facts patterns were repeatedly noted as particularly common in this period,[401] and in keeping with the march of orthodox medicine and the increasing specialisation of orthodox practitioners,[402] each concerned risks resulting from the increasingly invasive reach of medical science. They thus serve as a window into how the courts applied the developing jurisprudence set out above in the context of the advances in treatment and medical technology in the early twentieth century.

### (A) X-Rays and diathermy

These technologies, which were having their first sustained impact on healthcare in this period, raised particular challenges for both medical practitioner and the courts. The use of radiation-based technology straddled both diagnosis and treatment, testing the courts' willingness to question practice in both. Why was this the case? These technologies allowed, in some cases literally, a novel view into the body, but they also offered a more definitive way of diagnosing many patients or revealing, crucially, what had been missed in the process of diagnosis.[403] Equally, the fact that they were developing as a treatment protocol put them at the forefront of heroic medicine in the era and this was thus apt to present an area where the courts could exploit disagreement over accepted practice.[404] Further, the *technical* basis of radiation-based treatments opened practitioners to the risk that it would be regarded by courts as less readily compassable as truly *medical* in nature and, thus, open to greater challenge.

The use or omission of X-rays as a diagnostic tool was a common problematic case.[405] Certainly, early on, the courts were willing to accept that the additional use of an X-ray was not, according to accepted practice, a necessary part of the

401 Ebermayer (1924) 110–111; Goldhahn / Hartmann (1937) 79; Hübner / Warneyer (1939) 172.

402 Weisz (2006) 105–127.

403 Goldhahn / Hartmann (1937) 159–160; Hübner / Warneyer (1939) 34.

404 Bremer (1934) 14, noting that the duty to stay on top of new developments was of particular importance for those involved in radiotherapy and X-rays given that these areas were characterised by a rapid change in outlook. See 6 HRR 1930, 1097, where the *Reichsgericht* held that personal inexperience with radiation therapy was no answer to a claim that it had been negligently deployed, injuring the patient, Goldhahn / Hartmann (1937) 203. Certainly, those who were specialists, *Röntgenärzte*, were expected to stay connected to the developing literature. See *RG 03.09.1935* where the defendant's fault lay in not following, in 1926, the guidelines provided in 1924 by the *Deutsche Röntgengesellschaft*, Hübner / Warneyer (1939) 151–152. See also *RG 05.04.1932* 8 HRR 1932, 1643.

405 Grödel / Klopfer (1925) 2–3.

standard of care and were unwilling to challenge that,[406] and indeed that as long as treatment was carried out in accordance with the state of the art, that liability could be avoided.[407] Yet as the availability of the equipment spread, the *Reichsgericht* was more willing to take an aggressive position on the level of care that patients could expect.[408] In *RG 22.12.1922* the fault of the defendant was said to lie in merely restricting his diagnostic investigation to an external investigation and not, as the court put it, testing that result against an X-ray of the injury, there a misdiagnosed dislocated hip. In finding that the defendant was indeed at fault, the court emphasised that the hospital was equipped with the 'most modern remedies'; that the X-ray could reveal the, '...true nature of the plaintiff's injury';[409] and that in doing so it could protect *both* the plaintiff and the defendant against the regrettable outcome that had eventuated. They also noted that whilst this was only a 'very minor error', that was sufficient to ground liability.[410] The decision received a mixed reaction, with some medical commentators arguing that it set a very high standard of care for practitioners to meet,[411] others noting that it was only the coincidental availability of the X-ray that justified the result,[412] and others concerned that the court had missed the point that the patient's insurer ought to be consulted first.[413] Amongst lawyers, the reaction was more positive,[414] and it was the basis for further similar decisions.[415] Subsequent decisions, often concerning fractures,[416] saw the court uphold liability for a failure to undertake the correct X-ray quickly enough,[417] and remit cases on the basis that lower courts had failed to consider whether the omission of an X-ray was, itself, negligent. In one such case, the *Reichsgericht* emphasised that the court had overlooked the fact that the medical evidence

406 Goldhahn/Hartmann (1937) 169–170, discussing *OLG Hamburg 31.03.1917*. The court accepted that the X-ray would have made no difference to the choice of treatment. See however *Schumacher's* argument that good practice did require an X-ray for all possible fractures, *Schumacher* MMW 1931, 65.

407 Ebermayer (1924) 111, discussing *RG 01.10.1912*.

408 Hübner/Warneyer (1939) 34.

409 The court also later described X-rays as 'infallible', criticised as layman's puff by *König*, König/Kostlin (1937) 62.

410 *RG 22.12.1922* (1923) 52 JW 603.

411 Goldhahn/Hartmann (1937) 155.

412 *RG 22.12.1922* (1923) 52 JW 603, commentary from *Straßmann*.

413 *RG 22.12.1922* (1923) 52 JW 603, commentary from *Thierlich*, contra Goldhahn/Hartmann (1937) 158 suggesting that given the likelihood that a claim in negligence would result omitting an X-ray, it was better to proceed in most cases.

414 Ebermayer (1930) 137; Bremer (1934) 16; König/Kostlin (1937) 62.

415 *RG 20.06.1930* (1931) 60 JW 1466.

416 Hübner/Warneyer (1939) 35, noting that by comparison only two decisions concerning lung infections could be found.

417 *RG 23.02.1934*, Goldhahn/Hartmann (1937) 155.

considered an X-ray necessary, although it conceded that was not the case for all serious injuries.[418] As *Ebermayer* pointed out in the context of injuries from overexposure, although the courts would not retroactively apply a contemporary standard of care to a historic case,[419] the clearer the guidelines about dosage, the easier it was to assess if a practitioner had been at fault.[420] This dynamic could be seen at work in *RG 12.03.1931* where the court was unable to identify a recognised rule for radiation therapy dosage, but, nevertheless, held the practitioner at fault.[421]

Alongside scholars,[422] courts had suggested that the practitioner's locality would naturally be a relevant factor in setting the standard of care. But whilst this was often used to try and justify a lower, less modern standard of care,[423] in the context of X-rays it was used to ensure that patients were getting the benefit, as the court understood it, of medical advances.[424] Even where the court did not explicitly emphasise the easy availability of such technology, some feared that reliance on experts who tended to be seated at the most modern and well-equipped institutions would informally impose a considerably higher standard of care on their less well-equipped brethren than was just.[425] The *Reichsgericht* was similarly unreceptive towards the argument that an X-ray, although available, had not been undertaken on a child with a broken elbow due to resource constraints during hyperinflation. Given the injury, short of direct orders from the relevant insurance fund or the patient's (or guardian's) explicit rejection, a practitioner could not be excused for their failure to use a, '…necessarily essential examination'.[426]

418 Ebermayer (1930) 125–126, discussing *RG 03.05.1927* and *RG 22.03.1927*; Goldhahn / Hartmann (1937) 170–172, disputing that there was any case in which, in advance, an X-ray could be said to be necessary.

419 *RG 16.06.1931*, Goldhahn / Hartmann (1937) 206; Hilger (1951) 35.

420 Ebermayer (1930) 142.

421 *RG 12.05.1931* 7 HRR 1931, 1748. See also *RG 03.03.1936*, Hübner / Warneyer (1939) 37 where disagreement over the possible interpretation of an X-ray was met with the court finding fault in the failure to go back and re-image the wound; Hübner / Warneyer (1939) 116.

422 Rabel (1904) 11; Rümelin (1913) 11–12, contrasting it with Swiss practice which, he noted, applied the same standard in each; König / Kostlin (1937) 48, 53–54; Hilger (1951) 33. On locality and the objective standard of fault see Deutsch (1963) 30.

423 *OLG Celle 19.01.1912*, reported in Ebermayer (1924) 85; *RG 07.01.1938* (1938) 67 JW 2203. See also the unsuccessful defendant's argument in *RG 16.10.1934*; v Gunkel (1935) 621.

424 König / Kostlin (1937) 48. See also *RG 03.07.1934* where fault turned on the failure to use available diagnostic microscopy, König / Kostlin (1937) 60.

425 König / Kostlin (1937) 64; Hübner / Warneyer (1939) 114.

426 *RG 29.09.1936*, reported in Goldhahn / Hartmann (1937) 217–218.

Reliance on the availability of the necessary resources presented a particular problem given that the courts could hold a referring practitioner liable for the negligence of his colleague, who might be insufficiently equipped to provide that service.[427] Equally the courts created a rigorous set of duties incumbent upon the supervising practitioner to oversee the setting up of the equipment and filters rather than simply delegating treatment to ancillary staff.[428] Nor was it an answer that a more senior specialist had concurred with the initial diagnosis where treatment remained the responsibility of the defendant junior.[429]

Throughout the 1930s, the use of X-rays as a diagnostic tool became increasingly important as a means of avoiding liability,[430] albeit one could not simply deploy an X-ray pro forma; the results had to actually be examined.[431] Nor was it enough to simply offer radioscopy.[432] Such was the ubiquity of X-ray related injury that one 1935 study revealed that of 238 claims against medical practitioners 129 of them had involved a claim based on the omission or incorrect use of X-rays.[433] In some situations, the courts imposed a duty to re-image an injury with a further X-ray to check an initial diagnostic and treatment choice. To that end, the *Reichsgericht* held that where treatment was clearly not improving an injury, it was imperative to latterly employ an X-ray,[434] and it could be necessary to revisit an initial diagnosis in the face of ongoing pain even where a X-ray had been undertaken initially.[435] Equally, although it was insufficient to show that a practitioner had merely omitted an X-ray when there

427 *RG 03.06.1921* RGZ 102, 230; Goldhahn / Hartmann (1937) 158; Ebermayer (1930) 142.

428 *RG 16.09.1927* RG 118, 42= (1927) 56 JW 2844; Ebermayer (1924) 112, reporting *RG 24.03.1917*. A more lenient, if hard to distinguish, line was taken where the fault concerned a purely technical feature of the treatment, there the placement of the plates. *RG 19.01.1933* RGZ 139, 255; Hübner / Warneyer (1939) 150–152.

429 *RG 03.03.1936*, Goldhahn / Hartmann (1937) 161–162.

430 Gródel / Klopfer (1925) 3, suggesting that the rise in cases dated from the 1920s. This is supported by *Ebermayer* and it is notable that his first edition in 1924 singled out X-ray treatment in the contents page for particular coverage, Ebermayer (1924) 110–111; Ebermayer (1930) 142; Hübner / Warneyer (1939) 34 f.

431 Goldhahn / Hartmann (1937) 160, discussing *RG 20.07.1930*. See also, at 164, *LG Berlin 21.04.1931*.

432 Hübner / Warneyer (1939) 35.

433 Goldhahn / Hartmann (1937) 154–155, stressing the importance of using X-rays during treatment.

434 *RG 24.01.1933*, Goldhahn / Hartmann (1937) 161; Hübner / Warneyer (1939) 35, 39.

435 See also *RG 03.03.1936*, Goldhahn / Hartmann (1937) 161–162: 'The persistent severe pain of the plaintiff must already have given cause to take a new X-ray and to reassess the diagnosis'; *RG 23.02.1934*, Hübner / Warneyer (1939) 40–41.

was nothing to suggest the initial diagnosis was incorrect and the usual lag of time whereby an injury might be allowed to develop and settle had not passed, it would be otherwise where the diagnosis was less clear.[436] It was in the context of these cases that the court expressly emphasised the severability of fault from the *Kunstfehler*, discussed above,[437] although it should be noted that the willingness of the courts to critically engage with the expected standard of treatment did nothing to alleviate the plaintiff of the need to demonstrate that X-raying the injury would have avoided the resulting harm.[438] Alongside failure to X-ray the patient, injuries from incorrectly administered radiation treatment itself, excessive exposure and the resulting burns, were also common cases in this period,[439] and equally saw the court both exploit an absence of accepted practice and explicitly acknowledge the severability of the legal and medical discourses.[440]

### (B) Retained foreign objects

The root cause of the surge in cases concerning retained foreign objects lay in the maturation of modern surgical technique and facilities. But, as will be shown, their analysis as a legal problem reveals a forum where the German courts were, again, willing to impose their own view of medical behaviour in the teeth of medical expertise. There is an overlap with the preceding section in that the courts at times relied on the availability of X-rays as a check on the practitioner's assessment of whether anything had been retained, but much more so we see a tension between practitioners' desire to analyse these cases as ones in which the exigencies of emergency outweighed the need to take care in the moment and the courts' increasing attempts to ensure that broader safety measures were used to safeguard the patient.

The topic had slightly longer roots in the legal sources, helped by coverage of the Swiss *Bundesgericht's* 1904 decision and, after anaesthetic, its independence from a particular medical development,[441] but it was a topic where medical and legal opinions diverged unlike in any other.[442] In commenting on that 1904 decision, *Rümelin* had, as noted above, assumed that this would be an area where

436 *RG 17.03.1939* Seuffert's Archiv 93, 260.

437 *RG 23.02.1934*, Hübner / Warneyer (1939) 40–41.

438 *RG 28.03.1930* RGZ 128, 121; Goldhahn / Hartmann (1937) 166.

439 Bremer (1934) 20; Hübner / Warneyer (1939) 114, 149.

440 *RG 18.10.1930*; *RG 12.05.1931*, both reported in Hübner / Warneyer (1939) 152–152. In the former, the court rejected evidence from a leading textbook as to appropriate dosage.

441 *Ebermayer* reported that there had been 200 cases in the previous 20 years, Ebermayer (1924) 83.

442 Hübner / Warneyer (1939) 94.

there ought to be clear rules whose breach would clearly be a *Kunstfehler.*[443] That would prove, in part, incorrect. Similarly, *Ebermayer's* 1924 commentary on a 1913 decision from the *LG Königsberg* suggested that the question here was whether there were any circumstances in which leaving an object behind would not be regarded as negligent.[444] As it transpired, the answer was yes. Given the circumstances of the operation had required the rapid closure of the abdominal incision, the *Landesgericht* there had denied the claim.[445]

Where this was not the case, however, matters might differ. In *RG 09.07.1913*, where a 60-100cm gauze swab was retained, the court was happy to hold the defendant hospital responsible for the negligence of the operating surgeon, adopting a seemingly prescriptive position. Although the relevant expert had denied that there had been gross fault in the defendant's actions, there had, nevertheless, been a failure to provide the care required which, by the *Reichsgericht's* logic, would have avoided any retention. As they put it:[446]

> 'Whether through the combination of more safety measures or by other means, the defendant must have found a way whereby the retention of the swab was prevented and the removal of all bandages from the wound could be guaranteed.'

An appeal that the operation had to take place at speed because there had been no anaesthetic to hand was rejected on evidential grounds alongside a finding that, in any case, this was the fault of the hospital themselves. Finally, relying on their approach in *RG 01.03.1912*, the court held that the defendant had failed to provide an account of how the accident could have happened without fault on their part.[447] The decision is remarkable for its forthrightness in setting a high standard of care contrary to the relevant expert evidence;[448] the basic position was that, in the absence of extenuating circumstances, all materials had to be removed to avoid negligence.[449]

443 Rümelin (1913) 15 n 2.

444 Ebermayer (1924) 81–82.

445 Ibid. 82. *Ebermayer*, at 83, criticised a similar decision on the same lines in *RG 14.07.1913* where the court held that a lower standard of care should be applied in these cases, but abandoned the position subsequently, Ebermayer (1930) 91–92.

446 *RG 09.07.1913* RGZ 83, 75.

447 It should be noted that, as in *RG 01.03.1912*, the *Reichsgericht* here stressed that this approach did nothing to upset the ordinary burden of proof, *RG 09.07.1913* RGZ 83, 75. Equally, the practitioner appears to have failed to lead any evidence themselves to contradict the plaintiff's version of events, Mansfeld (1915) 334, 339.

448 Thus, causing a considerable degree of disquiet in medical circles, Mansfeld (1915) 334, 338.

449 See also the suggestion to this effect in *OLG Karlsruhe 22.12.1928*, Goldhahn / Hartmann (1937) 81.

By the end of that decade, this position was softening, with different emphasis put on the basic standard set out in *RG 01.03.1912.*[450] In *RG 17.10.1919,*[451] the *Reichsgericht* dismissed the plaintiff's appeal, focusing on the superseding nature of complications during the surgery necessitating swift closure and noting this time that, in such circumstances, items might indeed be retained despite the greatest degree of care on the defendant's part.[452] It also rejected the request for a senior expert opinion on the point given the first instance finding that the three expert witnesses were leaders in this field, laying heavy emphasis on the need to have evidence from those with direct knowledge of the risks in undertaking such surgery.[453] The evidence had endorsed the defendant's practice of leaving the corners of swabs hanging out of the wound or clipping them to the incision. The plaintiff argued that the defendant ought to have counted the items in, and out. Rejecting this, the *Reichsgericht* accepted the finding that, given counting would take place after closure thus risking a re-opening, it posed just as much danger to the patient as sewing items inside.[454] In any case, the circumstances of the case were sufficient to defeat the claim.[455] Commenting on this, *Ebermayer* stressed that the need to take into account the exigencies of medical practice that the defendant had faced was of particular resonance in these cases and that they could only be decided on a case to case basis.[456] Indeed he refuted the claim by a judge of the *OLG Munich* that forgetting an item would, except for the presence of 'totally extraordinary circumstances', always result in a finding of fault.[457] Rather, such were the many vagaries of surgery that any mere occurrence would, he argued, suffice to deny a finding of negligence.[458]

Whilst the distinction between those decisions was accepted as hanging on intra-surgery emergency,[459] and such cases were familiar examples in the

450 *RG 01.03.1912* RGZ 78, 432.

451 *RG 17.10.1919* RGZ 97, 4.

452 *RG 17.10.1919* RGZ 97, 6; Bremer (1934) 20.

453 *RG 17.10.1919* RGZ 97, 6.

454 Ibid. 5.

455 See also *RG 06.01.1928*, reported in Ebermayer (1930) 92. There, a sliver of the surgical shears had snapped off but could not be located before it became necessary to close. Although later located and removed, the claim was thrice rejected on the basis of the circumstances of the surgery and that, in any case, it was unforeseeable that the shears would break; Goldhahn / Hartmann (1937) 115.

456 Ebermayer (1930) 91; König/Kostlin (1937) 77, noting, poetically, that surgery was not simply a game of chess.

457 Schiedermair (1928) 280. See also Goldhahn / Hartmann (1937) 79–80 who were critical of the piece as inappropriate.

458 Ebermayer (1937) 2084. See also Goldhahn / Hartmann (1937) 106–107.

459 Mansfeld (1915) 334, 338, who noted, at n 1, its similarity to *BG 03.06.1904*; Bremer (1934) 20; König/Kostlin (1937) 48; Hübner/Warneyer (1939) 99.

literature,[460] later decisions in the period narrowed focus onto accepted medical practice, returning to the claim in *RG 17.10.1919*, that there was no way to guarantee removal of every item;[461] an opinion which, perhaps unsurprisingly, had been strongly endorsed in the medical literature by senior surgeons.[462] In *RG 20.06.1930* the court held that a practitioner was obliged to undertake an X-ray where a tube disappeared during re-dressing and an attempt to locate it manually was fruitless.[463] It was a failure to provide the care required that the defendant discounted the possibility that the tube had fallen into the wound and had not critically reviewed his assumptions rather than waiting to see if the patient's recovery stalled.[464] Further decisions required the defendant to lead some evidence that measures had been taken to ensure the wound remained uncontaminated rather than simply being able to rely on the assumption that items might be retained during even the most careful procedure.[465] Nor could a defendant surgeon plead that a swab might have been introduced without his knowledge by an assistant as they were expected to have control over the whole theatre.[466]

Imposing a requirement to count items or otherwise secure them became an important battleground. In *RG 16.01.1934*,[467] the court endorsed an expert opinion to the effect that, in the knowledge of the potential difficulties of the operation, the defendant practitioner ought to have personally counted the swabs before and afterwards to ensure that nothing, including the offending 97 x 45 cm item,[468] was left behind. They rejected the counterarguments that a count

460 König / Kostlin (1937) 48, discussing *OLG* Hamm 15.05.1933 and *KG 27.12.1931* which saw claims dismissed because of the supervening circumstances of the surgery.

461 *RG 17.10.1919* RGZ 97, 4; Ebermayer (1930) 92.

462 Karg (1928) 2082; v Haberer (1926) 97, noting that even he, then one of the leading surgeons in the German-speaking world, had lost items six times in 8,343 cases; Goldhahn / Hartmann (1937) 87.

463 *RG 20.06.1930* (1931) 60 JW 1466; Bremer (1934) 19.

464 Hübner / Warneyer (1939) 101, who saw the case as on all fours with *RG 22.12.1922* (1923) 52 JW 603. See also *RG 12.11.1935* (1936) 65 JW 644 where the case was remitted, in part, to consider a similar argument.

465 Goldhahn / Hartmann (1937) 104–105, reporting an undated 1930 decision of the *LG Hanau*. See also König / Kostlin (1937) 76–77, discussing *OLG Köln 13.02.1931* where the court held, contrary to the expert opinion, that delegating counting of the materials to assistants was not enough to avoid the claim. This requirement appears to have run contrary to the practice in many hospitals, Goldhahn / Hartmann (1937) 90–91.

466 Goldhahn / Hartmann (1937) 104–105, reporting an undated 1930 decision of the *LG* Mannheim.

467 *RG 16.01.1934*, Seuffert's Archiv 88, 140.

468 Goldhahn / Hartmann (1937) 109.

should only be undertaken where an operation had gone badly and that the operation had, despite the error, saved the patient's life.[469] The decision was fiercely criticised,[470] but its impact flowed through into later cases. In *RG 12.11.1935*, the court noted that it was precisely because items in the cavity might, from suffusion with blood, be difficult to locate, that further safety measures might be required so as to guard against the resulting danger to the patient.[471] In *RG 09.10.1936*, the court disregarded the sudden worsening of the patient during surgery – the heart of the expert evidence – focusing instead on the fact that the defendant had undertaken no safety measures, either counting or affixing the various items, during surgery; this was sufficient for a finding of fault given that a surgeon was required to take 'particular measures' to guard against the risk.[472] Indeed the hospital's own safety procedures, ignored by the defendant, had required a count to be undertaken.[473] Nevertheless, a number of studies in the period give an insight into the considerable degree of disagreement within medical practice as to exactly what, beyond the surgeon's nous, would help.[474] One oft-cited study surveyed 60 hospital heads to find that only two required a count for swabs and only eight for larger abdominal packs, including the surveyor themselves,[475] and, despite the persistence of the problem, there appeared to be no majority behind any particular safety measure.[476] Indeed some denied that there was any reasonable control possible where an operation required a huge number of bandages.[477]

Medical practitioners looked to *RG 16.10.1934* for reassurance.[478] There, a piece of a catheter, which had been broken during a previous operation but was assumed to have been accounted for, necessitated a later operation whereupon it

469 *RG 16.01.1934*, Seuffert's Archiv 88, 141.

470 Goldhahn / Hartmann (1937) 108–109, noted that the decision was contrary to the customs of the majority of clinics and surgeons and squarely blamed the expert; König / Kostlin (1937) 49, 76, 79, describing the decision as fundamentally mistaken, inexplicable and having paid too little attention to the difficulty of the surgery.

471 *RG 12.11.1935* (1936) 65 JW 644; Hübner / Warneyer (1939) 102–108.

472 Hübner / Warneyer (1939) 113.

473 Goldhahn / Hartmann (1937) 113–115. See also *LG Eisenach 21.11.1935* where the court enforced a need for special accounting when it came to counting such items.

474 Goldhahn / Hartmann (1937) 82.

475 König / Kostlin (1937) 76. See also the various medical studies reported in Goldhahn / Hartmann (1937) 84 f.

476 Goldhahn / Hartmann (1937) 87, 92–94; Hübner / Warneyer (1939) 94. The main contenders against counting appeared to be numerous different ways to tag, clip or bind parts of the items hanging outside the wound or post-operation X-rays.

477 Goldhahn / Hartmann (1937) 83.

478 *RG 16.10.1934* Seuffert's Archiv 89, 48; (1935) 64 JW 273.

was recovered.[479] The plaintiff argued that there had been negligence in the failure to X-ray given the fragment could not be located manually.[480] Having failed to defeat the claim for medical costs and 15,000 RM in damages for pain and suffering before the *OLG*, the defendant appealed on the basis that all the medical evidence presented in the case unanimously reported that no surgeon would have undertaken an X-ray in such circumstances. The *Reichsgericht* remitted the case as evidencing procedural impropriety; the *OLG* had, it transpired, failed to grapple with the various expert opinions. However, the *Reichsgericht* also rejected the defendant's claim that the operation had taken place in extenuating circumstances. Indeed, they noted that, despite the fact that the hospital was relatively small and such cases were rare there, the situation was far from urgent and that an X-ray had been available.[481] Whilst celebrated in some quarters as a welcome corrective,[482] it was seen by others in medical practice as a merely qualified victory given that, to their chagrin, the *Reichsgericht* had maintained the possibility that accepted practice might, in the right circumstances, be challenged.[483] Indeed, a similar appeal was rejected on exactly these grounds shortly thereafter; the lower court having held that the defendant's degree of carelessness was simply too great despite expert evidence to the contrary.[484] Equally, as shown in a subsequent decision, paying heed to the experience of medical practice in establishing the standard of care owed to the patient was a process that could just as well, as it did there, serve to establish a practitioner's negligence.[485]

None of this should be taken as suggesting that the courts ceased entirely to be sympathetic in cases where events overtook the orderly close of surgery. In *RG 12.11.1935*, where a suspected infection turned out to be tuberculosis and thus required an unplanned emergency hysterectomy, which saw two 20 x 25cm swabs retained, the *Reichsgericht* confirmed that the circumstances of a surgery could defeat an allegation of negligence,[486] and that the simple fact that objects

479 v Gunkel (1935) 620.

480 Ibid. 621.

481 Ibid. 621.

482 Kallfelz (1935) 606–607, complaining that the courts often ignored practitioners' views for fear they were biased or had an interest in the case. See also König/Kostlin (1937) 49–50; Goldhahn/Hartmann (1937) 122, who, somewhat excessively, took the case as authority for the proposition that expert evidence was thus of 'decisive importance'; Kallfelz (1938) 2204, 2205.

483 v Gunkel (1935) 622.

484 *RG 30.10.1936* reported in Hübner/Warneyer (1939) 113–114. There, where a 50cm plug had been left inside the patient, the court held there had been a *Kunstfehler* in the face of all medical testimony to the contrary.

485 *OLG Munich 29.01.1938* 14 HRR 1938, 725, citing *RG 16.10.1934*.

486 *RG 12.11.1935* (1936) 65 JW 644.

were retained was not, in itself, negligent.[487] But they placed greater emphasis on the need for supervening events to have substantially and suddenly disrupted the defendant's entire focus.[488] As the court acknowledged in *RG 09.10.1936*, there was a foreseeable risk of complications with any abdominal surgery.[489] Furthermore, the court could reframe the question and require a defendant to show they could not have foreseen the actual condition beforehand and changed course accordingly,[490] albeit that claim failed there.[491]

### (C) Assessment

The two situations examined in this part reveal the reality of the doctrinal shifts outlined in the preceding parts of this chapter. In each, the courts shifted towards a footing that saw them challenge and undermine medical expertise; fault came to be increasingly defined in their own terms rather than, as had been the case, inevitably tied to the contours of medically accepted practice.

In the case of X-rays, this flowed from the courts' view of what a patient was entitled to expect from the institution they were being treated in as the technology spread throughout the burgeoning hospital system and the centre of gravity shifted, irreversibly, away from the home. Equally it evidenced a simplistic, non-medicalised view of the utility of X-rays with medical evidence that it was not customary to X-ray a patient in a given scenario met by the courts' insistence that the X-ray could, and indeed should, operate as a panacea against the resulting harm. That many of these cases concerned broken bones is unsurprising; offering a forum where that claim was inevitably stronger and the diagnostic reality fraught with difficulty. The nature of attainable medical knowledge was changing and, with it, the courts' willingness to scrutinise a core area of *medical* behaviour, diagnostic assessment, even if that diagnosis itself relied on the use of simple technical means. Thus, practitioners were not simply

487 Emphasised in *RG 9.10.1936* König/Kostlin (1937) 55; Hübner/Warneyer (1939) 99.

488 Hübner/Warneyer (1939) 105.

489 Hübner/Warneyer (1939) 112.

490 Goldhahn/Hartmann (1937) 82, discussing *RG 12.11.1935*. Hübner/Warneyer (1939) 107. Those, such as *Goldhahn* and *Hartmann*, at 112, who appear only to have relied on the short form of the report heartily endorsed it as confirming a focus on surrounding events, but *Hübner* and *Warneyer* saw it rather, at 102, as confirming, '...particularly strong requirements for the duty of care and concentration of the operating surgeon.' It is submitted that the latter reading is the better of the two. Certainly, the case was very poorly received in the medical literature, see Hübner/Warneyer (1939) 108–110.

491 Hübner/Warneyer (1939) 110–111.

expected to offer appropriate treatment, but to critically reflect on their decisions and actions, with the X-ray offering them, in the courts' view, the ability to do so.

In the case of retained objects this standard setting process saw a dual shift in that the safety measures surrounding surgery were subjected to a greater level of scrutiny as to their use and execution, alongside a decreasing emphasis on the potential vagaries of surgery. In the teeth of clear disagreement and uncertainty within the associated medical discourse, the *Reichsgericht* was willing to impose a prescriptive requirement for some sort of safety measure beyond simple reliance on the defendant surgeon to avoid leaving an item behind. This represented a fundamental attack on the legal understanding of the nature of medical behaviour and revealed a clear difference between the medical and legal discourses surrounding medical error. Medical willingness to focus on the context surrounding the treatment was clear: The legal analysis of the medical act focused less on the intimacies of surgery itself. The end goal was not the survival of the patient at any cost up to death, but rather securing protection for them throughout the entire process of treatment. If that required the courts to stimulate the development of safety measures, or, again, require critical self-reflection from an otherwise confident (if mistaken) surgeon, then that was a task to which they were willing to turn.

The common rhetoric from *RG 01.03.1912* that medicine did not allow machine-like precision, did not mean, as it had been understood amongst many of the scholars in this period, that the mere fact that patients' bodies could be capricious was sufficient to lower the standard that the law imposed, nor was this a response when technological advances in medical treatment were capable of providing such precision, or at least the judicial conception of it. Indeed, it is notable in these case-studies that the very language of the *Kunstfehler*, objectively conceived, was beginning to disappear, at least as they were dealt with in the *Reichsgericht*. Far more so, the subjectivist reading was coming to define the contours of liability here and, with it, the imposition of a judicially-driven view of what the care required in the circumstances meant in practice.

## 5. The impact of National Socialism

Although the seizure of power by the Nazis in March 1933 usually marks a violent shift in most historical narratives, what *Cocks* characterises as the Third Reich's black-hole-like effect on German history,[492] this does not appear to be the case for the analysis of medical error by the German courts. As *Riegger* notes, the explicit impact of the Nazi takeover on the law relating to the subject of this

492 Cocks (1997) 1.

study can be identified in the legislative changes in medical organisation and discipline examined in chapter one.[493] Within that legislative programme, and often in deceptive rhetorical service of a long-held aim of orthodox practitioners,[494] a range of provisions bent the regulatory and disciplinary apparatus surrounding medical practice to the ultimate aims of the regime.[495] The long-sought unified organisational regime for orthodox medicine came at the cost of submitting entirely to the Nazi state.[496] Yet, given organised medicine and medical practitioners played an intimate role, not only in implementing but in originating the racial and biological ideologies that underpinned the atrocities of the Nazi regime,[497] this raises a natural inference that this corruption implicitly influenced legal development throughout this period. Although there were moves towards replacing the *BGB*, these were never implemented, and the basic legal framework governing medical error remained the same throughout;[498] any such influence would therefore have to be identified in the application or interpretation of this framework.

Whether this was indeed the case, however, is harder to parse in practice, and there is certainly scant evidence to suggest such influence on our precise subject matter here. For one, both in form and substance, the case law of the *Reichsgericht* in this area, as will be examined in greater detail below, suggests just that. As to form, none of the post-1933 case law relied on here utilises the rhetoric or terminology of the regime;[499] it resembles the case law of the preceding decades

493 Riegger (2007) 118.

494 Grunberger (1971) 221, noting the overlap between Nazi policy and the economic aspirations of many low-paid orthodox practitioners; Kater (2002) stressing personal occupational incentives as a means of advancement; Leichter (1979) 134–135.

495 Maehle (2016); Hubenstorf (1993) 43 f.

496 Leichter (1979) 135; McClelland (2002) 223–227.

497 See generally Lifton (1986); Leichter (1979) 133, noting the desire to control health insurance given its Social Democratic roots; Kater (1989) 35 ff; See Bock (1997) on the pre-history of surgical sterilisation in the Weimar period, and, at 160, the high degree of involvement in administering the new public health offices charged with enforcing the racial hygiene laws; on the pre-legal-history of these issues see Eser (1990) 25–28 f.

498 Riegger (2007) 132; Schiemann (2013) 2789–2790.

499 The glossary provided by *Majer* has proved an invaluable source here, see Majer (2003) 933-946; see also, Stolleis (1998) 64 f, who unpacks the role of community ('*Volksgemeinschaft*') in restructuring and reinterpreting the existing law. The only suggestions of its relevance here are, firstly, the passing reference to the fact that the relevant unorthodox treatment for diphtheria meant that it was not inherently illegal given the '*Reichsgesundheitsamt*' guidelines in *RG 19.03.1937* (1937) 66 JW 3089, and, secondly, the emphasis placed on the fact that treatment had been taking place in the industrial quarter of Rhine-Westphalia in *RG*

in almost every way other than the increasing frequency of cases concerned with problems arising from surgery and the use of technology, issues that are broadly incidental to the rise of the Nazi regime.[500] As to substance, the court pressed on with the business of separating the medical discourse around error from the legal one. This process of disentanglement, as we have seen, ultimately empowered them to challenge received medical behaviours and exploit medical disagreement by substituting their own ideas of what 'required' care under § 276 *BGB* entailed. If the 'medicalised killing'[501] of this period resulted, in part, from allowing orthodox practitioners the freedom to operate unchecked – often by aligning the idea of individual health with that of the '*Volk*' or '*Volkskörper*'[502] – then the analysis of *accidental* medical injuries that emerges from this period suggests a different approach there.[503] Indeed, looking beyond the subject matter of this study into other, closely-related areas of medical liability in this period, a similar picture emerges. It was, likewise, in the Nazi era that the *Reichsgericht* sharpened both its nascent case law on reversing the burden of proof in some medical liability claims,[504] and, for the first time, allowed successful claims on the basis that a practitioner had failed to disclose risks inherent in a successful operation, a line of doctrine built on emphasising the importance of the patient's consent to undergo treatment.[505]

Two interlocking factors may explain this jarring duality. First, although a considerable number of medical practitioners were involved in implementing the Nazi programme at home, at the front, and in concentration camps,[506] everyday medical practice continued.[507] It is likely that the huge drain of medical talent towards those theatres – and the accelerated training programme

07.01.1938 (1938) 67 JW 2204 as one justification for holding there had been no fault.

500 Lawrence (2006) 372. For the impact of these issues in other systems during the same period see Hondius (2010).

501 Bock (1997) 149.

502 Ibid. 155–156; Leichter (1979) 134.

503 *Stolleis* notes that it was not uncommon within civil law for some areas and topics to more thoroughly absorb Nazi thinking than others, see Stolleis (1998) 69.

504 Helbron (2001) 23–24.

505 Ibid. 80–82; see also Eser (1990) 23, noting, perhaps counterintuitively, that a meaningful disclosure duty was only widely accepted in the standard works on medical liability in the 1930s; Riegger (2007) 125.

506 Grunberger (1971) 220–221.

507 As *Bock* concludes, alongside the emerging state infrastructure focused on implementing mass murder, there was a, '…more or less modern, more or less normal twentieth-century welfare state' available to 'valuable' kinds of persons, see Bock (1997) 172; Lifton (1986) 418 ff on the idea of this sort of 'doubling' as a means of understanding the psychology of medical participation in the regime.

that necessarily resulted in order to try and balance it[508] – led to a decline in the quality of service for the 'ordinary *Krankenkasse* patient', thus risking lowering the standard of medical care provided in practice as the needs of the '*Volk*' came before the needs of individual patients.[509] But it is less obvious that this would have an immediate effect on the *legal* analysis of medical error. If understood to be a widespread problem, it may have provided a tacit justification for the courts easing the burden on plaintiffs and, equally, may supply an alternative explanation for the continued rise in cases before the courts during this era. But tracking a rise in cases to a particular cause here is guesswork at best and it is certainly the case that the rise continued a trend reported before the Nazi redistribution would have taken effect.[510] Equally, there is support for the idea that in the case of the medical practitioners there were pre-existing, underlying features of their occupational development in the decades preceding the Nazi takeover that predisposed them to participate in the atrocities that would follow.[511] If that is the case, then, again, it would downplay (but not rule out) the extent to which a change in the interpretation of the law on the basis of a change in medical behaviour might be expected after 1933.

Secondly, a key factor may simply be that, in the cases that reached the courts, the plaintiff was a patient who was lucky enough not to have fallen into one of the categories of persons against whom the regime oriented itself. As *Majer's* study makes clear, the separation in law of the populace into 'Germans' and 'non-Germans' was a vital part of fully implementing the regime's goals.[512] This may explain both the absence of any identifiable Nazi rhetoric in these cases and the effect of these cases in opening the way to better affording the patient–-plaintiff the protection of the law. The latter would be in keeping with the fact

508 Grunberger (1971) 220; Leichter (1979) 136.

509 Grunberger (1971) 221, noting the rise by 1936 of the insured patient to practitioner ratio from 450:1 to 600:1. This was particularly acute in some major cities where the removal of essentially all Jewish medical practitioners caused immediate problems, see Leichter (1979) 136. Although the general health of the population did improve on some measures throughout the Nazi era, see Grunberger (1971) 222–226.

510 The perceived rise in cases concerning medical error in this period partly contrasts with the emphasis placed on not suing for personal losses in the interests of '*Volk*', see Rothe / Naumburg (1937); but, equally, there were signals from within legal administration that in claims concerned with occupational misconduct, settlement was to be avoided as contrary to Nazi ideology, an idea welcomed in the literature on medical liability as guarding against spurious claims, see König / Kostlin (1937) 2.

511 Lifton (1986) 22 ff; Leichter (1979) 134–136; Bock (1997); Lawrence (2006) 374–375.

512 Majer (2003) 56–73; Rüthers (2017) 110; Stolleis (1998) 14; Bock, 170.

that whilst the various legislative changes were often intended to target 'non-Germans' directly,[513] or indirectly,[514] those fortunate enough to be regarded as 'Germans', indeed to be treated as persons at all, benefitted from the notional privilege of the law's protection.[515] Certainly where the plaintiff fell outside this privileged category, and was afforded access to the regular courts at all,[516] judges were more willing to creatively apply spurious interpretations of the civil law to deny the claim.[517] This process often relied on the general clauses of the *BGB* to supply the access point for them to do so.[518] Whether the norm provided in § 276 *BGB* was itself capable of such easy manipulation is unclear, but, on the face of the code, the standard of care required in a given situation was open for the court to simply declare.[519] Yet, for the subject matter of this study, we know that the German courts did not take this approach, given judicial reliance on the medical discourse to unpack what § 276 *BGB* meant; here they were not starting from such malleably open provisions as § 242 *BGB* or § 826 *BGB*. It may be that the continued path towards asserting the ultimate irrelevance of that approach was driven in this era by a desire to better manipulate § 276 *BGB*,[520] but it is unclear why then the result would not be the simple dismissal of the medical discourse altogether rather than, as we have seen, its gradual side-lining. Where the *Reichsgericht* did consider shaping the general civil law in the context of medical liability to better fit Nazi goals, it did so by openly trading in language that stressed the need to sublimate the health or productivity of the individual to that of the '*Volk*' and, furthermore, the role of medical practice in supporting,

513 Majer (2003) 58–64.

514 Ibid. 98 f, noting that the definition of those deemed caught by the statutes concerning sterilisation and marriage was so broad as to grant the authorities, in effect, unlimited scope to decide; see also, Müller (2001) 121–122.

515 Majer (2003) 523–524.

516 Rachlin (2013) 80; Majer (2003) 399–400, detailing the withdrawal of legal aid from Jewish plaintiffs; Maehle (2009) 126.

517 Müller (1991) 115–119, discussing examples from contract and property law in which Jewish plaintiffs were stripped of their rights. As *Müller* notes, the absence of a clear legal foundation did not impede 'resourceful judges' from getting to the desired result; see also Majer (2003) 383–397.

518 Rüthers (2017); Schröder (2002) 25; *Stolleis* notes that this process of reinterpretation was often easier than introducing new terms or concepts, Stolleis (1998) 17, 65; Rachlin (2013) 80.

519 It is perhaps worth noting that when they tried to change the *BGB* it was wrongfulness rather than fault that underwent the greatest change, again to align what was unlawful with the interests of the state.

520 Although it should be noted that the putative provisions of the *BGB*'s replacement, the *Volksgesetzbuch*, retained the fault requirement but altered the understanding of unlawfulness to encompass behaviour contrary to the interests of the '*Volk*', see Schiemann (2013) 2789–2790.

first and foremost, the goals of the state. Even still, to treat in such terms did not automatically entail submission to them. In *RG 19.06.1936*, the court grappled with the issue of a putative *Operationsduldungspflicht*, or duty to submit to medical treatment.[521] There,[522] the plaintiff had lost his arm following an apparently unwanted injection from the defendant. In answer to the lower court upholding such a duty on the basis that the *RÄO* had aligned medical practice with national policy, the *Reichsgericht* demurred and upheld the patient's claim. Not only had the regulatory legislation done nothing to alter the fundamentally civil law character of the practitioner-patient relationship[523] – one long underpinned by the need for consent to justify medical treatment – any exception to the general requirement of consent hinged on the potential for real risk to public health.[524] Tying it to the abstract goal of a healthy '*Volk*' was, simply put, too uncertain a standard to stand on its own.[525] Indeed, a further justificatory analogy to the Law for the Prevention of Hereditarily Diseased Offspring of 1933 was rejected given the requirement there, in § 14, for danger to the pregnant woman; neither could this limited exception be generalised to cover the case at hand.[526] Later, lower courts gradually sought to broaden the boundaries of this so-called duty but, again, and in contrast to the subject at hand, with rhetoric clearly emphasising the primacy of the '*Volk*'.[527]

521 Claimed to stem from the operation of §§ 242 and 254 *BGB*, Goldhahn/Hartmann (1937) 186; on the more common, and persisting, analysis of contributory negligence in failing to undergo medical treatment recognised in German law see Hilger (1951) 58–61; Eser (1990) 18 n 60.

522 RGZ 151, 349.

523 RGZ 151, 352, a position the court continued to uphold, see *RG 03.12.1941* RGZ 168 207; *Maehle* characterises both decisions as defensive, given their need to reconcile their result with the implications of the *RÄO* and rightly notes they were of no use to those who were persecuted by the regime, see Maehle (2009) 126–128.

524 RGZ 151, 352–353. The case earned a commentary from *Kallfelz* in which – although he accepted the principle of consent as the key to avoiding liability here – he rebuked the court for failing to take sufficient heed of the new order of interests under the Nazi regime in order to create an exception, Kallfelz (1937) 3114 f.

525 RGZ 151, 353.

526 RGZ 151, 354. The case was viewed by one of the leading works on medical liability as confirming, as had several cases before that point, the court's seminal decision in *RG 31.05.1894* RGSt 25, 375; Goldhahn/Hartmann (1937) 6.

527 Goldhahn/Hartmann (1937) 193–194, noting successful claims before the *Reichsversicherungsamt* relying on industrial workers owing a duty to the new state to ensure their capacity to be fit for work. Such injuries were also known to have led to sterilisation on grounds of diminished economic capacity, see Grunberger (1971) 225.

Alongside the corruption of medical thought and practice, many in the legal system proved equally willing participants in the Nazi regime.[528] Thus the mere fact that the courts post-1933 continued on the path set for them in the preceding decades of the century cannot be taken as unalloyed evidence of judicial beneficence in bending the civil law to the protection of patients as a whole, and the absence of clear evidence as to how the courts would have treated a 'non-German' plaintiff denies us a clear comparison. Given the regime's desire to assert control over all aspects of citizens' lives, it could be that the continued distancing of legal and medical concepts of error from one another simply served as a way to re-assert the primacy of the court for less beneficent, or simply arbitrary,[529] reasons and, given longer, this would have become more obvious. But, as we have seen, there is evidence of the normative standard the *Reichsgericht* was prepared to enforce, which suggests some sense of wishing to protect patients nevertheless, and the idea that the courts were here opening up this analytical space to impose greater paternalism, at best, would sit oddly with developments in the closely-related topic of disclosure liability noted above. A stronger case can be made that the various regulatory changes, in that they formalised the status of unorthodox practitioners, and sought to undermine specialism in favour of generalists within orthodox practice, supported legal equivalency between bodies of medical knowledge whether orthodox or otherwise.[530] But even there, key decisions pre-date the Nazi era.

The fact that cases on medical error continued to be heard before the general civil courts (not, for example, the *Erbgesundheitsgerichte*, of which, by 1936, there were 223, established to administer the sterilisation legislation and staffed by panels of three 'judges', two of whom were, in fact, medical practitioners),[531] and hinged on applying the unreconstructed *BGB*, meant that an analytical space remained for the legal analysis of medical error to remain undisturbed by

528 Kater (2002) 80, giving the figures as 45% party membership in medicine and 25% amongst lawyers. As with medical practitioners, there is evidence that personal ambition played a role in explaining this, see generally Jarausch (2013).

529 Müller (1991)138–139.

530 Weisz (2006) 124–126.

531 Lifton (1986) 25, 27, noting the 'considerable chaos and arbitrariness' that lay beneath the veneer of the 'legal' system set up to administer this system; Bock (1997) 159, notes that the establishment of the separate court structure was the most revolutionary amongst the measures that cemented the coincidence of medical interests and those of the regime in that they elevated medical practitioners to a position of formal legal authority. This is supported by *Müller* who suggests that the legal members often wholly deferred to the medical 'judges', see Müller (2001) 123.

broader ideological changes within the legal system and its operators.[532] By contrast, and in line with *Stolleis'* finding that the degree to which various areas of doctrine were penetrated by Nazi ideology varied,[533] it may be that there was simply no easy way to cast claims for compensation for accidental injury in the course of consensual treatment as an issue that was intimately connected with medical matters that more readily attracted the interest of the regime, such as 'genetic and racial hygiene', or indeed any sufficient reason to upend existing jurisprudence here.[534] As will be shown in the concluding chapter, the law post-1945 drew heavily, and seemingly without question, on the case law of the *Reichsgericht* covered in this period, suggesting that any impact was, at least in practical terms, folded into the continuity of the law and, as *Stolleis* notes was the case for much of civil law, this area too retained its core.[535]

Thus, whilst *Riegger* perhaps goes too far in suggesting that Nazi ideology had no influence on the development of the law here,[536] whatever else was the impact of the Nazi era, it was during this period – which ironically witnessed the notional occupational triumph and centralisation of orthodox medicine[537] – that the decisive break with the medical discourse surrounding error, so associated with it, occurred. Although there are plausible ways in which the same pattern of legal development may have resulted under the influence of the regime, there is credible evidence to suggest an unbroken chain and the relatively autonomous operation of what *Fraenkel* dubbed the 'normative' legal system in this part of medical liability.[538]

## 6. Conclusions

Such is the story of how liability for medical error was devised in the structures of the *BGB* and applied under it. During a period where the practice of medicine

532 As Rachlin notes, '...ordinary civil litigation was conducted by the regular courts in a more or less regular manner, although Jews and other *Untermenschen* (subhumans) were denied access to the courts as unworthy of German law', see Rachlin (2013) 80. Which is not to conclude that the ordinary civil courts were not, in their own way Nazified or capable of being a ready means to the regime's ends, see Steinweis/Rachlin (2013) 2–3.

533 Stolleis (1998) 73.

534 Bock (1997) 149, 161. An obvious, related, contrast would be the effective abolition of medical confidentiality in order to allow, amongst other things, practitioners to report hereditarily ill patients to the authorities, see Leichter (1979) 134; Maehle (2016) 90–97.

535 Stolleis (1998) 17.

536 Riegger (2007) 132–133.

537 Kater (2002) 80.

538 Fraenkel (2017).

settled into its modern form, we see an explosion in the volume of surrounding literature on the subject. To a much greater degree than the previous century, there was an active literature and a sense amongst those who wrote on the topic that it was an area in which the contemporary law, and its application, were ripe for challenge. Senior judicial and academic figures considered the subject worthy of further investigation and the extent to which medical liability, that most basic and ancient of problems with which a system of liability has to contend, featured as a topic in this period puts the lie to the idea that medical liability is somehow a 'problem' born in the latter half of the twentieth century.[539] In part this continued focus was clearly driven by the fact that this period witnessed, in comparison to the nineteenth century, an explosion of litigation with the *Reichsgericht* given repeated opportunity to clarify their approach to fault.

Although the period started with *Rabel's* reassurance that the new code threatened only more of the same for medical practitioners, the reality was, in practice, very different. Yet this was not because the law changed in a fundamental, substantive way upon the introduction of the code but, more subtly, that the change affected by the code came in the clarity which it provided to both plaintiff and defendant as to the nature of the relationship between them. The growing pains of the previous century gave way to fully fledged systematisation in which the lack of clarity that had plagued earlier scholarship was gradually replaced with rigorous certainty as to the nature of the legal relationship between practitioner and patient. Even still, the duality of actions required for the recovery of all potential heads of damages persisted; the unfortunate result of an unrelated decision as to the availability of damages for pain and suffering and the concurrency of obligations within the structures of the civil law as a whole, and a decision which saw the courts reject the idea of a medical right of intervention in constructing their approach to wrongfulness under § 823 (1) *BGB*. But the controversy over the contractual nature of the relationship was settled beyond any doubt. The remarkable flexibility inherent in the German law of contract allowed it to easily reflect the myriad forms the practitioner-patient relationship could take, and settled the question of how that relationship would, conventionally, be framed. The emergence of a literature surrounding the '*Arztvertrag*' and, indeed, the bloom of literature on the subject of medical liability, presaged what would come to be formally recognised in the decades following, which is that out of the general provisions of the code, scholars and judges were increasingly honing a particular approach to the liability of medical practitioners. The *BGB* provided, as a successful code ought to, a relatively clear

539 Hondius (2010) 8.

answer to a long-standing area of disagreement. The default practitioner-patient relationship was encapsulated best, as had been the emerging consensus in the later *gemeines Recht*, by a service contract. The complications of trying to formally separate different models of medical practice from one another using the black-letter law were gone. Alongside that, however, was a less obvious decision, that medical practice was compassable within the general provisions of the *BGB*, and that there was, formally, no such thing, yet, as an '*Arztvertrag*'.

A further contribution of the *BGB*, which only becomes obvious when one sets, as this study attempts to, the period in the context of the law that had preceded it, was its shifting of the centre of gravity for analysing medical error away from the criminal law and firmly towards the civil law. It was in this period that the civil law became, as it remains, the nexus of the legal analysis concerning 'everyday' incidences of poor treatment. That is not to say that the use of the criminal law ceased altogether, it remained, certainly in the closely related topic of disclosure malpractice, of foundational importance, and, as noted above, continued to be closely connected to unlicensed practice in its various forms. Nevertheless, the characteristic of medical liability as a civil law problem was the prevailing consequence of this period, and one that remained, crucially, formally unaltered by during the Nazi period. This permitted, despite the high degree of involvement in the regime amongst both medical practitioners and lawyers, the law here to continue broadly along the path it had been set on in the preceding decades and, in time, forced the courts to grapple with how the civil law would respond to rapid advancements in medical technology and power.

As for the approach to fault, we have mapped both significant continuity and significant change in its legal analysis. The formal definition of fault flowed naturally from that basic set of decisions about the categorisation of the practitioner-patient relationship, firmly settling the arguments of the Pandectist era in favour of simple fault. But despite the apparent clarity of § 276 *BGB*, the analysis above reveals that there was continued tension as to the relevance of accepted medical practice, with a considerable number of commentators emphasising the need to pay significant heed to both the mores and broader context of medical practice. Certainly, there was continuity with the nineteenth century in the use of the *Kunstfehler* as an important informal categorising concept within the analysis of fault in the medical context. Yet it is fair to say that the understanding of the *Kunstfehler's* legal relevance, and indeed its very definition, quickly came under pressure in the early decades of the twentieth century. Taken at its most narrow, and traditional, it threatened to supplant negligence as defined in § 276 *BGB* altogether, elevating medical discourse to congruency with the boundaries of liability. As it transpired, the medical definition received into the law in the course of the nineteenth century gradually yielded to the courts' own as it became clear that there were limits to the relevance of adherence to generally accepted practice. The process was gradual; there was no overnight breakdown in the wake of a single, seminal decision. Neither was the concept, as conventionally understood, abandoned entirely. Nor, importantly, was the process without rationale, and we have identified a clear eddy and flow within the numerous *Reichsgericht* decisions in this area. Rather, as the courts asserted their willingness, in some situations, to disregard accepted medical practice, they both recognised the instability and pluralist nature of medical practice and discourse, and, in its place, emphasised their own view of the obligations inherent to the practitioner-patient relationship. Fundamentally, as is revealed in the two case studies presented above, this process represented a challenge to what constituted *medical* behaviour in the first place, as idiosyncratic personal practice was becoming subsumed within the broader analytical category and institutional, technology-driven setting of 'healthcare'. With that came a different set of expectations to those, which practitioners had collectively imposed on themselves. When set against the earlier parts of this study, the direction of travel was clear: The practice of fault, the central control on the scope of medical liability, was, in principle, decoupled from simply not doing what it *was* that other practitioners would have done, and reframed so as to reflect the *Reichsgericht's* view of patient safety. There was no explicit rhetoric of 'patients' rights' in this era, yet we have clearly mapped the emergence of a more patient-oriented approach in the definition and application of medical error.

# Conclusion

The goal of this book has been to explain how a subtle, but fundamental, feature of the German law arose in practice. How did the interpretation and definition of medical error become seperable from what it was that medical practitioners themselves regarded as accepted behaviour, and, in doing so, allow the courts to define the scope of acceptable behaviour? The foregoing has presented the evolution of the both the law and the surrounding social history of medicine and medical practice. We may now consider both the role this collective evolution played in underpinning the later German law and what it has revealed about the drivers of legal development here.

## 1. Developmental themes

Several different developmental themes emerge. Some speak to more abstract features of the law here, others to more material aspects of the law and the world it operated in. The nineteenth century was a generally turbulent period of maturation for both German law and medicine and, as this study demonstrates, medical liability and the legal understanding of fault therein was fundamentally affected by the relationship between these spheres during this period, by the contextualisation of each *by* the other.

Perhaps the most obvious, and often overlooked, theme to emerge here was the increasing prevalence of medical error before the courts. As we have seen, much of the debate in the nineteenth century centred around the relevance of the mechanism for demanding payment for medical services. Cases concerning medical error being raised as a counterclaim to a demand for payment were more familiar in that era. As the twentieth century dawned, the growth of literature on the subject seems to have been driven, at least in part, by a surge in the number of cases and, increasingly, claims were straightforwardly based on the patient's desire for compensation. Since the *Fall Horn*, there had been a steady rhetoric about, and fear of, excessive liability that was often used as justification for adopting a *culpa lata* standard. This became markedly more fraught over the first half of the twentieth century. The underlying reasons for this surge are hard to pinpoint and there is no single, silver bullet which offers clear explanation. Certainly, the rapid increase in the number of patients with access to medical care in that era seems plausible, but the simple clarity offered by the *BGB* ought not to be overlooked as a necessary factor here. A broader social change, not limited to the subject of medical liability, is also likely relevant; as *Hondius* puts it, '…the growth of medical liability needs to be located in a change of social attitudes'.[1] This process is a long-acknowledged driver behind the twentieth century's increase in litigation as patients gradually substituted awe and deference with expectation and entitlement.[2] Although scholarship usually focuses on the increase in actions around the 1970s,[3] and the parallel emergence of the various national patients' rights movements that formed the clearest outward expression of this shift in social values,[4] at least some of the underlying factors were present in this earlier period: the *BGB's* role in promoting the sort of liberal, individualistic thinking that heightened expectations amongst patient;[5] the increasing technical sophistication of orthodox medical practice;[6] the beginning of its anonmysation as care shifted into hospitals;[7] and the continued[8] – indeed under the Nazis, formalised[9] – role of unorthodox practice in the marketplace, may have influenced attitudes towards expertise amongst patients and, crucially, their lawyers.

A second, and dominant, theme is the abstract nature of the constellation of formal rules within which the practitioner-patient relationship was captured. Medical liability – indeed 'medical law' itself – can suffer from something of an identity crisis in that it is often aggregated across specific rules and those of a more general nature, which are then applied in the relevant medical context.[10] That dynamic is clearly visible here as, over the course of the nineteenth century, the way in which liability was regulated lost the specificity that had earlier characterised it. The model of the *Carolina*, the paradigm of a specific rule, found only poor reflection in the nineteenth century as the relevance of the defendant's status as a medical practitioner became relegated to an aggravating factor of an otherwise general offence. Within civil law, where specific rules had no relevant historical precedent, whilst the nineteenth century witnessed some claims that a *sui generis* solution could be fashioned, there was ultimately little support for this and, as the *BGB* confirmed, medical liability was simply a contextualised application of the general civil rules.

1 Hondius (2010) 10.
2 Ibid. 9–11; Püster (2013) 101–103.
3 Helbron (2001) 17; Katzenmeier (2002) 28 n 161; Hondius (2010) 9.
4 Hondius (2010) 10.
5 Mansel (2000) 1.
6 Katzenmeier (2002) 28–29; Bell / Ibbetson (2012) 91–95; Taupitz (1991) 55, noting its effect in demystifying medicine.
7 v Bieberstein (1974) 249 ff; Zepos / Christodoulou (1983) 42.
8 McClelland (2002) 227, on the destructive impact on medical professionalisation of the Nazi era.
9 See above chapter 1, 3 (A) iv.
10 Hall (2008) 625.

A third theme is the relevance of the criminal law as a practical tool for regulating medical liability diminished with the arrival of the *BGB*. The shift both intellectually and practically, in the form of the relatively large increase in civil litigation which took place in the early decades of the twentieth century, is clear, the reasons for this considerably less so. A plausible explanation may be found in the received memory of the *Carolina* as identifying the appropriate forum for regulating injurious treatment, but it also speaks to the weakness of the civil law in this earlier period and its underuse relative to the twentieth century. On the other hand this is perhaps unsurprising given the blistering confusion which suffused the civil law before the arrival of the *BGB* and the compensatory incentive offered by the criminal law was quickly outstripped by the availability of damages for pain and suffering after that point. Furthermore, this flow, from the criminal law into the civil, is also clearly visible in the conceptual development of the law here. The *Kunstfehler* came of age in the nineteenth century, largely driven by the discussions related to the criminal law and decisions of the *Reichsgericht* in the context of criminal prosecutions. The speed with which the civil law became the centre of gravity for both the intellectual and practical assessment of the discussion is then surprising, but does speak to the very flexibility of the *Kunstfehler* as a conceptual device and, importantly, one that did not iterate as the legal basis for its assessment changed.

A forth theme is the link between legal regulation of medical practice and liability is clear. An ironic counterpart to the emergence of modern medical practice was the formal recognition, in 1869, of an open market for medical services. Even post-1935, victory was short lived with formal recognition of a parallel unorthodox path in the form of the *Heilpraktiker.* Indeed, dislike of the model of state control represented by the *Gewerbeordnung* 1869 could not halt the breakdown of the older, Romanised contractual analyses, which we have seen plagued the civil law in this period. The fee schedules that characterised orthodox medical practice denied a more straightforward route to a categorisation, which might have more easily allowed a lower, formal standard of care to be applied in practice. Furthermore, the instrumentalist response of the *Reichsgericht* to the state of medical regulation could not reasonably have been predicted. Rather than accept the pluralism of the medical marketplace, with the various risks and benefits that accompanied it, the court began an uneasy process of imposing liability to protect unwary patients against the dangers which accompanied it. Unable, in the post 1871-world, to do so by means of enforcing a ban from practice, they resorted to relying on their interpretation of otherwise general liability rules. In practice, the standards of orthodox practice supplied the necessary means of achieving this end, certainly as it related to the lowest tiers of medical practitioner. As had been the case with the *Carolina*, the regulation and liability of medical practitioners went hand in hand; the latter was a means of enforcing the former. Yet the fact that some orthodox practitioners also offered 'natural' and other less orthodox remedies alongside, or despite, their knowledge of the university-based scientific medicine which characterised the age, created a clear obstacle to continuing this approach. The concession that the idea of '*Schulmedizin*', previously synonymous with university-based practice, had become detached from any particular strand of practice, that the treatment offered by the practitioner themselves would supply the rule against which the court would judge them, marked a clear shift from the nineteenth-century stance. Even still, the idea that the court was willing, in some situations, to enforce compliance with orthodox practice where a practitioner had knowledge of it, evidenced their attempts to ensure that the basic minimums of modern medicine were complied with where possible.

Finally, and vitally, the changing nature of how fault was analysed as it related to medical practice over this period: Fault moved from a standard which was often formally indulgent of medical practice, requiring gross fault before an action would be countenanced, towards simple fault. Indeed, some of the raft of codifications over the nineteenth century came rather to equate failure to comply with one's occupational duty with gross fault as a factor which aggravated rather than triggered liability. Yet particularly within the scholarship of the nineteenth century, both legal and medical, there was a vocal insistence that the formal standard of fault ought to require something beyond merely simple fault, with some willing to work backwards from that towards whatever category of action best reflected that stance. Nevertheless, as the century closed, the formal hegemony of simple fault was a given. In practice, however, the position in the nineteenth century had always adopted an indulgent approach towards the interpretation of whatever the formal standard was. Even before the relatively settled acceptance of *Virchow's* definition of the *Kunstfehler*, the law in practice hewed closely to a sociological approach to the fault standard. The *Kunstfehler* supplied the necessary conceptual armoury to sustain that view, thus retarding the development of an alternative approach until the early twentieth century. As is clear from both the *Fall Horn* and the other expert opinions examined in this study, medical practitioners had been granted a high degree of control over the definition of fault in practice. As we reach the end of the period under consideration, that informal indulgence began to break down. Empowered both by changes in the procedural rules underpinning the relevance of expert evidence and their own activism, the *Reichsgericht* constructed an interpretive discourse of medical error in which the *Kunstfehler*, as previously understood, came to be modified and supplemented, and a new balance between a sociological approach and one underpinned by a court-driven ethic of patient safety was struck.

## 2. Drivers of development

Having mapped the dominant developmental themes of this study, we may draw attention to the main drivers of the law here. We will consider first those drivers internal to the law before turning to the surrounding social context and considering briefly how this study speaks to different existing models of explaining legal development.

Turning first to legislation we find it was of decreasing direct relevance here beyond, as one would expect, clarifying the various academic debates surrounding how the practitioner-patient relationship ought to be categorised. In that sense, and in keeping with the vocation of the age, as that framework of the law of obligations became increasingly general, medical practitioners lost the privilege of specific formal rules concerning liability and instead had to rely on their informal interpretation. Yet, as noted above, even if the *BGB* reflected the *fin de siècle* consensus as to categorisation, it might be that it's chief contribution was not a change in the content of the law itself but rather the clarity it provided.

Equally, scholarship ultimately played a limited role here. The authors of the *gemeines Recht* were, as we have seen, mired in an esoteric battle over how to reconcile the Roman law with contemporary medical practice, an endeavour which often saw the former take precedence over the latter, thus retarding serious academic treatment of the subject. Even *Hefke* and *Zimmermann*, whose works stand as the signal contributions to the subject, offered conflicting accounts of how the practitioner-patient relationship ought to be categorised and, unsurprisingly, the appropriate fault standard. Although the early twentieth century witnessed an explosion of scholarship on the subject, no grand theory, no scholarly architecture, emerged. Rather, the subject remained characterised by an approach that preferred to construct its taxonomies around the various sorts of anatomical injury which might be sustained rather than offering an abstract, rationalised framework for legal analysis.

That failure of scholarship to abandon its self-imposed Roman constraints earlier and engage fully with the difficult questions medical liability presented ultimately leaves us with a tale of judges and courts, the *Reichsgericht* in particular, as the main legal driver of the development of the law. Judges clearly felt themselves more and more capable of developing the law in practice to achieve what *they* regarded as an appropriate standard of care for patients. The underlying rationale behind the regulatory framework of the *Gewerbeordnung* 1869 was largely ignored when it came to liability until the 1930s, and although happy to borrow from the parallel medical discourse, they refined it in due course to clarify a considerable measure of judicial control over fault. Indeed, it speaks volumes that the leading author on the subject in the early twentieth century, *Ebermayer*, was a judge not an academic.

Turning now to features, which lie outside the law, it was ultimately the work of orthodox medical practitioners in defining, cultivating and vociferously defending the *Kunstfehler*, which played the key role in the eventual shape of the law here. Whilst the *Kunstfehler's* legal historical roots lay in the *Carolina*, the law and lawyers bore scant responsibility for its resurgence and, as would prove key, its definition and elevation within the medical discourse. That was of vital importance as it maintained the liminal space whereby the courts could draw on the *Kunstfehler* as an interpretive aid but, precisely because it remained an informal feature of the jurisprudence here, remained capable of allowing future courts to delimit its relevance in an easier fashion than would have been the case had it ever been given formal status as the benchmark for medical error. Thus, the importance of the *Fall Horn* and its fallout cannot be overstated. In due course, the subsumption of the *Kunstfehler* within the legal discourse as a means of achieving specificity within a framework of general rules provided the nexus within which the *Reichsgericht* could work; the boulder against which it could push. In defining the *Kunstfehler* in a manner that paid no heed to the forum within which it was applied, be it civil, criminal or disciplinary liability, practitioners themselves sowed the seed of their own regret as the courts placed limits on what had always been merely an interpretive rather than a formal device. That is not to say that the courts might not have reached an equivalent position from first principles, but in supplying them with an abstract concept – a delight to the German legal mind – it offered one model of fault, which ultimately provided the clay from which an alternative could be sculpted.

Finally, it is important to end by noting the changing nature of 'medicine' itself. Techniques and procedures which had once been unthinkable became commonplace. Advances in surgery and the advent of antiseptics and anaesthetic tremendously increased the power and promise of medical treatment. The dawn of X-rays and radiology provided, literally, a novel view of the patient's body, revealing what had long been hidden but, at the same time, providing an evidential basis for one's actions to be critiqued in retrospect and, as noted above in relation to changing social attitudes towards claims of occupational authority, demystified a process that had long gone unseen. That some of these developments appeared as problematic areas within the case law is thus unsurprising; new technologies are often a source of litigation.[11] But the connection between the *Reichsgericht's* reassessment of the *Kunstfehler* and these cases was no coincidence, and, it is submitted, suggests that these features played an important role in justifying the court's choices.

11 Bell / Ibbetson (2012) 38–39.

How does this schema of development speak to common analytical frameworks for assessing legal development?

For those who would focus on the law as isolated from, but capable of radically changing, wider society, this study has little to offer. *Watson's* dominant narrative of legal transplants, that the legal class in different societies engage with one another in developing the law,[12] only provides the thinnest explanatory veneer here. The effective transplantation of the classical Roman law into the German law of obligations is a defining feature of German legal life. But its impact in this area was little short of catastrophic. Far from providing a workable set of rules, failure to swiftly enough account in law for the obvious fact that medical practice in ancient *Rome* was not that of the nineteenth century in Germany left many scholars engaged in a fruitless endeavour of trying to reconcile the law of one with the practice of the other until events overtook them.

For structuralists such as *v Caenegem*, whose institutional focus identifies the leading legal source within various systems,[13] our results are equally counter-intuitive. Far from scholarship being the dominant voice in the German legal choir, judges have proven to be the protagonists here. That this is a feature of modern German medical liability has long been acknowledged,[14] but their efforts in this period, in keeping with evidence from other areas of nineteenth- and early twentieth-century doctrine,[15] have been overlooked in favour of an emphasis on the modern 'crisis'. Accounts of the intellectual development of a system, or its dominant characteristics, are only ever generalist in nature and when the same points are examined in a particular context – one 'impressed by moral views or values'[16] – the picture may, as here, be different.

For systems theorists, who would suggest that the law operates as a closed loop, autopoietically isolated from the wider environment, this study offers little support.[17] It is submitted that the law's reliance on a concept re-born and re-worked within an external, medical discourse irreparably weakens that central hypothesis. It may be that when viewed over the twentieth century the eventual abandonment of the *Kunstfehler* altogether could be seen, as systems theory would suggest,[18] as the law adapting in its own fashion. Or, less plausibly, that the ultimate root of the concept in the *Carolina* reveals a recurring but still ultimately *legal* rather than *medical* discourse that was, in the period under

12 Watson (1993).

13 v Caenegem (1987).

14 Katzenmeier (2002) 77.

15 See generally Falk / Mohnhaupt (2000), in particular the contribution from *Zimmermann* and *Verse* on the *BGH*'s early influence on delict.

16 Zweigert / Kötz (1998) 40.

17 Luhmann (2008).

18 Bell / Ibbetson (2012) 14.

examination, simply modified to take account of key contemporary changes. Yet it remains the case that the necessary cause of the concept's rebirth and rationalisation was the medical discourse that emerged in the wake of the *Fall Horn*. Far from inhabiting a separate intellectual space, the law in this period and its operators were intimately connected with the broader social context medical regulation and practice.

Considerably more legal scholarship focuses on explaining the relationship between changes in the law and wider society than on the effect of social change on the law itself.[19] Perhaps it is often harder to parse, but it is submitted that this study offers a context within which that dynamic operated as the fundamental driver of the law here. *Renner's* suggestion that legal rules may be incredibly resilient to fundamental changes in the environment they seek to govern is, to a degree, apt.[20] The confusion in the formal basis for the practitioner-patient relationship undermines the idea that the law here was not, to a degree, in flux in some areas, but this must be balanced by those legislative pockets, culminating in the *BGB*, which indeed provided a clear answer, often with the practical effect of imposing liability for simple fault. From that point on, the framework of the formal rules was fixed and, on the face of it, generally applicable. Nevertheless, this masked the evolution of assessing fault in practice from informally indulgent to the modified version that we have seen emerged in the later life of the *Reichsgericht*. The law proved itself to be highly flexible in its adoption and then delimitation of the *Kunstfehler*, easily reflecting the vast changes in the status and role of medical practitioners within wider society.

## 3. Change and continuity after 1945

It is the 'happy privilege' of the legal historian that they can choose a convenient cut off for their work and, indeed, in many cases this will emerge naturally from the subject itself.[21] In the case of this study, that is not so. The narrative that has been presented did not truncate at 1945 as is attested to by the vast literature concerning '*Arzthaftung*' that emerged throughout the latter half of the twentieth century,[22] and the attendant rise in cases before the German courts that has become the norm.[23] As noted in the introduction, the period considered in this

19 Cotterrell (1984) 53–54.
20 Renner (1949).
21 Ibbetson (1999) vi.
22 Katzenmeier (2002) 1; Katzenmeier / Laufs / v Lipp (2015); Riegger (2007) 168, 233.
23 See the number of cases reported in Petersen (1962) 194. This was particularly the case where it concerned claims brought before the civil courts, see v Brandis / Pribilla (1973) 18. Separately, *Pribilla* suggested that, despite this, the public

study has been greatly overlooked as an influence on the later law. Equally, as we cover the development of the law during the takeover of the state by the Nazi regime and, indeed, conclude with its fall and the abolition of the *Reichsgericht*, it is right that we offer a brief outlook on how the evolution of the law that has been uncovered here relates to what would follow. Thus, we now briefly consider change and continuity in the law post-1945.

Simply put, the retreat from the idea that the internalised, medical view of error encapsulated in the concept of the *Kunstfehler* was determinative of the contours of liability continued apace in the post-war legal landscape, clearly building on the foundation created by the *Reichsgericht*. In some of its earliest judgments, the freshly empowered *Bundesgerichtshof* explicitly adopted the position of the *Reichsgericht* on the relationship between a practitioner, institution, and patient, and, likewise, the approach towards the assessment of medical error.[24] In *BGH 11.04.1951*, the court confirmed the role of delict in providing a residual claim for an insured patient who had been treated by a practitioner not approved by their own insurance fund.[25] There, the patient suffered a spinal injury when they slipped into unconsciousness and fell off the examination table following administration of a local anaesthetic. Whilst the contractual protection created by the *Reichsgericht* would stretch to provide third-party patients with a claim against a hospital, the only duty owed in contract by such a practitioner was to the institution not the patient.[26] Nevertheless, where such a practitioner took on treatment it would raise a simple duty to avoid injury to the patient's health under § 823 *BGB*. Establishing the rhetoric of the *Kunstfehler* as the threshold test for fault, and drawing on the pre-war work of the *Reichsgericht*,[27] this duty would be breached where a practitioner failed to comply with generally recognised rules of medical practice, as they had done here in failing to direct the patient to lie back following the injection.[28] Notably the judicial panel included *Hans Drost*, whose 1951 text with *Arthur Hübner*[29] was an updated version of the latter's influential pre-war work on the subject with *Otto Warneyer*.[30]

Whilst the narrowest ratio of that 1951 decision spoke only to the constellation of duties surrounding the practitioner-patient relationship in the new state,

perception of a huge rise in cases of medical liability outstripped reality, see Pribilla (1971) 70. See also, Deutsch (1978) 5–8.

24 Katzenmeier (2002) 273: 'The touchstone of medical liability, for a considerable time and into the decades post-war, the "*Kunstfehler*".'

25 *BGH 11.04.1951*, BGHZ 1, 383

26 *BGH 11.04.1951*, BGHZ 1, 383, 386, citing *RG 27.09.1915*, RGZ 165, 106.

27 *RG 04.07.1916* reported in Ebermayer (1930) 136.

28 *BGH 11.04.1951*, BGHZ 1, 383, 386–387.

29 Hübner/Drost (1955).

30 Hübner/Warneyer (1939).

the following year, in *BGH 27.11.1952*, the court drew heavily on the preceding case law, which we have explored, in a case that centred wholly on setting the correct standard of fault for a medical practitioner.[31] There, a dentist was sued for the injuries sustained by his patient when they were allowed to swallow an unsecured 4cm needle during a root canal procedure. The subsequent successful claim, again in delict for non-pecuniary losses, was appealed all the way to the *Bundesgerichtshof* where it was upheld. The crux of the appeal was that the defendant was not duty-bound to use an approach which would have seen the needle secured and, thus, his failure to have done so could not sound as fault. Rejecting this, the court stressed that the fact that it may have been customary to avoid such safety measures due to the resulting discomfort to the patient and the increased duration that depended from their use,[32] was, simply, insufficient to defeat a finding that the defendant had fallen short of providing the required (which is to say '*erforderlich*') degree of care. As they put it:[33]

> 'From the fact that expert practitioners of dentistry ordinarily work with unsecured needles, the conclusion may be drawn that the defendant demonstrated the degree of care customary within his occupation. Yet, as noted, this is not determinative. Rather, more decisive is whether the objective required care has been observed. Presently, the protection of patients from incidents during treatment that threaten avoidable injury is the highest imperative.'

As they made clear, the key decisions of the *Reichsgericht* about the basic definition of a *Kunstfehler* were adopted,[34] alongside the clear water that had, in the preceding two decades, been put between that medical discourse and the legal concept of fault. Whilst, noting *RG 07.01.1938*,[35] it would often be the case that they may be contiguous, it was, just as the *Reichsgericht* had increasingly come to clearly articulate, ultimately irrelevant whether the defendant's conduct evidenced a *Kunstfehler* or not.[36]

*BGH 27.11.1952* was also notable for its rejection of any difference in the standard of care that could be expected from a '*Dentist*' like the defendant, rather than the more rigorously, and academically, trained '*Zahnarzt*' who, it was argued, represented the university-based body of thought that supported the sort of safety measures in contention. The former could not, in law, offer a lesser

31 BGHZ 8, 138.

32 Ibid. 138, 139.

33 Ibid. 138, 141.

34 The court cited *RG 12.10.1934* (1935) 64 JW 115; *RG 21.06.1940* (1940) DR 1949; *RG 12.05.1931* 7 HRR 1931, 1748; *RG 22.03.1932* 8 HRR 1932, 1828; *RG 22.12.1922* (1923) 52 JW 603; *RG 04.02.1938* (1938) 67 JW 1246; RG *08.04.1940* RGZ 163, 129.

35 (1938) 67 JW 2203.

36 BGHZ 8, 138, 140.

degree of care than the latter. In coming to this result the court relied not just on regulatory legislation from 1952, which had treated them as coordinate,[37] but the long-standing acceptance before 1952 that either rank of practitioner was as important in practice to the delivery of public healthcare, both being allowed to participate in insurance practice equally.[38] Thus, *BGH 27.11.1952* has come to be viewed as the mark, early on, of the *Bundesgerichtshof's* rigorous approach towards assessing medical error.[39] Yet when put in the context of this study, it reveals the high degree of continuity between the achievements of the *Reichsgericht* and the starting position of its successor.

To further situate the contribution of this study to understanding the later development of the law, it is clear that the shift from the language of the *Kunstfehler* to the modern language of the *'Behandlungsfehler'* marked the culmination of the process we have investigated, rather than a late twentieth-century innovation. Indeed, it was a gradual rather than a sharp phenomenon and, as this study reveals, much of the key process of disconnecting the legal from the medical discourse was achieved under the *Reichsgericht*, with the *Bundesgerichtshof* simply following through on the initial disjunction of the medical and legal discourses. Furthermore, as has been demonstrated in the preceding chapters, academic criticism of both the utility and the extra-legal nature of the concept was not uniquely confined to this later period. Ultimately, the inability to settle on any better understanding than that sometimes these medical and legal discourses concerning error would map perfectly and that sometimes they would not, did not provide much by way of rational guidance to solidify the concept against further criticism.[40] Indeed, scholarly criticism

37 *Das Gesetz über die Ausübung der Zahnheilkunde*, 31st March 1952, BGBl I 221. Indeed, part of the aim of this legislative initiative was to restrict the ability of unorthodox practitioners to engage in dental care at all, see Meyer-George (1988) 12.

38 BGHZ 8, 138, 139. Whether this approach could be stretched to cover unorthodox practitioners such as the *Heilpraktiker* was, later, the subject of much discussion, contrast Meyer-George (1988) 81 ff – arguing that whilst this sort of broad reading of medical competency may be appropriate in the context of dentistry it would be inappropriate with medicine – with Eberhardt (1986) 110, who saw *BGH 27.11.1952* as signalling an identical standard of care for *Heilpraktikers* as their more orthodox medical brethren. The difficulties with the existence of a formalised class of unorthodox practitioners continued throughout the post-war period, see Bockelmann (1966) 1145.

39 Deutsch (1976) 2291 n 38; Laufs (1977) 73 n 2, 75; Giesen (1983) 12, 13 n 68, 15 n 83; Pelz (1997) 43; Katzenmeier (2002) 274 n 11; Stauch (2008) 43–44.

40 Katzenmeier (2002) 274, noting the continued absence of a generally accepted definition throughout the later twentieth century.

concerning its definition again began to mount during the 1960s.[41] *Bockelmann*, in an oft-cited part of his 1968 textbook, challenged both the utility and doctrinal need for any overlap between – let alone equation of – legal fault and the *Kunstfehler* as the *Bundesgerichtshof* had adopted it. Once the law had recognised a broad degree of clinical freedom in the choice of possible approaches,[42] and that there could be liability for core medical behaviour without the need to demonstrate that there had been a *Kunstfehler* – a situation he took *BGH 27.11.1952* as confirming[43] – then all that the courts were required to do was to was to clearly articulate the abstract standard to which practitioners would be held, a process he felt, somewhat generously, had begun in *RG 22.03.1932.*[44] Indeed, looking back on the literature of the late 1930s he viewed these works as simply evidencing the start of a necessary process of concretising the various situations in which a medical practitioner could be liable as examples of this emerging judicial principle.[45] Noting that definitional controversy had continued into the post-war era – and reflecting shades of the discussion surrounding *Haberland's* earlier work[46] – *Pribilla* stressed the danger of allowing the *Kunstfehler* to morph into an unintended form of strict liability for medical error.[47] His was the first comprehensive review of the literature in the post-war era, and it found him emphasising the need to arrange the law so as to preserve flexibility of choice for medical practitioners, rather than binding them to a given 'rule' of practice in a particular situation.[48] As with *Bockelmann*, he repeated the call for greater efforts to articulate what the abstract standard of care would require in concrete situations once one accepted that the medical discourse was not decisive,[49] although this is difficult to reconcile with his suggestion to adopt a Scandinavian-style compensation system overseen by a

41 v Brandis / Pribilla (1973) 12. Although, as *Riegger* notes, strains of this could be found in the medico-legal literature in the immediate post-war period as well, Riegger (2007) 15 and *Engisch* had warned of a backslide towards a narrower view of the *Kunstfehler* as early as 1958, see Engisch (1958) 22.

42 A situation he noted could be justified in that the alternative would unnecessarily stifle medical progress rather than, as he suggested had been assumed, having anything to do with the resumption of restrictions on medical practice throughout the 1930s, see Bockelmann (1968) 87 n 9.

43 Bockelmann (1968) 86 n 6.

44 8 HRR 1932, 1828.

45 Bockelmann (1968) 88 n 19, citing König / Kostlin (1937); Goldhahn / Hartmann (1937); Hübner / Drost (1955); and Perrett (1956).

46 See above pg 174, n 237.

47 Pribilla (1971) 72.

48 Ibid. 75–76.

49 Ibid. 79.

panel of independent medical experts who would judge whether there had been a breach of the expected standards.[50]

This pressure continued into the late 1970s as further attempts were made to restrict or abolish the received understanding of the *Kunstfehler* by one of post-war Germany's medical law titans, *Erwin Deutsch*. Noting that *BGH 27.11.1952* had taken on the status of a *'ständige Rechtsprechung'*,[51] and echoing *König's* earlier efforts,[52] he suggested that doctrine would be considerably clarified if the concept was simply restricted to denote a special form of medical error consonant with the breach of an existing court-declared *Verkehrspflicht* or the breach of a protective regulation caught by § 823 (2) *BGB*.[53] Outside of these areas, the court could police medical error as it saw fit.[54] This was robustly countered by *Dieter Giesen* – an equal colossus of scholarship in this area – as an attempt to unjustly restrict the potential scope of medical error by enacting, in all but name, a special rule for medical practitioners compared to the case of other occupations.[55] Beyond such doctrinal discussions, some scholars came to be openly uneasy with the semantic atavism of the language of *'Kunst'* to describe what had become an overwhelmingly *scientific* model of medicine in practice.[56] Finally, given the increasingly dynamic nature of medical practice over the latter half of the twentieth century, tying medical error in law to a failure to have complied with accepted rules of medical practice, often adopted at the start of a practitioner's career, became widely viewed as unnecessarily risking hindering medical progress.[57]

Notwithstanding the mounting academic consensus that the idea of a *Kunstfehler* could, at least in legal terms, be dispensed with entirely, it made its way into the first two editions of the leading modern textbook on medical law, *Adolf Laufs'* 1977 work *'Arztrecht'*. In a chapter entitled *'Kunstfehler und Sorgfaltspflichtverletzung'*[58] he conceded the *Bundesgerichtshof* had adopted the

50 Pribilla (1971) 89.
51 Deutsch (1976) 2289, 2291.
52 See above pg 180, n 281.
53 Deutsch (1976) 2291–2292.
54 Ibid. 2292; Katzenmeier (2002) 275, n 26.
55 As *Katzenmeier* notes this was likely an overly strong reading of *Deutsch's* position, which he viewed as rather advocating, '...not the privileging of the medical fraternity, but rather the shaping of the material rules of liability according to the peculiarities of the medical sector.' Katzenmeier (2002) 275–276. Indeed, *Deutsch's* later writing may be read as vindicating that view, see Deutsch (1978) 1659; Deutsch (1995) 480.
56 Katzenmeier (2002) 274 n 13; Deutsch / Schreiber (1985) D 36.
57 Ibid. 275 n 21; Riegger (2007) 15; Bockelmann (1968) 87.
58 Renamed in later editions *'Arztfehler und Haftpflicht'*, see Laufs (1993) 263.

pre-war definition,[59] but – cribbing heavily from *Bockelmann* – stressed its disutility where there were no generally accepted rules and emphasised that an existing medical consensus in favour of a particular course of action could not satisfy a practitioner's responsibility to assess in *each* situation whether that was merited or not.[60] Indeed, the *Bundesgerichtshof* was in the process of developing a body of case law, perhaps over-generously described as substantial by *Laufs*,[61] repeatedly confirming that liability could arise despite the absence of any breach of the accepted medical rules by the defendant and unpacking the normative standard of care that would be expected from medical practitioners.

As *Bockelmann* saw it, the admonition in *BGH 27.11.1952* that, in cases of uncertainty, a practitioner had to show 'great care', provided a hint as to the normative standard the German courts would seek to enforce in interpreting *§ 276 BGB*.[62] This phrase had, as noted in chapter five, originated in *RG 22.03.1932*.[63] Although *RG 22.03.1932* was occasionally referenced separately from its citation in that later case,[64] the courts increasingly sought to better articulate what it meant in practice to replace formal cant with substantive doctrine, despite the obvious retreat from certainty that this would herald.[65] This process was visible as early as the mid-1950s when, in *BGH 17.02.1956*,[66] the court rejected the argument that a practitioner who followed a particular medical school could ignore the greater safety offered by other treatments.[67] The case was particularly striking given the fact that both possible treatments – one conservative, one interventionist – were a recognised part of contemporary medical science and, as such, there could be no talk of a *Kunstfehler* in the narrower sense of a breach of an accepted rule.[68] Rather, predictably drawing on *BGH 27.11.1952*, the finding of fault was freestanding and the *Bundesgerichtshof* emphasised the practitioner's duty to assess why, in each *particular* situation, a certain treatment was justified, particularly where there was a difference of

59 Laufs (1977) 73; v Brandis/Pribilla (1973) 12.

60 Ibid. 74, 75 n 8. This was repeated in the second edition, see Laufs (1978) 84–85.

61 Laufs (1977) 75.

62 Bockelmann (1968) 87; Laufs (1977) 74–75.

63 8 HRR 1932, 1828.

64 Deutsch (1995) 135, writing in 1963.

65 Pelz (1997) 44. As is apparent from any modern textbook, the focus has since turned to mapping categories of error, a rather more fact-driven pursuit, see Katzenmeier (2002) 277 n 36; Riegger (2007) 16.

66 (1956) 6 VersR 224.

67 This stance was further tightened in the case of non-orthodox practitioners who, building on *RG 19.03.1937*, were required to use widely-used and proven orthodox treatments, see *BGH 21.06.1960*, (1960) 13 NJW 2253.

68 Pelz (1997) 43–44.

medical opinion.[69] Again, in *BGH 13.10.1964*,[70] the court emphasised that the absence of a *Kunstfehler* was no answer to a potentially successful action if, separately, '…not everything had been done which, according to the rules and experience of medical practice, must be done for the protection of the patient from bodily harm.'[71] This process was almost certainly aided by the emerging protection of patients' rights as expressed in the burgeoning post-war jurisprudence on disclosure of risk.[72] Equally, and intimately tied up in this process, the considerable judicial emphasis on the constitutional guarantees of dignity and bodily integrity provided for by the *Grundgesetz* 1949 provided a touchstone for post-war developments here.[73]

Beginning with *BGH 27.09.1977*,[74] the court signalled the start of a formal move away from the remaining conceptual baggage of the *Kunstfehler* and towards the language of the *Behandlungsfehler*.[75] There, using the term *Kunstfehler* in quotation marks as simply a synonym for fault,[76] the court noted not only that there could be no automatic assumption that compliance with the accepted Hippocratic method would avoid a finding of fault, but also that the court was entitled to rigorously scrutinise expert evidence and construe it in line with its underlying logic – as the court saw it – not simply its explicit text.[77] By the end of that decade, the court was avoiding the term altogether.[78] As to how a *Behandlungsfehler* was to be understood, the court's proffered definition in *BGH 10.03.1987* has found widespread acceptance.[79] There,[80] in an unsuccessful claim regarding botched knee surgery which, it was argued, had later led to the amputation of the plaintiff's leg, the court clarified that a defendant practitioner's liability depended on:[81]

69 Bockelmann (1968) 86 n 6; Laufs (1977) 74.
70 (1965) 18 NJW 345.
71 (1965) 18 NJW 345, 346.
72 Most visible in the seminal *Myom* decision *BGH, 28.11.1957* (1958) 11 NJW 267; Stauch (2008) 107 ff.
73 Stauch (2008) 100.
74 (1978) 31 NJW 587.
75 Riegger (2007) 16.
76 (1978) 31 NJW, 588.
77 Deutsch (1978) 31 NJW 1657, 1658.
78 Riegger (2007) 16; Dunz (1980) 22; Laufs (1993) 269, noting that it was now simply a factual description of a legal category.
79 Giesen (1990) 1056; Katzenmeier (2002) 277 n 35; Katzenmeier/Laufs/Lipp (2015) 336.
80 (1987) 40 NJW 2291.
81 *BGH 10.03.1987*, (1987) 40 NJW 2291, 2292.

> '...whether in the precise situation, considering the medical proficiency and experience that may be demanded from him, the practitioner had made a justifiable decision concerning the diagnostic and therapeutic measures undertaken and carefully executed these measures.'

As *Giesen* put it in his seminal 1983 monograph, the *Bundesgerichtshof* had moved on from the idea of the *Kunstfehler* as adopted in *BGH 27.11.1952*. Not only had it, overwhelmingly, been substituted for the concept of a *Behandlungsfehler*,[82] this was to be judicially construed in light of the abstract standard in § 276 *BGB* and nothing more.[83] Indeed, in doing so the court had decisively confirmed a much broader reach for the idea of medical error, freed entirely from the notion that accepted standards within medical discourse could constrain a finding of fault.[84] Repeating his earlier criticisms, *Giesen* went further and noted that to allow any other such understanding of the concept would not only be for the *Bundesgerichtshof* to enshrine paternalism – a position it was, by then, clearly set against – but would also abdicate any independent responsibility to shape the contours of liability.[85] Drawing on the examples provided in the final decade of the *Reichsgericht*, the fact that it was now a judicial standard not a medical one was beyond contestation.[86]

## 4. A wider lesson

The answer to the question posed in the introduction reveals a complicated set of overlapping factors which, when taken together, offer an explanation of the law's development. That question did not address itself to the other features of medical liability, which emerged in this period, and more research on these topics would, undoubtedly, present a more nuanced picture than that proffered here. It is hoped that this volume offers the reader an insight into a particular model of liability and legal development in what was, and remains, a core concern of the private law, medical error.

There is no need for a broader conclusion than that offered above, but should one seek a wider lesson it is this: The iteration of legal rules that govern the behaviour of any social group is contingent upon whether and how that group is

82 Giesen (1983) 12 n 55; Laufs (1993) 269.

83 *Deutsch* remained less optimistic about this change, arguing that the old tension had simply been shifted to the lack of certainty about how the standard would be enforced in practice, and that it was only the widespread presence of insurance that permitted this sort of approach, see Deutsch (1995) 480.

84 Giesen (1983) 12.

85 Ibid. 14–15.

86 Ibid. 15, citing *RG 08.04.1940* RGZ 163, 129 and *RG 04.02.1938* (1938) 67 JW 1246.

acknowledged by the law and, once acknowledged by law, that original model may linger long after it ceases to be apposite.[87] Here, that process was informed by views of what medicine was, who both medical practitioners and, belatedly, patients were, and the role that each was expected to play within the healthcare system. These are not static values and as they change, or others come to the fore, current models must be reassessed. Failure to appreciate how this process has unfolded renders our scrutiny of the current law incomplete. Understanding how and why the law has developed ensures that our analysis of the law is better informed – accounting not simply for easily visible changes but also the developmental inertia and relevant drivers within a system – and may, it is hoped, prompt other systems to reflect on their own development in this area and question whether those previous choices remain appropriate.

87 Watson (1988) 80.

# List of Abbreviations

| | |
|---|---|
| AcP | Archiv für Civilistische Praxis |
| AGO | Allgemeine Gerichtsordnung für die Preußischen Staaten 1793 |
| ALR | Allgemeines Landrecht 1794 |
| BayObLG | Bayerisches Oberstes Landesgericht |
| BayStGB | Bayerisches Strafgesetzbuch 1813 |
| BG | Bundesgericht |
| BGBl | Bundesgesetzblatt |
| BGH | Bundesgerichtshof |
| BGHZ | Entscheidungen des Bundesgerichtshofs in Zivilsachen |
| BPO | Prozessordnung in bürgerlichen Rechtsstreitigkeiten für das Königreich Bayern 1869 |
| BStGB | Bayerisches Strafgesetzbuch 1861 |
| DR | Deutsches Recht |
| EPE | Entscheidungen des Preußischen Ehrengerichtshofes für Ärzte vol 1 (1908) |
| HRR | Höchstrichterliche Rechtsprechung |
| KG | Kammergericht |
| JW | Juristische Wochenschrift |
| LG | Landgericht |
| MMW | Münchener Medizinische Wochenschrift |
| NJW | Neue Juristische Wochenschrift |
| OAG | Oberappellationsgericht |
| OLG | Oberlandesgericht |
| PStGB | Preußisches Strafgesetzbuch 1851 |
| RG | Reichsgericht |
| RGBl | Reichsgesetzblatt |
| RGSt | Entscheidungen des Reichsgerichts in Strafsachen |
| RGZ | Entscheidungen des Reichgerichts in Zivilsachen |
| RRGSt | Rechtsprechung des Reichsgerichts in Strafsachen |
| RStGB | Reichsstrafgesetzbuch 1871 |
| RStPO | Reichsstrafprozeßordnung 1877 |
| RZPO | Reichszivilprozeßordnung 1877 |
| SBGB | Sächsisches Bürgerliches Gesetzbuch |
| StGB | Reichsstrafgesetzbuch 1871 |
| VersR | Versicherungsrecht |
| WRV | Weimarer Reichsverfassung |

*Translation note*

Statutory titles and text have been left in German, as have terms of art that cannot easily be rendered in English. Everything else has been translated by the author, unless otherwise stated.

# Bibliography

## Cases

### Germany

#### *Ehrengerichtshof für Ärzte*

*EGHÄ* 30.05.1902 EPEÄ (1908) 165
*EGHÄ* 30.05.1902 EPEÄ (1908) 138
*EGHÄ* 01.12.1902 EPEÄ (1908) 81
*EGHÄ* 04.05.1903 EPEÄ (1908) 87
*EGHÄ* 05.05.1903 EPEÄ (1908) 139
*EGHÄ* 11.01.1904 EPEÄ (1908) 89
*EGHÄ* 08.11.1904 EPEÄ (1908) 166
*EGHÄ* 02.12.1905 EPEÄ (1908) 99
*EGHÄ* 14.05.1906 EPEÄ (1908) 140
*EGHÄ* 15.05.1906 EPEÄ (1908) 107
*EGHÄ* 15.05.1906 EPEÄ (1908) 108
*EGHÄ* 14.05.1906 EPEÄ (1908) 82
*EGHÄ* 07.01.1907 EPEÄ (1908) 85
*EGHÄ* 08.01.1907 EPEÄ (1908) 166
*EGHÄ* 28.05.1907 EPEÄ (1908) 142

#### *Regional Courts*

*OAG Lübeck 20.07.1849* Seuffert's Archiv 3, 158
*OAG Lübeck 25.11.1865* Seuffert's Archiv 20, 343
*Cassationshofes zu Wolfenbüttel 01.05.1855* Seuffert's Archiv 9, 299
*OAG Oldenburg 22.02.1875* Seuffert's Archiv 31, 297
*OLG Celle 19.01.1912*
*OLG Hamburg 31.03.1917*
*OLG Karlsruhe 22.12.1928*
*OLG Hamburg 03.04.1928*
*KG 05.01.1929* (1929) 58 JW 2287
*OLG Celle 11.01.1929*
*OLG Frankfurt a. M. 25.01.1929* (1929) 58 JW 2289
*OLG Stuttgart 12.07.1929* 5 HRR 1929, 1909
*LG Berlin 21.04.1931*
*OLG Köln 13.02.1931*
*LG Frankfurt a. M. 27.03.1934* (O 436/32)
*OLG Königsberg 14.09.1934* 11 HRR 1935, 721
*OLG Karlsruhe 31.05.1935* (2 W 82/35)
*OLG Munich 29.01.1938* 14 HRR 1938, 725

*Reichsgericht*

*RG 18.03.1880*
*RG 08.06.1880* RGSt 1, 446
*RG 25.10.1881* RGSt 5, 74
*RG 12.04.1882* RRGSt 4, 313
*RG 04.06.1883* RRGSt 5, 403
*RG 03.07.1884* RRGSt 6, 506
*RG 03.10.1884* (1890) 53 Vierteljahrsschrift für gerichtliche und öffentliche Medicin 371
*RG 04.11.1886* RGZ 18, 173
*RG 14.01.1887* RGSt 15, 181
*RG 18.09.1888* RRGSt 10, 493
*RG 26.10.1893*
*RG 31.05.1894* RGSt 25, 375
*RG 23.02.1900* (1900) 29 JW 302
*RG 10.04.1905* RGSt 38, 34
*RG 27.03.1906* RG 63, 104
*RG 30.10.1906* RGZ 64, 232
*RG 11.06.1907* RGZ 66, 143
*RG 03.12.1907* RGZ 67, 182
*RG 27.05.1908* RG 68, 431
*RG 15.07.1908* (1908) 38 JW 579
*RG 14.03.1911* Seuffert's Archiv 67, 101; (1911) JW 449
*RG 01.03.1912* RGZ 78, 432; Seuffert's Archiv 74, 432
*RG 25.06.1912*
*RG 01.10.1912.*
*RG 09.07.1913* RGZ 83, 75
*RG 19.06.1914* RGZ 85, 183
*RG 01.06.1915* (1915) 44 JW 916
*RG 27.09.1915* RGZ 165, 106
*RG 04.07.1916*
*RG 24.03.1917*
*RG 23.09.1918* RGZ 93, 302
*RG 15.02.1919* RGZ 95, 16
*RG 13.10.1919* RG 88, 433
*RG 17.10.1919* RGZ 97, 4
*RG 04.05.1920*
*RG 03.06.1921* RGZ 102, 230
*RG 22.12.1922* (1923) 52 JW 603
*RG 20.12.1923* RGZ 107, 386
*RG 08.01.1926* RGZ 112, 290
*RG 22.03.1927*
*RG 03.05.1927*
*RG 16.09.1927* RG 118, 41; (1927) 56 JW 2844
*RG 06.01.1928*
*RG 18.01.1929*
*RG 26.11.1929* RGZ 126, 253
*RG 06.12.1929* (1930) 59 JW 1595
*RG 27.09.1929* RGZ 125, 374
*RG 28.03.1930* RGZ 128, 121
*RG 20.06.1930* (1931) 60 JW 1466.
*RG 05.07.1930* (1931) 60 JW 1466
*RG 08.07.1930* RGSt 62, 263; (1931) 60 JW 1483

*RG 20.07.1930*
*RG 18.10.1930*
*RG 12.05.1931* 7 HRR 1931, 1748
*RG 01.12.1931* RGSt 67, 12
*RG 16.06.1931*
*RG 29.02.1932* (1933) JW 2062
*RG 22.03.1932* 8 HRR 1932, 1828
*RG 05.04.1932* 8 HRR 1932, 1643
*RG 24.01.1933*
*RG 19.01.1933* RGZ 139, 255
*RG 16.01.1934* Seuffert's Archiv 88, 140
*RG 08.02.1934* 10 HRR 1934, 786
*RG 23.02.1934*
*RG 03.07.1934*
*RG 12.10.1934* (1935) 64 JW 115
*RG 16.10.1934* Seuffert's Archiv 89, 48; (1935) 64 JW 273
*RG 03.09.1935*
*RG 12.11.1935* (1936) 65 JW 644
*RG 03.03.1936*
*RG 29.09.1936* RGZ 152, 175
*RG 09.10.1936*
RG *19.06.1936* RGZ 151, 349
*RG 24.11.1936* RGZ 153, 280
*RG 15.01.1937* 14 HRR 1938, 857
*RG 19.03.1937* (1937) 66 JW 3087
*RG 04.02.1938* (1938) 67 JW 1246
*RG 07.01.1938* (1938) 67 JW 2203
*RG 17.03.1939* Seuffert's Archiv 93, 260
*RG 08.03.1940* RGZ 163, 129
*RG 21.06.1940* (1940) DR 1949
*RG 03.12.1941* RGZ 168, 207

### *Bundesgerichshof*

*BGH 11.04.1951*, BGHZ 1, 383
*BGH 27.11.1952*, BGHZ 8, 138.
*BGH 17.02.1956*, (1956) 6 VersR 224
*BGH, 28.11.1957*, (1958) 11 NJW 267
*BGH 21.06.1960*, (1960) 13 NJW 2253
*BGH 13.10.1964*, (1965) 18 NJW 345
*BGH 27.09.1977*, (1978) 31 NJW 587
*BGH 10.03.1987*, (1987) 40 NJW 2291

## Switzerland

*SBG 03.06.1904*, *Karrer v Bircher*, (1904) 30 Entscheidungen des Schweizerischen Bundesgerichts 304

## Books, articles and chapters in edited collections

A Alker, *Der preußische Zivilprozeß* (Ernst Günther, Lissa, 1846)

L Arndts, *Lehrbuch der Pandecten* (JG Cotta, München, 2nd ed 1855)

L Arndts, *Lehrbuch der Pandekten* (JG Cotta, München, 5th ed 1865)

FC Arnold, *Praktische Erörterungen aus dem Rechtsgebiete* (JJ Palm and Ernst Enke, Erlangen, 1853)

E Arztbach, *Grundfragen der ärztlichen Kammergesetzgebung und Berufsgerichtsbarkeit und ihr Verhältnis zum Grundgesetz unter besonderer Berücksichtigung der historischen Entwicklung des ärztlichen Berufsrechts* (Marburg, 1960)

M Anders / B Gehle, *Das Recht der freien Dienste: Vertrag und Haftung* (De Gruyter, Berlin, 2001)

E Auerbach, 'Autorität ärztlicher Gutachten im Strafprozesse', (1899) 4 Deutsche Juristen-Zeitung 482

Bacharach, 'Die Beweislast des Arztes', (1915) 44 JW 819

F Bauridl, 'Beitrag zur Lehre von dem Rechtsverhältnisse zwischen dem Arzte und dem Patienten' (1874) 15 Zeitschrift des Anwaltvereins für Bayern 328

J Bell / D Ibbetson, *European Legal Development: The Case of Tort* (CUP, Cambridge, 2012)

K-H Below, *Der Arzt im römischen Recht* (CH Beck, München, 1953)

AF Berner, 'Körperverletzung', (1867) 19 Gerichtssaal 30

G Beseler, *Kommentar über das Strafgesetzbuch für die Preußischen Staaten und das Einführungsgesetz vom 14. April 1851* (Weidmann, Leipzig, 1851)

G Beseler, *System des gemeinen deutschen Privatrechts* (Weidmann, Leipzig, vol 2 1853)

M v Bieberstein, 'Überlegungen zur Haftung bei Heilbehandlung', in F Hauss / R Schmidt (eds), *Festschrift für Ernst Klingmüller* (Verlag Versicherungswirtschaft, Karlsruhe, 1974) 249

R Bilstein, *Das deliktische Schadenersatzrecht der Lex Aquilia in der Rechtsprechung des Reichsgerichts* (Juristische Schriftenreihe, Münster, 1994)

P Birks / G McLeod, *Justinian's Institutes* (Duckworth, London, 1987)

J Bleker, 'To Benefit the Poor and Advance Medical Science: Hospitals and Hospital Care in Germany 1820–1870', in M Berg / G Cocks (eds), *Medicine and Modernity: Public Health and Medical Care in Nineteenth- and Twentieth-Century Germany* (CUP, Cambridge, 1997) 17

CB Bloemertz, *Die Schmerzensgeldbegutachtung. Medizinischer Leitfaden für Ärzte, Juristen und Versicherungsfachleute* (De Gruyter, Berlin, 4th ed 1984)

F Blume, *System des Geltenden Privatrechts* (Adolph Marcus, Bonn, 1852)

JC Bluntschli, *Deutsches Privatrecht* (Literarisch-artistische Anstalt, München, vol 2 1854)

G Bock, 'Sterilization and "medical" massacres in National Socialist Germany', in M Berg / G Cocks (eds), *Medicine and Modernity: Public Health and Medical Care in Nineteenth- and Twentieth-Century Germany* (CUP, Cambridge, 1997) 149

P Bockelmann, *Strafrecht des Arztes* (Georg Thieme, Stuttgart, 1968)

P Bockelmann, 'Das Ende des Heilpraktikergesetzes', (1966) 19 NJW 1145

G Bohne, 'Bemerkung zu RG 01.12.1931', (1933) 62 JW 1775

TN Bonner, *Becoming a Physician: Medical Education in Britain, France, Germany and the United States, 1750–1945* (OUP, Oxford, 1995)

C v Brandis / O Pribilla, *Arzt und Kunstfehlervorwurf* (Wilhelm Goldmann, München, 1973)

KH Bremer, *Die Zivilrechtliche Haftung des Arztes* (H&J Lechte, Emsdetten, 1934)

E Breuer, *Das Verhältnis der Ärzte und Fachärzte zur Gesamtbevölkerung im Deutschen Reich und in der Bundesrepublik Deutschland in der Zeit von 1825–1958* (Hochschulschrift, München, 1963)

TH Broman, *The transformation of German academic medicine 1750–1820* (CUP, Cambridge, 1997)

G Brüggemeier, *Haftungsrecht: Struktur, Prinzipien, Schutzbereich* (Springer, Berlin, 2006)
A Brinz, *Lehrbuch der Pandekten* (Andreas Deichert, Erlangen, 1857)
A Brinz, *Lehrbuch der Pandekten* (Andreas Deichert, Erlangen, 2nd ed 1882)
F Bruck, *Zur Lehre von der Fahrlässigkeit im heutigen deutschen Strafrecht* (Wilhelm Koebner, Breslau, 1885)
W Buckland, *A Text-Book of Roman Law: From Augustus to Justinian* (CUP, Cambridge, 3rd ed 2007)
WF Bynum, 'The rise of science in medicine, 1850–1913', in WF Bynum / A Hardy / S Jacyna / C Lawrence / EM Tansey (eds), *The Western Medical Tradition 1800–2000* (CUP, Cambridge, 2006) 111
R v Caenegem, *Judges, legislators and professors* (CUP, Cambridge, 1987)
J Casper, *Practisches Handbuch der gerichtlichen Medicin* (August Hirschwald, Berlin, vol 2 1857)
G Cocks, 'Introduction', in M Berg / G Cocks (eds), *Medicine and Modernity: Public Health and Medical Care in Nineteenth- and Twentieth-Century Germany* (CUP, Cambridge, 1997) 1
R Cotterrell, *The Sociology of Law: An Introduction* (OUP, Oxford, 1984)
C Crawford, 'Legalizing medicine: early-modern legal systems and the growth of medico-legal knowledge', in M Clark / C Crawford (ed) *Legal Medicine in History* (CUP, Cambridge, 1994) 89
F Dahn, *Deutsches Privatrecht* (Breitknopf & Hartel, Leipzig, vol 1 1878)
G Dannemann, *An Introduction to German Civil and Commercial Law* (BIICL, London, 1993)
H Dankwardt, 'Die locatio conductio operis', (1874) 13 (= NF 1) Jahrbücher für die Dogmatik des heutigen römischen und deutschen Privatrechts 1
H Dankwardt, 'Der Arbeiter-Vertrag', (1875) 14 (= NF 2) Jahrbücher für die Dogmatik des heutigen römischen und deutschen Privatrechts 228
W Danz, *Handbuch des heutigen deutschen Privatrechts* (FC Löflund, Stuttgart, vol 5 1799)
M Danzer (ed), *Das Bayerische Landrecht vom Jahre 1756 in seiner heutigen Geltung* (J Schweizer, München, 1894)
D Daube, 'Review of K.H. Below, Der Arzt im Römischen Recht', (1955) 45 The Journal of Roman Studies 179
Deneke, 'Zur gerichtsärztlichen Behandlung von Kunstfehlern', (1888) 15 Aerztliches Vereinsblatt 253
R Dettmeyer / J Preuß / B Madea, 'Malpractice – The role of the forensic pathologist in Germany', (2004) 144 Forensic Science International 265
H Dernburg, *Pandekten* (HW Müller, Berlin, 1886)
H Dernburg, *Pandekten* (HW Müller, Berlin, 3rd ed 1892)
E Deutsch, *Fahrlässigkeit und erforderliche Sorgfalt* (Carl Heymanns, Köln, 1963)
E Deutsch, 'Medizinische Fahrlässigkeiten', (1976) 29 NJW 2289
E Deutsch, *Medizin und Forschung vor Gericht* (CF Müller, Heidelberg, 1978)
E Deutsch, 'Reform des Arzterechts', (1978) 31 NJW 1657, 1659
E Deutsch / HL Schreiber, *Medical Responsibility in Western Europe* (Springer, Berlin, 1985) D 36
E Deutsch / HJ Ahrens, *Deliktsrecht* (Carl Heymanns Köln, 4th ed 2002)
A Diurni, 'Die Arzthaftung von gestern und das Medizinrecht von heute in rechtsvergleichender Perspektive', in HJ Ahrens / C v Bar / G Fischer / A Spickhoff / J Taupitz (eds) *Medizin und Haftung: Festschrift für Erwin Deutsch zum 80. Geburtstag* (Springer, Berlin 2009) 85
A Diwald, *Grundriss des Deutschen Privatrecht* (Self-published, Wien, 1905)
A Dochow, *Die Buße im Strafrecht und Strafproceß* (Jena, 1875)

F Dross, 'Health Care Provision and Poor Relief in Enlightenment and 19th Century Prussia', in OP Grell / A Cunningham / R Jütte (eds), *Health Care and Poor Relief in 18th and 19th Century Northern Europe* (Ashgate, 2002) 69

MD Dubber, 'The German Jury and the Metaphysical *Volk*: From Romantic Idealism to Nazi Ideology', (1995) 43 American Journal of Comparative Law 236.

W Dunz, *Aktuelle Fragen zum Arzthaftungsrecht unter Berücksichtigung der neueren höchstrichterlichen Rechtsprechung* (RWS, Köln, 1980)

D Dwyer, *The Judicial Assessment of Expert Evidence* (CUP, Cambridge, 2008)

L Eberhardt, 'Die zivilrechtliche Haftung des Heilpraktikers', (1986) 36 Versicherungsrecht 110

L Ebermayer, *Arzt und Patient in der Rechtsprechung* (Rudolph Mosse, Berlin, 1924)

L Ebermayer, 'Zur Fahrlässigkeitsfrage beim Zurücklassen von Fremdkörpern in der Bauchhöhle', (1928) 48 Münchener Medizinische Wochenschrift 2084

L Ebermayer, *Der Arzt im Recht* (Georg Thieme, Leipzig, 1930)

L Ebermayer, '*Ärztliche Kunstfehler*', (1932) 61 JW 3305

I Ebert, *Pönale Elemente im deutschen Privatrecht* (Mohr Siebeck, Tübingen 2004)

M Eccius, *Preußisches Privatrecht* (Reimer, Berlin, 7th ed vol 2 1896)

L Edelstein, 'The Distinctive Hellenism of Greek Medicine', (1966) 40 Bulletin of the History of Medicine 197

A Ehrenzweig, 'Die Kunstfehler der Medizinal-Personen', (1892) 30 Assecurranz-Jahrbuch 1

CF Eichhorn, *Einleitung in das deutsche Privatrecht mit Einschluß des Lehenrechts* (Vandenhoeck & Ruprecht, Göttingen, 5th ed 1845)

C Emmert, *Lehrbuch der gerichtlichen Medizin* (Georg Thieme, Leipzig, 1900)

F Endemann, *Lehrbuch des bürgerlichen Rechts* (Carl Heymanns, Berlin, 8th ed 1903)

K Engisch, *Die rechtliche Bedeutung der ärztlichen Operation* (Gustav Fischer, Jena 1958) 22

W Ernst, 'Negligence in 19th Century Germany', in E Schrage (ed), *Negligence: The Comparative Legal History of the Law of Torts* (Duncker & Humblot, Berlin, 2001) 341

A Eser, 'Zum "Weg der Forschung" im Recht der Medizin', in A Eser (ed), *Recht und Medizin* (Wissenschaftliche Buchgesellschaft, Darmstadt, 1990) 1

J Evelt, *Das preußische Civilrecht* (Ferdinand Schöningh, Paderborn, 1854)

U Falk / H Mohnhaupt (eds), *Das Bürgerliche Gesetzbuch und seine Richter* (Klostermann, Frankfurt am Main, 2000)

O Fischer, *Lehrbuch des preußischen Privatrechts* (J Guttentag, Berlin, 1887)

E Fischer-Homberger, *Medizin vor Gericht: Zur Sozialgeschichte der Gerichtsmedizin* (Luchterhand, Darmstadt, 1988)

Flesch, 'Die rechtliche Natur der Buße des Reichsstrafgesetzbuchs', (1876) 28 Der Gerichssaal 278

G Flügge, *Das Recht des Arztes* (Urban & Schwarzenberg, Berlin, 1903)

F Förster / ME Eccius, *Theorie und Praxis des heutigen gemeinen preußischen Privatrechts* (Georg Reimer, Berlin, 5th ed vol 2 1887)

F Förster, *Theorie und Praxis des heutigen gemeinen preussischen Privatrechts auf der Grundlage des gemeinen deutschen Rechts* (Georg Reimer, Berlin, 3rd ed vol 1 1873)

F Förster / ME Eccius, *Theorie und Praxis des heutigen gemeinen preußischen Privatrechts* (Georg Reimer, Berlin, 6th ed vol 2 1892)

F Förster, *Preußisches Privatrecht* (Georg Reimer, Berlin, 6th ed vol 2 1892)

F Förster, *Theorie und Praxis des heutigen gemeinen preussischen Privatrechts auf der Grundlage des gemeinen deutschen Rechts* (Georg Reimer, Berlin, 3rd ed vol 2 1873)

M Foucault, 'La politique de la santé au XVIIIe siècle', in M Foucault (ed), *Les Machines à guérir, Aux origines de l'hôpital moderne* (P Mardaga, Brussels, 1979) 222

E Fraenkel, *The dual state: a contribution to the theory of dictatorship* (OUP, Oxford, 2017 trans EA Shills)

D Franzki, *Die Beweisregeln im Arzthaftungsprozeß* (Duncker & Humblot, Berlin, 1982)
U Frevert, 'Professional Medicine and the Working Classes in Imperial Germany', (1985) 20 Medicine, History and Society 637
P Fromherz, 'Haftet der Arzt auf Schmerzengeld?', (1912) 108 Archiv für die Civilistische Praxis 435
J Fürstenthal, *Real-Encyclopädie des gesammten in Deutschland geltenden gemeinen Rechts* (August Rücker Berlin, vol 1 1827)
A Fuld, 'Die Vernachlässigung der Aseptik und Antiseptik als ärztlicher Kunstfehler', (1898) Aerztliche Sachverständigen-Zeitung 351
G Geiß, 'Beitrage zur Erörterung criminalistischer Fragen', (1838) Archiv der Criminal Rechts 573
HG Gengler, *Lehrbuch des deutschen Privatrechts* (Theodor Bläsing, Erlangen, 1854)
CF Gerber, *System des deutschen Privatrechts* (Gustav Fischer, Jena, 17th ed 1895)
CF Gerber, *System des deutschen Privatrechts* (Friedrich Mauke, Jena, 5th ed 1855)
CF Gerber, *System des deutschen Privatrechts* (Friedrich Mauke, Jena, 2nd ed 1850)
J v Gerlach, 'Das Arzthaftungsrecht in der Antike', in HE Brandner (ed), *Festschrift für Karlmann Geiß zum 65. Geburtstag* (Carl Heymanns, Köln, 2000) 389
O v Gierke, *Deutsches Privatrecht* (Duncker & Humboldt, Leipzig, vol 3 1917)
D Giesen, 'Wandlungen im Arzthaftungsrecht', (1990) 45 Juristenzeitung 1053
K v Gunkel, 'Fahrlässigkeit und ärztliches Verschulden', (1935) Deutschen Ärzteblatt, 620
D Giesen, *International Medical Malpractice Law, A Comparative Law Study of Civil Liability Arising from Medical Care* (JCB Mohr, Tübingen, 1988)
D Giesen, *Wandlungen des Arzthaftungsrechts* (JCB Mohr, Tübingen, 1983)
CF Glück, *Ausfuhrliche Erläuterung der Pandecten nach Hellfeld* (JJ Palm, Erlangen, vol 10 pt II 1808)
CF Glück, *Ausfuhrliche Erläuterung der Pandecten nach Hellfeld* (JJ Palm, Erlangen, vol 11 pt II 1809)
CF Glück, *Ausführliche Erläuterung der Pandecten nach Hellfeld* (JJ Palm, Erlangen, vol 15 pt II 1814)
CF Glück, *Ausfuhrliche Erläuterung der Pandecten nach Hellfeld* (JJ Palm, Erlangen, vol 17 pt II 1816)
R Goldhahn / W Hartmann, *Chirurgie und Recht* (Ferdinand Enke, Stuttgart, 1937)
J Gordley, *Foundations of Private Law* (OUP, Oxford, 2006)
C Gossler, *Ueber der Rechtsverhältnis zwischen einem Kranken und seinem Arzte* (C Salfeld, Berlin, 1814).
E Graf, *Das ärztliche Vereinswesen in Deutschland und der deutsche Ärztevereinsbund* (Vogel, Leipzig, 1890)
J Grimm / W Grimm, *Deutsches Wörterbuch* (Leipzig, vol 24 1854)
F Grödel / F Klopfer, *Gesetzbuch und Ärztlicher Röntgenbetrieb* (Julius Springer, Berlin, 1925)
R Grunberger, *A Social History of the Third Reich* (Weidenfeld and Nicolson, London, 1971)
H v Haberer, 'Zur Frage bei Operationen vergessener Fremdkörper', (1926) 198 Deutsche Zeitschrift für Chirurgie 96
Haberland, 'Ärztliche Kunstfehler', (1932) 61 JW 3304
Haebler, 'Zur Lehre von den ärztlichen Kunstfehlern', (1898) 18 Aerztliche Sachverständigen-Zeitung 370
M Hall, 'The Legal and Historical Foundations of Patients as Medical Consumers', (2008) 96 Georgetown Law Journal 583
HA Hammelmann, 'Expert Evidence', (1947) 10 Modern Law Review 37
W Hanauer, 'Ein ärztlicher Haftpflichtprozess wegen schlecht geheilter Schulter-Luxation', (1897) 21 Aerztliche Sachverständigen-Zeitung 423

H Hälschner, *Das gemeine deutsche Strafrecht* (Adolph Marcus, Bonn, vol 2 1884)
G Hänel, *Lehre vom Schadenersatzrecht* (Leipzig, 1833)
JC Hasse, *Die Culpa des römischen Rechts* (Adolph Marcus, Bonn, 2nd ed 1838)
A Haug, 'Die Neue Deutsche Heilkunde', in J Bleker / N Jachertz (eds), *Medizin im Dritten Reich* (DÄV, Köln, 1989)
H Hausmaninger, *Das Schadenersatzrecht der lex Aquilia* (Manz, Wien, 5th ed 1996)
J Heimberger, *Strafrecht und Medizin* (CH Beck, München, 1899)
A Hefke, 'Über den Beweis der culpa bei Kontraktsklagen', (1883) 3 vol 2 = NF 13 Archiv für praktische Rechstwissenschaft 1
A Hefke, 'Der Arzt in römischen und im heutigen Recht', (1886) 3 vol 3 =NF 14 Archiv für praktische Rechstwissenschaft 1, cited as Hefke (1886a)
A Hefke, 'Haftung des Mensor nach römischen Recht und nach heutigem Recht', (1886) 3 vol 3= NF 14 Archiv für praktische Rechstwissenschaft 153, cited as Hefke (1886b)
A Hefke, 'Das Wesen des damnum inuria datum', (1886) 3 vol 3= NF 14 Archiv für praktische Rechstwissenschaft 212, cited as Hefke (1886c)
O Hegener, *Das Vertragsrecht des Arztes* (Richard Schoetz, Berlin, 1925)
H Helbron, *Entwicklungen und Fehlentwicklungen im Arzthaftungsrecht* (Herbert Utz, München, 2001)
K Heldrich, 'Der Arzt in römischen Privatrecht', (1939–1930) 88 Jherings Jahrbücher für die Dogmatik des bürgerlichen Rechts 139
K Hellwig, *Die Stellung des Arztes im bürgerlichen Rechtsleben* (A Deichert, Leipzig, 1905)
A Henke, *Lehrbuch über die gerichtliche Medizin* (Berlin, 3rd ed 1821)
A Henke, *Abhandlungen aus dem Gebiete der gerichtlichen Medicin, als Erläuterungen zu dem Lehrbuche der gerichtlichen Medicin* (FA Brockhaus, Leipzig, 2nd ed vol 4 1830)
CFT Hepp, *Die Zurechnung auf dem Gebiete des Civilrechts* (CF Osiander, Tübingen, 1838)
H Hildebrand, *Stellung, Pflichten und Gutachtertätigkeit des Arztes* (Richard Schoetz, Berlin, 1925)
E Hilger, *Die zivilrechtliche Haftung des Arztes für ärztliche Kunstfehler* (Hochschulschrift, Köln, 1951)
H Hirte, *Berufshaftung* (CH Beck, München, 1996)
E Hondius, *The Development of Medical Liability* (CUP, Cambridge, 2010)
M Hubenstorf, 'Von der "freien Arztwahl" zur Reichärzteordnung – Ärztliche Standespolitik zwischen Liberalismus und Nationalsozialismus', in J Bleker / N Jachertz (eds), *Medizin im "Dritten Reich"* (DÄV, Köln 2nd ed, 1993)
A Hübner / H Drost, *Ärztliches Haftpflichtrecht* (Springer, Berlin, 1955)
A Hübner / O Warneyer, *Haftpflichtfälle aus der ärztlichen Praxis in juristischer Beleuchtung* (Julius Springer, Berlin, 1939)
C Huerkamp, *Der Aufstieg der Ärzte im 19. Jahrhundert* (Vandenhoeck & Ruprecht, Göttingen, 1985)
C Huerkamp, 'The Making of the Modern Medical Profession, 1800–1914: Prussian Doctors in the Nineteenth Century', in G Cocks / KH Jarausch (eds), *German Professions 1800–1950* (OUP, New York, 1990) 66
KF Hufnagel, *Mittheilung aus der Praxis der würtembergische Civilgerichte* (Tübingen 1846)
DJ Ibbetson, *A Historical Introduction to the Law of Obligations* (OUP, Oxford, 1999)
DJ Ibbetson, 'How the Romans Did for Us: Ancient Roots of the Tort of Negligence', (2003) 26 University of New South Wales Law Journal 475
S Jacyna, 'Medicine in Transformation, 1800–1849', in WF Bynum / A Hardy / S Jacyna / C Lawrence / EM Tansey (eds), *The Western Medical Tradition 1800–2000* (CUP, Cambridge, 2006) 11
N Jansen, *Die Struktur des Haftungsrechts: Geschichte, Theorie und Dogmatik außervertraglicher Ansprüche auf Schadensersatz* (Mohr Siebeck, Tübingen, 2003)

N Jansen, 'Developing Legal Doctrine: Fault in the German Law of Delict', in N Jansen (ed) *The Development and Making of Legal Doctrine* (CUP, Cambridge, 2009) 1

K Jarausch, 'The Conundrum of Complicity: German Professionals and the Final Solution', in A Steinweis / R Rachlin(eds), *The Law in Nazi Germany* (Berghahn, New York, 2013) 15

R v Jhering, 'Culpa in contrahendo oder Schadenersatz bei nichtigen oder nicht zur Perfection gelangten Verträgen', (1861) 4 Jherings Jahrbücher für die Dogmatik des bürgerlichen Rechts 1

H Joachim / A Korn, *Deutsche Ärzterecht* (Franz Vahlen, Berlin, vol 1 1911)

R Jütte, 'The Professionalisation of Homeopathy in the Nineteenth Century', in J Woodward / R Jütte (eds), *Coping with Sickness: Historical Aspects of Health Care in a European Perspective* (Sheffield, 1995) 45

W Kahl, 'Der Arzt im Recht', (1930) 59 JW 1545

M Kalisch, *Die Kunstfehler der Ärzte* (Veit & Co, Leipzig, 1860)

W Kallfelz, 'Anmerkung zu RG 19.06.1936', (1937) 66 JW 3314

W Kallfelz, 'Anmerkung zu RG 07.01.1938', (1938) 67 JW 2203

W Kallfelz, 'Zur Frage der Sorgfaltspflicht des Arztes bei operativen Eingriffen', (1935) Münchener Medizinische Wochenschrift 606

C Karg, 'Zur Fahrlässigkeitsfrage beim Zurücklassen von Fremdkörpern in der Bauchhöhle', (1928) 48 Münchener Medizinische Wochenschrift 2082

M Kaser, *Das Römische Privatrecht* (CH Beck, München, 2nd ed vol 1 1971)

MH Kater, 'Professionalization and Socialization of Physicians in Wilhelmine and Weimar Germany', (1985) 20 Journal of Contemporary History 677

MH Kater, *Doctors under Hitler* (University of North Carolina Press, Chapel Hill, 1989)

MH Kater, 'Criminal Physicians in the Third Reich: Toward a Group Portrait', in FR Nicosia / J Huener (eds), *Medicine and Medical Ethics in Nazi Germany* (Berghahn, New York, 2002) 77

C Katzenmeier, *Arzthaftung* (Mohr Siebeck, Tübingen, 2002)

C Katzenmeier / A Laufs / V Lipp, *Arztrecht* (CH Beck, Nördlingen, 7th ed 2015)

H Kehr, *Ärztliche Kunstfehler und mißbräuchliche Heilbehandlung: Eine strafrechtdogmatische Untersuchung zu Artikel 134 der Carolina* (Görich & Weiershäuser, Marburg, 1972)

F Keidel (ed), *Handausgabe des Bürgerlichen Gesetzbuchs auf Grund von J v Staudingers Kommentar* (Julius v Staudinger, München, 3rd ed 1931)

R Kessler, *Die Einwilligung des Verletzten in ihrere strafrechtlichen Bedeutung* (J Guttentag, Berlin, 1884)

T Kiefer, *Die Aquilische Haftung in 'Allgemeinem Landrecht für die Preußischen Staaten' von 1794.* (Centaurus, Pfaffenweiler, 1989)

K Kober / T Engelmann / K Geiler (eds), *J v Staudingers Kommentar zum Bürgerlichen Gesetzbuch und dem Einführungsgesetz* (J Schweitzer, München, 9th ed vol 2 1929)

G Köbler, 'Vom Arzt im Recht zum Arztrecht', in B-R Kern / E Wadle / K Schroeder / C Katzenmeier (eds), *Humaniora: Medizin–Recht–Geschichte* (Springer, Berlin, 2006) 157

A Kollbrunner, *Die Rechtliche Stellung des Arztes* (Aschman & Scheller, Zurich, 1903)

F König / H Köstlin, *Haftpflicht des Arztes* (JA Barth, Leipzig, 1937)

A Korn, 'Kann die Haftung des Arztes für Operationen oder innere ärztliche Behandlung durch Vereinbarung ausgeschlossen sein', (1912) 16 Das Recht 413

J Krähe, *Die Diskussion um den ärztlichen Kunstfehler in der Medizin der neunzehnten Jahrhunderts* (Marburg, 1984)

K Kubella, *Patientenrechtegesetz* (Springer, Berlin, 2011)

F Kudlien, 'Die Unschätzbarkeit ärztlicher Leistung und das Honorarproblem', 14 (1979) Medizinhistorisches Journal 3

A Kühner, *Die Kunstfehler der Ärzte vor dem Forum der Juristen* (Knauer, Frankfurt am Main, 1886)
A Kwaschik, *Die Parteivernehmung und der Grundsatz der Waffengleichheit im Zivilprozess* (Mohr Siebeck, Tübingen, 2004)
A Labisch, 'From Traditional Individualism to Collective Professionalism: State, Patient, Compulsory Health Insurance and the Panel Doctor Question in Germany 1883–1931', in M Berg / G Cocks (eds), *Medicine and Modernity: Public Health and Medical Care in Nineteenth- and Twentieth-Century Germany* (CUP, Cambridge, 1997) 35
A Laufs, *Arztrecht* (CH Beck, München, 1977)
A Laufs, *Arztrecht* (CH Beck, München, 2nd ed 1978)
A Laufs, 'Arzt und Recht im Wandel der Zeit', (1986) 4 Medizin Recht 163
A Laufs / A Eichener, 'Ursprünge einer strafrechtlichen Arzthaftung', in E Jayme et al (eds) *Festschrift für Hubert Niederländer* (Carl Winter, Heidelberg, 1991) 71
A Laufs, *Arztrecht* (CH Beck, München, 5th ed 1993)
C Lawrence, 'Continuity in crisis: medicine 1914–1945', in WF Bynum / A Hardy / S Jacyna / C Lawrence / EM Tansey (eds), *The Western Medical Tradition 1800–2000* (CUP, Cambridge, 2006) 247
HM Leichter, *A comparative approach to policy analysis: health care policy in four nations* (CUP, Cambridge, 1979)
T Lenoir, 'Laboratories, medicine and public life in Germany 1830–1849', in A Cunningham / P Williams (eds), *The laboratory revolution in medicine* (CUP, Cambridge, 2002) 14
RJ Lifton, *The Nazi Doctors* (Basic Books, New York, 1986)
K v Lilienthal, 'Die pflichtmässige ärztliche Handlung und das Strafrecht', in *Festgabe Bekker* (Haering, Berlin, 1899) 56
J Lister, 'Antiseptic Principle of the Practice of Surgery', (1867) 351 British Medical Journal 9
F v Liszt, 'Strafrecht und Strafprozeßrecht', in R Stammler (ed), *Systematische Rechtwissenschaft* (Teubner, Berlin, 1906) 195
Lobe / Oegg / Schliewen / Seuffarth (eds), *Das Bürgerliche Gesetzbuch mit besonderer Berücksichtigung der Rechtsprechung des Reichsgerichts* (Walter de Gruyter & Co, Berlin, 8th ed vol 2 1934)
T Loewenfeld, 'Inästimabilität und Honorierung der artes liberales nach römischen Recht', in *Festgabe für J W v Planck* (Christian Kaiser, München 1887) 365
T Löwenfeld, 'Über den Dienst-, Werk-, und Auftragsvertrag nach dem Rechte des *BGB*', in Adams et al (eds), *Gutachten aus dem Anwaltstande über die erste Lesung des Entwurfs eines Bürgerlichen Gesetzbuches* (W Moser, Berlin, 1890) 893
N Luhmann, *Law as a Social System* (OUP, Oxford 2008 trans K Ziegert)
CE McClelland, *The German experience of professionalization* (CUP, Cambridge, 2002)
A-H Maehle, 'Professional Ethics and Discipline: The Prussian Medical Courts of Honour, 1899–1920', (1999) 34 Medizin Historisches Journal 309
A-H Maehle, *Doctors, Honour and the Law: medical ethics in Imperial Germany* (Palgrave, Basingstoke, 2009)
A-H Maehle, *Contesting Medical Confidentiality* (Univeristy of Chicago Press, London, 2016)
D Majer, *'Non-Germans' under the Third Reich* (Johns Hopkins University Press, Baltimore, 2003 trans PT Hill / EV Humphrey / B Levin)
HP Mansel, 'Eigen- und Fremdveranwortung im Haftungsrecht – Zu den außerjuristischen Triebkräften der Haftungsverschärfung', in P Gottwald / E Jayme / D Schwab (eds), *Festschrift für Dieter Heinrich* (Giese King, Bielefeld, 2000) 425
K Mansfeld, 'Zur Haftung des Arztes wegen Pflichtverletzung', (1915) 5 Leipziger Zeitschrift für Deutsches Recht 334

B Markesinis, 'An Expanding Tort Law: The Price of a Rigid Contract Law', (1987) 103 Law Quarterly Review 354

BS Markesinis / H Unberath / A Johnston, *The German Law of Contract* (OUP, Oxford, 2006)

BS Markesinis / H Unberath, *The German Law of Torts* (OUP, Oxford, 4th ed 2002)

U Mattei / T Ruskola / A Gidi, *Schlesinger's Comparative Law* (Foundation Press, 7th ed 2009)

B Matthiaß, *Lehrbuch des bürgerlichen Rechtes* (O Häring, Berlin, 5th ed 1910)

H Melies, *Die Strafrechtliche Behandlung der Kurpfuscherei* (Max Welzel, Köln, 1929)

Merner, 'Aus langjähriger Gerichtspraxis', (1888) 49 Vierteljahrsschrift für gerichtliche und öffentliche Medicin 32.

Meusel-Gotha, 'Kann dem practischen Arzt die Beibehaltung der altern Wundbehandlung mit Charpie und Salbe unter Umständen als Kunstfehler angerechnet werden?', (1880) 7 Aerztliches Vereinsblatt 196

T Meyer, Das *ärztliche Vertragsverhältnis* (Rostock, 1905)

M Meyer-George, *Die zivilrechtliche Haftung des Heilpraktikers* (Frankfurt am Main, 1988)

Ministry for Medical Affairs (ed), *Lehrbuch der Geburtshülfe für die Preußischen Hebammen* (August Hirschwald, Berlin, 1878)

Ministry for Medical Affairs (ed), *Preußisches Hebammen-Lehrbuch* (August Hirschwald, Berlin, 1892)

CJA Mittermaier, 'Beiträge zur Lehre vom Beweise durch Sachverständige', (1819) 2 Archiv für die civilistische Praxis 119, cited as Mittermaier (1819a)

CJA Mittermaier, 'Beurteilung der neuesten criminalistischen Schriften', (1819) Neues Archiv des Criminalrechts 355, cited as Mittermaier (1819b)

CJA Mittermaier, *Grundsätze des gemeinen deutschen Privatrechts mit Einschluß des Handels-, Wechsel- und Seerechts* (Philipp Krüll, Landshut, 1824)

CJA Mittermaier, *Grundsätze des gemeinen deutschen Privatrechts mit Einschluß des Handels-, Wechsel- und Seerechts* (G Joseph Manz, Regensburg, 6th ed vol 2 1843)

CJA Mittermaier, 'Die strafrechtliche Verantwortlichkeit der Ärzte, Wundärzte, Apotheker und Hebammen wegen Kunstfehler oder anderer Handlungen oder Unterlassungen in Bezug auf Ausübung ihrer Kunst', (1853) NF Archiv des Criminalrechts 1

CJA Mittermaier, 'Die Lehre von der strafrechtlichen Verantwortlichkeit der Medicinalpersonen und die Stellung der Sachverständiger bei Begutachten der daraus bezüglichen Fragen geprüft', (1858) 10 Der Gerichtsaal 1

CJA Mittermaier, *Grundsätze des gemeinen deutschen Privatrechts mit Einschluß des Handels-, Wechsel- und Seerechts* (1892–3)

F Mommsen, *Beiträge zum Obligationenrecht* (CA Schwetsche & Son, Braunschweig, pt III 1855)

JL Montrose, 'Is Negligence an Ethical or a Sociological Concept?', (1958) 21 Modern Law Review 259

P Mossler, 'The discussion on general clause or numerus clausus during the preparation of the German Civil Code', in E Schrage (ed), *Negligence: The Comparative Legal History of the Law of Torts* (Duncker & Humblot, Berlin, 2001) 361

B Mugdan, *Die gesammten Materialien zum Bürgerlichen Gesetzbuch für das Deutsche Reich* (R v Decker, Berlin, vol 2 1899)

I Müller, *Hitler's Justice* (IB Tauris, London, 1991 trans DL Schneider)

M Neal / J Morgan, 'The Professionalization of Everyone? A Comparative Study of the Development of the Professions in the United Kingdom and Germany', (2000) European Sociological Review, 9

B Nicholas, *An Introduction to Roman Law* (OUP, Oxford, 1975)

V Nutton, 'Medicine in the Greek world, 800–50 BC', in L Conrad / M Neve / Nutton / R Porter / A Wear (eds), *The Western Medical Tradition 800 BC to AD 1800* (CUP, Cambridge, 1995) 11, cited as Nutton (1995a)

V Nutton, 'Roman Medicine 250 BC to AD 200', in L Conrad / M Neve / V Nutton / R Porter / A Wear (eds), *The Western Medical Tradition 800 BC to AD 1800* (CUP, Cambridge, 1995) 39, cited as Nutton (1995b)

V Nutton, 'Healers in the medical market-place: towards a social history of Graeco-Roman medicine', in A Wear (ed), *Medicine in Society* (CUP, Cambridge, 1992) 15

V Nutton, 'Continuity or rediscovery? The city physician in classical antiquity and medieval Italy', in A Russell (ed), *The Town and State Physician in Europe* (Herzog August Bibliothek, Wolfenbüttel, 1981) 9

V Nutton, 'The patient's choice: a new treatise by Galen', (1990) 40 Classical Quarterly 235

V Nutton, 'Two notes on immunities', (1971) 61 Journal of Roman Studies 52

P Oberhammer / T Domej, 'Germany Switzerland, Austria (ca 1800–2005)', in CH v Rhee (ed), *European Traditions in Civil Procedure* (Intersentia, Antwerp, 2005) 103

O Oesterlen, 'Kunstfehler der Ärzte und Wundärzte', in J Maschka (ed) *Handbuch der gerichtlichen Medizin* (Laupp, Tübingen, vol 3 1882) 589

K Oliphant, 'Medical Malpractice and Compensation: Comparative Perspectives', in K Oliphant / R Wright (eds), *Medical Malpractice in Global Perspective* (De Gruyter, Berlin, 2013) 513

L Oppenheim, *Das ärztliche Recht zu körperlichen Eingriffen an Kranken und Gesunden* (Benno Schwabe, Basel, 1892)

FC Oppenhoff, *Das Strafgesetzbuch für die Preußischen Staaten* (Georg Reimer, Berlin, 5th ed 1867)

FC Oppenhoff, *Das Strafgesetzbuch für die Preusischen Staaten und das Gesetz über die Einführung desselben* (Georg Reimer, Berlin,1872)

FC Oppenhoff, *Die Rechtsprechungen des Königlichen Ober-tribunals in Strafsachen* (Georg Reimer, Berlin, vol 18 1877)

O Palandt (ed), *Beck'sche Kurz Kommentare: Bürgerliches Gesetzbuch* (CH Beck, München, vol 7 1939)

FJ Pelz, 'Verschulden- Realität oder Fiktion', in A Laufs / C Dierks / A Wienke / T Graf-Baumann / G Hirsch (eds), *Die Entwicklung der Arzthaftung* (Springer, Berlin, 1997) 41

M Pennitz, 'Ius quaestium tertio: German Legal Doctrine and Practice in the 18th and 19th Century', in E Schrage (ed), *Ius quaestium tertio* (Duncker & Humblot, Berlin, 2008) 251

W Perrett, *Arzthaftpflichtrecht* (Urban &Schwarzenberg, München, 1956)

P Petersen, 'Die Haftung des Arztes in der Rechtsprechung des Bundesgerichtshofes', (1962) 40 Deutsche Richterzeitung 194

BW Pfeiffer, *Practische Ausführungen aus allen Theilen der Rechtswissenschaft* (Hahn'sche Hofbuchhandlung, Hannover, vol 7 1844)

H Philips, 'The German Code of Civil Procedure', (1895–1896) 21 Law Magazine and Law Review 271

O Pribilla, 'Der ärztliche Kunstfehler', in A Mergen (ed), *Die juristische Problematik in der Medizin* (Goldman, München, vol 3 1971)

H Prütting, 'International Sources of German Civil Procedure', in M Deguchi / M Strome (eds), *The Reception and Transmission of Civil Procedural Law in the Global Society* (Antwerp, 2008) 249

GF Puchta, *Lehrbuch der Pandekten* (JA Barth, Leipzig, 1838)

GF Puchta, *Vorlesungen über das heutige römische Recht* (Bernhard Tauchnitz, Leipzig, 4th ed vol 2, 1855)

GF Puchta, *Lehrbuch der Pandekten* (JA Barth, Leipzig, 9th ed 1863)

D Püster, *Entwicklungen der Arzthaftpflichtversicherung* (Springer, Berlin, 2013)
E Rabel, *Die Haftpflicht des Arztes* (Veit & Co, Leipzig, 1904)
R Rachlin, 'Roland Freisler and the Volksgerichtshof', in A Steinweis / R Rachlin (eds), *The Law in Nazi Germany* (New York, 2013) 63
O Rapmund / E Dietrich, *Arzthaftpflichtsrecht, Ärztliche rechts- und gesetzeskunde* (Georg Thieme, Leipzig 2nd ed 1913)
K Renner, *The Institutions of Private Law and their Social Functions* (Routledge & Kegan Paul, London 1949 trans A Schwarzschild)
G Ritter von Rittershain, *Die Heilkünstler des alten Roms und ihre bürgerliche Stellung* (Lüderitz, Berlin, 1875)
H Rodegra, 'Medizinhistorische Untersuchungen zur Problematik des ärztlichen Kunstfehlers und der Arzthaftung', (1986) 43 Gesnerus 61
AR Rothe / LR Naumburg, 'Schadenersatzpflicht und Gemeinschaftsgedanke', (1937) 66 JW 1449
J Rückert, 'vor § 611. Die Regelungsprobleme und Lösungen seit Rom im Überblick', in M Schmoeckel / J Rückert / R Zimmermann (eds), *Historisch-kritischer Kommentar zum BG* B (Mohr Siebeck, Tübingen, vol 3, 2013) 700, cited as Rückert (2013a)
J Rückert, 'Dienstvertrag mit Arbeitsvertrag', in M Schmoeckel / J Rückert / R Zimmermann (eds), *Historisch-kritischer Kommentar zum BG* B (Mohr Siebeck, Tübingen, vol 3, 2013) 823, cited as Rückert (2013b)
AF Rudorff (ed) *Pandekten von GF Puchta* (JA Barth, Leipzig, 7th ed 1853)
AF Rudorff (ed) *Pandekten von GF Puchta* (JA Barth, 9th ed 1863)
M Rümelin, *Haftung in Klinischen Betrieb* (Mohr, Tübingen, 1913)
B Rüthers, *Die unbegrenzte Auslegung* (Mohr Siebeck, Tübingen, 8th ed 2017)
R Sacco, 'Legal Formants: A Dynamic Approach To Comparative Law', (1991) 39 American Journal of Comparative Law 1
FC v Savigny, *Das Obligationenrecht als Theil des heutigen römischen Rechts* (Veit & Co, Berlin, vol 2 1853)
J Scarborough, *Roman Medicine* (Cornell University Press, Ithaca, 1969)
J Scarborough, 'Romans and Physicians', (1970) 65 The Classical Journal 296
Schäffer, 'Ob und unter welchen Voraussetzungen für geleistete dienste und verabreichte Alimente eine vergütung auch ohne vorgeriges versprechen einer solchen angesprochen werden kann', (1850) NF VII *Zeitschrift für Civilrecht und Prozeß* 1
M Schäffer, 'Ueber den Einfluß des Criminalurtheils auf den Civilpunkt', (1854) 37 Archiv für die civilistische Praxis 152
MJ Schermaier, '§§ 276–278 Verantwortlichkeit des Schuldners', in M Schmoeckel / J Rückert / R Zimmermann (eds), *Historisch-kritischer Kommentar zum BGB* (Mohr Siebeck, Tübingen, vol 2, 2007)
J Schiedermair, 'Fragekasten', (1928) 6 Münchener Medizinische Wochenschrift 280
G Schiemann, 'Unerlaubte Handlung', in M Schmoeckel / J Rückert / R Zimmermann, *Historisch-kritischer Kommentar zum BG* B (Mohr Siebeck, Tübingen, vol 3, 2013) 2711
Imke Schröder, *Zur Legitimationsfunktion der Rechtsphilosophie im Nationalsozialismus* (Peter Lang, Berlin, 2002)
T Schirmer (ed) *Pandekten von GF Puchta* (JA Barth, Leipzig, 12th ed 1877)
E Schmidt, *Einführung in die Geschichte der deutschen Strafrechtspflege* (Vandenhoeck & Ruprecht, Göttingen, 3rd ed 1995)
R Schmidt, *Die Strafrechtlichte Verantwortlichkeit des Arztes für verletzende Eingriffe* (Gustav Fischer, Jena, 1900)
E Schumann, '*De medicis et aegrotis-Arztrecht im Frühmittelalter*', in HJ Ahrens et al (eds) *Medizin und Haftung: Festschrift für Erwin Deutsch zum 80. Geburtstag* (Springer, Berlin, 2009) 545
JA Seuffert, *Praktisches Pandektenrecht* (Stahel Buchhandlung, Würzburg, 3rd ed 1852)

L v Seuffert, 'Zivilprozeßrecht', in R Stammler (ed), *Systematische Rechtwissenschaft* (Berlin, 1906) 162

J Shaw, 'Informed Consent: A German Lesson', (1986) 35 The International and Comparative Law Quarterly 864

E Siebenhaar, *Commentar zu dem bürgerlichen Gesetzbuch für das Königreich Sachsen* (Leipzig, vol 1 1864)

E Siebenhaar, *Lehrbuch des Sächsischen Privatrechts*, (Leipzig, 1872)

E Siebenhaar, *Commentar zu dem Bürgerlichen Gesetzbuch für das Königreich Sachsen* (JC Hinrich, Leipzig, 2nd ed vol 2 1869)

H Silber, 'Operae liberales', (1939–1930) 88 Jherings Jahrbücher für die Dogmatik des bürgerlichen Rechts 161

H Simmer, 'Principles and Problems of Medical Undergraduate Education in Germany during the C19th and early Twentieth Centuries', in C O'Malley (ed) *The History of Medical Education* (University of California, Berkeley, 1970) 173

G Simon, 'Von der Wirkung des Criminalerkenntnisses auf die Entscheidung des Civilpunktes', (1856) 39 Archiv für die civilistische Praxis 247

CF Sintenis, *Das Practische Gemeine Civilrecht* (Carl Focke, Leipzig, vol 2 1847)

CF Sintenis, *Das Practische Gemeine Civilrecht* (Bernhard Tauchnitz, Leipzig, 2nd ed vol 2 1861)

CF Sintenis, *Das Practische Gemeine Civilrecht* (Leipzig, 4nd ed, vol 2 1886)

T Soergel (ed), *Bürgerliches Gesetzbuch nebst Einführungsgesetz* (W Kohlhammer, Stuttgart, 5th ed 1931)

T Soergel (ed), *Bürgerliches Gesetzbuch nebst Einführungsgesetz* (W Kohlhammer, Stuttgart, 7th ed 1939)

R Spree, 'Quantative Aspekte der Entwicklung des Krankenhauswesens', in A Labisch / R Spree (eds), *Einem jeden Kranken in einem Hospitale sein eigenes Bett* (Campus, Frankfurt, 1996) 51

R Spree, *Health and Social Class in Imperial Germany* (Berg, Oxford, 1988 trans S McKinnon-Evans / J Halliday)

M Stauch, *The Law of Medical Negligence in England and Germany, A Comparative Analysis* (Hart, Oxford, 2008)

M Stauch, 'Medical Malpractice and Compensation in Germany', in K Oliphant / R Wright (eds), *Medical Malpractice in Global Perspective* (De Gruyter, Berlin, 2013) 179

M Stauch, 'The 2013 German Patients' Rights Act: Codifying Medical Malpractice Compensation', (2015) 6 Journal of European Tort Law 85

P Stein, *Roman Law in European Legal History* (CUP, Cambridge, 2000)

A Steinweis / R Rachlin, 'Introduction: The Law in Nazi Germany and the Holocaust', in A Steinweis / R Rachlin (eds), *The Law in Nazi Germany* (Berghahn, New York, 2013) 1

O Stobbe, *Handbuch des deutschen Privatrechts* (W Hertz, Berlin, 2nd ed vol 3 1885)

O Stobbe, *Handbuch des deutschen Privatrechts* (W Hertz, Berlin, 3rd ed vol 3 1893)

M Stolberg, 'Alternative Medicine, Irregular Healers and the Medical Market in Nineteenth Century Bavaria', in R Jütte / M Eklöf / MC Nelson (eds), *Historical Aspects of Unconventional Medicine* (EAHMH, Sheffield, 2001) 139

M Stolberg, 'Health Care Provision and Poor Relief in The Electorate and Kingdom of Bavaria', in OP Grell / A Cunningham / R Jütte (eds), *Health Care and Poor Relief in 18th and 19th Century Northern Europe* (Ashgate, 2002) 112

M Stolleis, *Law under the Swastika* (University of Chicago Press, Chicago, 1998 trans T Dunlap)

F Straßmann, 'Ärztliche Kunstfehler', (1932) 61 JW 3305

G Strohal (ed), *Planck's Kommentar zum Bürgerlichen Gesetzbuch nebst Einführungsgesetz* (De Gruyter, Berlin, 4th ed pt II 1928)

R Stürner, 'Beweisregeln und freie Beweiswürdigung im Zivilprozess der Europäischen Staaten', in T Lobinger (ed), *Festschrift für Eduard Picker zum 70. Geburtstag* (Mohr Siebeck, Tübingen, 2010) 809

Superarbitrum der Königlichen wissenschaftlichen Deputation für das Medicinalwesen, 'Fahrlässige Tödtung durch Kunstfehler', (1854) 6 Vierteljahrsschrift für gerichtliche und öffentliche Medicin

Superarbitrum der Königlichen wissenschaftlichen Deputation für das Medicinalwesen, 'Geburtshülflicher Kunstfehler?', (1858) 14 Vierteljahrsschrift für gerichtliche und öffentliche Medicin 1

J Taupitz, *Die Standesordnungen Der Freien Berufe: Geschichtliche Entwicklung, Funktionen, Stellung Im Rechtssystem* (De Gruyter, Berlin, 1991)

R Teufel, *Der Arztvertrag: eine Untersuchung der privatrechtlichen Beziehungen zwischen dem Arzt und dem Kranken* (JF Bofinger, 1919)

K Tillmanns, *Strukturfragen des Dienstvertrages* (Mohr Siebeck, Tübingen, 2007)

W Thilo, *Die Strafgesetzgebung des Großherzogthums Baden* (CT Groos, Karlsruhe, 1845)

JAC Thomas, *Textbook of Roman Law* (North Holland, Amsterdam, 1976)

KA Unterholzner, *Quellenmäßige Zusammenstellung der Lehre des römischen Rechts von den Schuldverhältnissen, mit Berücksichtigung der heutigen Anwendung* (JA Barth, Leipzig, vol 2 1840)

KA v Vangerow, *Lehrbuch der Pandeckten* (RG Elwert, Marburg, 7th ed 1869)

FH Vering, *Geschichte und Pandekten des Römischen und heutigen geminem Privatrechts* (Franz Kirchheim, Mainz, 4th ed 1875)

FH Vering, *Geschichte und Pandekten des Römischen und heutigen geminem Privatrechts* (Franz Kirchheim, Mainz, 5th ed 1887)

H-D Viel, *The New Complete Code of Hammurabi* (University Press of America, Lanham, 2002) 647

R Virchow, 'Kunstfehler der Aerzte', in R Virchow (ed), *Gesammelte Abhandlungen aus dem Gebiete der öffentlichen Medicin und der Seuchenlehre* (August Hirschwald, Berlin vol 2 1879) 519

S Vogenauer, 'An empire of light? Learning and lawmaking in the history of German law', [2005] 64 Cambridge Law Journal 481.

HJ Wagner, 'On the prehistory of the German Society of Legal Medicine', (2004) 144 Forensic Science International 89

A Walter, *Spezialisierung und Sorgfaltsstandard im Arzt- und Anwaltshaftungsrecht* (Ernst und Werner Gieseking, Bielefeld, 2004)

A Watson, *Failures of the Legal Imagination* (University of Pennsylvania Press, Philadelphia 1988)

A Watson, *Legal Transplants: An Approach to Comparative Law* (University of Georgia Press, Athens, 2nd ed 1993)

P Weindling, 'Medicine and modernisation: the social history of German health and medicine', (1986) 24 History of Science 277

P Weindling, 'Public Health in Germany', in D Porter, *Social Medicine and Medical Sociology in the Twentieth Century* (Rodopi, Amsterdam, 1997) 119

A Weinrich, *Die Haftpflicht wegen Körperverletzung und Tödtung eines Menschen nach den im Deutschen Reiche geltenden Rechten* (Carl Heymanns, Berlin, 2nd ed 1902)

G Weisz, *Divide and Conquer: A Comparative History of Medical Specialisation* (OUP, Oxford, 2006)

O Wendt, *Lehrbuch der Pandekten* (Gustav Fischer, Jena, 1888)

F Wengler/H Brachmann, *Das Bürgerliche Gesetzbuch für das Königreich Sachsen* (Rostberg, Leipzig, 1878)

GW Wetzell, *System des ordentlichen Civilprocesses* (Bernhard Tauschnitz, Leipzig 3rd ed 1878)

R Wetzell, 'Crime and Criminal Justice in Modern Germany', in R Wetzell (ed) *Crime and Criminal Justice in Modern Germany* (Berghahn, New York, 2014) 1
F Wieacker, *A History of Private Law in Europe* (OUP, Oxford, 1995 trans T Weir)
B Windscheid, *Lehrbuch des Pandektenrechts* (J Buddeus, Düsseldorf, vol 2 pt I 1865)
B Windscheid, *Lehrbuch des Pandektenrechts* (J Buddeus, Düsseldorf, vol 2 pt II 1866)
B Windscheid, *Lehrbuch des Pandektenrechts* (J Buddeus, Düsseldorf, 3rd ed 1870)
B Windscheid, *Lehrbuch des Pandektenrechts* (J Buddeus, Düsseldorf, 3rd ed pt II 1873)
B Windscheid, *Lehrbuch des Pandektenrechts* (J Buddeus, Düsseldorf, 4th ed pt II 1875)
B Windscheid, *Lehrbuch des Pandektenrechts* (Ebner & Seubert, Stuttgart, 5th ed vol 2 1879)
B Windscheid, *Lehrbuch des Pandektenrechts* (Rütten & Loening, Frankfurt am Main, 6th ed pt II 1887)
P Zepos/P Christodoulou, 'Professional Liability', in A Tunc (ed), *International Encyclopaedia of Comparative Law* (JCB Mohr, Tübingen, vol 11 pt 1 1983) 6–1
F Zimmermann, 'Ueber das Rechtsverhältnis zwischen dem Arzte und dem Patienten', (1873) 56 Archiv für Civilistische Praxis 222
R Zimmermann, *The Law of Obligations* (OUP, Oxford, 1996)
R Zimmermann, 'Savigny's legacy: legal history, comparative law, and the emergence of a European legal science', (1996) 112 Law Quarterly Review 576.
R Zimmermann/D Verse, 'Die Reaktion des Reichsgerichts auf die Kodifikation des deutschen Deliktsrechts (1900–1914)', in U Falk/H Mohnhaupt (eds), *Das Bürgerliche Gesetzbuch und seine Richter* (Klostermann, Frankfurt am Main, 2000) 319
R Zimmermann, *Roman Law, Contemporary Law, European Law: the civilian tradition today* (OUP, Oxford, 2001)
E Zitelmann, *Die Haftung des Arztes aus ärztlicher Behandlung* (Georg Thieme, Leipzig, 1908)
K Zweigert/H Kötz, *An Introduction to Comparative Law* (OUP, Oxford,1998 trans T Weir)

## Un-attributed Periodical Articles and Reports

*Allgemeine Gerichtsordnung für die Preußischen Staaten* (G Reimer, Berlin, pt I 1822)
(1853) 3 Vierteljahrsschrift für gerichtliche und öffentliche Medicin 20.
Obergutachten des Königlichen Medicinalcollegii für Pommern, 'Zwei Obductionsberichte, betreffend zwei verfolgte sogenannte Curpfuscherfälle', (1858) 14 Vierteljahrsschrift für gerichtliche und öffentliche Medicin
'OAG Lübeck', (1862) 4 Kritische Vierteljahresschrift für Gesetzgebung und Rechtswissenschaft 137
'Der Entwurf einer Straf-Prozess-Ordnung für das Deutsche Reich', (1875) Aerztliche Sachverständigen-Zeitung 28
'Die Antiseptik vor Gericht', (1885) 12 Aerztliches Vereinblatt 39
'Gutachten (juristisches) über die 5 Deneke'sche These betr. Kunstfehler' (1888) 15 Aerztliches Vereinsblatt 266, (1890) 53 Vierteljahrsschrift für gerichtliche und öffentliche Medicin 371
'Die Strafrechtliche Verantwortung der Aerzte', (1894) 21 Aerztliches Vereinsblatt 573
'Prozesse gegen Kurpfuscher', (1896) 23 Aerztliches Vereinsblatt 447
'Schadenersatzanspruch gegen den Arzt wegen Gesundheitsschädigung', (1896) 23 Aerztliches Vereinsblatt 444
'Fahrlässige Tödtung in Folge unzureichender Hülfeleistung bei einer schweren gynäkologischen Operation', (1896) 2 Aerztliche Sachverständigen-Zeitung 232

'Fahrlässige Tödtung durch Unterlassung', (1896) 2 Aerztliche Sachverständigen-Zeitung 516
(1897) 24 Aerztliches Vereinsblatt für Deutschland 301
'Obergutachten der Königlichen wissenschaftlichen Deputation für das Medicinalwesen, betreffend ärztlichen Kunstfehler', (1897) 3 Aerztliche Sachverständigen-Zeitung
'Zur Haftpflicht der Ärzte', (1897) 3 Aerztliche Sachverständigen-Zeitung
'Ob die Behandlung der H. seitens des Dr N. gegen die annerkannten Regeln der Heilkunde verstösst; Fahrlässige Tödtung von Seiten des Arztes durch unterlassene Entfernung einer Messerklinge aus dem Gehirn', (1898) 4 Aerztliche Sachverständigen-Zeitung
(1898) 4 Aerztliche Sachverständigen-Zeitung 204
(1898) 4 Aerztliche Sachverständigen-Zeitung 356.

## Theses

T Riegger, Die historische Entwicklung der Arzthaftung, (Unpublished Thesis, Regensburg, 2007)

# Index of terms